AF478117

THE WRITING LIFE

The Writing Life

Journals, 1975–2005

GEORGE FETHERLING

Edited by Brian Busby

McGill-Queen's University Press
Montreal & Kingston • London • Ithaca

© McGill-Queen's University Press 2013
ISBN 978-0-7735-4114-6

Legal deposit first quarter 2013
Bibliothèque nationale du Québec

Printed in Canada on acid-free paper that is 100% ancient forest free
(100% post-consumer recycled), processed chlorine free

McGill-Queen's University Press acknowledges the support of the Canada
Council for the Arts for our publishing program. We also acknowledge the
financial support of the Government of Canada through the Canada Book
Fund for our publishing activities.

The author gratefully acknowledges the support of the Canada Council
for the Arts.

Library and Archives Canada Cataloguing in Publication

Fetherling, George, 1949–
    The writing life: journals, 1975–2005 / George Fetherling; edited by Brian Busby.

    Includes index.
    ISBN 978-0-7735-4114-6

    1. Fetherling, George, 1949–. 2. Authors, Canadian (English) – 20th century – Diaries.
3. Authors, Canadian (English) – 21st century – Diaries. 4. Canada – Intellectual
life – 20th century. 5. Canada – Intellectual life – 21st century. I. Busby, Brian John
II. Title.

PS8561.E834Z47 2013   C818'.5403   C2013-900556-0

Frontispiece: photo by Barry Peterson
This book was typeset by Interscript in 10.5/14 Sabon.

Contents

Preface

I've always been attracted to writers' diaries and the way they let us into the actions and thoughts of the persons doing the scribbling. In the proper hands, such books also become part of a literary sub-genre that is defined most of all perhaps by its flexibility. If a writer's journal is an honest document it likely contains not only embryonic ideas and notes-to-self but also minor revelations, anecdotes, gossip, self-deluding fictions, and bits of postdated social history – all manner of stuff. The journals of authors as different as Virginia Woolf and Jean Cocteau, to name two contemporaries who wouldn't have liked each other in the least, are mosaics of this sort, despite their vast differences in intent and tone.

Beginning in the 1970s, a generation of feminist scholars began publishing fully annotated editions of Woolf's diaries: in all, five fat volumes (appearing more or less at the same time as six more of her letters). But this worthy project came at the expense of the one-volume selection, *A Writer's Diary*, which Leonard Woolf had edited back in 1953, a dozen years after his wife's suicide. The academic Woolf specialists were highly suspicious of his motives, believing that he was burying unpleasant truths by carving out a manageable single volume from the great mass of manuscript. But in fact the two camps were engaged in quite distinct tasks that happened to involve the same trove of material. Whereas the scholars valued completeness, the widower pursued readability. The *Writer's Diary* he stitched together was designed to be enjoyed rather than studied. It tried to show what being an author was actually like in a certain place and time.

This book has a similar motive. It is distilled from notebooks covering thousands of pages. From these, Brian Busby has selected entries that seem to him to show how one generally unsuccessful writer managed to peck out his work and somehow support himself during the period that is often referred to as Canada's cultural renaissance (and continuing a bit into – what to call it? – the après-renaissance). It is about living the writing life and surviving thereby, but it deals as much with other people as it does me. At certain points, more. Oscar Wilde said that his friend Frank Harris, the author of *My Life and Loves*, had been a guest in all the great homes of England – once! You get the picture. I believe that the reader will find here not only many Canadian literary figures, and a few foreign ones, but also a seasoning of politicians, entrepreneurs, philosophers, actors, broadcasters, and so on.

But I hope that *The Writing Life* won't be confused with the journals that writers have kept with the intention of naming as many conspicuous public figures as possible. Those of the aesthete Cecil Beaton (1904–1980) are examples of how journals are sometimes used this way, for social observation. So are the equally voluminous ones of the popular novelist Arnold Bennett (1867–1931). Such journals tend to smack of an attitude that might be paraphrased as "Great men and women who have known me." Bennett's, however, are of additional interest in that they created a vogue for the published journals of living writers, at least in the middle-brow universe, just as those of his French contemporary André Gide were doing in the high-brow one.

Is it possible to think of journals as art? I once put the question to my artist friend Vera Frenkel, who said no, not any more than statues in parks can be considered sculpture. The comparison with public statuary seems especially apt in the case of those endless formal diaries that certain personages have kept as strictly as a religious observance for the purpose of ensuring their posthumous fame: the diaries of people such as Beaton and Harold Nicolson or, from a different part of the English galaxy, the Labour politician Richard Crossman. Vera went on to say: "Gossip and self-revelation – interchangeable, perhaps – are endlessly intriguing, and for me, can appear in fairly rough-and-ready form without losing any interest." Most of us feel the same, I'd bet.

Despite being drawn to journals as a reader, I didn't begin to keep one until I had been writing for a decade; and when I did finally adopt the practice, I did so in odd circumstances and not for the customary reasons. I have suffered all my life from a physiological speech disability I call dysphonia, to distinguish it from the psychologically triggered one known as stuttering or, more genteelly, stammering. (Arnold Bennett had the same affliction, which provided more reason for Virginia Woolf to mock him.) In 1974 I was writing for the *Toronto Star* when a new managing editor was brought in (in that era, they came and went with astonishing speed) and I lost my small and unenviable position as the paper's book review columnist and general cultural dogsbody. Two colleagues there, independently of each other, reported to me that the m.e. had said that the paper "already has a guy who can't talk" and didn't require a second. In his crude Australian way – he had worked for Rupert Murdoch and was about to do so again – he was referring to one of my friends, Sid Adilman, an entertainment writer who suffered terribly from a speech handicap but bravely earned his living on the telephone every day, gathering information about people with boldface names. After a normal period of complaining about being mistreated – but not too loudly, I hope – I returned, after quite a long absence, to speech therapy, which I had first encountered in 1954, age five.

Speech therapy is far from being one of the precise sciences and is susceptible to the usual trends and fads. At the time to which I allude, journaling was in fashion. One was supposed to keep a daily record of all the dreaded pauses, elongated syllables, and awful little animal throat noises that befell one in the course of going to the bank and the post office or ordering lunch. In time, so the theory went, invisible patterns would become apparent like watermarks, giving warning of when danger was most likely to strike. I duly went along with this for a while. In fact, such notations retain a place in my journal, which I continue to keep today, though on an imaginary pie chart they would constitute little more than a thin sliver. What the journal became instead, at least in my own perception, was a working document by someone trying hard to grow up as a person and as a writer.

I was twenty-six when I began the journal. Physically, I must have appeared to others as a tall, gangly fellow with long hair, gigantic feet, and an Adam's apple the size of a baseball: characteristics held together by a unifying awkwardness of utterance and manner. Not yet hard of hearing, I was certainly hard of knowing. I must have been careless as well, for at some point in the years covered here I lost the journal for 1976, no doubt in one of the many changes of residence reflected in the following pages. I suspect that the missing entries, should they ever turn up, would read very much like those of 1975, which now strike my ear as so many lies. By this I mean that they were written in a false diction as I attempted to convince myself that I was, if not the equal of my betters, then at least a younger version of them. This masquerade resulted in a risible tone of world-weariness that was utterly unsanctioned by actual worldliness. But then, at some point later in the 1970s, I began, tentatively, to find my own voice in the journal, which then became a more complex organism. My hasty entries took on some characteristics of an *aide-mémoire*, a bully pulpit, a commonplace book, a room in which to complain and confess, a vehicle for self-praise and self-castigation, and of course a storehouse of raw material for my books and other writings. This growth in the document itself was clearly a reflection of my own struggles towards what I then believed was maturity but now have been assured is the road to decrepitude.

I believe that Brian's selection gives a fair indication of the journal's flavour. What it can't do is show the journal as a tall stack of physical objects. As this too speaks to my method, let me quote Brian's description:

[The 1975 entries] are written on leaves torn from an appointment book and held together by a metal clip, while the next volume in the sequence consists of hundreds of cerlox-bound pages, most typewritten on the reverse of old CBC scripts and publicity releases. One more recent volume resembles a religious tract; it has been bound in black boards with the title *War News* stamped in gold on the front. Some of the journals have a professional appearance, being written in the lovely Moleskine notebooks favoured by Bruce Chatwin and others or in highly tactile ones made by Clairefontaine. One journal is actually bound in full calf, with raised bands. [I believe this was a gift from someone.] Many others, however, seem to make use of whatever stationery was nearest to hand, such as school exercise books evidently grabbed during travels but used only much later. For example, one journal is written in an exam book from the South Pacific and another, on the cheapest imaginable paper, appears to have begun life as a student's scribbler in – judging from the alphabet of the cover text – Burma.

Owing to the loss of 1976 (reward if found), *The Writing Life* covers 30 years in only 29 sections. At the beginning of each, I give a brief summary of my doings so as to help the reader along. But to complete the context I probably should say something of the years preceding 1975.

I began supporting myself with menial newspaper work when I was sixteen. I was a typical young bohemian of the time, seeking the comfort of people my own age who were interested in writing, the visual arts, and music. In 1967 I got a lucky break and went to work, briefly, as the entry-level employee at a brand-new Toronto publishing firm, House of Anansi Press, which, in ways that could not have been foreseen, came to seem the centre of productive ferment in Canadian writing. Anansi published a poetry collection of mine before the end of 1968, after which I appeared in a few anthologies and may have edited one or two, and wrote introductions to a few other books. Later I lived in London, trying to write a novel, and on my return learned that I could keep myself fed by reviewing books in the *Globe and Mail* and other places and by writing articles – on just about every subject you could imagine – for general-circulation magazines, of which Canada had quite a few in those days. When the journal begins, I had published two more poetry collections, both justifiably derided, and was struggling to insinuate myself into the literary world while supporting myself in a second world that scarcely knew of the first one's existence. I have described this period and its personalities more fully in a memoir called *Travels by Night*, published (with much difficulty, as the present book will recount) a generation later.

For bringing *The Writing Life* to its present state I am deeply grateful to my friends Brian Busby and Jean Wilson.

George Fetherling

THE WRITING LIFE

1975–76

I had been living for years in a section of downtown Toronto called the Annex, near the University of Toronto – at this particular time, in a communal house on Howland Avenue, one of three addresses I have occupied on that street alone. I was writing poems and trying to complete an utterly quixotic book about Ben Hecht (1893–1964), the American novelist, screenwriter, and Zionist. Whenever an opportunity arose, I reviewed books for the *Globe and Mail* and for magazines such as *Saturday Night* and *Books in Canada*. The height of good fortune was the occasional arts piece for either *Weekend* or *The Canadian*, competing rotogravure magazines carried in Saturday newspapers across the country. But all the above put together still left a big hole in my personal economy. I made up the shortfall with a bizarre array of uncredited tasks. I wrote manuscript reports for book publishers, captions for a photography book, anonymous restaurant reviews for a tourists' guide, publicity matter for the upcoming Olympics in Montreal, and "continuity" for a television documentary about the *New York Times*: those kinds of things. To husband my sanity, I began a serious cinema column in the *Canadian Forum*. One by-product of the *Forum* connection came just as a long postal strike threatened my survival. This was the offer to write introductions to dozens of classic films. Each week, one of these scripts was read – by someone else of course – on the local CBC television station. My records show that I received $49.05 for each one used.

WEDNESDAY, 15 JANUARY / TORONTO
Bob Fulford, at home with ague, calls late this morning, inviting me up for a talk.[1] The maid brings tea to the split-level den while we talk 3½ hours about *Saturday Night*, our own writing and other topics … Bob has become my good friend these past two or three years. As a result, there is some embarrassment in his discussion of business matters with me. But this is more than made up for in the frankness and conviviality of talks on other issues. He says at one point: "I think journalists in this country should be able to make as much money as any other professional. I can, but I have to do so many different things – really keeps me busy … A lawyer of my prominence would make a lot more than this. I make as much as an ordinary lawyer." I record these as very uncharacteristic statements. He's almost always self-effacing and seemingly unconcerned with monetary matters except in the way we are all concerned with them.

THURSDAY, 16 JANUARY / TORONTO
Last night went with Jackson to a party at Peter Pearson's house.[2] There talked with Rotstein, Colombo, Gzowski, movie people, and made lunch date with the actress Sue Petrie.[3] Later adjourned with Jackson to a screening of Robin Spry's *Action*, his NFB documentary on the October Crisis. A ludicrous public discussion, moderated by Gzowski, followed. Then with Jackson for spaghetti at Angelo's … Today I lecture, stop at Marty's bookstore and return home to work. At this writing I'm considering an all-night marathon.

SATURDAY, 18 JANUARY / TORONTO
Slow beginning. Breakfast at home. Buy art supplies. Some small work. In the evening I have a meal with Linda S at Switzer's deli on Spadina, then return to her place to talk, walking through the empty market: shuttered shops, splintered vegetable crates, frightened alleycats and

---

1 Robert Fulford (b. 1932), newspaper columnist and editor of *Saturday Night* magazine, 1968–87.
2 Peter Pearson (b. 1938), film director.
3 Abraham Rotstein (b. 1929), nationalistic economist; John Robert Colombo (b. 1936), "found poet" and trivia collector; Peter Gzowski (1934–2002), broadcaster and writer.

rain. We argue about Wyndham Lewis till 2 a.m., adjourning to buy freshly baked bagels. Then I return here, walking up deserted Spadina, still in the rain, turning on Bloor into crowds of men with fur-collared girlfriends. Work till dawn.

MONDAY, 20 JANUARY / TORONTO
Browse bookshops, then sit through six hours of a Building and Development Board meeting at City Hall with the class from Ryerson. Afterwards, dinner at Sai Woo to get the taste of municipal politics out of my throat. There is a new breed – "reformists" not reformers, rambling, perpetually angry and unbelievably authoritarian and puritanical. Fugitives from OISE [Ontario Institute for Studies in Education] who are based in sociology (a useless field) rather than law. Terrible administrators. I prefer the company of the Church Street panhandlers, who are more socially useful. Write my *Forum* column.

TUESDAY, 21 JANUARY / TORONTO
Turn in my *Forum* copy. It's sad that Michael Cross is leaving the magazine and the U of T to teach in Halifax.[4] The *Forum* has grown almost realistic under his editorship and also livelier and better designed. Besides, he's always seemed a good sort to have around: an academic who sees the foibles of academic life. Clean apartment. Stall landlord on rent. Read for Hecht project. Write.

MONDAY, 27 JANUARY / TORONTO
Marian Engel, now alas an avid literary politician, has to attend a meeting of the Metro Library Board, to which she's got herself appointed.[5] As a result, I teach her class at Vic on book reviewing. What a collection of people. A Christian zealot in the front row who immediately readjusts her skirt when I enter the room; a friendly but befuddled Englishman who insisted on calling me Old Sport (like Jay Gatsby!); and the usual assortment of homemakers seeking fulfilment. Still, I am glad to receive the fifty bucks.

4 Michael Cross (b. 1938), labour historian and professor.
5 Marian Engel (1933–1985), author of *Bear* and other novels.

WEDNESDAY, 29 JANUARY / TORONTO

Go with Susan Swan to see Paul Thompson's satirical sex revue *I Love You, Baby Blue*.[6] It is well staged and generally enjoyable but, like most revues, best when least serious. Once it plunges into moralism and twice more, by my count, into uncalled-for attempts at lugubriousness. But it also makes delicious fun of several recognisable Toronto types. Later to Sue's for roast beef in the shabby baronial drawing room, but return home early because her child is feeling poorly and I have to watch Tom Snyder do a show from Toronto concerning the CIA.

THURSDAY, 30 JANUARY / TORONTO

Stein and I teach our Ryerson [Polytechnical Institute] class after I've shopped at David Mason's [bookstore].[7] Later stock up on groceries as well, knowing that I must eat at home more often if I am stretching my few pennies. Terribly worried about mounting bills and mounting interest on many overdue ones. Devote some time to good work, then down to paperwork for the evening. Cold and lonesome.

FRIDAY, 31 JANUARY / TORONTO

Go see Bob F at the offices on Richmond, near Church, to which *Saturday Night* moved yesterday. He then takes me to lunch. Later I return to the office with him to discuss assignments: the seed of an article planted, a request accepted for a review of Woodcock's new book (then home to read it).[8] In the evening I go to Leonard Cohen's concert at Massey Hall. Jack McClelland is there. Likewise, Layton.[9] The music has improved and so has my liking for Cohen as a lesser charlatan's for a far greater one. Back here. To sleep at 4:30 a.m.

6   Susan Swan (b. 1945), author of *The Biggest Modern Woman in the World* and other novels.

7   David Lewis Stein (b. 1937), journalist and author of *Scratch One Dreamer* and other fiction.

8   George Woodcock (1912–1995), anarchist historian and man-of-letters.

9   Leonard Cohen (b. 1934), poet and songwriter; Jack McClelland (1922–2004), publisher of McClelland & Stewart; Irving Layton (1912–2006), iconoclastic poet.

SUNDAY, 2 FEBRUARY / TORONTO

My creditors besiege me. I total up $4,000 in pressing debts. Newgate has been torn down these many years fortunately. Still, I don't know what the end will be. I haven't a dime and more bills all the time. I have nothing to sell. Such thoughts, realisations, and worry consume this evening.

THURSDAY, 6 FEBRUARY / TORONTO

Lunch with Fulford with long discussion of the changes in writers' ambitions in the '40s and '50s on the one hand and the '60s and '70s on the other. In the evening Peggy A calls from her farm for a chat.[10] One of her sheep has died. I express sympathy.

SUNDAY, 9 FEBRUARY / TORONTO

Cook breakfast, write letters, read, work on poems. Indoors all day and all night. Melancholy provides most of the warmth. Stein drops by with his small daughter and a wild scheme to become publisher of the *Citizen* [a community newspaper]. Cook dinner. Eat it too.

FRIDAY, 14 FEBRUARY / SUDBURY

One beautiful moment. I am jammed in the back seat of a car outward bound from the Sudbury airport with Lorimer, who's never been here before.[11] The landscape passes: grey snow, mine tailings, a McDonald's arch on the horizon; I glance at Lorimer's face in the mirror and catch, for just a mini-second, an expression of "My God, *this* is the country I'm fighting for!"

Horrible reception but a fine meal, with Stein, Lorimer, Graeme Gibson.[12] Lorimer and I talk late into the night, distrustful of each other, which is all to the good.

10   Margaret Atwood (b. 1939), poet, novelist, and woman-of-letters; author of *The Edible Woman*, *The Handmaid's Tale*, *The Robber Bride*, etc.
11   James Lorimer (b. 1942), nationalistic publisher of James Lorimer & Co.
12   Graeme Gibson (b. 1934), author of *Five Legs* and other novels; mate of Margaret Atwood.

SATURDAY, 15 FEBRUARY / SUDBURY

Seminars relatively painless. Dave Godfrey speaks well. Lorimer also talks, and Matt Cohen and I give a class of sorts.[13] Graeme has an early reservation but desires a later one, so we switch identities and tickets. Fly home with Lorimer early evening, avoiding the banquet.

THURSDAY, 20 FEBRUARY / TORONTO

Deliver copy to Bob F, try to sell him on other ideas. *Saturday Night* is a madhouse of activity – phones ringing, unidentified humans running about with sheaves of proof. It warms my heart. This follows lunch with [an acquaintance] whom I help with her questions about first and early editions of De Quincey. Later talk with Robin Skelton, who's very funny if a bit pretentious.[14] In reference to his editing of the *Malahat Review* he says, "What's required of nepotism is the proper sort of nepot."

SUNDAY, 23 FEBRUARY / TORONTO

Call Gwen MacEwen and am invited to her place for coffee, her Greek husband being away (ominously?) in Montreal for some reason.[15] Poor Gwen. She's grotesquely puffed up and talking nonsense. Illustrating her technique of pain control, she spends the whole evening passing one hand slowly through the flame of a candle till it's black from carbon up to the wrist. Also present is a fellow Gwen introduces as a psychic, who insists I am a student and come from out west. Filled with sadness after seeing Gwen, I trudge these old neighbourhoods in the rain.

WEDNESDAY, 26 FEBRUARY / TORONTO

Dinner with Howard Engel.[16] His writing and what's more his publishing have taken giant steps since his break-up with Marian. His comment on his own poetry is that it is "like someone quietly going to pieces in the jungle." How Maughamish this sounds.

13 David Godfrey (b. 1938), writer and publishing entrepreneur, co-founder of House of Anansi Press and new press; Matt Cohen (1942–1999), author of *The Disinherited* and other novels.
14 Robin Skelton (1925–1997), poet and man-of-letters.
15 Gwendolyn MacEwen (1941–1987), poet and novelist.
16 Howard Engel (b. 1931), author of the Benny Cooperman mystery series; married to Marian Engel.

THURSDAY, 27 FEBRUARY / TORONTO
The postal strike has forced me to go against my principles and, flourish-
ing proof of receivables tied up in the mail, apply for a bank loan. This I
do in the morning. The verdict tomorrow.

Lunch with Charles Taylor, dear man, whose conversation sparkles
with anecdote.[17] For instance, the story of how he was conceived at the
Dorchester in London and how, when passing the hotel on the Hyde
Park side, he's careful to give it his Prince Philip wave, which he demonstrates. We talk of his progress on the third book, then browse SCM
[bookstore].

SATURDAY, 1 MARCH / TORONTO
Chinese food with Malcolm Lester and [an acquaintance].[18] Malcolm
leaves first and she and I are left to talk. She is a person it's safer not to
know, but having come to know her, I find it better that she side with me.
I detect no vicious streak but rather a wide vein of carelessness.

SUNDAY, 2 MARCH / TORONTO
Dinner at Roger [Hall] and Sandra Martin's with two of their friends.[19]
On arriving I have to borrow from Roger to pay the cabbie. Abstain
from drink. Leave early and cordially to write my overdue *Forum* piece.
Monday is my day for making the rounds, and the schedule is long and
arduous.

17 Charles Taylor (1935–1997), foreign correspondent and China hand, author of
Six Journeys and *Radical Tories*.
18 Malcolm Lester (b. 1938), publisher of Lester & Orpen Dennys and Lester
Publishing.
19 Roger Hall (b. 1945), historian, and his wife, Sandra Martin (b. 1952), journalist.

1977

In literary terms, my principal accomplishment during the year was publication of *The Five Lives of Ben Hecht* by the firm of Lester & Orpen. It received brief but friendly mentions in publications as different as the *New York Times* and *Variety*, but the reviews themselves were generally corrosive (and in time I came to understand why). As all that was taking place, I managed to get some reviewing assignments from the *Chicago Tribune* and the *Los Angeles Times*, to no lasting effect. As before, I turned down nothing that was offered, not even contributions to a mere newsletter of the arts. Yet it was in this period that I suddenly began to find my feet as a magazine journalist. What's more, a break came when a friend about to begin a sabbatical asked me to teach his first-year survey course in the journalism department at Ryerson. I thought that if I could maintain both writing and teaching for an entire year (in the event, for several years), I could scrape together a down payment on a house. So it was that in December I bought a small nondescript Annex house on Albany Avenue, within spitting distance of my past few addresses.

TUESDAY, 19 JULY / TORONTO
Today at the Press Club I lunch with Col. Jim McPhee, PR man and flack to Her Majesty the Queen. He was an RAF pilot in the war and flew survivors of Belsen and Dachau to England. He saw the camps, and explains his continuing hatred of Germans. The conversation has left me quite disturbed.

SATURDAY, 23 JULY / NEW YORK
Soaking wet in the rain in the old Village, now very largely gay. One shop, the Marquis de Suede, selling whips and collars. Good music.

People at the [*Village*] *Voice*. Some cabbies have removed the bullet-proof plastic shields. Pearl's unchanged in menu, only difference is decoration and clientele. Still perhaps the only good restaurant in New York deliberately closed Saturdays; it used to be said that this is because Pearl is orthodox Chinese. Late night stroll with Audrey [an old Toronto friend] up Fifth Avenue, past the library lions, past the moonshadow of the Empire State Building. Cafés in SoHo. People sleeping in Washington Square.

SUNDAY, 24 JULY / NEW YORK

Audrey and I stumble into a gallery opening fairly late at night. In old clothes, we load up on salmon and other foods, only to discover that the crowd isn't there for an opening but rather for a wedding reception. Leaving as quickly as possible, I have my hand shaken by an old man, obviously father of the bride. I feel I should give him an envelope. Instead, I mutter something about wishing them all the best. We beat it out of there and up an alley. At the twentieth anniversary they will be arguing about whose friends we were ...

In the old days one gave blood at Roosevelt Hospital for I believe $13-a-pint food money. Now one gives semen at the Bellevue sperm bank for $40 a wad? a jolt? A unit, in any event. I draw no conclusion from this change, except to say something vague about inflation.

MONDAY, 25 JULY / NEW YORK–TORONTO

Speech has been faltering, though I have not lost confidence. It was better in the morning and I hope will be better still tomorrow. I tell Audrey that I always have found our friendship rewarding and fulfilling. She laughs at this in the absence of any better response ... So again I leave New York: Tuli Kupferberg, living in wretchedness in a slum loft above a bar at Sixth Avenue and Spring Street, saying, "A bunch of us were invited to Wisconsin for a conference on the future but it turned out to be a recollection of the past."[1]

---

1   Tuli Kupferberg (1923–2010), New York experimental poet and member of the radical band The Fugs.

MONDAY, 12 SEPTEMBER / TORONTO
Spent much of today, like much of yesterday, sorting through old letters, diaries, and drawings. Letters mostly and most of them destroyed in the end. The ones to and from E and, to a lesser extent, B, broke my heart. F's so caring in her peculiar way and mine so selfish and full of imaginary woe. I wonder if I shall ever come to terms with my other (in this case, social) self and do something about the sickness she speaks of with such maddening accuracy. Looking earnestly at more recent relationships I think that I have become better the past year or two: more attentive to the feelings of others, less artificial in public. There remains the possibility, however, that such a view is caused by the addition to my problems of a newer, still more false, idea of myself: a sort of inverted cynicism. Although all the correspondents were younger in those days, as of course I was (painfully so) – still they were so right and I was so wrong. I carefully kept only a few letters from each, all of them innocuous. I would have myself believe that the selection was to protect their feelings but I know better; it was to protect me from myself. I also preserved a few letters from Woodcock, Earle [a former Toronto friend], and others that have special meaning. Now everything is neatly labelled and stored away. I feel cheap, as though I am foolish enough to believe I have now carefully rewritten my past and prettied it up a bit.

WEDNESDAY, 14 SEPTEMBER / SAN FRANCISCO
Ginsberg's Dublin Pub. Overseas banks. City Lights amid the massage parlours. I call up [a Toronto acquaintance] who has been living here since returning from Fleet Street, where she starved. Leaving the hotel in Sutter Street, I pick up a bottle of wine from the drug store. The reason for her reaction to me back in Toronto, she says, is that she was carrying on with her landlord-and-best-friend's-husband under the nose of her own husband. This now past and husband gone.

THURSDAY, 15 SEPTEMBER / VANCOUVER
Vancouver has grown for the worse. New buildings everywhere. The Doors in Chinatown, where once I ate for 90 cents a week, a daily bowl of rice and a plate of cold pork every so often, are closed, probably by the board of health. I liked the city better when it was everyone's retreat.

MONDAY, 10 OCTOBER / TORONTO

Thanksgiving weekend. On Friday evening, dinner with Linda Thorson after a performance of a play at the Bathurst Street Theatre (a converted church) in which she is starring.[2] Twenty, even 15 years ago theatres in renovated barns were popular; now this one in a church. And I see old churches being put to many other uses. Did the first trend signify at last the triumph of urban culture over rural and does the second indicate the final demise of the sectarian at the hand of the secular? I doubt it, but this is the kind of thought one can wholesale to impoverished editorial writers. The restaurant seems not to have suffered much by the change of management – its founder having moved to Florida. What Toronto really lacks, however, is a restaurant whose walls are papered in fading 8 x 10s of third-rate actors and corrupt aldermen, the sort of place at which sullen reporters and connivers eat lunch and whose owner routinely cashes everyone's paycheque.

FRIDAY, 21 OCTOBER / TORONTO

The other day I saw John Diefenbaker (who once threatened to sue me) in the lobby of the Radio Building on Jarvis Street, very tall and square-shouldered and expensively tailored in a shiny suit.[3] Only on television, when the focus is on the head, does he appear terribly feeble. He does, however, continue to look like a soup-stained old character, full of bluster and nostalgia for his triumphs of long ago.

I am now working several days each week at Church and Front in [Michael] de Pencier's magazine empire. I love that part of the city for its old buildings (made the proper size for people and not to match other buildings) and its traces of the time when King was Toronto's principal street. In the autumn weather, which is rapidly overtaking us, it is especially appealing. The other day I walked past the St Lawrence Hall and noted again the cast iron watering trough with its three levels: one for the horses, another for kids, and a third, lower one for dogs. How

2 Linda Thorson (b. 1947), Canadian actor, starred in the television series *The Avengers*.

3 John Diefenbaker (1895–1979), Progressive Conservative prime minister, 1957–63.

thoughtful of the Victorians in small ways such as this, how monstrous otherwise.

Chesterton's book on Browning: "It may be difficult to discover the principles of the Rosicrucians, but it is easier to discover the principles of the Rosicrucians than the principles of the United States."

I dislike the tone my voice is taking today.

1978

By becoming a first-time property owner, I also became, with a suddenness that shocked me, a major debtor. Before I could grow accustomed to living with a first mortgage I had to retire a second one. So my freelance life became even more hectic. I seemed to oscillate between two downtown intersections. At the corner of University Avenue and Dundas Street, I wrote a great deal for *Maclean's*, which had become a weekly under the editorship of Peter C. Newman. My subjects were books, film, music, and – a new category but one I had always been interested in – the media. At the same time I could be found most days near the intersection of Church and Front streets, where a large number of magazines were published. Among them was *Toronto Life*, where I peddled ideas as well as my own writing, produced "display copy" (headlines and decks), and performed assorted other functions. That autumn the magazine printed a 22,000-word piece of mine about office politics at the *Globe and Mail* that resulted in a low-level establishment furore. I repeated to myself a remark of Sam Spade's from *The Maltese Falcon*: "I don't mind a *reasonable* amount of trouble."

SUNDAY, 29 JANUARY / TORONTO

For about the past two weeks I have been settling into the house in the Annex. I am optimistic about being able to live well cheaply, which is perhaps the best defence as well as revenge. The Powers, so to call them, would have us eat chemically treated food and live with planned obsolescence, and all the rest of it. The answer is to become as self-sufficient as possible without abandoning what it is one thrives on and enjoys. The answer then is to become some sort of urban farmer, and I am full of schemes for living well, getting my work done and so on while paying next to nothing for food, fuel, and the like. Until spring I'll be spending time fixing the interior of the house. Stage one should be cooking one's own food and publishing one's own books. Stage two should be growing the food that one cooks and printing the books that one manufactures. At least I shall get to stage one. A process that began long ago is at length leading to where I feel I must go. At present, however, it's lonely in this big house. I seek someone to rent the top storey.

Recently Joey Slinger, the former gossip columnist of the *Sun*, now with the *Sunday Star*, was at the National Newspaper Awards banquet at which the keynote speaker was Diefenbaker. As it happens, Diefenbaker is (was) quite an avid reader of the column, and asked Slinger what trouble he had with libel actions. "We had a saying when I was a young lawyer," said Diefenbaker. "The greater the truth, the greater the libel." Replied Joey: "It's for that reason, sir, that I avoid the truth as much as possible." Both were amused at themselves.

WEDNESDAY, 8 FEBRUARY / TORONTO
Not even another person's relatives are so embarrassing as another person's patriotism.

Irish whisky leaves you not with a hangover but with a famine.

God laughs at both artists and politicians but He laughs louder at the politicians.

SUNDAY, 12 MARCH / TORONTO
I am confused about the purpose of this journal. I don't wish it to be a record of daily doings; I have my appointment book for that. Nor do I want it to become a *polished* rephrasing of current thoughts and anecdotes, though too often it is just this – I can't help myself. No, it should serve two functions. First, to reveal to me at some later time how I can improve, to explain better than I can now why my personality is as it is. Second, to allow me to permit the emergence of material that I can use elsewhere. The latter has already been the case on one or two occasions. The problem is finding the proper tone for later use. Pulling out all the stops and striking for honesty above all else may be excellent therapy, but is this the matter at hand? Isn't the point rather to set down raw

material? Not so raw that it's formless the next day and, even worse, with time. Not so well thought out as to be just more writing. The journal should be a *release* from writing.

WEDNESDAY, 17 MAY / TORONTO

Inwardly I've always felt that I would accomplish something significant. I have believed this with the glowing innermost part of myself that transcends mere rationality. What on this one plane was a sense of inevitability became, on other levels, constant disappointment, even bitter resignation. Some people, who've necessarily based their opinions on how I've talked, not on what I've thought, believed, depending on their own makeups, that I was a gentle idiot or pompous fumbler, destined either for mental disintegration or deserved come-downs. Their morality-by-rote told them to pity me; but the doggedness of the problem (caused by my refusal to stay silent) brought their contempt to the surface. When, on occasion, I have chanced to show promise or accomplish some minor feat, they have been forced to stare uncomprehendingly – to question their own judgement and my sincerity.

It is wrong to mock the afflicted. But it is foolish of the afflicted to appear on television.

Lunch today at the Courtyard with Peggy A. Her pointed comments surface like photographic images in a chemical bath after hours of conversation have ended. Or else like watermarks, I don't know.

FRIDAY, 22 SEPTEMBER / TORONTO

I have resumed this journal at last. I now have some sense of its usefulness, as I have several times pilfered ideas and observations from these pages for pieces I've been writing. I'm now at home with the fact that it's neither a daily record nor an exploratory exercise but rather good discipline. By writing at the end of the day I hope to take advantage of the odd mental alertness and capacity for wonder that accompany fatigue. This notebook I'll certainly find easier to maintain now that the weather is beginning to change; I've always worked best and most conscientiously in cold weather.

A certain segment of Albertans should be addressed as Reverend in the same spirit in which Kentuckians enjoy being called Colonel.

One must learn to make good use of every mood.

FRIDAY, 29 SEPTEMBER / TORONTO

Being a Canadian forces one to live in the present. This is one of the many benefits and an important one, I think.

SUNDAY, I OCTOBER / TORONTO

To the [Maple Leaf] Gardens to hear Neil Young.[1] His show opens with the staginess now demanded of big concerts. A group of Trappists with electric red eyes glowing under their hoods (actually, they represent characters from *Star Wars*) appears on stage and moves about giant speaker cabinets covered by cardboard housings painted to look like huge steamer trunks. In time, one of these casings is hoisted overhead to reveal Young, maybe fifteen feet above the stage, curled up in a foetal position atop the speaker, his head resting on a three-foot harmonica. He sings the first number from there after pretending to wake up and stretch. The audience lights candles, throws Frisbees, and smokes joints, as much lost in the past as Young himself. Although I don't stay beyond the first half I am glad to have heard him live. I now have a much better sense of how his high-blown lyricism goes together with his melodic gift. Still, his most accomplished songs (these are atypical ones melodically, such as "Old Man") are fine indeed. He frequently changes instruments, and wanders the huge stage troubadour-like as he performs. There is a minimum of chatter. He does not seem particularly impressed one way or another by the fact that this is the biggest possible auditorium in his old home town. He's come through so much, as so many have in terms of drugs, etc. But he's living in the past. I was too young to be anything but an onlooker back then, and I'm just now gearing up for what's ahead.

SUNDAY, 8 OCTOBER / TORONTO

A message from Sue Glover [the managing editor] to call her about the *Canadian Forum*. I expect her to tell me the magazine has had to postpone or suspend publication of the next issue. The magazine is peopled by sentimentalists inept at human relations. Two of them in particular manage to be very insulting whenever I see them. There has always been the feeling that the magazine is a private affair among gentlemen socialists,

---

1   Neil Young (b. 1945), Canadian musician and songwriter.

that working-class people and those who actually know a bit about journalism are unwelcome. They are suspicious of pop culture yet engaged in it, protectors of high culture, unwilling to let it fall into other hands.

SATURDAY, 14 OCTOBER / TORONTO

Notes on some novelists … 1) Graham Greene, in the names he picks for characters, flaunts his skill and flouts the subtlety that should inform it.[2] Thus in *The Third Man* he has an American searching for a perhaps nonexistent fellow countryman named Lime – nonexistent because, while the character is an American, he also in a way represents England in the Cold War: he's everywhere and nowhere, he's what's become of the limey. Similarly, in *The Quiet American* the American in question embodies all the worn-out stereotypical qualities of the US liberator of bygone times. The naïveté, the lust for being liked. He's like the characters of Ernie Pyle. His name is – Pyle. 2) Mailer is obsolete in terms of his career.[3] Worse than obsolete, anachronistic – no, extinct. He's the Famous Novelist, a nineteenth-century concept when the masses went in for the Zolas, the Dickenses, the Trollopes – all those verbose narrators who made people realise that their own civilisation, not simply the classical ones, could be the meat of powerful art. This all seems so silly when pulled out of context so sharply by Mailer's insistence on his own greatness. The shade of the big man with big ideals in an age of big events has become, quite simply, a blowhard. 3) Joyce Carol Oates is in one respect a reprise of Colin Wilson.[4] Wilson surfaced with his book *The Outsider* in 1956, a working-class kid living in a sleeping bag on Hampstead Heath. Reviewers gasped that a working-class lad who hadn't gone to university could have assimilated such wide knowledge of philosophy and art. In truth, Wilson had read nothing that wasn't available in paperback at the sort of English bookstore one finds in non-English-speaking cities, and what he'd done

2 Graham Greene (1904–1991), English novelist, author of *The Quiet American*, *The Heart of the Matter*, *Travels with My Aunt*, etc.

3 Norman Mailer (1923–2007), US novelist and commentator, author of *The Naked and the Dead*, *Armies of the Night*, etc.

4 Joyce Carol Oates (b. 1938), US novelist, author of *We Were the Mulvaneys*, *them*, etc.; Colin Wilson (b. 1931), English novelist associated with the Angry Young Men of the 1950s, author of novels, genre works, and books of popular psychology.

with the information was not amazing in the least. His success was made
by other people's shock at realising the poor fucking bastards were gaining on 'em. (Later, he did go on to prove himself a remarkable writer:
but now the kitchen sink school is passé in Britain, and he is ignored or
ridiculed.) Now in Oates we have a similar situation. A working-class
woman from Rochester, I believe, who astounded the elite with her presumption (and like Wilson, her hard work). In her case the effect has been
achieved through a body of writing. To hear her talk, to hear the accent
and the earnestness and studiousness with which she undertakes to answer simple questions, to ponder simple issues – this is the tipoff. To me,
it's also, variously, nostalgic and a bit disconcerting. (Like Wilson, she has
triumphed over what promised to be her early reputation; she's of course
a far more important writer and artist to say the least, though Wilson has
a decently curious mind.)

SUNDAY, 15 OCTOBER / TORONTO
I am the reverse of the fifty-year-old businessman of fiction, the one who
suddenly realises that he's spent his days chasing material success at the
expense of inner peace. I, conversely, have my intellectual, emotional and
spiritual lives in what seem increasingly to be pretty good shape. What I
want now is to be a success.

Magazine writing is more and more like acting. Actors get one or two
meaty roles and so acquire names – roles many others could fulfil just as
well. From then on it's a struggle to get parts that aren't seen as backslid-
ing into semi-professional status. One seems to develop in this post-star-
system environment only by becoming older, more familiar to the
audience. So it is with magazine writing. One gets the occasional assignment with a scrap of flesh on the bones. Between times it's a lot of fixing,
short pieces, impossible subjects and false diction. The difference is that
this business, being ruled by a few editors and trendies rather than, ultimately, by a democratic audience, sends you up instead of revering you
as an old-timer.

TUESDAY, 17 OCTOBER / TORONTO
I write this in the elation of fatigue, hoping some sense will still be apparent when I look at the page again in the morning. I am finishing a
marathon rewrite session at 3:30 a.m. It's dead quiet.

Some bright social historians of the future are going to begin defining the constant tension within pop culture as a continuation of the never-quite-resolved divergence of the Mods and the Rockers, taking their metaphor from early 1960s London. This difference in cultural outlook is apparently timeless: one sees it in books about aesthetes between the wars; one sees it in punk rock now. The latter interests me a great deal (though not musically, structurally as in the New Wave groups). Rather, it's the premise that's so appealing. Middle-class people were brought up to believe that working-class kids vomited on stage and wore safety pins in their noses. Here we have the same middle class paying through their own noses to see working-class ones pretending to satisfy their prejudices – paying and not really being any wiser. Beautiful.

To the Royal Alex to see Peter O'Toole and Jackie Burroughs in Coward's *Present Laughter*.[5] A highly enjoyable experience although afterwards I am struck at once by the memory of George Jean Nathan's piece recalling the source of Coward's jokes: vaudeville. O'Toole is marvellous, alternately graceful from the knees up and awkward from the knees down, or vice versa. I had not realised how much he acts with his body. Not quite a farce, not precisely a comedy of manners, this was one of those plays centred on a man who thinks himself rational and sophisticated but who's presently taking great delight in being flustered. The sort of role one associates with Cary Grant. Or at any event, the tone of voice.

FRIDAY, 3 NOVEMBER / TORONTO
There should be a derisive generic term for publishers, the equivalent of *quack* for doctors and *shyster* for lawyers.

TUESDAY, 28 NOVEMBER / TORONTO
Dinner with [an actor] for a little piece in *Maclean's* but actually to test myself. She is so like R who stole away one of her husbands. Now with a few years under my belt I see the little weaknesses and insecurities of this precise type of personality, but such knowledge is not so much limiting as it is complicating.

5   Jackie Burroughs (1939–2010), Canadian stage and television actor.

We meet at the Windsor Arms, naturally. She is there sitting cross-legged on the bed talking with a publicist who's from Sri Lanka. We have some tequila, she fields a few phone calls, we talk; the scene is very familiar from the example of others who carry their lives with them on the road. I go down to the Courtyard to wait while she changes. She finally comes down, with the publicist again, wearing a see-through Victorian dress. In time we are joined by some strays: the publicist's boyfriend; a boutique-owner and rocker I'd seen for years but whose name I still don't know; an owner of after-hours clubs; the after-hours club guy's sister, who's working on Tom Hedley's film; and Pierre Sarrazin, the brother of Michael and virtually his double.[6] Two Broadway big shots in their fifties stop by for a while as well; they are here to rent the theatre at Stratford for some off-season rehearsals.

The evening is riotous. [The interviewee] speaks of putting energy back into the system lest she risk a smack (she looks heavenward) from the Big Paw. She *becomes* a Tennessee Williams character when drunk, which is what we all quickly become. When the Courtyard closes, we all return to her room. The goings-on are still going on when I leave in the middle of the night. I return home thoroughly looped on champagne and repeated tequilas. My chore now is explaining to *Maclean's* how I let myself get stuck with the champagne bill for hundreds of dollars.

FRIDAY, 16 DECEMBER / TORONTO

At about 9 p.m. Jack Batten [journalist, who lived down the street] knocks on the door. He had been walking home when he saw a coatless old man passed out with his head in the gutter just one or two houses south of here; several other people before him had simply stepped over the fellow, Jack says. I take a look and see that the fellow has no watch, wallet, or ID. He is comatose and won't stir. Although there are no visible injuries we are cautious of moving him. I knock on [next door neighbour] Bill's door and he gets a blanket and calls the cops, who send an ambulance. No liquor on the breath and the eyelids, once the ambulance men get a light on his face, are those of someone who's ODed. Jack

---

6 Tom Hedley (b. 1943), expat Canadian screenwriter of *Flashdance*, etc.; Pierre Sarrazin (b. 1944), Canadian film producer; Michael Sarrazin (1940–2011), film actor.

continues on, and I go to a party in progress at Bill's. It is a predictable party full of women in expensive boots and peasant blouses who've just returned from living in the caves on Crete, of slightly older types who speak with mock gentleness and wear waistcoats over their undershirts. I get drunk and go home.

Lately my speech has been as bad as at any time in the past year. I'm getting resigned to the fact of being an emotional diabetic, carefully nurturing a particular healthful and cautious lifestyle.

1979

Much of my sustenance during the year came from the fact that this was the fiftieth anniversary of the 1929 stock market crash. *Weekend* magazine com-·missioned me to write something on the subject that would take up one entire issue. Of course I had no interest whatever in the stock market as such – no interest and no knowledge. But I've always been a keen student of the 1920s in other respects, and resolved to use the opportunity to write an essay-in-disguise about urban modernism in Canada (where the financial calamity differed in several fundamental ways from the events in United States). I ended up producing the manuscript of a small book, published the following year as *Gold Diggers of 1929*, from which *Weekend* took what it needed to fill what was to be, as it happened, the magazine's final issue. Such was my bread-work. On the other plane, I was tending to my poetry with the support and encouragement of Robert Weaver, the saintly figure in charge of literary pro-gramming for CBC Radio.

FRIDAY, 5 JANUARY / TORONTO
"I cried when they outlawed absinthe." A matter of moral hygiene, I suppose. Can those people renegotiate exile from time to time, like a mortgage? I dream dreams of long dead individuals who live only in dreams, which lose something on the page. Sophistication cannot save them. One says, "I'm trying to serve my sovereign as best I can."

SUNDAY, 28 JANUARY / NEW ORLEANS
I will have to come to terms with coming here. One's first impression is that the principal industry is decay, sometimes known as tourism. This adds to the romance, and I can easily see the attraction the place held for

[my father] GSF, who was so full of romantic yearnings without ever quite coming to grips with them. The almost simultaneous impression is that the city is very poor. A cross between Paris and Buffalo.

FRIDAY, 23 FEBRUARY / TORONTO

I'm getting back into my routine after many distractions, some illnesses and, for the past two days, some enervating and almost debilitating socialising. The night before last W threw a dinner party after spending a day or two preparing food. Don Cullen and his wife Janet were one couple.[1] She looks somewhat like R in that she has a triangular face and shows her upper gum when smiling. She seemed severe at first but this was shyness. Later, when towards the latter part of the evening my speech began to sputter, she became positively kind. One of those people who reacts that way when I'm *that* way. When everyone was going home I made the innocent mistake of suggesting lunch sometime when I'm around the CBC, where she works. Cullen piped right in and made it clear any lunch would be a threesome. I don't blame him.

WEDNESDAY, 13 JUNE / TORONTO

Gwen MacEwen calls to invite me to her place down the street to sit sweltering in the garden with her and Mike Zizsis and his friend, Zizsis being the editor of *Intrinsic*, an interesting, it seems to me, small lit magazine. Later the group of us go to a Greek greasy spoon way out Bloor Street. We begin to play a game, "Lloyd George Knew My Father," in which one figures by how many handshakes one is removed from great historical figures. I discover to my surprise, for instance, that I know three people who met Mao Tse-tung and one who met Hitler. And so on around the table for an hour or more.

SUNDAY, 17 JUNE / TORONTO

Audrey and I linger in a restaurant. How I long to figure out the mechanics of our friendship. I know her only as a fellow lover of the picaresque and the exotic, someone who is stubbornly resisting taking her turn at power. But what do I really know of how she feels and functions as a

---

1   Don Cullen (b. 1933), actor and former owner of the Bohemian Embassy coffeehouse in Toronto; Janet Inksetter (b. 1946), later proprietor of Annex Books.

woman, as a Jew? Still, I cannot complain. Our acquaintanceship is secure and comforting.

SUNDAY, 9 DECEMBER / TORONTO

Last night I was in someone else's dream in my own head. My spirit was inside the body and voice of a fifty-five-year-old balding overweight Englishman, a correspondent for the *Observer*. He (or I) was with another man – a diplomat or soldier – visiting the hostages in Iran. We walked one of them, a young woman, around the embassy courtyard so she could get some exercise. She was pretty badly dazed and I (or whoever it was) felt a great sympathetic and platonic affection for her.

Noted about myself in the third person, for convenience: Now that at last he has some minor facility in his writing, and a confidence in that facility, he takes a slapdash attitude towards mere money-work of the most boring sort but cherishes the opportunity to do the better sort of assignment. Both usually work out fine, though stuff done (however carefully) when the money need is greatest inevitably comes to grief.

SATURDAY, 29 DECEMBER / COLLINGWOOD

I seem to be entering one of my "good periods" wherein I exercise, eat cautiously, keep this journal, have kindly thoughts, and seek if not enlightenment then modest improvement. I alternate between such spells and others in which I'm lazy, avaricious, and guilty over paying so little attention to my other self. This see-saw act is my own personal manifestation of the tussles we all have between natural left and natural right, female and male, Canada and elsewhere. I feel as though I'm playing both parts in some ancient masque and sometimes get confused on stage.

Ramsay and Trisha invite us to their country place.[2] We leave hurriedly in a rented car and, through misdirection and incompetence, spend 4.5 hours making what should have been a ninety-minute journey. The house (near Collingwood) is one of those glamorous architect-designed jobs of redwood and glass, remote from everything. I am hesitant and circumloquacious in conversation, having my hands full keeping my

2 Ramsay Derry (b. 1939), editor and publishing consultant; Trisha Jackson (b. 1950), lawyer.

companion from slipping into the stridency that is her defence against tight social situations.

SUNDAY, 30 DECEMBER / TORONTO
The day an improvement on the last. I worry, however, that Ramsay thinks I talk too much about work, though it's he who always brings up the subject and pursues a line of questioning. Odd how natural Upper Canada small-T (I presume) tories, whom one would expect to disdain me, instead sometimes seem to cultivate me as a benign exotic: viz. Charles Taylor, John Lownsbrough, each in his own way.[3] The countryside is pleasant. We hike through the woods, around ponds, over lichen-covered rocks for a few miles. What hard scrabbling this must have been to the original farmers.

We return to the city in the evening to get an hour's rest before Marie and her husband arrive with another friend in tow. How I enjoy distancing myself and observing the process by which our generation is quickly assuming some influence in everyday matters. (I thought this again tonight when I noticed the local Bathurst Street greasy spoon has been sold to a young couple; nothing else in the place has changed, yet the difference is enormous; all of a sudden it's a refuge.) With Marie's husband, I find myself thinking constructively about my social inadequacies. He good-naturedly (and I believe sincerely, or certainly with elemental good sense) enjoys my innocently flirtatious relationship with his wife, who's overwhelmingly good-hearted and unintellectual. But there's a distance there, a struggle on both his part and mine to talk freely and behave with comradeship. I'm sure it stems from the feeling given off by my pauses and my poor eye contact when speaking: the feeling that even Carol [a speech therapist] has confessed to having about me as well. Anyway, on this occasion I made some minute progress in this regard. But I must work harder. My speech therapy has now made me so aware of all this, and I'm amazed at how for so many years I walked around like an egotistical robot offending by my attempts at familiarity (which no one recognised) and expecting everyone else to forgive my hamfistedness – or to ignore it entirely, to see through it in fact – when I did no such thing in return.

3   John Lownsbrough (b. 1946), magazine journalist.

1980

A book I edited as a tribute to my friend George Woodcock, the Vancouver man-of-letters, finally appeared as *A George Woodcock Reader* after being rejected, with agonising slowness, by various publishers. I pushed on with other literary projects, thanks in part to two Ontario Arts Council grants totalling $3,500.

TUESDAY, 1 JANUARY / TORONTO

Today is my thirty-first birthday. I'm just now arriving at the stage of always thinking of myself as younger than I actually am; what a reversal from just a short time ago. Also, I'm beginning to find myself a poor judge of age in others younger than me; where before I could determine 22 from 25 at a glance, or on the basis of a snippet of overheard conversation, now all such ages run together. Yet I am jolly about it all. Why shouldn't I be? My health overall is good, though I'm fighting off the residual effects of old abuses: a process easily mistaken for acute hypochondria. And I feel that I'm entering into a great decade for work, presuming always that I can make enough money with such ease as to let me finish 25 per cent of the projects I have lined up like railway commuters.

It's inevitable to cast back to what I was doing at the start of the 1970s by way of comparison with now. I was a few months back from London and Paris, living in an attic bachelorette on Bernard after quitting the Ford Hotel. The War Measures Act was in effect. I was waiting for those awful poems in [*Our Man in*] *Utopia* to get themselves published by Macmillan and writing a silly items-column for Peter Newman at the *Star*.[1] What a terrible time for me and the country.

---

1 Peter C. Newman (b. 1929), editor of the *Toronto Star* and later of *Maclean's* magazine; author of *The Canadian Establishment* and many other works.

SUNDAY, 13 JANUARY / TORONTO
Today I take up the regimen again after a week or more of sloth. Sensitivity to daylight and darkness, primitive religious feeling, politics – everything changes when my habits change.

How curious is politics in this interregnum period. Everything about Joe Clark is ridiculous except his principles. In this regard is he the exact opposite of Trudeau?[2] Or so some would say. I of course have no opinions on anything.

Recent dream: a rather dramatic one in which I'm being hunted down in Oakville or perhaps Mississauga as the assailant of John Bassett [former publisher of the Toronto *Telegram*]. It is night and I am innocent of the crime, though I seem to be carrying a long wire painted white, which might have been a weapon. The dream is remarkable because of the tightness of the plot; it is, in fact, a thriller, and even as I am among the action I pause to admire its cinematic slickness. It is in colour ... In another dream I have a bridge of silver teeth (left uppers) that falls out unexpectedly, making me fearful that the rest will fall out. This is similar to a rather more frightening dream I had about 1960 or so, wherein first one big-rooted tooth fell out on a table, followed by all the others in rapid succession. This time the loss is accompanied by mature concern rather than panic ... In yet another, I dream of [the magazine editor] Don Obe: an indication of how business life has lately entered my sleeping thoughts quite often.

TUESDAY, 15 JANUARY / TORONTO
Linda Pyke has died. I missed the story in the papers a few months ago because they made no reference to her being a poet, and only now have I heard the news from someone preparing a memorial programme for the CBC. Confined to a wheelchair most or all of her life, she was a small woman with withered legs and an obvious battle with her spirits. I took her to lunch once after reading some of her poems in the little magazines. (Macmillan finally published her collection *Prisoner* after Anansi and others turned it down as too Atwoodian.) Later I tried getting her a job, at her request, but wasn't able to locate anything in the editing field in a building equipped with lifts. I should have tried harder. It seems her

2   Joe Clark (b. 1939), Progressive Conservative prime minister, 1979–80; Pierre Trudeau (1919–2000), Liberal prime minister, 1968–79, 1980–84.

mother, with whom she lived, had died, and Linda decided to go back to school. She fell out of her wheelchair at York and cracked her head but lingered on a bit after that. She was 31. Bob F now tells me he's writing a memorial piece in *Saturday Night*.

My main interest in reading biography and the more journalistic sort of literary study has been to learn about the minutiae of public careers. I have always been fascinated to learn of other people's work habits – what hours they wrote, how they conducted their business, where exactly they fitted in on the stages of their time. I believe this interest has been partly aimed at locating habits worthy of emulation (or theft). But there's also a more pressing need: to make me rationalise, or conjure up, as the case may be, where I might stand or don't stand in regard to public-ness. All things considered an appalling propensity. But I shouldn't complain too much: in searching for these data I have learned a great deal of other things unintentionally. I've even perceived some changes in myself as reflected in the approach to such books; as I get older, I skip the childhoods in biographies; there's nothing to be learned in these passages that I haven't already learned by error.

SUNDAY, 10 FEBRUARY / TORONTO

Returned yesterday from a week in Nassau. Herewith some notes not found in Dupuch's *Bahamas Handbook and Businessmen's Annual*. The two casinos in town are the Playboy one in the Ambassador at Cable Beach and the Resorts International one sharing a building on Paradise Island with Loew's and the Britannia hotels. The former is the smaller and has the worse odds. The ads claim some of the dollar machines are set for 95 per cent return; in Canada or the States this statement would be enough to bring charges under advertising laws. What's more, the place is full of cops, both Bahamian uniforms with their red tunics and white topis and the more sinister house cops strolling about aimlessly in tight blue suits. The bar is small and costly and there are, I'm told, no working girls allowed on the premises, Hefner being at base a Puritan on the D.H. Lawrence level. The casino on Paradise Island (formerly Hog Island), then, is by far the better. The blackjack is good, and one at least stands a chance of modest profit by running a hundred in quarters through one of the diagonal-play machines. Or so it seems to me as I linger to watch the customers.

MONDAY, 3 MARCH / TORONTO
Last night I dreamed I was in Peking searching for John Fraser.[3] The city
was brilliant with natural light and alive with the mercantile commotion
one wouldn't expect to find there. My mission was obscure but sensitive.
Perhaps it involved the *Globe*. Anyway, when I got to Fraser (after following him from a distance) I discovered he was wearing a white suit –
and doing so without the slightest trace of affectation.

WEDNESDAY, 5 MARCH / TORONTO
Canadian intellectuals, both left and right, take surprisingly little interest
in Canadian popular culture despite their concern with all other variants
of art in the country. I see two reasons for this: 1) So used are they
to American pop kultch that they wish to believe the whole field an
American intrusion, in ways not true of, say, urban studies or feminism;
and 2) An interest in p.c. presupposes at least a subliminal appreciation
of democracy; and this is naturally seen to be the American, Jacksonian
rabbly kind of populism that stinks of weak beer and embodies all the
worst aspects of Diefenbaker and other phonies who entertain the people instead of forcing medicine down their throats.

SUNDAY, 30 MARCH / TORONTO
Today I saw the first wino of spring on Bathurst Street. (Where do they
go in the winter? Is it to the place to which taxis disappear when it
rains?)

TUESDAY, 1 APRIL / TORONTO
Unlisted telephone numbers: the initial sign of societal breakdown?

The power of any political philosophy can be drained by turning that
philosophy into a religion (exactly the reverse of what was the case cen-
turies ago). He who turns his back on his religion is a freethinker whose
intellect has outgrown his beliefs. But he who deserts the all-powerful
party is a traitor. Political heretics are the only kind left, as the worship
of power is now the only worship. Where once Paul Hellyer or Jack

3 John Fraser (b. 1944), China correspondent of the *Globe and Mail*, 1977–79;
later, editor of *Saturday Night* and master of Massey College, University of Toronto.

Horner would have profited from burning, they now must suffer the ig-
nominy of being ignored.[4]

FRIDAY, 4 APRIL / TORONTO
The Canadian scene in the 1970s: somewhat like the Grubstreet of
Ned Ward's time when private patronage had been half supplanted
by potboiling.

SUNDAY, 11 MAY / TORONTO
Lunch with Anne [Collins] and her best friend.[5] My speech staccato.
Individually I can, at times, interact with both of them. But I realise that
together I face the wall of their friendship – a friendship in which no one
else can participate. They humour me sometimes but most often they try
for the very thing I too am attempting: a feeling that we're all the same
generation, grown now into some kind of responsible position. We're all
in this mess together.

WEDNESDAY, 14 MAY / MINNEAPOLIS
A million or so is the population necessary to begin achieving some comfort; only then are there enough people to be interested in all the various
forms of activity, only then is there sufficient population that one does
not necessarily know all one's opposite numbers. There are still some
surprises left ... At first glance the city is all white, practically a breeding
farm for stewardesses. But matters pick up around Hennepin and
Seventh: some of the 200,000 Natives (mainly Sioux) who give it the
largest aboriginal population anywhere on the continent. (Do the racists
call them the equivalent of "Main Street Hawaiians," as in Winnipeg?)
Good industrial base, very prosperous, the people the Middle West
equivalent of healthy Californians. Like Toronto a decade ago, its saving
grace is that it's behind the times: few if any high-rises in the downtown
area, only in the suburbs. "We haven't even got Dutch elm disease yet,"

4 Paul Hellyer (b. 1923), MP, at various times a Liberal (twice), a Progressive
Conservative, an independent, and founder of his own Action Party; Jack Horner
(1927–2004), MP, Progressive Conservative and later Liberal.
5 Anne Collins (b. 1952), an editor at *Maclean's*, *Saturday Night*, and *Toronto
Life* magazines; later publisher of Random Knopf Canada.

someone tells me sadly. Socially and economically dominated by the Wayzata set, who are interlocking: the Daytons et al., the Cowleses. University is big (40,000 students) and Dinkytown a clean superstructure: thoughts of the very young Dylan, and Tom from Eau Claire. Canadians have scandalised the locals by taking over cable and by developing a big block of downtown. Meet a reporter on the *Star*. She is blonde and classically healthy looking. We rendezvous in her car when she can't get her cycle started, take in a female mud wrestler (her idea) and then pick up Chinese food to take back to her place. She is full of tiny prejudices about which she shows a curious pride. I stay over at her place though she won't make love. I take genuine comfort in her kissing my neck, stroking my hair. She drops me off after terrible tasting breakfast in the morning; later in the day I see her at a press conference and she's all business …

Sam Butler writes that one can't eradicate mouse ideas (today we'd say Mickey Mouse?), that the best one can do is to get a few cat ideas of one's own to keep them in check.[6] I think of this reading R's book and the embarrassing publicity she engineers to go with it. I think now that her U was a civilising influence on her (this seemed a preposterous notion when they were together). He kept her from North American tackiness, which is so much tackier than the European variety.

The technology changes but the professional slang drags on. Steamboats had cabooses, then railways had them. Steamboats had running boards, then autos had them. Planes had cockpits, now spacecraft have them. The nomenclature of the professional (so important in America especially) lingers as a way of showing connection to the past, which is the root of such professionalism. The modern military man thinking himself a horse soldier, the modern journalist thinking himself a daily newspaperman interested in daily news.

FRIDAY, 16 MAY / TORONTO
Stupid lunch last week with Howard [Engel] in which I fucked up so badly (so suddenly, too) that W had to come in and finish my sentences, like [the CBC television host] Fred Davis [on *Front Page Challenge*]

---

6   Samuel Butler (1835–1902), English novelist, author of *Erewhon*.

explaining away the latest gaucherie of Gordon Sinclair.[7] Make up for it now, being fairly coherent, though in the middle of one of these depressive spells that so ruin everything for me in the spring. It's okay, it's purely psycho-sexual.

Coins passing from hand to hand as a metaphor for the way history accumulates. Also: you're older than I am, you walk ahead, you've made it that far at least, I will make it there also; you are the measure that measures out my life; the difference in our ages is as much as I can grasp of the future.

Blood on the snow.

Even her phone messages sound pissed off.

SUNDAY, 18 MAY / TORONTO

Dinner with Peggy A at which she tells me the following story. A possible business associate was feeling sheepish and so invited Peggy and Graeme to dinner at the house. A few days before the event was to take place, however, the host was walking barefoot near there and contracted some bizarre sickness, not having read the warnings in the newspapers. P comments on [a colleague's] odd way of going through husbands and equivalent as though by changing the scene she can also change the plot.

There are many Torontonians who buy books only on Sunday, which has become the day for culture instead of worship – or if not culture exactly, then gracious living less highly profiled the rest of the week. Where once prominent individuals had their own pews at church, so now they have their favourite tables at the Courtyard. The devotion has receded, leaving only the theatre.

MONDAY, 19 MAY / TORONTO

Dream in which I am with Vera [Frenkel] and Oded [her husband] in what is partly New York.[8] We're walking west across lower Broadway, which opens into what I now take to have been the old farmers' market. Oded is himself but isn't speaking with his Israeli accent. We're all laughing but I sense they're angry with me for some unstated reason, in some

7 Gordon Sinclair (1900–1984), brash *Toronto Star* reporter and broadcasting personality.

8 Vera Frenkel (b. 1938), video artist and printmaker.

equally unstated way. bill bissett figures in the dream as a reference somehow.[9] The market becomes Russell Square in London.

My speech has been going along fairly well in this three-week period when the therapist has been away. But I *must* begin forcing the repetition and elongation when outside the laboratory. The other day I had an absolutely ideal phone conversation: the proper sentiments uttered the perfect way without hesitation or extraneous sound. How I remember forever the tiny triumphs. At lunch later I improved on my last performance with an editor. It's hard breaking these patterns: once I fuck up in someone's presence, I find it very difficult not to do so the next time I'm face-to-face with him or her. Would that this also worked in reverse.

TUESDAY, 3 JUNE / EDMONTON

Here once again and I like it much more each time, not the city itself but the city within the province within the west. I'm a westerner trapped in an eastern body, a sort of geographical Jan Morris.[10] [Note in 2012: I was utterly and totally mistaken.] In Edmonton everything is perpetually unfinished (recall Rupert Brooke or was it Dickens on Toronto?). Everything unfinished including the sky. When the lustre of newness is gone or paled by weather, the feeling of incompleteness still remains, as in unpainted lumber. Edmonton is not unravelling round the edges exactly like most other cities, for the ends were not woven to begin with.

Hurtig's neat little shop consists of his office (one entire wall of his personal press clippings two and three thick as in the Absinthe House in New Orleans and a signed photo of [Liberal politician] Walter Gordon). The shop itself is full of people, Albertan to their very socks, who call him sir or Mr Hurtig in every sentence.[11] He tries to put on a show for me: his driver deposits us at a too brief lunch in a restaurant where he's fawned over; he dictates a few letters and memos in my presence; that kind of thing.

9   bill bissett (b. 1939), experimental poet.
10   Jan (until 1972, James) Morris (b. 1926), English travel writer and journalist.
11   Mel Hurtig (b. 1932), bookseller and publisher.

WEDNESDAY, 4 JUNE / VANCOUVER
Vancouver as usual makes me feel free and drives me to the typewriter
in wonderful expectation, but I have come now to distrust the easy nostalgia it offers. The city is too much changed. The old skid row hotel I
lived in is now cleaned up – on the outside. Too much new development.
Why am I so attracted to Vancouver? Let me count the ways. I like the
streetlife, the way sleaze and wealth commingle. I like the way one sits in
a good restaurant and looks out over industry (in Toronto by contrast,
everyone is wealthy but no one works). And of course the natural setting. Vancouver is almost precisely the right size. It is sad, a good place
in a far larger much worse world. Graham Greene would understand it.

Hoffer's bookshop. In recent visits [Bill] Hoffer has sensed that I only
clam up when he lays his fake angst and westcoastism on me and so he's
grown more humane when I'm about. He actually sits down at the
Granville end of the store and we chat about books (he's just bought old
Fred Cogswell's library, Fred having finally returned from teaching in
Fredericton).[12] Various bizarre characters wander in and out as per usual. He tells me that [the poet] Stanley Cooperman is said to have shot
himself in order to prevent an increase in his alimony. (Who knows if
he's telling the truth?) I can't find her in the phone book. How I love old
Vancouver office buildings.

FRIDAY, 13 JUNE / TORONTO
Audrey from New York talking about a hack book she's writing pseud-
onymously for Ace: "The kind of a house where the editors are intimidated by waiters." She describes the programme at Columbia and I
remark that the people sound very white: "No, blanched almond."

MONDAY, 16 JUNE / TORONTO
Dream with the following elements: Peggy A, a trip to Vancouver, cam-
els, deadly serious Scrabble games (played, I believe, on an oversize black
and white Monopoly board), and passing out.

12   Fred Cogswell (1917–2004), New Brunswick poet.

It seems Don Bailey's wife Anne is dying of cancer, has from two months to two years, according to gossip.[13] She's 35. Howard denies it or minimizes it, but rumour from Woodcock and Harris is that Marian Engel has some form of cancer as well. K as well for sure. Sweet Lord help everyone.

A journal can be a form of religious observance. By sorting out oneself, but *forcing* the reflective element out on paper, one begins to allow for the vacuum to be filled.

SUNDAY, 22 JUNE / TORONTO
Gay communities: middle-class Chinatowns.

SUNDAY, 6 JULY / TORONTO
Sandy Ross [a journalist] still makes me terribly uneasy because of all his suppressed anxiety, yet I cannot deny that his legend looks appealing on paper. While on the *Ubyssey* [student newspaper] he wrote a song called "God and Social Credit" that won him some national acclaim as a satirist. He somehow parlayed the *Vancouver Sun* into *Maclean's* (he was a little late for the great Vancouver invasion of that magazine in its heyday). Very skilled, very sloppy and erratic, he dislikes writers who write with his style and assurance as he feels that they must therefore lack the hard information he covets. Has been known to appear in the office with a tenor banjo and sing an early 1950s country song, "When Jesus Tears the Iron Curtain Down." Looks like photographs of Jack London at thirty though he's 45.

MONDAY, 7 JULY / TORONTO
In a dream I see Earle Birney driving a taxi (a reference perhaps to his terrible accident in a cab sometime in the early 1970s); he waves and smiles but says nothing; he is considerably younger, as in the dust jacket photo from *Near False Creek Mouth*, long before I ever met him.[14]

13   Don Bailey (1943–2003), fiction writer, memoirist, and ex-convict; author of *Memories of Margaret*, etc.
14   Earle Birney (1904–1995), poet and novelist, author of *David and Other Poems*, *Turvey*, etc.

FRIDAY, 8 AUGUST / TORONTO
The American cities I've been to seem dirty and decaying, dotted with ignored monuments to the industry they chose over culture.

TUESDAY, 12 AUGUST / TORONTO
Audrey is here and says to me at dinner: "Things might have been better for me if I'd been Jewish in New York, which is a lot different from being Jewish in Boston, or if I didn't talk in this weird way. But what can you do?" Her absolute togetherness is something I've always admired (and wondered at) silently. Like that time I spent the night out at [a friend's] cottage. As she made my bed I got a look at her bookshelves: there was only one book on feminism and that was a poetry anthology. The experience ever since has made me like her but wonder at her and also fear for her. With Audrey, however, there's never been such fear or wonder, just awe, surprise.

Audrey and I go out for Chinese, then to dessert at the Courtyard. Paul Mazursky [the film director] is leaving as we enter. In show biz the less famous sleep with the truly famous as the big fishes eat the little ones.

Beth Appledoorn at Longhouse [bookshop] reports that Peggy A came in recently with her daughter Jess, aged about five. Beth sought to give the child a gift and fetched one of the international children's books whose pictures she thought Jess might enjoy. "But then I saw that she was reading one of the books on rape instead."

THURSDAY, 14 AUGUST / TORONTO
Lunch yesterday with Conrad Black.[15] He's very charming and perhaps relishes talking about writing, which we do. He tells me at last the inside story of the FP [newspaper chain] sale; thinks the *Globe and Mail*'s publisher [Roy] Megarry all right but believes he's been "seduced by the Geoffrey Stevens editorial types" into thinking the *Globe* an institution instead of a device for selling classifieds. Such is the role he enjoys playing; I respond by grimacing, as I am expected to do. Australians come up in the conversation and he tells me he's proposed to Rupert Murdoch

15 Conrad Black (b. 1944), Canadian financier and newspaper proprietor; later, Lord Black of Crossharbour.

that they go together in buying the *Chicago Tribune*.[16] Of Brigadier [Richard S.] Malone [former *Globe and Mail* publisher] he says: "He's not a man you could say felt, well, *hemmed in* by principles." Black is one smart fellow.

Earle Birney has attacked my temperate, affectionate piece on his book with a letter to Bob F almost as long as my review. Says I've no business dismissing the writers he's talked about since when they were alive I was yet to be born, a remarkable statement for a Chaucer scholar to make. I don't answer reviewers in print, however stupid, and expect others to take the same attitude. I phone him and soothe his aged ego a bit.

Virginia Woolf on Thoreau's works: "They are not written to prove something in the end. They are written as the Indians turn down twigs to mark their path through the forest." For that statement I can almost – almost but not quite – forgive her ridiculing Arnold Bennett's speech handicap.

FRIDAY, 15 AUGUST / TORONTO
That feeling you get when you're in the last free taxi during a rainstorm and speed splashing past others who by twos and threes are desperately, vainly trying to flag your driver: with such a feeling many people stride through life, with guilt and comfort doing violence to each other. I am not one of those.

SUNDAY, 17 AUGUST / TORONTO
Some people are more polite and only do what they do behind your back.

TUESDAY, 19 AUGUST / TORONTO
When I awake, Irving Layton is being interviewed on the radio. How comical and pathetic and phoney a figure he's now come to seem. One can almost visualise him puffing up to his full importance before answering each question. He doesn't talk, he intones and declaims. His voice sounds like Richard Burton having himself on.

16 Rupert Murdoch (b. 1931), Australian media mogul, owner of *The Times* of London.

WEDNESDAY, 20 AUGUST / TORONTO
Take [a literary colleague] to lunch today. As usual, it goes on too long so that my speech winds down after about an hour, worsening the impression. But I do manage to call him finally on the review. With sympathetic eyebrows, I say how sad it makes me that one with his obvious abilities and knowledge let himself be used as a cat's paw by a newspaper that has plausible reason to be disdainful of me.

The mind runs on even as I try to sleep with lights off. One must simply choose some arbitrary time at which to stop taking notice. Like a bank or the post office.

SATURDAY, 23 AUGUST / TORONTO
A weed should offer no affront to a gardener if it bears fruit, except for the fact that weeds are so random and out of any gardener's control. Thus the story of literary "reputation."

SUNDAY, 24 AUGUST / TORONTO
Three ages of prose. The *first* in which the written language is evolving separate from the spoken and becoming somewhat standardised. Here we find joy in being able to realise the strengths of speech in something quite different and with its own particular advantages. The *second* in which the oral tradition, having been lost sight of, is reclaimed a bit or at least put through the filter of prose. This is the age of the novel, which coincidentally is the age of wonder at all the civilisation by which the oral trad has been cut off. Ergo, to treat this civilisation as an almost natural phenomenon is the closest one can really come to nature; hence the naturalists and later the realists, to whom setting down the physical world in great detail assumes at times almost supernatural importance. The *third* is the present age, when the information of civilisation has so got out of hand that prose has become a machete for cutting through the verbiage and the bullshit and for finding (it is hoped) a little peaceful clearing. Thus prose has first aped its environment in awe, then relished and wondered at the manmade environment that replaced it, and finally has gone to war with the next-generation artificial environment that has in turn replaced the second.

TUESDAY, 26 AUGUST / TORONTO

Reading testimonials to the late Donald Creighton.[17] How rancid was his silly ancient Ontarioism, what a bigoted old bugger he was (the words aren't strong enough); and yet how fine his best book (the first – no that's unfair to the Macdonald biography) and how his various ethical and spiritual diseases will only enhance the work in time, giving it the flavour of a period piece, albeit one made of silver. His views concern me today because I sense again how at least a small portion of the prejudice directed at me is in some deep way because I lack a region. This ties in because Creighton was an aspirant to a certain class that in Ontario constitutes a psychic region, one as readily identifiable as the Maritimes or the Prairies or the North or the West Coast, one with its own accent, traditions, customs, mindset and, of course, gentry. The difference is that, whereas these other regions all want to separate from one another, Creighton's region wishes only that its inferiors would all go away somewhere and stop existing.

One always has a few friends and a few detractors, that's just the way it is. One can try to take care with the latter and befriend the former in return. But one can't really choose who's in which camp, not beyond a certain point.

FRIDAY, 5 SEPTEMBER / EDMONTON

Sitting in the kitchen with reporters waiting for the premier to deliver an address in the banquet hall. Jeff Sallot [of the *Globe and Mail*] is discussing the anomalies in the US constitution and their origin.

SUNDAY, 14 SEPTEMBER / TORONTO

Growing older and reading I realise what others must always have known: that the bright moments in any life, whether public recognition or personal triumph, must inevitably fall amid the usual long run of tedium and drudgery. The proper approach to this reality seems to be an acceptance of it: an understanding that the predictable workaday existence is what makes possible the sudden and unusually quite *un*predictable

17 Donald Creighton (1902–1979), historian, author of *The Empire of the St Lawrence* and a biography of Sir John A. Macdonald in two volumes.

relief. Reputation often consists of how one manages other people's recognition of such things.

For the past week I've been retching inwardly at the spectacle of Trudeau's sham constitutional conference. The full attention of the media has been focused on this non-event, which everyone (the public and most especially the media) sees for what it is but dares not identify. What amazes and amuses me in all their coverage has been the almost complete absence of PEI, the one province probably delighted to have been asked, to have been remembered at all. The Maritimes, I'm convinced, will ultimately prove the bane and the undoing of Trudeau-style centralism, not the mouthy West or contrarian Quebec. I can never forget how no one remembers them. This gives me hope that their grievance, when it comes, will be so unexpected as to be overpowering.

The University of Toronto is a pernicious influence on the life of this country, this province and most especially this city. It has no involvement with the community except in its capacity as perhaps *the* major slum landlord and destroyer of historic buildings. A breeding ground of snobbery of the worst sort. It's interesting, for instance, that whereas most great universities – Oxford, say, or Harvard – clutch the local bohemia around them like a cloak, the U of T keeps its distance and always has. Gerrard Street, Yorkville, now Queen Street for God's sake – always the bohemians have taken the cue and moved as far away from the campus as possible, for the two institutions stand for opposite, almost antipathetical principles.

TUESDAY, 16 SEPTEMBER / TORONTO

It seems odd to make an entry in this journal during daylight hours, even on this quiet afternoon when I have a chance to think and to hear the absence of sound around me. But even without thinking, I know that this journal is beginning, just beginning, to have some at least cosmetic effect on my disposition. I get a sense of having at least begun to work through some personal woes in these pages, and this is comforting.

SUNDAY, 21 SEPTEMBER / TORONTO

My faults have not been simply an excess of my few virtues, as is the case with many people I know; they've been a whole different set of things apparently, to observers, unrelated to my strong points, which they cloud over.

Waiting for the car on Bloor Street I run into [a poet]. All very pleasant until she makes a parting crack about my productivity. I lose both ways: she'd put me down if I worked less hard than she, and of course she puts me down when I work much harder. How odd it must be to see yourself as the norm and everyone else as variant. Human relations never her strong suit.

SATURDAY, 27 SEPTEMBER / TORONTO
George Hulme [a Canadian-born British playwright] is over from London and Charles Taylor and I lunch with him. A week in Canada has left him yearning for the rugged, and we leave him at a shop that stocks flannel hunting shirts and Hudson's Bay coats. Over drinks at the Pilot later, Charles is very free about his father, whose mind is beginning to slip. As we are leaving, Charles looks at my umbrella, which happens to be green, and says in sad admiration, "I've been trying to work up the courage to get one in brown."

The monastery and the mine shaft appeal to me equally because in neither (as I envision them) is one expected to speak.

Ramsay and I were talking of this at lunch: how writers in Canada (unlike those in the cultured continental traditions or the political American ones) pride themselves on not being part of the society, being aloof from and, they believe, better than the practical workaday people. Ramsay believes this is because they reconcile themselves to the smallness of the potential market and thus come to feel the whole thing is an almost intramural affair. It puzzles me that citizenship should be one of their great concerns for they are remote from it as usually practised. Rather, to them, citizenship is a sort of honorific they confer on one another to set themselves apart from the true and engaged citizens they deplore.

SUNDAY, 28 SEPTEMBER / TORONTO
Dinner with Peggy A and the mood between us somewhat sour. No doubt my fault. It's as though age is now a matter of concern between us – truly, not as she once considered it to be. "He's only a kid," she said of someone. "About 30 or so."

TUESDAY, 30 SEPTEMBER / TORONTO
Amused by: the verse epigraphs novelists use in their novels to show that they are cultured people, far deeper and better rooted in man's finer

instincts than anyone could ever guess. The epigraph is usually some silly thing from Byron; the novelist is usually a tough-guy realist of the most bankrupt sort.

It is a truism that disfigured Catholic homosexuals make the best confessional poets, proving torture when self-inflicted is its own reward.

Now take me, I've not exactly spent my life in Hart House, but I know few if any men who go around using the word *pussy* in cavalier fashion. Yet certain women (possibly from eavesdropping in raunchy men's magazines) persist in thinking the word is common currency and using it to show that the other sex has no secrets from them, that they are, as it were, one of the boys. But even the idiocy of this pales beside [a female editor's] use of *nookie* in conversation, a word known only to 1958 readers of Henry Miller.

The reason Bob F has always liked me (aside from exotic background – in his eyes) may be that I'm the only smart person he knows who's more socially awkward than himself.

When things go badly, we head for the cellar. When things go badly long enough, we head west. [Hans] Blumenthal's idea extended: when the wave of national energy goes west, does it then return eastward, changing as it passes over for the second time, like one of those handheld credit card machines? Is this so-called age of scarcity simply the beginning of the carriage return?

Dennis Lee: "Many spaces no longer belong to the ones who once filled them."[18]

I'm always amused at Dennis's free use of almost contemporary slang in daily conversation. It tends to be mellow slang and it forms a part of his special easy-going kind of articulation. I see it as the deliberate trappings of a devoutly religious man who's on the outside of the secular culture looking in; in this it reminds me of René Lévesque's Korean War–era American slang, which seems to creep into his conversation whenever he speaks English for the benefit of the press.[19] I keep thinking of Dennis only half a mile away on Summerhill and how little I see of him and how awkward and useless I feel when I do.

18   Dennis Lee (b. 1939), poet and essayist, co-founder of House of Anansi Press.
19   René Lévesque (1922–1987), separatist premier of Quebec, 1976–84.

THURSDAY, 2 OCTOBER / TORONTO

Coming out of the bookstore on Bloor, I meet [a poet]. Over coffee in the Italian restaurant we discuss Marian Engel. The stories are true, worse even than I'd heard: Marian does indeed have cancer. I am sorry and fearful for her on two counts: both out of dread of the whole subject (we fear cancer as our ancestors feared the devil; what if both, in fact, exist?), and out of what I hope is genuine sympathy for her. She and I discuss tales of Marian's legendary social awkwardness, for she truly is one of the few people beside whom I feel like an old smoothy at parties. From there we get onto her loose style of narrative. "Her books would be very differently received," I say at one point, "if this were the nineteenth century and they were published in weekly parts." Apparently this is an insight. For the rest of the conversation she keeps finding ways to pat my arm. I believe she feels for my faltering speech, for when the situation comes up she discusses it with a good sense and level head that I find uncommon. It is my fortune that I have within me the strange occult power to make women wish to touch my right arm and then disappear from my life.

SUNDAY, 5 OCTOBER / TORONTO

A poor, rough upbringing of bad food and no love either causes one to die young or to go on nearly as long as the well-born (though without, of course, the feeling that it's one's *right* to do so). It remains to be seen into which category I shall fall.

MONDAY, 6 OCTOBER / TORONTO

Recently I've been subject to dreams in which I cannot find the landmarks that I know should be in a particular place.

FRIDAY, 10 OCTOBER / TORONTO

I find myself disgracefully dysphonic through lunch and feeling not at all bothered by it (though I put on a good show to ease my companion's tension) and perfectly all right once I get out into the sunlight, away from a restaurant that is acclaimed despite its food, its service, and most especially its décor (which my luncheon-mate likens to that of a bordello; she admits never having been in a bordello, of course, and so leaves me to draw conclusions about ancestral memories).

Home tonight and read the "selected writings" of Creighton that Ramsay has edited. It is, I fear, mis-subtitled: it's rather a "literary remains" of the good nineteenth-century sort. One of Creighton's addresses printed therein is one of the greatest concentrations of cliché I can even remember seeing anywhere; and the whole is marked by an absence of anything resembling an idea or even an awareness of what ideas are for. Still, I suppose, a nice tribute on Ramsay's part to a departed old friend.

SATURDAY, 11 OCTOBER / TORONTO

A Saturday full of drizzle. Walking Bloor Street close to the buildings. Had to break in a new barber, a Portuguese. Stopped in to see Howard [Engel] and Janet and unfortunately got them out of bed.[20] Howard has had a relapse with his bad eye but he's childishly excited about his first book (the first should have been some years ago but Howard is a man of many old fears and insecurities). He pads round the house in a bathrobe and I can't help noticing that he has large and rather beautiful feet, the toes not crumpled from years of bad shoes like the rest of us.

My Chinese neighbours two houses away have long practised Far Eastern gardening methods in their back lawn. Now they've taken to doing strange things to ducks. For the past few days a barbecued bird, gutted and spreadeagled in pathetic imitation of the reverse of an old German coin, has been hanging on the clothes line.

Among thoughts *esprit de l'escalier*: The next time someone asks me sympathetically whether I will be able to cure my speech, I shall say: Cure? It's not a venereal disease.

SUNDAY, 12 OCTOBER / TORONTO

Thinking more about Creighton, I still believe the fact of the book is a better memorial than the contents. Creighton had his two forms: the major nineteenth-century book and the polished historical interpretive essay (rather than simply the research paper). Yet he was afflicted with this disease of wanting to be a person of general ideas, possibly because it harked back to some favourite period, though in truth it harked back

20 Janet Hamilton (1951–1998), fiction writer, author of *Sagacity*; married to Howard Engel.

best to early America more than to early Canada or early Britain. All this went along with a parallel and typically academic notion of not wanting to waste any ideas on mere journalism. The result: a lot of verbiage about not much in particular. Also, he failed to see how pure tory prose had become impure. He never saw that journalism had made it more epigrammatic, something on the order of Galbraith's, for instance, which is at once very high-toned and very modern, the sentences structurally simple (and looked at as sentences, boring) but redolent of the idea of the writer as a kind of amateur observer.[21] Trained in the academy, don't you know old boy, but not really of that world. Nor of the crass world of commerce and smoking cars; and indeed, finding the whole notion charmingly déclassé.

MONDAY, 13 OCTOBER / TORONTO
There's a kind of old Torontonian who will have you believe that even when the city was dreadfully imperial 1940s in style, it still presented to their (retrospective) eyes a lot of potential. They will have you know that *they* felt it was a sort of Belfast on wheels.

SATURDAY, 18 OCTOBER / TORONTO
Thinking more about Sandy Ross and how he has built up an often convincing façade of sophistication, or rather slickness and polish, but is secretly still a Vancouver boy frightened of Toronto (easier for the native-born to take such things seriously even though the stakes for them are so very much lower) and thinks I'm onto his game and mocking him, or else reminding him in his own mind whence he came, or perhaps thinking I am a convenient source of embarrassment at his own ruse.

I must go it alone because I am not part of a group and must not be part of a group because I must go it alone. Take some simple professional matters. One of the most significant developments of the era has been the way the young leftists have built their own superstructure, or machinery of recognition and development, quite apart from the universities. They have their own book publishers like [James] Lorimer, their own institutes, their own folk heroes, their own magazines, their own

21 John Kenneth Galbraith (1908–2006), liberal Canadian-born US economist, public servant, and author.

small-c culture almost, as the straights have so long had. I have no place in either camp, except perhaps when looked at historically.

SUNDAY, 26 OCTOBER / CHICAGO

The city is brittle and busy and yes windy. If the best face of London is its late Victorian highwater mark, then Chicago's is the 1920s. The evidence is everywhere. The old architecture was an original response to the commercial excitement. Walk up and down Michigan Avenue with W, pointing out this and that, examining the Wrigley Building and the Tribune Tower in detail. Then I walk over to look at the bullet scars on Holy Name Cathedral from the Capone attack on Weiss. O'Banion's flower shop stood across the street, and there is now a bar called O'Banion's nearby: a safe nostalgia to traffic in. I take W up to the Near North Side, up Lincoln, past the Biograph where Dillinger was killed, towards Altgeld. A pleasant chilly day. Only strip shows and peep shows and bookstores left on Rush Street because the massage parlours have all moved outside the jurisdiction of the local police, either out to the O'Hare area or else to places like Skokie and Cicero (shades of Capone and bootlegging).

Then we go to the [Ben] Hecht exhibit at the Newberry [Library], which takes up two floors and is wonderfully vivid: his Oscar, letters from [H.L.] Mencken, many photos I'd never seen. Also new to me is the fact that Hecht considered writing his autobiography (but in verse) as early as 1927. Then via an old Queen Mary omnibus (we ride on top) back to the Drake for the reception and dinner. W says she's never seen so many $1,000 dresses all together in one room, and indeed the place does seem lousy with Fieldses and such. We amuse ourselves cracking private jokes about the old coots and their cootessas and their young very white daughters who look like centrefolds from *Town and Country*. W remarks that [a friend in Toronto], seeing so many eligible bankers, would have a vaginal heart attack on the spot.

The banquet must feature 600 or 700 people, including two former governors of Illinois, only one of whom, curiously enough, has ever been indicted for anything. Helen Hayes[22] gives the keynote (I am mentioned

---

22 Helen Hayes (1900–1993), US stage and film actor, married to Hecht's some-time-collaborator Charles MacArthur (1895–1956).

in the preamble by a Newberry biggie) and makes the following points: that Hecht dyed his hair and kept a trainer on the premises at Nyack to keep his waistline trim, that he was cool to Rose towards the end (this between the lines), that the Hecht graves (Ben, Rose, and Jenny – but not Teddy) are in disrepair, that there was some difficulty getting BH into the cemetery when he died (because he was Jewish?), that Charlie [MacArthur] cried over the Palestine business and argued unsuccessfully for moderation on Hecht's part, that [Pascal] Covici at Viking lost *Child of the Century* to Simon & Schuster when he argued against Hecht's "obscenity" and prolixity, that this change cost the book a lot in sales (I don't understand this), that Hecht had many "concubines" who sometimes travelled with him and Rose but that Rose ran the household absolutely and was Hecht's first editor at all times, that Hecht always said he wanted to find the rarest book in the world (Poe's *Tamberlane*, cf. Starrett) in order to quit Hollywood. At one point, the audience was stunned into silence (at least I was) when Hayes made an uncalled-for attack on Israel and Begin.[23]

At the end of the talk I am introduced to Hayes and she asks me to send her a copy of the book. She begins to write out "Helen Hayes ..." and her address but stops and tears up the page, saying: "That's my professional name. I don't have a profession anymore." She then takes another sheet and writes out, "Mrs. Chas. MacArthur." I've never bought that "first lady of the American theatre" stuff but I find myself calling her "M'am" as though I were addressing my sovereign. She's 80 and quite funny and one of the very last survivors of her crowd.

Later, W and I have a nightcap with one of the curators who is bright and also dowdy-but-young. She tells me that Hecht was addicted to pain killers and that the staff found pads of blank Rx forms among the papers, as well as some evidence to suggest that he might have been having an affair with Nanette the secretary. There is also a fellow there who does a one-man Hecht show. Back at the Drake I hear sirens in the night and think of R: no one is famous in a dark hotel room. I have to get up at 5:30 a.m. to catch a plane to Edmonton by way of all sorts of small bizarre places in Minnesota and the Dakotas.

23 Menachem Begin (1913–1992), prime minister of Israel, 1977–83.

FRIDAY, 31 OCTOBER / TORONTO

See two people walking up the street and recognise them at once as being architects. One can always tell. They can't hide from me.

Why is the obvious taken by the devious as being so offensive?

I'm sick to death of all my interlocutors thinking that I'm stupid or that my speech is somehow contagious.

That old line about Halifax as a city that sleeps between world wars has a parallel in Toronto, which sleeps – restlessly, tossing and turning, muttering – between bunches of refugees attracted to it by the potential it offers for slumber and safety.

The closure moves, the great commotion in the House, have occupied me the past couple of days. Republicanism? How can people admire in Mackenzie King what they hate in Trudeau? Why can they not damn both pairs of eyes?

Alan Walker at *Maclean's* about some piece of copy: "We gotta news-ify this stuff."

MONDAY, 3 NOVEMBER / TORONTO

Spot Scott Symons across a restaurant on St Clair, and approach and say hello.[24] He stares a moment, so I introduce myself. (He's obviously forgotten dropping acid in the El Matador on Yorkville in 1968, when I much admired the design of his *Place d'Armes*. But then why should he remember?) He then says: "Do you still think I'm insane?" Me (laughing): "My God, I don't think I ever said that, did I?" He: "You almost did." This is all about a *Saturday Night* review of Charles [Taylor] in which I wrote nothing of the sort of course. A long awkward pause, and then he: "Well, I enjoy reading your work." He is in a denim vest and his beard is turning grey.

Meet Gwen [MacEwen] and some artist boyfriend of hers on Bloor and go to a greasy spoon where I encounter [an editor], as condescending and unworldly as ever (what a combination).

I am invited to dinner at Valerie Frith's (she is the daughter of a very charming Liberal lawyer who had his sentence commuted to life in the Senate). She warns me others will be there. When I arrive I'm greeted by

24 Scott Symons (1933–2009), novelist and sexual rebel.

Val Clery, and it takes me a while to realise that the two of them are a couple. This floors me. Also invited is [an editor] from Vancouver of whom Valerie says at once, "I don't think she'll like you." This person in question has a Vancouver look about her (private school variety), with that triangular face and prominent cheekbones. She has a condescending giggle.

THURSDAY, 6 NOVEMBER / TORONTO
Lunch today with Zolf.[25] He tells among other things non-stop: the story about the 15 statutes of Macdonald and Leslie Frost and that [Sir Izaak] Killam used to personally write many editorials for the *Mail and Empire*, etc.

SATURDAY, 8 NOVEMBER / TORONTO
I dream that I am returning old manuscripts to various people, some of them friends from long gone days. This chore is accomplished from an old factory in which other more normal activity is underway. The whole dream is fraught with the most lingering sort of melancholy and romantic pain. The mood is still with me long after the images and details have vanished.

SATURDAY, 15 NOVEMBER / TORONTO
I see [a journalist] on Bloor Street. He faces me from perhaps three feet away, pauses and then turns away in the most frightened manner. He really is a curious character. The last time he had that look in his eyes was when I passed him several months ago, he being in a phone booth and I on the sidewalk. Judging by his reviews, he seems now to be modifying his professional pose somewhat. In the past he was the uneducated hero and natural genius, the man of both culture and action equally. Now he appears to be playing down his intellectual superiority and cultivating the position of an honest working man looking at books from the outside as he scrapes the manure from his boots. If only he really knew the problems outcasts struggle with every day in the real world. We should be allies, he and I. But I could never drag him down to my level of reality.

25 Larry Zolf (1934–2011), CBC television commentator and political gadfly.

MONDAY, 17 NOVEMBER / TORONTO

Once again, what's this journal supposed to be? Therapy, a source for other writing, an exercise in honesty? Perhaps all three. Every time I sit down at it I fight the temptation to let it degenerate into a *chronique scandaleuse.*

TUESDAY, 18 NOVEMBER / TORONTO

"Spring is for poets. Autumn is for editorial writers ..." [A.J.] Liebling.

SATURDAY, 22 NOVEMBER / TORONTO

A great bout of anxiety this week. Peter Newman asks me to write a story for [a section editor at *Maclean's*] who was supposed to do it but has gone out of town and can't or won't be reached; I try to smooth everyone's feathers as I go along; but [the editor] returns, raises hell, gets Newman angry and then turns on me (a useless pursuit, this last – I've worked at the *Star* and am impervious to editors' insults specifically). I take the precaution (especially since the story *then* collapses for legal reasons) of dropping in on PCN to make sure everything is okay. He is *charming.* It's hard to take any satisfaction in the outcome, however, since *anyone* could out-politick [this particular editor].

Lunching with Bev Slopen, the agent and book chat columnist, I run into Conrad Black in a corner booth. I am a bit awkward, I'm afraid; in fact, my awkwardness has disturbed my thoughts the past few days. But he is of course smooth enough to cover for both of us. He is lunching with some pinstriped operator who looks as though he has just shot JR [a character in *Dallas*, a popular US television series].

MONDAY, 24 NOVEMBER / TORONTO

The party for [John] Fraser's book at the Four Seasons is a curious affair. Arriving fairly early on I am shunted off to talk with Fraser's mother, a charming woman of strong will. By the time I extricate myself, the place has filled with hundreds of people: Peter Newman, the book people, the *Globe and Mail* people, assorted preppies. I bump, almost literally, into Brigadier Malone, introduce myself at once and am quick to remind him that I defended him only last week against [former *Vancouver Sun* publisher] Stu Keate's attack. This causes him to warm considerably, in contrast to the last time I met him when he seemed to have moved all

the way across the room while still, somehow, shaking my hand, reluctantly. I suggest he could get up a jolly good libel action against Keate
(notice how quickly I slip into the *patois du pays*). He says no, that such
would involve raking up unpleasant family memories. [St Clair] Balfour
[chairman of Southam Newspapers] comes by, the Brig introduces him
to me, and Balfour blanches and walks away quickly. Malone then pro-
ceeds to tell me war stories such as what he said to Winston and what
Winston in turn told Max: that kind of thing. Says that McClelland and
Stewart is bringing out a book of his on economics. God help us. He is
jolly. I propose lunch sometime and then push off saying: "I must keep
moving, otherwise I'll be a target in this room." He seems to understand
and reacts appreciatively. Stumble into Charles Taylor, who is drunk as
a skunk and ageing rapidly. I suggest we leave and get some food. The
plan is foiled by the arrival of Lord Thomson, who recognises me (and,
by the look in his eyes, seems to remember that in *Maclean's* I recently
used his name and Al Capone's in the same sentence).[26] I feel as though
I should expect to be tossed a few coppers and told to get out of the way
of the carriage.

Finally I manage to get Charles out of the hotel and over to a restaurant. He spills the wine, spills the coffee, babbles on marvellously about
Al Purdy as a Folk Tory.[27] He begins choking on a piece of meat, turning
red in the face and blue or grey in the lips. I jump up, pull him to his feet,
and with a double fist between his ribcage and navel, give him three
sharp thrusts. I save him but at the cost of his expensive meal, which
comes spewing out onto the table linen. By this time he is repeating himself quite a bit. I manage to then get him out of *there* but he insists on
driving himself home. I dissuade him from this silly notion, envisioning
the headline HEIR TO FORTUNE SLAYS THREE IN AUTO. Instead I bring
him back to Albany Avenue where, while chatting with him, I make him
drink brandy and cocoa to make him sleepy and then trundle him off to
the upstairs bedroom for the night.

26 Kenneth Thomson (1923–2006), 2nd Baron Thomson of Fleet and newspaper
publisher.
27 Al Purdy (1918–2000), poet, author of *The Cariboo Horses*, *Wild Grape Wine*,
etc.

TUESDAY, 25 NOVEMBER / TORONTO

At 8:30 this morning Charles is up and dressed, cheerful and appreciative and absolutely none the worse for wear, or so it seems. I arrange for him to get a lift to his car. As he walks away, I see that he is wearing only one galosh.

SUNDAY, 7 DECEMBER / BERMUDA

Hamilton is vastly more metropolitan than Nassau, though equally old and visually somewhat similar: colonial streets fronting the harbour. The whole country has only 25 per cent the population of the Bahamas yet this city itself is much more liveable and has absolutely all the amenities. Why do I lust after these small places? Because I've found myself a failure in bigger centres? Certainly I've always been this way (my attraction for Wales, for instance, over England), preferring not only their present but their culture and their past. I feel this comes out of regionalism, that it derives from the same impulse as my stand on the current constitutional question. By extension, in fact, I believe I go to these smaller places in order to see Canada more clearly, or so I always come away thinking. It's easier to see the clockwork of the local power elite, for example, when the establishment in fact contains only a few dozen powerful people. Similarly, the cultural set-up and the economic fabric.

Graffito on one of those English knee-high walls: "Fock." Well, phonetically, yes … English school girls with shiny black leather shoes and white stockings and little uniform dresses. No nightlife at all in Hamilton. Bermuda retains its Englishness without finding it necessary to add any more for the tourist trade. Bobbies sent over from home. One of the last places to which young Brits on the make and confined by the economic atmosphere in London can repair and hope to make good and rise without a trace. The one scarce commodity is water. Small water-tank trucks constantly winding along the narrow roads lined with white, pink or blue stucco houses, each with a white tiered roof designed to channel the rainfall into storage barrels. Canadian influence present very little, which surprises me, but like Canada it has two cultures intertwined historically, unable to muster complete harmony. Running on the beach, exploring "caves" made by the action of the ocean upon the coral and limestone outcroppings. Election day.

MONDAY, 8 DECEMBER / BERMUDA

I pick up the *Royal Gazette* on the breakfast tray and read that John Lennon has been murdered.[28] I shout the news to W and when she comes into the room give her a few details: he was shot outside the Dakota by an autograph hunter. She at once sums up the situation correctly, namely that the act comes from the same instinct as the request for the autograph, that the guy wanted a share of the fame and not being able to have it decided to destroy what there was and supplant it with his own infamy. We're both very shocked; I try not to let on but in fact the news (which we follow by getting all the foreign papers it's possible to get every day) ruins the trip for me and leaves a queer feeling in my stomach still. Not because I saw Lennon a couple of times or because he was a symbol for the era, youth, etc. I find myself dwelling on the incident. There were simply too many holes to save him, he immigrated to the wrong America, imagine born in 1940 and with the middle name Winston – it's just all too ironic a statement on Britain and America. Oddly he was the only one of the four reared in a middle-class house, yet he was clearly the most working class in his outlook and allegiances. Mothers, ex-wives, kids – the lot is not an easy one.

TUESDAY, 9 DECEMBER / BERMUDA

I wait at the Phoenix for the New York papers. When they come I take them to a bar full of merchant seamen – Americans for the most part, one drunken Scot. I sit at the bar and read them and begin to cry, partly in joy at being able to do so at all. This evening I am sitting on the deserted ferry to Paget and Somerset. On the one side, the lights of the city, doing its best to be Christmassy in the semi-tropics. On the other, absolute cold fucking darkness with no reprieve.

MONDAY, 22 DECEMBER / TORONTO

Talking tonight to Tom Marshall:[29] his boyish awkwardness a) is different from mine, b) makes me feel better.

---

28 John Lennon (1940–1980), singer and songwriter, formerly of the Beatles.
29 Tom Marshall (1938–1993), poet.

WEDNESDAY, 24 DECEMBER / TORONTO
The final war will be between the Consultants and the Co-ordinators.

THURSDAY, 25 DECEMBER / TORONTO
I was always ten years ahead of everyone I knew in popular culture. Not realising this, they mocked me all the more. This placed still more distance between me and them, and kept me from even beginning to realise that I was ten years behind everybody else in self-knowledge.

SATURDAY, 27 DECEMBER / TORONTO
Easy come, easy go. All the civilisation we ever needed, wanted, or knew.

Lunching with [Douglas] Creighton when [a former colleague of mine] passes by and seeing who I'm with gives me an unreasonably big hello and rushes over to shake my hand feelingly.[30] The phoney. Creighton is a big likable chap of no special brain power, a lower-middle-class fellow who's made money unexpectedly, mispronounces all the French on the menu and seems to be getting very tired of the whole business. Pronounces Calgary as Cal Gary, like an American.

30 Douglas Creighton (1928–2004), co-founder and publisher of the Toronto *Sun*, a right-wing tabloid.

1981

As such financial disturbances always do, the recession of 1981–82 struck the economically vulnerable first and most severely. I was reduced to seeking out odd (and sometimes even bizarre) editorial assignments at various places across Canada and elsewhere. I survived, barely.

THURSDAY, I JANUARY / TORONTO

My thirty-second birthday. I reread the entries from last year and wonder how I could have grown an inch in that time, except perhaps in that my awareness of the need to do so has itself grown.

I walked into the Longhouse [bookshop] and came upon [Milton] Acorn saying out loud to absolutely no one, "I'll have that bastard's resignation!"[1] Seeing me he then shut up, and I bravely went about business at my own sweet pace, then left. Milton has not threatened to kill me for – it must be a year or two now. I feel unloved.

Poets are accepted in Canada as practically nowhere else in the West because of their place in an officially supported and popularly endorsed Canadian culture. Yet they're still bitter and argumentative as poets elsewhere are, because they have no audience as such, only a sanctioned role in the cultural scheme of things. I wonder whether those popular Russians like Voznesensky and the poetaster Yevtushenko have any appreciable degree of this same attitude even though they're said to draw hundreds of thousands of readers.[2] In other words, is it something one always finds in communities of poets regardless of what society they live in?

1   Milton Acorn (1923–1986), poet and agitator.
2   Andrei Voznesensky (1933–2010) and Yevgeny Yevtushenko (b. 1933), famous Russian poets of the late–Cold War era.

But I digress shamelessly. The point is that Milton is demented and, receiving no treatment of any kind so far as I know, gets worse year by year.

SATURDAY, 3 JANUARY / TORONTO
Ah, the best use of this journal in the short term: to allow me the satisfaction and discipline of writing *something* at least on those days (far too many of them) when I get nothing else accomplished.

It occurred to me the other day that I should change my name to George Fetherling; that is, drop my first name in favour of my middle one, as a sort of private homage to GSF. Trouble is that it wouldn't be so private. Another consideration is that "Douglas" is inappropriate in someone with no Scots ancestry whatever. (It also makes me sound like a golf pro.)

TUESDAY, 6 JANUARY / TORONTO
Poetry as a process atop a large body of painfully acquired self-knowledge: I am thinking particularly of Ginsberg's[3] journals.

SATURDAY, 10 JANUARY / TORONTO
Much troubled by fever until I took some quinine yesterday.

TUESDAY, 13 JANUARY / TORONTO
I feel that one should try to keep a record of dreams. To me this is as strict a tenet as keeping a year's food is for the Mormons.

SATURDAY, 17 JANUARY / TORONTO
Reading Dennis Lee and Purdy interviews after I'd just been contemplating the differences between eastern and western poets. Remember Bowering's remark about eastern joke poems?[4] Lee puts it well: eastern poets try to write sound individual occasional poems whereas western poets try for discontinuous flow. But to what extent is this regional conditioning, politics, teachers' influence, "schools"? The west generally

3   Allen Ginsberg (1926–1997), US Beat poet, author of *Howl and Other Poems*.
4   George Bowering (b. 1935), prolific BC poet.

hostile to the concept of the professional poet. Consider Birney in this regard. Much different in the States of course, though I daresay east and west are still separate and different. The curiosity about Rexroth is that he's a western poet who's always written eastern poems.[5] Reading Ondaatje's *Long Poem Anthology* I see how far I have to go.[6]

Let's face it. I'm the kind who, if he's ever going to win, must win on points.

MONDAY, 19 JANUARY / TORONTO
Lunch today with Dennis Duffy (that second *n* in his name will always give him away even more than his accent will).[7] He was charming but seemed to treat me just a bit too much like a student.

SATURDAY, 24 JANUARY / TORONTO
Last week one day I happened by 671 Spadina [the original home of House of Anansi Press] when one of its residents, who works at [the book trade journal] *Quill & Quire*, chanced to step outside. We chatted and I asked to be invited in to look around the old place. The memories! Of course, it looked smaller, and it's pretty run down now. We repaired to the Varsity [restaurant] (which *has* changed for the better) and spent an hour reminiscing independently of each other. Then the other day Woodcock kindly sent me a new book of his poems done by Cogswell. These two strains now go together in a dream in which Woodcock is reading something called the *French Canadian News* and busying himself with letters to and fro, and in which Dennis Lee is talking to Art Smith at some party at which several other writers are present.[8] The other bedside note to myself says, "Describe room – messy," but I don't remember what this means.

Again at Longhouse I run into Acorn who studiously avoids me. I don't make my escape too hastily.

---

5   Kenneth Rexroth (1905–1982), US poet, critic, and translator.
6   Michael Ondaatje (b. 1943), novelist and poet.
7   Dennis Duffy (b. 1938), professor and critic.
8   A.J.M. (Art) Smith (1902–1980), poet and anthologist.

MONDAY, 26 JANUARY / TORONTO
Displaying in full measure her belief in cheap public transit, [a friend] tells me she fantasises about being fucked on a TTC bus or streetcar. I mention that [a colleague] told me that she can tell in [her partner]'s novels which sex scenes stem from his own kinks and which are merely concessions to the intended audience; she just lets these things drop in conversation without any design to steer the conversation in a particular direction. One time she also told me casually he likes to cut her hair. "And it's not just the hair on my head."

SUNDAY, 8 FEBRUARY / SCHEFFERVILLE, QUEBEC
Two days in this dying mining town, sleeping in the bed in which Duplessis died.[9] The place withers away. I try to be merry among people whose only idea of a good time is to stay up all night drinking HBC rum (actually made by Seagram). When on the second day a storm comes up and Quebecair cancels out (as they do on any excuse), I hitch a ride in the two-person chopper down to Lab[rador] City, not following the railway line but flying as the crow doth, straight across the barrens, in order to make the destination by nightfall. We miss by 20 minutes or so, running in the utter darkness without lights. Lab City, when spotted at the end of Wabush Lake, seems like the skyline of Montreal, so much does it stand out in the utter devastation of the countryside. Surprisingly, I'm not shaky after the trip despite the almost gale-like conditions, including a 28-knot crosswind that nearly had our little chopper going sideways when the engine was trying to pull us forward.

TUESDAY, 10 FEBRUARY / SEPT-ILES
A despicable place, company town in the worst sense, a shopping mall, iron ore dust everywhere, everything closing down, everything already destroyed, not what Champlain had in mind. The locals introduce me to an Irishman who has a speech impediment, evidently believing we will bond. He brings in the other local sufferer. So there we are, three people who can't speak, carrying on a conversation down by the docks. What are the odds, I ask you?

9   Maurice Duplessis (1890–1959), Union Nationale premier of Quebec, 1936–39, 1944–59.

THURSDAY, 12 FEBRUARY / TORONTO
"The persistence of the dead in the living,/if recognized, makes us sane."
Tom Marshall.

SUNDAY, 15 FEBRUARY / TORONTO
Flow chart isn't working. Or rather, I am not. I face terror at the prospect
of so many simultaneous deadlines, for big work and small, within the
next 60 days.

Run into Salutin in the all-night Mexican restaurant.[10] He is with a
female video artist. I struggle as well as I am able to overcome his historically base opinion of me but of course merely end up reconfirming it.

SATURDAY, 21 FEBRUARY / TORONTO
I have fallen into the custom, whenever I see the death notice of some
author I've read, of taking down his or her books again in a kind of
tribute. Seeing that Fawn Brodie died, I reread her life of [the explorer
Sir Richard] Burton, an old favourite, and come on the following sentence: "In the end Burton had nothing to show for his summer's work
but his usual two-volume study." Laughter from the wings.

The difference between the foreigners and the infidels and how I am
actually only the former but am continually being accused of being the
latter.

A Toronto scene: I'm at the greasy spoon on Bathurst chatting up
someone when a Greek man comes over to me waving a paper with the
words "Two coffee no cream, one jelly doughnut." The staff soon gather
round, everyone very expectant and with much banter and loud talk;
finally I realise that the customer has been sent by his buddies to fetch a
take-out order but neither he nor the staff can read English; I'm surprised because the people who run the restaurant speak English quite
well – always friendly, fluent, good neighbours. Another one: In the
Bloor doughnut shop in the middle of the night, a drunken First Nations
fellow in some kid's old high school jacket is drinking coffee with a
young Black guy with an afro the size of a basketball and a younger

10   Rick Salutin (b. 1942), playwright and political commentator.

Chinese-Canadian kid, probably a foreign student. They fall to arguing, not one of them understanding the other two.

SUNDAY, 25 FEBRUARY / VANCOUVER

Spend the night at Rob's on Davie with the hookers calling out to one another in the street below. The old Vancouver feeling in me that I must write here, that I could make a refuge here quite easily. But then I must disabuse myself of the idea that I can do only one thing at a time. Wander round endlessly in the atmosphere of rainy tolerance and 1912 architecture. Continue downtown where there is a party for local friends. It is a bit strained.

SUNDAY, 8 MARCH / MONTREAL

When writing business takes me somewhere on someone else's tab, the level of my accommodation rises considerably. Put up at the Ritz, I dream that I am in Montreal at the Ritz but that the room is the one [a friend] and I had that time, must have been '69 or '70. Waking up, I panic that I am not in the room to which I retired last night.

FRIDAY, 27 MARCH / TORONTO

Dinner with Bill Toye of Oxford University Press at the Don Quixote.[11] We discuss the plight of a common friend (the plight being that he deludes himself into thinking he's capable of jobs he's not capable of and so does nothing and starves). Then he tells me of a recent visit to Art Smith, who's in a home in Montreal. "He lay there on the bed, looking at the ceiling. I'd been warned on going in that he looks very bad, but I'd not really been prepared to see him dying. He just seemed to go downhill after his wife died. I brought a *New Yorker* and tried to read several stories to him, but after two of them he waved to me to stop, he didn't care for them. Then I picked up the *New York Times* book section and asked if he'd care to hear the review of [Joseph] *Conrad and the Nineteenth Century*. Was he interested in Conrad? 'Oh yes,' he said. When I finished the review, he looked over at me and said, 'We'll have to read that book!'"

11   William Toye (b. 1926), Oxford University Press editorial director, 1969–91.

SATURDAY, 28 MARCH / TORONTO

As I finish dressing at the Y on Spadina, I spot Matt Cohen as he heads for the showers with a towel clutched around his skinny frame. "I didn't know you were in this neighbourhood," I say.

"I'm not but I keep a membership here. I'm writer-in-residence at Victoria this year."

"Under Dave Godfrey?"

"Yes."

"How is he?"

"Well, he's just into computers now, you know."

"Yes, I saw the anthology he put together. How does he reconcile only being into computers with being head of creative writing?"

"Well, he demands that his students just be into computers also."

SUNDAY, 12 APRIL / TORONTO

My dreams are all so credulous.

One of the most beautiful women I've ever seen I saw one afternoon about 1970 in the subway. She got off at Spadina (my stop that day) and I followed her down past Bloor, mesmerised. When she spoke Greek to someone, though, I lost interest and went away sickened at my own prejudice, or rather perhaps at how reality had punctured my daydream. I think of this and also of the time, must be seven or eight years ago, that I was expecting a fight to break out in the greasy spoon I was in late at night: very much yelling and bantering, and rough stuff just below the surface. But then I saw that all the guys had post office flashes on their jackets. It made me feel safe. How ridiculous.

Where was I two weeks ago when I heard the news that Reagan had been shot?[12] I was in the back of a taxi driving along Bloor by the Colonnade. I told the driver, a Black man, that I was relieved that it was a white guy doing the shooting, else hell *would* have broken loose in the aftermath.

The other night the silence became like the roar of the sea.

12 Ronald Reagan (1911–2004), US president, 1981–89.

FRIDAY, 10 APRIL / TORONTO

Enright tells me some producer (not [Mark] Starowicz) asks him for a writer who can contribute to the arts package on CBC.[13] Enright suggests me and the fellow is interested. Then E says, "There's only one thing, his speech falters a bit." The producer looks disgusted: "We can't have that!"

SATURDAY, 11 APRIL / TORONTO

[A colleague] and I are walking along Bloor to Bay and for some reason he starts telling me about his marriage etc. What is it about me that makes people I don't know well want to get my advice on their sex lives (not that [the person in question] actually asks for advice) when my own is such a mess and when the consensus always has been that my speech makes people too uncomfortable and that I am impossible to talk to even about trivialities?

MONDAY, 20 APRIL / TORONTO

Dinner tonight with Gore Vidal who seems to us as charming and cordial as he ever gets with outsiders (look at what he writes about even his few old friends like Tennessee Williams).[14] W reports that he flashed a curious look for an instant on the first occasion my speech faltered but that he took in the situation in a mini-second. "He's a gentleman from the inside out" is her comment. Generally the session went very well: I (haltingly) talked ideas while W charmed it out. When he's amused (and not always just at his own remarks) a marvellous and intelligent and feminine smile engulfs the lower part of his face ... He's well informed about Canada, which was pleasant for a change. When he spoke of being from a region ancestrally where many people are descended from Roman legionnaires, I could see the connection at once. His head would look perfect on a coin, says W. My thought is that as a young man he must have looked like a gigolo but now, at 56, he looks instead like a very successful bank embezzler, with a hint of a wry grin betraying the fact that he's always got away with it. He suggests someone who is both a Fellow of the

13   Michael Enright (b. 1943), CBC Radio journalist.
14   Gore Vidal (1925–2012), US novelist and essayist, author of *Myra Breckinridge*, *Burr*, etc.

Royal Society of Literature and a Guy, so to speak, of the American Institute of Arts and Letters. He makes me think of Chesterton's remark about GBS: he generates light but not heat.

FRIDAY, 24 APRIL / TORONTO
Lunch the other day with Jack David.[15] I back off contributing to the big critical project, claiming to be just a passed-over old newspaper johnny unequal to the task. I must say he and I hit it off.

Mike, the Bathurst Street barber from Trinidad, plays tapes of early 1960s rock and roll whenever I'm in his shop, and we try to catch each other out on trivial points about groups and labels of the period. We're the same age, and this banter has proved useful, transcending many differences. (Such is the power of cultural imperialism!)

TUESDAY, 28 APRIL / VANCOUVER
Dinner at the Woodcocks. George: looking old now, false teeth, very Muggeridgey mouth. Inge: robust German with terrible bronchial cough and guffaw mixed as one. Jack Shadbolt: a fine leonine head, strong opinions on all sorts of subjects about which he's totally uninformed, very unpainterly and big, kids George about being on the left. Doris S: wonderful Ontario accent and manner, straight, earnest, decent, like a middle-aged Jan Walter.[16] Paul Wong [who] runs Bau-Xi Gallery on coast and in Toronto. His wife: 40-year-old anglo, looks younger ... I arrive first and have an hour of literary and other chat with George in his den, not so many books as I would have imagined, the old portable manual typewriter he uses for all purposes set up on a large folding table. He says his health is fine now, he attributes his heart attack in the '60s to the stress of teaching two new courses and writing three books all at once – I'd have thought that if anyone could do that, he could ... Cocktails then dinner in the small dining room of this very English house ($14,800 20 years ago, now because of land worth $200,000, according to "estate agents") filled with objects from travels ... Topics from George

15   Jack David (b. 1946), publisher of ECW Press.
16   Ingeborg Rozkelly Woodcock (1917–2003), political activist; Jack Shadbolt (1909–1998), visual artist; Doris Shadbolt (1918–2003), gallery curator and art historian.

then and after dinner range from art patronage in 15th-century Germany
to the iconography of the wild roses on Hornby Island as opposed to
that of those on the mainland – all this without the slightest trace of ar-
rogance or brashness or even awareness of what it is he's doing ...
Woodcocks have a clawless cat named Alfie that looks like Groucho
Marx and that they took in from the pound years ago when it appeared
the creature would be killed. Inge and I feed the raccoons on the back
porch: a nightly ritual.

WEDNESDAY, 29 APRIL / TORONTO
Today I have the first tangible evidence to support the years of rumours
that Jack McClelland is getting old fast, is slowing down and getting
tired, is contemplating retirement. After the meeting of the [Writers']
Trust directors, he said that he's bought three acres next door to Berton's
estate in Kleinburg and is planning to sell the house on Dunvegan.[17]
"Out in the country," he said, "I won't be able to get drunk every night,
which has been my lifestyle for the past 35 years." He looks terrible,
just awful.

THURSDAY, 30 APRIL / TORONTO
Last night went to Galen Weston's house, which was even more of a
mansion than I had been expecting.[18] He said that the 18th-century
sporting canvases in the library where we talked are in fact too big for
the room but had been brought over from the "small castle" he formerly
occupied in Ireland.

MONDAY, 6 MAY / TORONTO
John Fraser full of scuttlebutt, as usual. Someone has left her husband
for an Australian woman, someone else (male) is coming out of the closet
less dramatically, a third person plays host not to orgies exactly but
"orgy brunches." All this aside, and under the preppy exterior, Fraser
turns out to be capable of excellent practical advice. We run into Doug
Creighton, who doesn't remember my name at first but twigs when I ask

17   Pierre Berton (1920–2004), historian, journalist, and media celebrity.
18   Galen Weston (the elder) (b. 1940), executive and financier associated with
Loblaws, Holt Renfrew, and other companies.

him what he thought of the *Sun* piece in *Saturday Night* (which he says he liked).

Each day we become more and more American, like a ruin falling down a stone at a time.

THURSDAY, 7 MAY / TORONTO
David Walker at the Albany Club who gossips most indiscreetly about the likes of Ken Thomson ("the young Thomson") and Julian Porter ("the young Porter").[19] The senator has known every prime minister from Laurier to the present, disliking all the Grits and advising all the Tories. After lunch he takes me upstairs and shows me all the Sir John A. relics. I am never less than polite but think, "What the hell am I doing here?"

TUESDAY, 12 MAY / TORONTO
See Northrop Frye in Murray's [restaurant] today, paying his tab at the cashier's; we speak a few moments; he looks to be in better health, and with a finer complexion, than I remembered.

THURSDAY, 14 MAY / TORONTO
Elwy Yost.[20] The sort of person who thinks one enters a monastery in order to lose weight.

TUESDAY, 9 JUNE / TORONTO
Awake today with a phone call at about 8:30 a.m. and notice that I am almost incapable of coherent speech for the first time in months. Sure enough, the rest of the morning is rough, but I tough it out on the phone and by the afternoon the worst seems to be over. Curious.

THURSDAY, 11 JUNE / TORONTO
Lichens growing on the tombstone.

[A friend] says that on his first date with [his future wife], in Montreal, he bought her a dog; a man was exhibiting the creature in the old market with a sign that read, in French, IF YOU DON'T BUY HIM I'LL HAVE TO

---

19 David Walker (1905–1995), Progressive Conservative MP and senator; Julian Porter (b. 1936), lawyer.
20 Elwy Yost (1925–2011), cinephile and television presenter.

KILL HIM. Later, he, she and the dog all moved in together. This is a useful story.

SUNDAY, 28 JUNE / TORONTO
How I used to write with my legs twisted around the chair in squirmy agony, waiting for the words to pick up momentum, waiting for the gears to shift, then never revising. No wonder the results were all so awful.

SATURDAY, 1 AUGUST / TORONTO
One of the worst evenings of theatre I've ever attended took place in the form of a political satire by Charles Taylor and Scott Symons at a Ukrainian hall on College Street. The subject is Jim Coutts.[21] Introduced by Charles, an actor in drag impersonates Coutts' aunt from Alberta. Later, after remarks by Symons, a tiny actor wearing braces imitates Coutts himself. An audience of about 75 persons roars with ennui (the others having walked out, shocked at discovering the affair was not a Citizens for Coutts rally, as had been advertised). The highlight is a musical number, and the cast joins to form a chorus line. Unaccountably, Charles is the only member who is out of step.

Going away Monday to Labrador. Must leave the phone off the hook a week.

FRIDAY, 11 SEPTEMBER / TORONTO
Trisha [Jackson] and Ramsay [Derry]'s wedding party at the University Club, very black tie, haute Anglican. I keep expecting W to say precisely the wrong thing but in fact she performs quite well except for asking Robertson Davies what his new novel is about.[22]

WEDNESDAY, 16 SEPTEMBER / MANCHESTER
Manchester is even bleaker now than it was when the smokestacks were busy. Some streets are burned out and boarded up, especially Moss Side,

21 James Coutts (b. 1938), principal private secretary to Prime Minister Pierre Trudeau, 1975–81.
22 Robertson Davies (1913–1995), novelist and playwright, author of *Fifth Business*, etc.

of course. The old Corn Exchange has been converted to antique deal-ers' stalls but the building itself not improved. Meet W at the railway station, go to the car and proceed to drive to the Lakes. I feel quite re-strained as I usually do when I travel in company.

FRIDAY, 18 SEPTEMBER / LAKE DISTRICT

A tense moment when W begins haranguing me. I can see the wheels going round in her head till finally she decides that she had better straighten up as she's stuck with me in the middle of England, a place totally foreign to her: Only I know the way out.

TUESDAY, 22 SEPTEMBER / LONDON

Train ex Manchester pro London and stay at a small hotel in Halfmoon Street. Walking round London. W absolutely insufferable the whole time, making me vow silently never to travel with her again if I can help it. I will stay on a couple more days alone.

SATURDAY, 26 SEPTEMBER / LONDON

The safety demonstration on British Air includes the exhibition of an inflatable life jacket. The stewardess indicates how the belt is to be tied in a big bow, and then she notes the presence of a child's whistle in a special little pocket at the front. Presumably the purpose of the latter is to summon a bobby in the middle of the North Atlantic.

SUNDAY, 27 SEPTEMBER / TORONTO

Thinking of Peggy A, who's throughout the Sunday papers, makes me think that authors should either not let themselves be written about at all if they can help it or be written about often, so that no one isolated piece can do terrible harm.

When I look at Can lit and find no one of my sort in it, I must take that to mean that there's a place for me, not that there is no such place or no others such as me.

TUESDAY, 29 SEPTEMBER / TORONTO

A visiting author from eastern Europe says unto me: everything in Canada is named after Indians and yet I see no Indians in the streets. I reply: let that be a lesson to us all.

SUNDAY, 11 OCTOBER / TORONTO

My historical interests incline this way: sometimes towards assassins and misfits, sometimes towards poets and misfits; [Lee Harvey] Oswald and [Walt] Whitman; people who leave behind effects much more interesting than their main work and create more mystery than they solve.

The price of flexibility is a short attention span.

FRIDAY, 23 OCTOBER / TORONTO

I see Howard Engel being taken up as a cutie-bear by the establishment on account of his detective books, and this depresses me and makes me feel sorry for him even while I am glad of his success.

SATURDAY, 7 NOVEMBER / TORONTO

On my way from Britnell's [booksellers] to the supermarket today, I stop in to see poor Peter Martin at his bookstore.[23] He is raging drunk, turning on all the customers. It isn't quite noon.

Colombo gives me his stack of new books. The bibliography of Algernon Blackwood is interesting, but John's prose contains the following sentence: "A period of sickness, drug-taking, criminal proceedings, visions, and near starvation came to an abrupt end when he joined the *New York Times* as a reporter." Some would argue on the contrary that's when the visions and criminal behaviour began.

TUESDAY, 10 NOVEMBER / TORONTO

Yesterday a letter from Woodcock, who seems to have had another heart attack, or something very similar, and is now in somewhat dodgy health again.

23   Peter Martin (1934–2003), publisher, later bookseller.

1982

My private life took a dramatic turn when Janet Inksetter (hereinafter J) and I became domestic partners. Professionally, however, the scrounging continued.

WEDNESDAY, 14 APRIL / TORONTO
J and I have been living together now since before Christmas. This is the big news, and a dozen times a day I think of things about her that I want to put down in these pages. The truth and the pattern will emerge over time, I guess. The fact to set down now is that we both emerged *relatively* unscathed from our respective arrangements: her last partner on balance was civilised. In the midst of all this, however, W got in a huff and decided to keep her distance after running out, calling me and then hanging up in anger, sending me a crackpot note, barging in when she knew I was away and insulting Earle [who was housesitting].

FRIDAY, 16 APRIL / TORONTO
This journal is really me talking to myself, scheming a sustainable posture, working it all out silently in the absence of anybody with whom to discuss problems face to face. It is, I suppose, an extension of the way I would lie in my bed as a child and attempt, for hours on end, to figure out my options for the next day's survival. In fact, I cannot help but think of that time in the corner upstairs, behind a pile of furniture, when I actually kept a journal – a seven-year-old's journal – setting down how I had been hounded that day.

WEDNESDAY, 28 APRIL / TORONTO
Yesterday, as an act of friendship, I went to a noontime reading by Janet Hamilton (she shared the stage with Graeme Gibson). It disturbs me to see Janet craving the literary life. She is far too good and sensible a person to wallow in all that business and come out bitter like the rest, as she inevitably will. Which leads me to ponder my own condition. When this current year of financial matters is at a close, I must return to work but only with my ultimate aims sorted out. Do I want the renown as I once thought? Absolutely not. I'm too vulnerable, and besides fame consists largely of television, a medium of which I'm incapable. Do I want standing? Not if it means the niggling, in-fighting, and bitterness of the literary world with its destroyed personalities. A little respect wouldn't hurt, and this will come from writing that is more accomplished and more honest. Such writing, and not the rewards of it, must be my goal.

SATURDAY, 29 MAY / MONTREAL
Returned last night from a quick trip to New Hampshire on business, getting a ride across the border from Montreal where I've now returned. Hanover, as the seat of Dartmouth [College], depressed me, as all college towns do: thousands of fresh smart-assed 22-year-olds. The countryside lovely, thinly populated, thickly wooded, lots of granite, many tiny islands in the various rivers. Possibly a good place to hide one day, good place to practise my defensive posture. So noted.

WEDNESDAY, 8 SEPTEMBER / NEW YORK
I have patched things up with Audrey and got her views on the W business, swearing her to secrecy on my own. Stay uptown, but even then my distance (no longer nostalgia) evident with regard to the city. Owing to some new twist in the bylaws, the city is suddenly full of Far Eastern (that is, Korean) bath houses. Junkies grabbing one's arm outside Carnegie Hall and other sociological vignettes.

1983

In this case, the following few entries tell the story of the year cogently. I got married and struggled to maintain the household, even resorting to an unhappy period writing speeches about government arts policy (such as it was) – the thought of which still gives me a chill.

SUNDAY, 2 JANUARY / TORONTO

Howard Engel comes to dinner. He's batching it this week as Janet, who has been suffering a numbing depression for six months, is off in Halifax seeing a friend. He and I have been discussing all this in detail for the past week or so. The poor guy fears for the marriage. In that regard I'm so fortunate now. J and I have been together more than a year, and the wonderful aspects of the relationship deepen. Her divorce is set for January 21st.

THURSDAY, 27 JANUARY / NASSAU

I'm struck once again by how when I travel I relish the smaller freedoms, which become so much more important when the bigger ones are removed. This is related somehow to my wish always to simplify my life: fewer positions, fewer possessions, less responsibility, more good living, a nest egg to draw on. Of course, the search for that nest egg, and the constant survival schemes I concoct in my head, cost me dearly in time and energy that could best be applied elsewhere.

THURSDAY, 3 FEBRUARY / TORONTO

Matters have improved somewhat this past month. J's divorce came through painlessly and the finances, though still wobbly in the extreme, do not provoke quite the same panic as before, though this may well be because the panic has now become routine. The visit from Earle was a productive one, and as of this week we have tenants living in the basement, which helps with the bills. Looking back over the month, I'm amazed at the vigour with which I've moved to save myself. I have a truly formidable array of outlines, ideas, and requests in circulation.

FRIDAY, 18 FEBRUARY / TORONTO

Riding along Davenport in the middle of the afternoon I see Dave Godfrey strolling along in a raincoat, briefcase in hand. Same gait as before, same body, though a bit hunched over, it seems to me. I feel so bad for Ellen [Godfrey] and him about their son's death that way.[1] I sit way back in the cab so he can't possibly see me. I don't want to intrude on his grief.

Seated at my escritoire, contemplating reliques.

THURSDAY, 24 FEBRUARY / TORONTO

So downcast that since Tuesday I have done nothing but sit in the office all day and most of the night. The problems are obvious: the collapse of a book project has ruined my financial prospects, and J is so depressed she can't look for work. Yet in my bright moments I marvel at how, all the same, I've managed to keep afloat, with a complicated system of deferred payments I have devised. But the pressure is on. So this journal is becoming more important, as I need a place to talk out loud to myself.

These days I have the sure feeling, which as I've had several times in the past, often for long periods, that I'm washed up. Yet I must hark back to the old examples and take a certain perverse martyr's delight in each setback and rejection; for I have learned that such is the way to wait out the troubles and eventually re-emerge from the shadows. There are even moments and days when I positively delight in the safety of my obscurity.

---

1 Ellen Godfrey (b. 1942), publisher, and writer of true-crime and detective fiction.

MONDAY, 16 MAY / TORONTO

J and I were married today at Old City Hall, in the interfaith chapel directly across the corridor from the place one goes to check in with one's parole officer: the two clienteles mingle in the spaces between until they are indistinguishable one from the other. The wedding went smoothly whereupon the party – bride, bridegroom, best man, maid of honour, bridesmaid – went to Chinatown for the traditional wedding dim sum. Earle, here for a few days with one of his daughters, was best man; later, over dinner, he and I have a long and melancholy conversation about his family problems.

TUESDAY, 17 MAY / TORONTO

A dream about Earle and me in Singapore, he getting badly beaten by spivs because of cowardice on my part. I interpret this as meaning I should help him more in his crisis. I have recounted the dream to him.

THURSDAY, 19 MAY / TORONTO

I learn that K died of a heart attack on 16 May. He was my first *patrone*.

FRIDAY, 20 MAY / TORONTO

I dream of K as a young man, long before I met him.

MONDAY, 30 MAY / TORONTO

The past three months have been difficult and eventful. Two months ago, J's mother learned that she has cancer and has been in hospital ever since except for one two-day visit here. Naturally this illness has put J under enormous pressure and taken most of her time some days.

My financial position continues to be very precarious to say the least. I struggle from week to week.

THURSDAY, 30 JUNE / TORONTO

New thoughts on work after interviewing Gzowski some weeks ago for a piece and then interviewing Bob F about Gzowski: how hard they work, taking all kinds of jobs beneath their talents. I must return (and I believe I am so returning) to the idea of the dignity of work, the honest toil of taking whatever small writing tasks present themselves or can be conjured up as opportunities.

SUNDAY, 3 JULY / TORONTO
Layton seemed most original and outrageous (and least tiresome and sad) during the salad days of John Diefenbaker, whom he so much resembled: they were both egotistical buffoons made so perhaps by some early privations and by comparison with people who had more fully integrated personalities. Similarly, Peggy A has clearly been the major poet of the Trudeau era. They are both possessed of fabled intelligence; both are famed for their cool but are likely to see it, in extreme instances, shattered under duress and the natural assertion of their authority. Who, then, will be the poet of the Brian Mulroney epoch? Who indeed.

TUESDAY, 25 OCTOBER / PITTSBURGH
Crack of dawn departure for Buffalo, most of which has now been torn down. This devastation and the much publicised subway in progress would seem to constitute the new era of hope about which one hears quite a good deal but of which one sees little hard evidence. I am reasonably comfortable in the old industrial culture; its ragged cityscapes are familiar, and I know the folkways. Tie up some infrastructure before flying to Pittsburgh where I'm met by [a friend], who's less tired and nervous than I've seen him recently. On the way back to his place we stop for a long talkative session in a grungy bar with gaudy advertising stuff on the walls but good food of the sort it has. [His wife] is away taking a course and he has been on his own in the big house for weeks. The place stinks and is terribly messy. I bed down in the downstairs game room. He says he will drop me off in the morning.

FRIDAY, 28 OCTOBER / TORONTO
Breakfast at the Westbury with Woodcock on one of his rare – very rare – visits here. I am dysfluent, mainly because of lack of sleep, and this is the first time he has seen me in such a state; but I manage all right in the end. He is busy on a dozen projects which will all come to fruition, is off to Australia soon, and so on. He seems smaller and more worn, but is receptive to humour and eager for news of the outside world.

SUNDAY, 30 OCTOBER / TORONTO
Vera [Frenkel] comes to dinner. She is broken up by her separation. Earle
here too. He seems to be coming apart a bit. I look over at J and marvel
at my good sense and good grace.

WEDNESDAY, 2 NOVEMBER / TORONTO
My second day working as a speech writer in the cultural sector and I
steal time for these quick lines. But I am interrupted …

1984

Freeing myself from the speech-writing job while regretting the loss of its $2,320 per month, I was hard at work on two manuscripts. One incorporated new poems and earlier unpublished ones with others taken from two previous collections and assorted broadsheets and chapbooks. The other project was a collection of my arts journalism on Canadian topics.

WEDNESDAY, 21 MARCH / TORONTO
My contract is to expire on 30 March whereupon I am to begin a six-month period (renewable) at two days per week for speech-writing work of the simplest sort. But today the situation becomes so intolerable that I have to quit. No need to recount the whole business here except to say that I find myself in a terrible squeeze and feel unable to carry on the remaining six days until gaining my freedom. I go to a movie.

THURSDAY, 22 MARCH / TORONTO
I am officially out of town by prior arrangement, and believe that I am bearing up well, yet am oddly angry with myself for what I have done.

SUNDAY, 8 APRIL / TORONTO
I read over the above entry and feel that it has completely missed the point. The point is that, on more than one occasion and for the first time in, oh, years, it seems, I felt well up inside me the need for a histri-onic, cleansing experience of the sort with which quitting is associated. When I was younger I often felt this, which I should imagine is very much what goes on during midlife crises, now so popular. And that basically is what I did. Stupid, of course, but it was also a renewal, a

rebirth; and what's wrong with that if it works? Peggy A used to remark on this tendency of mine – it was she who applied the word *histrionic* – and opined that it was both destructive and self-destructive, as it was at the time, perhaps totally. But now that I am older and have settled somewhat, like a building's foundation, I can certainly see the positive applications as well. In any event it is my nature – not my devoir but my nature certainly. Besides, the wages of sin are generally insufficient.

FRIDAY, 13 APRIL / TORONTO
My short-term financial worries are lessened as I now have a $10,000 writing contract and the general freelancing might be said to have improved greatly. I am angry at that part of me that sees my quitting as irresponsible. On two other occasions I have had the semblance of a job only to lose it: at one of the newspapers through my own lack of self-awareness and general immaturity, and at one of the magazines of the day, ditto. Here at least I have been the master of the situation. My personality was not holding me back, not much anyway, and my speech was bearing up quite well indeed under such pressure (better than it has done since then, in fact). It was as though I feared the steady slide into middle age and had to throw over the job. This still rankles me. To date I have had two different and quite vivid dreams about the situation. In each I have given a good account of my actions to the other people involved and convinced them and myself. But what's done is done. Perhaps [John] Fraser was correct in saying, as he has more than once, that I am simply not suited to a real job.

FRIDAY, 20 APRIL / TORONTO
To ease the tension J and I take a week in Bermuda, which we can do only because Christopher Ondaatje kindly lends us his condominium there.[1] Virtually nothing has changed and I see a lot more of the place than last visit. Pretty tense most of the time, however, and then had a near-complete speech collapse Tuesday last, J observing that the last time I flew the same thing happened the day after returning. The good aspect of the trip was that J certainly seemed more rested after it. One curious

1   Christopher (later Sir Christopher) Ondaatje (b. 1933), philanthropist and author, brother of Michael Ondaatje.

incident gave me a funny feeling during our time there. I had a dream in which Earle, Susan Sarandon, J, and I were in a film together. My notes run this way. It seemed to involve the actor who gave away the cheques in *The Millionaire* television series, a volume of love letters to Bernard Shaw on the shelf, and interview techniques used in what is really an epic film-within-a-film. The special effects were explained by Sarandon; we were in an old cinema with a wonderful Italian Renaissance screen; she encouraged me to ascertain that the silly costumes had been padded … In the morning I told J, by way of passing absurdity, that I dreamt that the two of us, Earle and Sarandon were in a film. She replied, "I suppose we were all married to one other." There was something about coupons and free samples being hoarded as well.

1985

J and I purchased Annex Books, a second-hand bookshop in Bathurst Street, round the corner from our house. She converted it into a true antiquarian shop, specialising in Canadian literature, while I remained the silent partner (or, as we joked, the vice-president in charge of heavy lifting and rodent disposal). The shop became a popular meeting ground for Canadian and visiting writers. My book *Variorum: New Poems and Old 1965–1985* received the first favourable review I had ever had for literary work, followed a short time later by an equally favourable one for *The Blue Notebook: Reports on Canadian Culture.* I felt suddenly, and briefly, reprieved.

SUNDAY, 30 MARCH / TORONTO

Lately have come to know Geoff Hancock and Gay Allison.[1] He's hostile to the past but I don't see the careerist some others do, though I see the freelancer who must get by, for I have a memory. She is more fascinating. She seems to have a speech problem that she has internalised; of course, the eyes give it away; that's how I of course must seem to others when I'm not actually dysfluent: the unnatural expression, the unnatural diction. People must think they're dealing with a zombie.

MONDAY, 8 APRIL / TORONTO

The kind of writer whose reputation improves after death, assuming it survives, because the memory of his personality fades, leaving only the personality of the works. Not because of any prophetic quality in the

---

1 Geoff Hancock (b. 1946), editor of *Canadian Fiction Magazine*; Gay Allison (b. 1943), poet.

writing but because his contemporaries saw the person they met and not the person whom even the writer was disappointed to see alone on the page – so unhuman and non-human, he thought to himself at the time.

1986

A busy and productive year as Annex Books grew in importance as a hub of bookish activity and I painted furiously and published a book-length poem, *Moving towards the Vertical Horizon*. I also began research for *The Gold Crusades: A Social History of Gold Rushes 1849–1929*, which took me to Australia for the first time. Simultaneously I was editing *Documents in Canadian Art*, an anthology published the following year, and writing for *Literary Review of Canada* and other new periodicals, including the weekly *Now*, where I launched its first books column.

TUESDAY, 3 JUNE / TORONTO

Peggy A is in a good mood but weary from months of promotion and family illness. Difficult to remember that she's so close to 50: skin smooth, moist-looking as always; she's very thin now, face seems to have changed shape somehow. Tells me Gwen [MacEwen] is back on the bottle and other similar bad news. Her contemporaries are ageing even if she isn't. Tries to convince me that Robin Skelton, being a warlock, could cast a pregnancy spell for J. I demur. She is completely serious about everything as usual. Later she comes into the shop and looks about, promising to sell J her review copies etc. One must admire her loyalty to old friends. I think she believes this *is* friendship, that thing she's read about all her life. I wonder who her really deep friends are, aside from Charlie Pachter and one or two others I can think of.[1]

---

1 Charles Pachter (b. 1942), visual artist and entrepreneur.

SATURDAY, 19 JULY / TORONTO

Returning from a week or so at a writers' workshop in Kingston, a place
I last knew before its economic revitalisation. Very pleasant now, one
entire street near St George's Cathedral is actually *in* the 19th century,
not simply a token of it: an intense emotional experience to find it one
day while the mind is elsewhere. The workshop itself: decent poetry sessions once I got going, some talented people; my book-reviewing talk a
rather large flop; but the cultural journalism workshops I managed to
salvage once I got through the first day. Much time for study and relaxation. With help from what I read, I actually achieved some understanding of how to re-engineer myself. Also, Neil Reynolds at the *Whig* and I
discuss a job at the paper, something like writer-in-residence.[2] Helwig
bends over backwards to be sociable, inviting me to dinner with Tom
Marshall at his (David's) beautiful old stone row house.[3] He is relaxed.
Candid about Maggie and about his other daughter, too, who's gifted in
science.[4] Proud. He and Nancy, who manages the Grand Theatre, reminisce about their early days, with Tiff Findley and others, in a touring
troupe of actors.[5] Marshall becomes ever more difficult to carry on a
conversation with due to, first, his inability to stick with one subject for
an entire sentence and, second, his habit of stopping in each sentence to
giggle. Thinking I must be exaggerating the impression, I shut off com-
prehension for five minutes by actual count and listen for the giggles;
sure enough, every sentence. He seems a lonely fellow, surely the last gay
male to remain in the closet. (I recall that time he made a pass at Jim
Christy in my kitchen, according to Christy. An excellent way to have
got one's jaw broken.[6])

During the workshop I fall into the custom of breakfasting with
Monica Hughes and Janet Lunn, the former enormously funny and clini-
cally bright in a particularly English way, the latter a person of whom
I had always been somewhat frightened (I suppose because of her

2　 Neil Reynolds (b. 1940), editor of the Kingston *Whig-Standard* and later of the
Saint John *Telegraph-Journal*, the *Ottawa Citizen*, and the *Vancouver Sun*.

3　 David Helwig (b. 1938), novelist and poet.

4　 Maggie Helwig (b. 1963), writer and peace activist.

5　 Nancy Helwig (b. 1938), arts administrator; Timothy Findley (1930–2002), author of *The Wars* and other novels.

6　 Jim Christy (b. 1945), writer and adventurer.

husband) but whom I now see differently.[7] She has a genuine talent for saying unexpected things. With the straightest face imaginable she told me how appalled she was that her grandchildren weren't being taught "The Rime of the Ancient Mariner" at school but rather Simon & Garfunkel "because they're supposed to be 'where it's at' as the young people say."

TUESDAY, 22 JULY / TORONTO
Lunch with Diane Turbide.[8] Her loyalty to *Quill & Quire*, not now in one of its strong periods, is affecting, because it is the blind patriotism one always has towards the first magazine or paper on which one has worked. Yet the pay's so poor that she's considering jumping ship.

TUESDAY, 23 JULY / TORONTO
To Hamilton for a day with the Whitemans.[9] A show of Hamilton artists' work in which Deborah [Whiteman] has a piece; a Hamilton retrospective at the HAG [Hamilton Art Gallery]; a tour of Whitehern, family home of the McQuestens, including T.B. McQ, the trust officer and later patron of J's father. The gallery especially interesting on account of the way Hamilton for much of the century seems to have had more women artists than Toronto, painters at least. With sculpture the reverse would be true but then I imagine a good feminist critic could make the case that this is because sculpting relates to the birthing experience etc.

SUNDAY, 7 SEPTEMBER / TORONTO
Writing this at the borrowed studio in the laneway behind Palmerston, a refuge.

Dinner party last night with the Whitemans and the LePans.[10] I'm not really good at hosting despite comparison with how bad at it I used to be. Get nervous, tell the same stories more than once, say all the wrong

---

7   Monica Hughes (1925–2003), science fiction writer; Janet Lunn (b. 1928), author of *The Hollow Tree* and other books for children.

8   Diane Turbide (b. 1956), *Quill & Quire* review editor; later, editorial director of Penguin Canada.

9   Bruce Whiteman (b. 1952), poet and rare-books librarian, author of *The Invisible World Is in Decline*.

10   Don LePan (b. 1954), founder of the publishing house Broadview Press.

things. J no help at all, slipping into her mother's voice and accent. Delighted at LePan's anti-Americanism; our common ground for the future, I'm sure. Heather [LePan] still somewhat suspicious of me, but then she's most unhappy to be living in Canada, is homesick for England (yet they're trying to buy a house).

FRIDAY, 17 OCTOBER / TORONTO

Reading more Eric Hoffer.[11] Because he favoured the war, hated intellectuals and liberals, etc., I disagree with him but don't hate him in the least. Instead I'm closer to the position of Bob F, who told me once he loved Hoffer for the way he "scratched out his ideas." Indeed. Also, I'm sorry that he had to live in isolation, remote from those he despised, amid workingmen with whom he had nothing in common. So he lived in his own notebooks and in the books he read. The classical picture of the scholar: Erasmus.

Further to the above, many perceptive people see me at what I believe is my best and most vigorous but react as I do to myself when I am very tired.

WEDNESDAY, 29 OCTOBER / TORONTO

To Sutton Place in the evening for a charity dinner given by David Silcox.[12] He always seems civilised, with a sophistication based on candour, yet slyly cynical sometimes as well. David McFadden[13] there, honest working class. Joy Kogawa, who doesn't say a word (one still gets a sense of her overwhelming good heart), Chapelle Jaffe, whose perfume is lovely, and Eli Mandel, who is recovering from a stroke last Dominion Day.[14]

11   Eric Hoffer (1898–1983), US political philosopher and social critic, author of *The True Believer*.
12   David Silcox (b. 1937), critic and art world figure, at various times associated with arts agencies on the municipal, provincial, and federal levels; later, head of Sotheby's Canada.
13   David McFadden (b. 1940), poet.
14   Joy Kogawa (b. 1935), poet and novelist, author of *Obasan*; Chapelle Jaffe (b. 1949), stage and film actor; Eli Mandel (1922–1992), poet, teacher, and critic.

FRIDAY, 31 OCTOBER / TORONTO
Lunch with [an acquaintance]. Once that would have been impossible. I've now mellowed enough to see the muddle and lack of smarts that much of her former aggression sought to hide. A perfectly pleasant time, though she's become a bit of a social climber. Does it well, too.

SATURDAY, 8 NOVEMBER / TORONTO
A party this evening at [John] Lownsbrough's house. A very moneyed crowd in surroundings the same. Terrific art. Charlie Pachter rude to me as usual, and actually threatens me from across the main room as J and I are leaving. Enright is in good form, and his wife, I now realise, dislikes the world in general more than me in particular.

WEDNESDAY, 12 NOVEMBER / TORONTO
We take Vera [Frenkel] to dinner to mark her birthday a couple of days late. She's having a difficult time. Looking at her state helps me see my own more clearly.

TUESDAY, 18 NOVEMBER / TORONTO
Meet [a colleague] on my way to perform errands. Difficult, sometimes ignorant man, convinced of his superior civilisation etc. I put up with his insults for half an hour or so and come away better for information gained in the process. Later, I even begin to see the context of his barbs. Feel sorry for him.

WEDNESDAY, 19 NOVEMBER / TORONTO
J and I got to the launch for Roy MacLaren's book.[15] [A common friend] pregnant. Sandra Martin there, overtures of friendliness. Roy at his most charming. Lots of big Grits, including the Rainmaker.[16] One left expecting severe showers.

15 Roy MacLaren (b. 1934), MP who served the Trudeau, Turner, and Chrétien governments before becoming high commissioner to Britain; author of *Canadians in Russia* and other books.
16 Keith Davey (1926–2011), long-serving campaign director of the federal Liberals, nicknamed the Rainmaker for his problem-solving skills.

FRIDAY, 21 NOVEMBER / TORONTO
An advisory panel most of the day at the OAC [Ontario Arts Council]. I have new respect for Sarah Sheard.[17] I manage to make an ass of myself only intermittently.

TUESDAY, 25 NOVEMBER / TORONTO
Bob F comes to the shop towards the end of the day, then I take him to the studio for a preview of Saturday's show. Helpful comments along predictable lines: doesn't think much of me as a colourist etc., likes the works on paper. Buys a collage, one of the most expensive items.

WEDNESDAY, 26 NOVEMBER / TORONTO
Lunch today with [a colleague]. I'm always at my best (not that my best is any too good) in such one-to-one situations when I can encourage a confidential tone and give the impression that the meeting is a welcome bit of sanity and a respite from the cold craziness of the world. With a party of even three, however, I'm correspondingly hopeless. J and I to the office-warming of the new *Saturday Night* building in King Street. A large claustrophobic party. Doug Gibson is pleasant.[18] Later, a late Chinese dinner.

[Eric] Hoffer says one must not lose misfit status no matter how tempting the replacement offer, for that's the way we become part of mobs and other destructive mass movements. Compare with Hegel's slave mentality. More to the point one shouldn't lose one's misfit status because it is the essence of the tradition of, for example, Christ and Lee Harvey Oswald and all who resemble them.[19]

SUNDAY, 30 NOVEMBER / TORONTO
To the Whitemans' in Hamilton for dinner. The only bad moment came when Deborah in her naïveté lets slip a comment about my puny origins. Bruce has the good sense to be embarrassed at the revelation, but I carry the hurt still.

17 Sarah Sheard (b. 1953), novelist, author of *Almost Japanese*.
18 Douglas Gibson (b. 1943), McClelland & Stewart publisher.
19 Lee Harvey Oswald (1939–1963), alleged assassin of John F. Kennedy.

MONDAY, 1 DECEMBER / TORONTO

[A friend] tells me he lusts after Val Ross (he's always telling me he lusts after someone) and is returning, more or less, to the church.[20] Appalling table manners and spirited conversation. Very fast with the language, very facile, but not so sophisticated as that suggests. Confesses that he is terrified of speaking to Raymond Souster, a neighbour.[21] I don't feel it is my place to comment or even roll my eyes.

FRIDAY, 5 DECEMBER / TORONTO

Back last night from three days in New York (J's birthday present): some of her sights and some of my own; hers of course uptown, mine downtown. The veneer of prosperity seems a little thicker than when I looked last. Comfortable dinner with Audrey and her husband and afterwards a drink at their place in the Village that I once felt so at home in. Being in, say, the Gotham Book Mart makes me realise how at home I was in the sort of bohemian atmosphere that grew on the underside of old-fashioned industrial society.

TUESDAY, 9 DECEMBER / MONTREAL

Two days here. The city slowly acquires the same sense of second-class political and economic demography as Winnipeg. Long chat in hotel. Screw-up later in plane departures because of snow and I move to the Queen E [Queen Elizabeth Hotel] for one more night.

MONDAY, 22 DECEMBER / TORONTO

A wonderful three-day visit from Earle and his present wife. I admire his joy in good culture whether high or low, his critical pleasure in it, his mind and its workings, his warm place in the past as a spot from which to live out the present usefully. Altruistically I'm glad to observe this new marriage. Selfishly I take pleasure in him because I can always learn from him and from the way he teaches.

20 Val Ross (1950–2008), journalist and author.
21 Raymond Souster (1921–2012), poet, author of *Ten Elephants on Yonge Street* and many other books.

1987

I worked persistently on book projects and visual art. In December, I rented an apartment in Kingston, preparing to become the so-called writer-in-residence (and, later, literary editor) at the *Whig-Standard*, returning to Toronto on weekends.

FRIDAY, 2 JANUARY / TORONTO
A slightly belated New Year's Eve booksellers' dinner at Gail Wilson's, where Marty Ahvenus is in fine form, full of good bookselling stories and references to some old Toronto characters.[1] For example, Sterling Jones (a sleazy coin and medals dealer of the 1950s), Harcourt Slime (another of the same), and Walter the Signer (responsible for the artists' signatures on countless 19th-century European chocolate box paintings, which signatures of course would come to light only after a cleaning by the dealer). Story of Walter's involvement in trying to sell a painting "by Rembrandt's brother."

SUNDAY, 11 JANUARY / TORONTO
Leo Stein: "The historian investigates his facts, the autobiographer just remembers them." U.S. Grant in his memoirs: "That's the way I remember these things. Let those who remember them otherwise write what they remember …"

Relationship between sickly sweet memories of youth and Vancouver.

---

1 Martin Ahvenus (1928–2011), antiquarian bookseller with a shop in Queen Street.

Lunch Thursday with [a colleague] who says of her new editorial board: "I feel like the group leader guiding a bunch of Amish people through Times Square."

WEDNESDAY, 21 JANUARY / TORONTO
Reading Pierre Berton the same as watching [the Hollywood actor] Charlton Heston: barbershop Nietzscheans, bankrupt, is it actually possible that they believe any of it themselves?

Working the bookshop and the former Cuban culture minister, here to read at some poetry conference, comes in, chats, 65 and tired looking, knows Woodcock (of course), buys some Atwoods for the train and leaves.

MONDAY, 26 JANUARY / TORONTO
A National Book Festival jury, sealed up all day in the Park Plaza with Michael Ondaatje, Libby Scheier,[2] a librarian from London whose name I never catch, and Sarah Sheard, the group leader. Predictably, lovably, Michael the only one who hasn't done his homework. Scheier turns out to be aggressive and rather intense but no doubt with underlying strength. Reading SS is difficult. Much more there than the delightful middle-class ordinariness remembered or created so artfully in her book. One could study her face for a long time and have nothing revealed.

In the evening, Dave Powell [environmentalist and former housemate] comes over to borrow my overcoat to wear to his father's funeral. Tells me of how his father's life arrived at its final stage without causing undue alarm; there was a completeness and a sense of accomplishment.

SUNDAY, 8 FEBRUARY / TORONTO
J's been in England while I've minded the shop, and alone tonight, with a blizzard coming on, I sit in the window of the curry restaurant and watch the owner distributing rock salt broadcast from a big sack as at home he might have done with seed.

2 Libby Scheier (1946–2000), poet, author of *Second Nature* and other works.

[A colleague] returns to his office a few minutes late, having got into an argument with the blind man selling newspapers at Queen and Spadina.

[An acquaintance] dressed as though she does all her shopping at boutiques whose names suggest Newfoundland outports: Heart's Delight, Unspeakable Passion, Modesty Forbids, One-Size-Fits-All.

SUNDAY, 1 MARCH / TORONTO

"One of my greatest pleasures in writing has come from the thought that perhaps my work might annoy someone of comfortably pretentious position. Then comes the saddening realization that such people rarely read." John Kenneth Galbraith in his memoirs.

MONDAY, 9 MARCH / TORONTO

Speech has been pretty good for a couple of days despite the surprisingly harsh blow of the turn with the other booksellers who keep upping prices on books we'd agreed to buy and then of having to speak with Harold Town on the phone.[3] But today everything falls apart most magnificently because of the following nightmare, which I write down at 6:18 a.m.: I have been hanging out with [fellow prisoners] but now I'm on the run from them and others, hiding in abandoned factories that look down on the high street from the east, running from one to the next, avoiding the cops because I know that no one arrested there for anything is let go. At length I'm taken in by a hippie band, male and female, six or eight strong, who live in a huge hangar-like studio. Sexual and other adventures. But then after a year or so perhaps, suddenly I'm in one of the fleet choppers attacking and strafing them. J is as upset about this as I am and my defence is weak – very disturbing. I believe the nightmare has arisen as a warning about involvement with certain others and about writing a memoir I am considering after [book publisher] Jan Walter encouraged me.

"Rather choose rough work than smooth work, so that only the practical purpose can be answered, and never imagine there is reason to be proud of anything that may be accomplished by patience and sandpaper." Ruskin, *The Stones of Venice*.

3   Harold Town (1924–1990), visual artist, member of Painters Eleven.

MONDAY, 16 MARCH / TORONTO

Woodcock dream/nightmare in which I am at his house in Vancouver whereupon he announces that he is a member of the Vancouver Filmmakers Cooperative and has made a video. It is a colour documentary about Vancouver office buildings, old and new: the Sun Tower, that wonderful wedding-cake on West Pender with green icing on the cupola, and a number of others. We drink a bit. The ocean laps outside. He is packing his books and announces he is dying. He embraces me and slaps my back. "Take care of yourself, lad," he cries, and I cry too.

SATURDAY, 23 MAY / SYDNEY, NSW

Anzac Day in Kings Cross, a terrible skirl of pipes, the Vietnamese woman who runs the restaurant I'm sitting in rushes to the door to see what's happening, and a short ragged line of pipers mis-marches past: "Waltzing Matilda" of course.

Rather a banana monarchy than a banana republic.

Kings X: crazy man, screaming to himself, walking up the street with a huge shark's head, recently severed, in a shopping cart being pulled behind him; people avoid the stench and the blood and so he begins using it as a weapon with which to attack his fellow pedestrians.

MONDAY, 15 JUNE / TORONTO

Ondaatje reading at the music gallery, big crowd even in the balcony, a party; I feel very paranoid. My tolerance decreases.

In the bookshop I ask the woman if I can help her. "No, just bruising," she replies.

SATURDAY, 27 JUNE / TORONTO

Much angst involved this past week in the sale of *Saturday Night* to Conrad Black and Bob F's resignation. J actually weeps when she reads my letter to Bob.

Picasso created a worldwide public image of himself (largely true but irrelevant to fellow artists) as someone life-loving and almost life-giving, a celebrant and a celebrator, incredibly fecund, never flagging in his job of recording his own joy with life. Basically a pop culture attitude. This is what people see in [Charlie] Chaplin – along with the idea (oddly American) of art made from the most democratic materials.

Rexroth (compare with remark on [Leonard] Cohen): "… I can re-member when the only Bach you could get without ordering the records from His Master's Voice in Canada was the 'Air for the G-String [*sic*].'"

FRIDAY, 7 AUGUST / TORONTO

A long lunch today with Bob F to hear his account of the recent events at *SN*. I am shocked by how depressed he is, a day's growth of grey stubble on his face, talking of his failure. Says the Reichmanns [a family of wealthy property developers] had intended to buy the magazine earlier but backed out when [a business journalist] wrote that piece about them. I had a real sense of Bob's awareness that the generations have turned. He has had the predictable offers from the *Star* and the *Financial Post* (that last one so painfully reminiscent of what happened to Sandwell).[4] All very sad. I do everything wrong, giving him that old cheque as a memento, letting him pay for lunch (because not to have done so would have been worse). Yet there is a real vein of nitty-gritty candour.

FRIDAY, 21 AUGUST / TORONTO

J goes with Ann Mandel to [her husband] Eli's office at York and buys his books. He has had two more strokes and has had to retire. Ann tells J he can still write, using his left hand on the keyboard, but cannot speak. This gives me an odd and highly unpleasant feeling. E was the person who had the most difficulty with my not being able to talk: a long story from long ago, nearly 20 years, but a real enough problem all that while.

More on Bob F at our lunch: Mentions that he likes rose-gardening. Said, "When I was young we knew precisely what good painting was. It was painted on East 10th Street between Second and Fifth or was painted elsewhere but with the same look …" The sentence trails off. Could the missing words be "but we were wrong"? Tells story of getting his own radio show on CHUM, then the lowliest of the radio stations, when he was 15, reporting school news. Later became apparent that he got the job because a man named Fulford owned the station and the person who hired him thought he was that Fulford's son.

---

4 B.K. Sandwell (1876–1954), editor of *Saturday Night*, 1939–51; ended his career on the *Financial Times*.

SATURDAY, 22 AUGUST / HAMILTON

Here to see Bruce and Deborah [Whiteman]. My luck has always been bad with them, never speaking well when we meet; one day they'll be surprised when I catch them on a good day. They apologise when Thera, aged six, keeps making bilingual puns.

SATURDAY, 29 AUGUST / TORONTO

See [a long-ago acquaintance] on Bathurst. He's become a wino. I make the mistake of speaking to him by name, embarrassing him in front of his alky companions.

Bob F's dignity always fragile but think of how he bore up when the magazine suspended publication, when [his ex-wife] Jocelyn died, when he resigned. Notice how his speech is less formal around me, because he lets his guard down, doesn't have to stand on ceremony – this compensates, in his eyes, I believe, for my general unease, which would tend to remind him of his own.

Have to call [a colleague] for a bit of information. After the usual long babbling about his career, he makes some crack about people's entries in *Canadian Who's Who*. Apparently all he has to do these days is to sit around reading it. After the call, I take his card out of the Rolodex. Dangerous stuff. Bad medicine.

TUESDAY, I SEPTEMBER / TORONTO

Bad day today with the new financial reverses, then a dreadful review of *Documents in Canadian Art* in the *Whig*, which certainly complicates matters grandly. Scanning the shelves I see that I haven't published a book that hasn't resulted in at least one wildly destructive and abusive review, save only *Variorum* (so far, though [Tom] Marshall's review might qualify in effect if not in design). Which is not to deny that some have also received decidedly warm notices, notably from Adachi.[5] Further headache today from a letter from Bob H, very condescending.[6] I write a somewhat postdated reply, address and stamp it, and will decide in a few days whether to post it. It may well turn out that the proper course is not merely to hold off but also to ignore any eventual

5 Ken Adachi (1929–1989), *Toronto Star* books columnist.
6 Bob Hilderley (b. 1952), publisher of Quarry Press.

follow-up letter from him. We'll see. I can't help thinking that Kingston is going to be more of a test than I usually imagine, what with all these bad relationships awaiting me, and that's without even considering who else there might be, particularly at Queen's.

Five or six days ago, a three-month-old kitten that had been abused by the people upstairs fell partway through one of the ceiling tiles at the shop after being trapped in the crawl space up there for two days. J named him Norman and adopted him, took him to the vet. He was almost blind with conjunctivitis and the vet feared he might have leukaemia. J nursed him tenderly for several days but, though he had a few bouts of playfulness, chasing imaginary mice and the like, the little creature died during the night on Sunday. J found him near his water bowl and has been terribly upset, as am I. Yesterday afternoon in the pouring rain I dug a grave in the garden behind the shop and we buried him. It's hard to forget the image of the stiff little corpse so disconnected from the world. His life was so short and unhappy that I can barely restrain my tears.

WEDNESDAY, 9 SEPTEMBER / TORONTO
"Reading a manuscript that's not properly punctuated is like driving in a town where the traffic lights don't work, or rather, where some of them work and some of them don't." So says [a colleague].

The birds are forced to do the dirty work, deliver the messages.

WEDNESDAY, 14 OCTOBER / TORONTO
On my way up Yonge Street to deliver the ms [*The Gold Crusades*] to Macmillan, I bump into Al Purdy. We do coffee. He tells me that Avie Bennett, meeting him for the first time, played a comedic role and said something like, "So you like baseball. You're a real person after all, not one of these arty people I have to deal with around here."[7] He invited Al to the next Jays game. A big box with 25 or 30 people eating and drinking. "I'd never been to a place like that," Al says. He also tells a funny story of being asked by the protocol people at Queen's Park whether he would allow himself to be inducted into the Order of Ontario, of which he had never heard. He thought it was some practical joke, but no. Thirty

7   Avie Bennett (b. 1928), at the time, chair of McClelland & Stewart.

or so athletes (Ben Johnson), scientists ([John] Polanyi), artists, and the like were created OOs. "I needed a dress suit and was going to rent one but it cost $75 and we found I could buy one for $110. I also needed dress shoes and found a second-hand pair but they were two sizes too small and made noise. I took them off under the banquet table and left them there."

SUNDAY, 18 OCTOBER / LONDON
A whole week in London, getting back into it. I know now that this is my refuge in a political emergency. More exiles, more crumbs of work, the centre of civilisation. Yet how long before my weakness rises up over the environment like a sunrise? Geography, alas, does not change the basic problems but only provides a new venue.

SATURDAY, 31 OCTOBER / TORONTO
Before I go to visit Earle, J and I are invited to Peterborough for dinner with Tom Symons and his wife Chris, following a Broadview [board] meeting.[8] We ride down with the MacLarens, and J afterwards notes that Roy's charm is his roughness, so unexpected in one with such lapidary credentials. I also like his moral candour. First lunch at the LePans', which is pleasant (Lee [MacLaren] very animated in her recollection of Khartoum), followed by a drive to the office for the business meeting, which is inconclusive, itself followed by a reception there for the local literati that appears to be a success in its own terms. Then we troop off, with the others following, to the Symons' house, Marchbanks, built *circa* 1845 and purchased by them from Robertson Davies long ago. A large library, some interesting pictures (two Homer Watsons), a portrait of an ancestor who commanded the ship that took Napoleon to Elba, staring down on us round the dinner table. Making polite dinner chat, I ask if Peterborough still contains any physical traces of its mid-19th-century literary culture, as exemplified by Susanna Moodie.[9] Symons answers, "You're sitting at her dining table." He is inscrutable in that English way, no intensity, no emotion, everything joviality and smoothness. LePan has

8   Tom Symons (b. 1929), educator and public intellectual.
9   Susanna Moodie (1803–1885), author of *Roughing It in the Bush*.

too much to drink and says inane things in defence of free trade, but the host perfectly flawless in his handling of the situation.

Symons tells a story of travelling with Armand Hammer to Washington on a mission for the United World Colleges, which wished to buy an extensive property in New Mexico owned by the Roman Catholic Church.[10] The presiding bishop at the Church's real estate office first said that it wasn't for sale but gradually warmed to the possibility. Hammer placed a doctor's satchel on the desk and asked the bishop whether the Church would part with the property for the contents of the bag, sight unseen. The bishop sized up his man and agreed. The bag contained us$1 million, "a slightly generous price but not overly so," according to Symons.

Symons' voice quite like that of his younger brother [Scott], whose photo, I noticed, hangs above the toilet, whereas reminders of their grandfather Perkins Bull were scattered about generously.[11]

When Roy at table explains that he is a vegetarian and begs leave to have salad only, Symons confides in a most conversational tone that "the PoW" has said that he, [Prince] Charles, is now vegetarian also. Lee and I look at each other knowingly.

Then I am off to see Earle. At one point I check into a hotel for a few hours and it is brought home to me there how good my urban security and survival skills in fact are – but that what I must work on are the interactive skills so as to prevent some of the occasions on which others are needed. That I am so strong in the former area is perhaps a crutch. No, I'm certain of it.

SUNDAY, 1 NOVEMBER / ITHACA

The road to Ithaca, early in the morning, raining. Puddles under the underpass. Dark clouds roll in like a regrettable past, like blackmail. New barn abuilding: a hopeful thought amid the desperation. One large clump of yellow on the hill, like a black dog with one white paw.

Ithaca at end of the day: the bus depot is an old train station. Alone there with '60s hits on the ticket agent's radio. Echoes like a shower stall.

10 Armand Hammer (1898–1990), US billionaire industrialist.
11 Perkins Bull (1870–1948), natural resources entrepreneur and amateur historian.

Bugs drawn to the filthy glass globes glowing with an equally dirty yellow light beneath.

TUESDAY, 3 NOVEMBER / BUFFALO

Flying from Binghamton to Buffalo on a 19-seat commuter plane I am across the narrow aisle from Victor Borge.[12] Shortly after takeoff I notice that he is writing the numbers one through 10 on a sheet of paper and begins a list of some sort. But he very shortly dozes off, and I sneak a look at the list. It reads: "1) Overture ..." The rest is blank. He sleeps all the way to Buffalo and his concert appearance.

TUESDAY, 10 NOVEMBER / TORONTO

The end finally came for poor Heywood [the dog] last Thursday. She had been growing weaker and weaker, refusing any nourishment as well as medication, and hadn't been able to walk or indeed stand up for two days. I spent one bad night with her when I believe she was in a lot of pain. We had been hoping that she might go naturally from her bad heart or one of the little strokes she's been having. When the tumours began to press on her vitals even harder and there was probably renal failure, we knew what had to be done. I sent J to the shop while I waited for the vet to come – it was like a scene from a Gothic novel, anticipating her approach with her sinister black bag. She first gave H a tranquiliser, which took effect in 15 minutes or so, and then the fatal injection, as I watched, comforting her and weeping. When the body was wrapped and boxed and the vet gone, I walked over to the store (the cold seemed to freeze my tears) and stayed there while J returned home and took the remains to the Humane Society to be cremated. The mourning continues, though last night we took the traditional advice and got a puppy: Dexter by name, about 50 pounds at eight months, part lab retriever and part German short-haired pointer. He has a goofy expression (tongue hanging out the side of his muzzle) and big sad eyes. He is white except for a black head. He looks like Sylvester Stallone playing Othello. Yo! Desdemona.

---

12 Victor Borge (1909–2000), Danish-born US concert pianist and musical satirist.

SATURDAY, 14 NOVEMBER / TORONTO

Breakfast yesterday with Joe Nickell, in town for a TV taping for a few hours.[13] How middle-aged! Like my father. I see my own decay and mortality in the sags and ravages of his face. But as with me, his sense of moral responsibility has increased with age. Now detecting forgeries as an expert witness, and perhaps embarrassed by his past as a Pinkerton, and so on. A fine fellow, not too interested in money, only in being useful in his way. I felt good seeing him, but then I had lunch with Bill French (to tell him my Kingston news) and came away feeling very paranoid because he showed he remembers me when I was very young.[14] Contrast with Joe, a contemporary, who was naïve right alongside me in our twenties.

More on Joe. When he went back (having always intended to wait for an amnesty), his brother, a former Marine, wouldn't speak to him. In all these years they have been in the same room together only twice: at their father's deathbed and again at his funeral; on neither occasion did his brother speak to him. But Joe carries on. He's been back in the States for 11 years now, says if asked he always says he made the right decision [on Vietnam] and would do it again; people are still sometimes cold, but aside from one anonymous death threat over the phone he's had no trouble, looks people right in the eye, always offers his hand first and if they take it, fine; the cheerful approach works for him much of the time.

SUNDAY, 15 NOVEMBER / TORONTO

Fearing the worst with Bill French's column on Monday (why do I get so worked up so far in advance? – I seem to be getting worse as I become more acutely conscious of my actions); but then I must toughen myself and prepare for more publicity as of old, however much I hate it.

MONDAY, 16 NOVEMBER / TORONTO

Last night I dreamt of picking up a copy of a redesigned *Globe* (the nameplate black on a yellow rectangle) and reading Bill French's fancy prose description [of my *Whig* appointment], with all the details wrong.

13   Joe Nickell (b. 1944), poet and former magician and detective; later, a debunker of paranormal activity.
14   William French (1924–2012), *Globe and Mail* books columnist, 1958–1990.

But this morning the actual piece proves fine (I read it on the front porch at 7 a.m.); not the precise emphasis one would wish for but then we didn't take out an ad: I can hardly expect to influence the copy. Everybody who knows what it means will see it; others (mere business associates say) will not. Perfect.

TUESDAY, 17 NOVEMBER / TORONTO
Today's *Whig* has the news on the front page. I want to take credit for a tricky situation well handled, but in truth it was a matter of good luck.

TUESDAY, 24 NOVEMBER / TORONTO
A party for Charles Ritchie at Ramsay and Trisha's house.[15] Half a valium and I am in fine form. My God I actually enjoy myself, and chat quite happily with the various old dears (John Holmes, for instance).[16] Fraser is there, harried looking under the weight of his new responsibility as editor of *Saturday Night* and thus the confidant of monarchs and prime ministers. He is suddenly greying but wears a superb suit of some bulky black wool with cloth-covered buttons on the waistcoat in a quite 19th-century manner. He says he's seeking a fiction editor and I put in plugs for people I think would be good candidates.

Goethe (Kronenberger's translation): "Everybody wants to be somebody; nobody wants to grow."

TUESDAY, 1 DECEMBER / TORONTO
Reuben [Zellermayer, a sculptor] from next door comes over to the house with the news that he has just come from Gwen's place where the coroner had taken away her body. He is badly shocked and, curiously, this is the first time we have ever seen him so articulate: the violent emotion forces out the words. My mind begins retrieving bits about Gwen of course. Her extraordinary gift for languages (teaching herself not merely Greek but Arabic, and well enough to translate Arabic tales), the time she picked up a guitar and instantly began playing (having taught herself to play the violin, she transposed etc.), that time

---

15 Charles Ritchie (1906–1995), diplomatist and diarist; ambassador to the US and United Nations, and high commissioner to Great Britain.
16 John Holmes (1910–1988), diplomat and scholar.

I discovered the portrait of me she'd done. How she changed her birth-place from Winnipeg to Toronto. One time she went on an unlikely whimsy kick and pursued her newfound whimsical side with complete earnestness. I still see her at No. 52. More memories to follow no doubt.

MONDAY, 28 DECEMBER / TORONTO
J says Bob F has always liked me because I'm vulnerable. Thinking about this I see that the same can be said of others who have befriended me. A pretty small audience, though, these collectors of vulnerability.

1988

Juggling competing responsibilities in Kingston and Toronto proved difficult. For six months, I contributed, heavily, to virtually every section of the *Whig-Standard*, writing on books, film, art, and music of course, but also doing travel pieces, political columns, and magazine features. One week I even had something in the home décor section; another time, to bridge a visual art shortfall, I rushed home on my lunch hour and painted a picture for the cover of the weekly *Whig-Standard Magazine*. I also produced a great many editorials, particularly those on politics and developments in Britain and Europe. After six months, I was made the literary editor. This change ignited protests from locals accustomed to a type of literary journalism different from my own. Somewhere in here I published *The Crowded Darkness*, a book of cinema criticism. To occupy my spare time, and to relieve some of the pressures I was under, I began drafting, tentatively and discontinuously, what eventually became *Travels by Night: A Memoir of the Sixties*.

FRIDAY, 1 JANUARY / KINGSTON
I spend (expend) my thirty-ninth birthday alone playing music and listening through the wall to the young soldiers in the next apartment.

Kingston has many shingles outside lawyers' offices, etc. These creak in the wind in the middle of the night when it's stormy: one of the sounds of the 19th century.

SATURDAY, 2 JANUARY / TORONTO
Before catching the bus to Toronto, I stop in at the newsroom and chat with the person, who looks about 17, doing the night police calls. It was like talking to a female version of myself at that age. Same job.

I must look fearsome. People never take the seat next to me on the bus or train even if it's the next to last one free. Sometimes waitresses and others look at me very carefully, with controlled alarm. This must be a different flaw in my character from the one that makes people give me pots of jam at Xmas – hundreds of the damn things.

WEDNESDAY, 6 JANUARY / KINGSTON

Whig: one day at work, then a break for New Year's, then back to feeling my way in these surroundings. Helped out by a libertarian with coke-bottle glasses who takes me under his wing, no doubt his right wing. He had been the new boy until I arrived. He was an Ottawa mathematics professor who was hired as an education writer because Neil, in a way that is typical of his mad genius, liked the letters-to-the-editor he wrote from time to time, which the *Citizen* in Ottawa had declared incomprehensible. Today, for instance, he has an editorial whose subject is the speed of light. Apparently he's in favour of it. I've always been a gravity man myself, preferring the tangible. Today I ask Neil how I'm doing and he makes a circle with his thumb and forefinger, referring to my long piece on why a hereditary Senate would result eventually in a chamber that is in regional and gender balance. Bizarre, totally bizarre. Good to be back on a paper.

When the Group of Seven reinterpreted the transcendentalism of Emerson and Thoreau – that one seeks enlightenment by going out and looking at one's own here-and-now – the result was inherently good. When the Beats did it the result was inherently malevolent. Why? Quality of here-and-now the Americans had to work with. Beats didn't hate America. They hated Eisenhower but loved America. The difference more apparent than real. Whitman would have loved Eisenhower. Eisenhower would have loved Whitman, too, if his ghostwriters had included ghostreaders to read him what Walt had written.

Squeaky F was recaptured last week after escaping from Alderson.[1] I know her mistake. If it's snowing hard enough there to cover your tracks it's snowing hard enough to make those mountains impassable. Also, no conifers to speak of there; hardwood, mostly tulip poplar. So they could

---

1   Squeaky Fromme (b. 1948), attempted assassin of US president Gerald Ford.

spot her from the next hill, never mind dogs, never mind search planes, much less heat sensors. She should have busted out in high summer. Caves to hide in during the day, plenty of berries, paw-paws; gone down the river at night. Get far away fast.

THURSDAY, 14 JANUARY / KINGSTON

Whig: on the seventh Arthur Lower[2] died at 98 and there was panic as the paper prepared to give him four pages, but the tributes were forced down to only two pages when a block of Princess Street caught fire – flames a hundred feet high. The following Monday, the first session in the boardroom with an outside guest: the principal of Queen's, who looks like Mr Carlson on [the television comedy] WKRP and whose hands shook as he spoke and who was daringly candid on all the subjects about which he was reasonably certain we knew the dirt anyway (a tactic not calculated to work well in a room full of newspaper editorial people). Can't tell how I'm doing, but I grow to like and respect Harvey [Schachter, associate editor].

FRIDAY, 15 JANUARY / KINGSTON

Very odd visit from J, her first to see me in Kingston. She is so nervous that I can't talk, of course, and that makes her even more tense. She bursts into tears.

SATURDAY, 16 JANUARY / KINGSTON

Today J has a nervous stomach, keeps saying that Kingston is working class and that I have all the characteristics of the adult children of alcoholics as listed in *Newsweek* (I look up the article and am appalled). My God is that what she thinks of me? Things are not working out well. The realisation has naturally left me feeling empty and concerned.

WEDNESDAY, 20 JANUARY / KINGSTON

Lunch at Chez Piggy in which I find myself called on to assume the role of my companion's counsellor re his fear of AIDS and general *problemas sentimentales*.

2   Arthur Lower (1889–1988), historian, author of *Colony to Nation*.

THURSDAY, 21 JANUARY / KINGSTON

On the phone J gives an account of the memorial service for Gwendolyn [MacEwen] (néc Wendy, I am surprised to learn). It seems to have been conducted with some dignity. When I myself die, I realise again with a shudder, the memorial service can be held in a phone box. Everything about me seems to conspire to forbid acceptance even in death, and if that's the case in big cosmopolitan Toronto, you can imagine how well I'm fitting in at Kingston, though a small breakthrough this week when Bronwen Wallace holds the door for me when I have my hands full of books and coffee (still won't talk to me though).[3]

FRIDAY, 22 JANUARY / KINGSTON

About ten of us have 55 minutes alone with Mulroney in the board-room.[4] I'd only seen him once before, that time in Montreal; today he seems old, tired (his voice, like mine, breaks down to a low unmodulated growl when he's fatigued). It strikes me that when he was young he must have looked like the young Peter Worthington; now he looks like a 50-year-old Jay Leno.[5] After seeing him, I have short snatch of music going through my head but can't place the melody. (Later: It finally comes to me. It is Marlene Dietrich singing "See What the Boys in the Back Room Will Have.")

THURSDAY, 28 JANUARY / KINGSTON

The asbestos ceiling was pulled down in the editorial writers' office. Now the same is being done in the newsroom. The chaos multiplies.

SUNDAY, 31 JANUARY / KINGSTON

Return tonight from a much better trip to Toronto than the last one. Stop at the paper on my return to find a note from Brenda Large, written on Friday, asking me to meet her so that she can pass along some confidential information.[6] I naturally imagine that I'm in trouble but

---

3　Bronwen Wallace (1945–1989), poet and short story writer, author of *The Stubborn Particulars of Grace* and other works.
4　Brian Mulroney (b. 1939), Progressive Conservative prime minister, 1984–93.
5　Peter Worthington (b. 1927), founding editor of the *Toronto Sun*.
6　Brenda Large (b. 1942), *Whig-Standard* political reporter.

on reaching her at home learn that Harvey S has been saying nice
things about me to her – that I'm working so hard etc. and will be
asked to stay.

MONDAY, I FEBRUARY / KINGSTON
Forgot to say White Rabbit the first thing on waking this morning.

THURSDAY, 18 FEBRUARY / KINGSTON
Harvey finds me working at a terminal when he comes in at 7:00 a.m.
and when I leave an hour or so later he makes a crack. "Nice of you
to drop in," he says sarcastically. I reply, "It's when you don't see me
that I'm working hardest. In that respect, I resemble the Viet Cong."
It's true: hours of reading every day for the book column. Once I get
some sleep, however, I return for a few hours. The scene is tense. So I
do an editorial overnight and leave it for him in the system. At night,
talk with Brenda.

FRIDAY, 19 FEBRUARY / KINGSTON
Harvey has asked me to speak with Barry about the quality of his writing: a difficult assignment. I do my best. Make suggestions, offer help.

SUNDAY, 21 FEBRUARY / KINGSTON
J here and we go to the place of Stephen Heinemann the book scout
and buy some stuff. A very '60s apartment: the kitchen painted in a
bright industrial yellow enamel, secondhand furniture, books and dust
everywhere, artefacts, objects, a rat under the bathtub, a picture of
Jimi Hendrix hung in the bedroom. A warm environment on a bitterly
cold day.

SUNDAY, 28 FEBRUARY / KINGSTON
Have to get some large pictures to Kingston for the show tomorrow and
didn't have any means of crating them, so I hire [an acquaintance] to
drive me and them down in his taxi at 10:00 a.m. I ask him not to smoke
pot openly when driving along the 401 and he explodes into curses. Very
sarcastic and unpleasant. "I've never known *what* you are," he says at
one point with great contempt. Accusations of triviality etc. I stay calm,
seeing no point in any other reaction.

TUESDAY, 1 MARCH / KINGSTON
Brenda comes over, doesn't like others but wants to buy the painting with the white pitcher in it. So much linseed oil that it will take months to dry.

WEDNESDAY, 2 MARCH / KINGSTON
I believe someone should take [one of the reporters] out for a beer and comfort him about his being let go (or, technically, his not being picked up for another term). He is distraught to say the least, as I always was in similar situations in my own twenties. I give him my best advice but I don't know if he'll listen. I never listened either.

SATURDAY, 5 MARCH / TORONTO
Dinner with Bruce and Deborah [Whiteman] downstairs but Deborah is distant, cold, suspicious and bored most of the evening, it seems to me. First thought: her saying, "Oh God, do I have to spend another evening with that horrible Fetherling?" Second: that they'd been arguing about something else. Comes out in conversation that Thera has been ill, fevered, etc. I think she didn't want to have a social evening for that reason. Awkward all around. They should have cancelled or postponed the get-together.

THURSDAY, 10 MARCH / KINGSTON
Paul-André Comeau, the editor of *Le Devoir*, at lunch today in the boardroom.[7] A sort of Québécois Fulford, the crisis of liberalism, the wringing of hands over what to do about the Young People. Sounds like Bob did 15 years ago before he became so conservative. Even looks a bit like Bob did in 1973.

WEDNESDAY, 16 MARCH / KINGSTON
Arthur L. Davies had a poem on the letters page about the arrival of spring.[8] Alas, he wrote too soon, but a pleasant change from the correspondents who've been kidnapped by space aliens or fear homosexuals.

---

7 Paul-André Comeau (b. 1940), journalist, educator, and Quebec's diplomatic representative in France.
8 Arthur L. Davies (1903–1996), former *Whig-Standard* publisher.

MONDAY, 21 MARCH / KINGSTON

Bronwen [Wallace] stops me on the street, praises the piece on Elsa Gidlow.[9] That certainly makes me think that her opinion of me may be moving a bit higher.

TUESDAY, 22 MARCH / KINGSTON

Lunch with Peter Dorn, convivial but lonely, I believe, and with a genuine love of writing as well as of design.[10] Stories about Barker Fairley.[11] Invites me to his farm. In the evening go to the Picasso film with [a friend]. It seems that at [the friend's] instigation her husband impregnated the woman she went to stay with.

WEDNESDAY, 23 MARCH / KINGSTON

[A colleague] crying on my shoulder again about office politics. A pleasant and gentle man with a respect for other people's abilities, but he creates these nerve storms for himself.

THURSDAY, 24 MARCH / KINGSTON

The system is down when I arrive at the office at eight in the morning. If it doesn't come up by late afternoon, we set type in Brockville. But no, it doesn't come to that. I run into [an acquaintance] in the A&P and we go for a drink. She looks much the same (wonderful hair) but dressier now as befits a faculty member, but with broken-out skin and limping badly from arthritis. She pretends to remember nothing of our old business. I have my doubts. But I am friendly and sincere as can be and for once leave matters right where they should be.

FRIDAY, 25 MARCH / KINGSTON

Dinner with Stephen Heinemann. The instant each dish of Chinese food arrives he quickly sticks his nose right into it, smelling for freshness. Funny habit, no doubt the result of his early days in Shanghai. I believe I'm entering a bad patch of a few days.

---

9 Elsa Gidlow (1898–1986), Canada's first openly lesbian writer, author of *Elsa: I Come with My Songs* and *Ask No Man's Pardon*.
10 Peter Dorn (b. 1932), graphic designer.
11 Barker Fairley (1887–1986), scholar, portrait painter, and poet.

SATURDAY, 26 MARCH / KINGSTON
The bad patch continues. I get into a spat with auction people at the Hopkins sale at City Hall and walk out just as the books are coming up (after I'd wasted the whole day waiting). I must realise the special disadvantages under which I labour when I'm run-down or tired, or have missed a meal or a night's sleep, or when I find myself in a stressful situation without a copy of the script.

TUESDAY, 29 MARCH / KINGSTON
A long talk with [historian] Donald Swainson, a lovely man. Later, on a walk, [an acquaintance] tells me that she's gone so far as to arrange and fund her husband's passades but that he avoids serious affairs lest he have to move out and go to work. Tentative first signs of spring. In the evening, an interview with one of the local worthies in his enormous Victorian house filled with such things as a dozen of Bonaparte's dishes and two tiny dark canvases he insists are Constables.

TUESDAY, 12 APRIL / KINGSTON
Managing editor. The very sound of it is tautologous.

MONDAY, 23 MAY / KINGSTON
Bus strike has me stuck here for the holiday, feeling lonely and missing J. See Brenda, who lets drop an explanation for the cold shoulder I received from some people months ago: Neil's secretary left a memo with my salary figure lying on her desk, engendering resentment all round.

TUESDAY, 9 AUGUST / KINGSTON
Bruce [Whiteman] has come for a visit, and I read him a section of the memoir in progress.

Earle never condescending when I ask him a question whose answer he's surprised I don't know. A slight look of astonishment for a second, or perhaps a check to see if I'm serious in asking, and then his teaching voice kicks in.

FRIDAY, 19 AUGUST / KINGSTON
Liked it better when the world was closed off, when you stood in Finland and looked across the frontier into the USSR, knowing you were looking at

what was dangerous because it was so unknowable. Everything is opening up politically but with no corresponding opening up of the culture, no flowering; purely a business convenience. The excitement is in China, Korea, Latin America: everywhere but here, the North American backwater.

MONDAY, 5 SEPTEMBER / KINGSTON

I feel that the memoir, as impractical a project as it is, may actually cure me of my past, the way previous books have cured me of my interest in their subjects. Maybe the trick is to write but not publish these merely therapeutic projects.

If the end is near I don't want to rush out and gobble experience anymore. I've spent years getting this routine I like. Let me carry on with it.

Neil: I seem to be totally unused to having my knowledge respected.

SATURDAY, 26 NOVEMBER / KINGSTON

Worried about Woodcock since when in Vancouver last week I telephoned and got Inge who told me he has had another heart attack. So I write down this from Derek Stanford's book *Inside the Forties: Literary Memoirs, 1937–1957*: "I had contributed to George Woodcock's anarchist magazine *Now*, and very much respected George with his quiet gentle manners. Like me, he had worked on the land at Cambridge in the early years of the war, and had then, with amazing industry, turned out one pamphlet after another in which he set forth the anarchist programme: on railways, on agriculture, on factories, etc. These were not rabble-rousing statements which the public mind associates with his brand of politics, but reasoned and reflective arguments, fed with a full sufficiency of facts. It always seemed to me that George and not the more dynamic Alex Comfort was the rightful lineal descendant of Herbert Read, about whom he was to produce an excellent book in 1972. Muriel [Spark] also liked and admired George. She had met him regularly as a reviewer in her days at *The Poetry Review*, and used to say that he and his wife must be very much in love for him to be able to write so much in the cramped quarters of their tiny abode without their strangling each other. When George went as an academic to teach in a Canadian university – since when he has remained in Canada – the English literary scene lost a lot. Nobody who knew him in his English days, unless they had been informed, would have recognized that he was Canadian-born."

Remember also the George Melly [English jazz singer and celebrity] story, or Ferlinghetti's telling the *Sunday Times* that he went to Whitechapel Alley on a pilgrimage when he was in London recently.[12]

WEDNESDAY, 21 DECEMBER / KINGSTON

Wayne Grady tells me the following story about Marian Engel, whom he had known in his *Books in Canada* job, etc. and whom he assumed knew him as well.[13] She approached him at a party and told him that Margaret Laurence was on the bottle again and that she and Peggy were worried.[14] Later in the conversation she said, "I enjoyed your new book." Wayne thanked her.

Not able to leave well enough alone, Marian added, "It made me think of Mackenzie King in an entirely new way."[15] Wayne thought to himself, "Mackenzie King? *The Penguin Book of Canadian Short Stories*? I have *no* idea what she's talking about." So he asked, "How is that?"

She replied, "I hadn't realised Canada kept all those Jews out of the country."

She thought he was Irving Abella, the author of *None Is Too Many*, to whom he bears only the slightest resemblance, having a black beard but being much thinner and younger.[16] He gently put her right but she was wounded despite his best efforts. The next morning an obviously embarrassed lawyer phoned him at *Books in Canada* with the message that he was calling on behalf of Mrs Engel to say that if he ever published what she told him about Margaret Laurence she would bring the full weight of the law down on him.

12   Lawrence Ferlinghetti (b. 1919), US publisher and poet.
13   Wayne Grady (b. 1948), journalist, author of books on the environment, and translator.
14   Margaret Laurence (1926–1987), author of *The Diviners* and other novels.
15   William Lyon Mackenzie King (1874–1950), Liberal prime minister, 1921–26, 1926–30, 1935–48.
16   Irving Abella (b. 1940), historian and professor, author of *History of the Jews in Canada*.

1989

The pattern continued: voracious reading and writing and ricocheting between two cities. I published a new collection of poetry, *Rites of Alienation*, and began a book about Canadian songwriters, to be called *Some Day Soon*.

FRIDAY, 6 JANUARY / KINGSTON
A giant tragedy of errors.
   "My friends all call me Bob. Or they would if I had any."

WEDNESDAY, 11 JANUARY / KINGSTON
Return here tonight to read the boards of the *Magazine*, the usual routine, only to find a note that one of the local hostiles had phoned to make further wild allegations and shout obscenities. I do him the courtesy of ignoring the message.

SUNDAY, 22 JANUARY / KINGSTON
For *Some Day Soon*: short attention span created mostly by the vice of fashion, the demands of the incessant need of the pop kultch industries. Their ideas are bio-degradable, it's merely their packaging that's not. This is in the nature of liberal technocratic societies.

SATURDAY, 4 MARCH / KINGSTON
Drafting a new chapter of the memoir. Dave [Godfrey] and Dennis [Lee] at Anansi – I admired them both, though differently, for they were quite different creatures. Dave, the *precision* of his cynicism. Dennis likes poets only until they achieve their majority; this rankled me for years, but I know now that we all need our methods of staving off death and this

was his. His prehensile interest in toryism. [George] Grant, [Graeme] Gibson et al. were writing from a far more elevated class position than he was.[1]

FRIDAY, 24 MARCH / KINGSTON

I've liked working in the newsroom (of course I like puppies, too). But I'm not sure I wish to continue for much longer when each phone call brings new chaos and generalised nastiness. Today, however, is quite the opposite in its tenor (but the same in its effect). The point in any case is that I'm into one of my periods of darkness, a rite of purification: a thousand tiny suicides. "Cast down your silence and follow me." But what is it that's being expunged, what am I treating with such acts of cauterisation? Am I responding to an injury? Induce bleeding to assess the flow, then suture the wound. The rollercoaster effects of these days are hard on the body, of course. They underscore the fact that, okay, I have no long-range plan, but perhaps none is possible. We must proceed from one crisis to the next.

TUESDAY, 9 MAY / KINGSTON

The important point I've learned these past couple of months is that it's foolish and childish at my age to keep seeking approval. Supply myself with satisfaction by making my own work and let that be enough to lubricate me. Now if only I can make myself remember the lesson the next time terror strikes.

WEDNESDAY, 10 MAY / KINGSTON

Rexroth on Tolstoy: "From the beginning of organized society, or at least from the beginning of written documents, there have always been people who challenged and rejected this state of affairs [the Social Lie]. Usually they have been members of the Establishment themselves; Buddha and Tolstoy were both princes. Obviously the mute inglorious sufferers who have always borne the burden of 'The System' are unknown to history, except in moments of social turmoil when some renegade from the ranks of the literate and privileged has spoken for them.

1   George Grant (1918–1988), nationalist philosopher, author of *Lament for a Nation*.

It is hard to say of any given period of history or of any people, even our contemporaries, how acceptable the actual bulk of society finds the principles upon which it is organized. As a matter of fact, most people except politicians and authors work out for themselves, in secret, ways of living which ignore organized society as much as possible. After five or six thousand years much of life is still private, extraordinarily resistant to the mechanisms of civilization, even, or perhaps especially, in the most powerful and authoritarian states. What is called 'growing up,' 'getting a little common sense,' is largely the learning of techniques for outwitting the more destructive forces at large in the social order. *The mature man lives quietly, does good privately, assumes personal responsibility for his actions, treats others with friendliness and courtesy, finds mischief boring and keeps out of it. Without this hidden conspiracy of good will, society would not endure an hour.*" [my italics]

MONDAY, 15 MAY / KINGSTON

My conclusion is that my spirits are recovering faster these days, until I get a bizarre fax followed by the same text in letter form. I save the former, because thermal fax paper fades away in time, but I destroy the latter more permanent communication. My response to severe criticism from these yahoos coexists uneasily with my genuinely short attention span for praise. V. Woolf writes of such matters well in her diary.

The way I always sneak into Toronto, making my secret rounds, only to return to Kingston and do the same – dropped off blocks from where I intend to go, avoiding the camera in the lobby, midnight data-checks of the system and so on and so forth – demonstrates my need for safety through security, having, as I do, no other way to protect myself.

FRIDAY, 19 MAY / TORONTO

J and I celebrate our sixth anniversary a week late. Last year we ran into Robin Skelton and dragged him along to our anniversary dinner (telling him that this seemed only fair, seeing that he had been excluded from the honeymoon). This year we find ourselves invited to a party for him at the home of [a Toronto arts figure]. She and everyone else in fine form, [and] Robin looking dazed as usual. When we enter, poor Sylvia [Skelton] lets the cat out of the bag about the [Michael] Ondaatje portrait I bought for J. The artist is there, delighted to have made a sale. I know how that is.

I ask Robin what books he has coming out or in the works and he withdraws a neatly numbered list of 20 titles. Running me through it, he curses that he has forgotten one. Later still, another stray occurs to him. We leave before the count reaches 23. He is voluble and oddly charming, less nervous than when more wary of his companions. His knack for attracting helpful women in Toronto to be his agents and promoters has always amazed me.

Walking back home, J sees a dozen or so good packing boxes, ideal for books, in someone's rubbish at the kerbside and so we cart them along with us.

TUESDAY, 23 MAY / KINGSTON

Talking to Vera [Frenkel] on the phone about some experimental film critic she knows – rather, some critic of experimental film. "He's got God by the short hairs," she says.

Pizarro's body mummified in Lima cathedral. Think of Stalin, Mao, Roy Rogers' horse. A possible theme park if some American businessman could bring them all together, no doubt in Florida.

More insults from one of the Kingston orthos today and instantly I am back in the state I experienced a month or so ago: the sense of moving slowly, as though wrapped in some huge opaque membrane. It's not an unpleasant sensation actually, merely one that drains off the sense of being alive and acute. Sensation of twilight – crepuscular gloom.

THURSDAY, I JUNE / KINGSTON

An interview last week with Malcolm Ross, who's still very upright and hardy.[2] "No, you're wrong," he would say whenever I was wrong. But old men should never wear camelhair jackets: they always look frail in them. I remember once interviewing Callaghan and his c.h. had a two-inch tear in one of the seams, which robbed my attention for an hour.[3] The poor man had no one to look after his wardrobe.

2   Malcolm Ross (1911–2002), editor of the New Canadian Library paperback series.
3   Morley Callaghan (1903–1990), novelist and short story writer, author of *The Loved and the Lost* and *That Summer in Paris*.

Lunch last Friday with [David] Silcox. I like him. He *understands* patronage, knows how that world works and equally how art works. Rare creature.

Section 319 of the Criminal Code, the part prohibiting public incitement of hatred.

George N. Kates in *The Years That Were Fat: Peking, 1933–1940*: "I have never seen old age more grandly self-respecting, or more self-justifying. The modern Westerner loses enormously by not comprehending what high ranges, both of appearance and conduct, are accessible to those who have actually cultivated their later years. This single mistake, and the consequent mismanagement of all our possibilities from middle age onward, puts us worlds apart from those Chinese within the traditional system. The last part of life we tend to abandon even to despair, whereas for the Chinese it is a summit, for the very reason that it has been built by human wisdom alone upon a notoriously fragile and transitory base."

TUESDAY, 6 JUNE / NAPANEE
I've always liked the view of this place one gets from the train, the old walled jail (nicely defensible) and the rear end of the courthouse with its cupola poking through the foliage. In fact, a redneck town. I need a drink, which doesn't make my stay any happier, though I go down by the Napanee River, where I see a garter snake in the grass and a big turtle sunning itself on a rock mid-stream, its neck outstretched as far as it will go. Fetherling's nature trip.

MONDAY, 19 JUNE / KINGSTON
Formerly it was my elders who judged me and found me lacking so much; now my contemporaries. I need to perform a tough-minded audit of myself, quite unsentimental, relative to what can only be called the avuncular biz plan, new facts to fill an old void, which itself follows from previous collapses and reassessments. Real worth of a financial cushion as it affects mood. Be helpful to those younger: a framework to do so, without becoming an old bore. Memoirs.

"In casting himself as the second Vasari, Filippo Baldinucci chose a troublesome role, and one for which he was ill-prepared. Baldinucci's birth was insignificant; his education was mediocre; and his artistic expertise was uncertain. Since his search for patronage was continually frustrated, he was forced to attempt increasingly aggressive and ingenious schemes of self-promotion. Filippo also suffered bouts of chronic depression and was prey to destructive religious obsessions." *After Vasari: History, Art, and Patronage in Late Medici Florence* by Edward L. Goldberg.

TUESDAY, 20 JUNE / KINGSTON
Following the news like watching an ant farm.

TUESDAY, 27 JUNE / KINGSTON
I'm confusing everyone, and if polarising opinion in the process, at least making potential supporters into real ones whom one must stand by – without of course making the matter worse. Truth is that I arrived with a plan that is proceeding well enough without being exposed: working less for more money; more time means more freelancing and so the ability to save the salary and refill coffers, while in the bargain producing some reprintable stuff for a collection. All this an elaborate subsidy for my real (!) writing.

FRIDAY, 14 JULY / KINGSTON
Until recently I had never taken seriously the notion of "control" as that which the grown-up children of alcoholics and others feel compelled to exert on their environment and the people in it. But lately I have come to see how by doing something to help me think my way through this (though logic is not always a useful tool in such matters) I can at least make my professional life happier. For aren't all the freelance scrapes about my needing to exert control over the work in every particular? I should have taken the lesson from *The Blue Notebook*: that the stuff simply must exist as awful journalism and then be cleaned up and tallied every few years to allow for evaluation and perhaps even give it a bit more permanence. Existence will be better if I can keep this thought in mind and be less intense about the immediate use of the material.

FRIDAY, 28 JULY / KINGSTON
J returns from the book-buying on the Coast, having seen the Woodcocks, whom she said treated her like a daughter-in-law, and the Skeltons,

where she luxuriated in the family atmosphere. "I called them Mr and Mrs Woodcock and they called me Mrs Fetherling. Inge calls George 'George Woodcock.'" And in Victoria: "One evening the family was talking about whether or not the daughter was pregnant, but Robin didn't understand what the subject of the conversation was. He was preoccupied trying to get the recliner to stop turning on him."

SATURDAY, 26 AUGUST / TORONTO
I walked into the Greeks' to meet up with J at breakfast and she was in tears reading the *Globe*. The end had finally come for Bronwen Wallace on Friday (I was already in Toronto) and there was a tribute by Dennis Lee in the paper. We were all hoping she would recover; I raised a sum of money for her round Kingston in the expectation that she wouldn't be able to work while convalescing.

SUNDAY, 27 AUGUST / KINGSTON
If put in a PoW camp, I would immediately begin to tunnel. Having a secret project to keep me sane is very much part of my makeup, always has been. In any case, my scheme at the moment, though of small importance financially and not without a certain danger, fills this need. I could write an essay upon projects, like Defoe![4]

A big example this week of amateur editing of my stuff brings frustration to the surface again, but I must welcome these opportunities to show that I can let go, as I welcome my tunnel-digging activities, which have become a game.

SATURDAY, 2 SEPTEMBER / KINGSTON
I am tense during Bronwen's memorial service. If I'm being completely honest I have to confess that I was jealous of her personality, doubly so because it didn't signal superficiality in her case. How I wish I had more of what she had. Might well have developed that way if it weren't for dysphonia, but what can you do? The world belongs to the likable, who are not necessarily the competent. The tyranny of the cheerful! People are frightened, insecure, and rush to embrace any sign of friendliness. I

4   Daniel Defoe (1659–1731), English journalist and novelist, author of *Robinson Crusoe*.

can't quite manage to project this because people naturally respond uneasily to my speech and I take their reaction as condescension (I think they're mocking me when they laugh nervously).

Though speaking of ego, the events last night were saved by my reverting to egolessness, one of my adrenalin-driven responses whenever danger jumps out at me. As the antagonist was acting emotionally, I knew better than to react logically merely for the easy triumph of winning on points. Life would have been better without King Street [the *Whig*'s office] this morning, especially so as I was in no condition to assemble a better response, one more conducive to understanding, but I believe that time will work its usual magic and that the process will begin soon enough – certainly before this weekend is out. Must keep from playing it out loud as I walk along. Too young to have such a past and too young (dignified? don't I wish) to be forced into reliving such incidents from it. Breathe deeply.

Can't hold a job for the same reason can't be hypnotised: stubbornly refuse to concentrate because of need to avoid putting all my attention in one basket – in case it's impounded and I become dependent on others, whom I wish to behave as I would if I were able to do so.

If I must find within a kind of individualism that satisfies my anti-Americanism and is to some extent suitable to my unusual personality, then I could do worse than to have the [Al] Purdy example there, not as a model, but as a suggestion of the range of possibilities: his crude antiquarianism and the place he has made for himself outside the usual circles at no apparent sacrifice to his being recognised.

TUESDAY, 7 NOVEMBER / KINGSTON
Two weekends ago, J and I were in Ottawa for the antiquarian bookfair. One night we went out to Maison Henri Berger with Bruce [Whiteman], because of whose jeans we were given an intimate private dining room upstairs, with a buzzer to summon the waiter and a view of the Peace Tower in the distance across the river: the sort of room that Frank Harris might have enjoyed. I took ill at the fair the next day, and not being able to wait many hours for the train, took a taxi back to Kingston ($165), where, subsequently, 'flu and bronchitis set in. For several days there I was quite rotten, and only today, after going to a doctor and getting some erythromycin, do I begin to feel a bit better. Must recover fully by next week in order to go to London.

1990

I spent the first part of the year on several long overseas assignments: looking at the Soviet Union on the eve of what most experts accurately predicted would be its disintegration, and taking the Trans-Siberian Railway to Beijing for the first anniversary of the Tiananmen Square massacre, before going to Shanghai and snaking up the Yangtze River to Sichuan. When I returned, I published *The Rise of the Canadian Newspaper*, a historical monograph on how news, as a commodity, came to be thought of in terms of daily units rather than an unbroken flow (to which it has now reverted). A busy time for me, but a troubled one for the *Whig*, an institution about which I resolved to write a book.

THURSDAY, 2 AUGUST / TORONTO

"He was a man of very extraordinary genius. He has generally been treated by those who have spoken of him in print as a madman. But this is a mistake and must have been founded chiefly on the titles of his books. He was a man of fervid mind and of sublime aspirations: but he was no madman; or, if he was, then I say that it is so far desirable to be a madman." De Quincey, "A Peripatetic Philosopher"[1]

FRIDAY, 26 OCTOBER / KINGSTON

We learn today that the *Whig* is being sold to Southam, news that seems to put an end to a chapter in my professional life, though I'm hoping to hold on to the job (and the book project) as long as I can. Much depends

[1]   Thomas De Quincey (1785–1859), English essayist, author of *Confessions of an English Opium Eater.*

on whether Neil stays. It takes courage to see spring at the end of these dark economic winters, to actually believe, rather than simply to remember, how the cycle of expansion and recession is built into a credit economy like this.

MONDAY, 29 OCTOBER / TORONTO

Robin Skelton is visiting. At one point mentions that WASP Air Canada flight attendants, spotting his all-black outfits, his long greying beard, and the saucer-sized silver pentacle he wears on a chain round his neck, automatically bring him the kosher meal: part of their evident plan to get ahead in the corporation by showing initiative. Also, a visit with Earle and his spouse of the moment. I wonder if he is sad to see me age, as I am him.

THURSDAY, 8 NOVEMBER / WINNIPEG

From Vancouver, where I find George [Woodcock] looking much healthier, I come here for [an arts council] jury. The city seems bleak to me, with much evidence of homelessness; bankers' row and the area round the old Grain Exchange remind me of Shanghai in that they speak of the great age of prosperity, spanning the 1920s, though the epoch seems nearer to the present on the Bund, quite frankly, than it does at Portage and Main. Winter is upon us, and I huddle.

At the jury there were three people, two WASPs, one Jew, all of whom had grandparents or great-grandparents who had some involvement in the events of 1919 [General Strike].

MONDAY, 19 NOVEMBER / TORONTO

A dilemma: I have often been dismissed as a phoney when I use up my daily ration of speech energy to attempt vivacity; conversely, when I stay silent (as with Ramsay and [John] Fraser – two recent examples), I seem boring beyond belief.

THURSDAY, 6 DECEMBER / TORONTO

My instinct was right. I was to have had first pages of the travel book [*Year of the Horse*] from Summerhill [Press] on 14 November. Call today only to learn that the business is being shut down because of Gordon's [Gordon Montador] failing health due to AIDS. The succession plans he made previously are no longer going to be followed.

FRIDAY, 7 DECEMBER / KINGSTON
For my book on the paper [*A Little Bit of Thunder*] Neil kindly lends me
his correspondence files, and I come upon his memo to Michael Davies
when he was negotiating to hire me.[2] It cheers me considerably. Also
find his memo to one of the orthos, which I never knew about, telling
him to stop blaming me for his troubles. The fact remains, though, that
I am tired of this endless cycle of bad luck and good luck in irregular
alternation; it wears me down.

MONDAY, 24 DECEMBER / TORONTO
Bad period of stress and middle-aged sleeplessness these past couple of
weeks. Several nasty interpersonal incidents at the *Whig* caused by
blood, chemistry and everyone's uncertainly about the future of the
paper.

Robert Nozick (ordinarily a crank) in *The Examined Life*: (1) "After
an ample life, a person who still possesses energy, acuity, and decisive-
ness might choose to seriously risk his life or lay it down for another
person or for some noble and decent cause. Not that this should be done
lightly or too soon, but some time before the natural end – current health
levels might suggest an age between seventy and seventy-five – a person
might direct his or her mind and energy toward helping others in a more
dramatic and risky fashion than younger, more prudent folk would venture." (2) "Calling an act 'creative' characterizes it only in relation to the
materials it actually arose from, the earlier experiences and knowledge
of the creator, not in relation to everything that has preceded it in the
history of the universe."

One of the first things that happens to a dead body, one of the things
with which the undertaker must deal, is that the eyes turn to liquid.
Sometimes I swear I can feel the process beginning or see it starting in
other people I pass on the street.

Several rainy days in a row, bad for dogs and painters.

SUNDAY, 30 DECEMBER / TORONTO
Several times each week as I walk down the Bathurst Street hill on my
way back from the gym I find myself with a view of 19th-century Toronto

2   Michael Davies (b. 1936), proprietor of the *Whig-Standard* and philanthropist.

down below, in the distance: the provincial parliament and the tower of the old College Street fire hall poking up above the tree tops all alone. A few steps farther and the illusion is destroyed by the modern buildings that suddenly explode into view.

1991

With my ties to Kingston fading, I focused on Toronto once more, and published several new books, including *Year of the Horse: A Journey through Russia and China*, and a poetry collection, *The Dreams of Ancient Peoples*.

FRIDAY, 4 JANUARY / TORONTO

Dinner last night with George Galt and Alyse [Frampton] at a Greek place they like on the Danforth and then with them to a party at [Michael] Ondaatje's.[1] The usual O crowd is there: the Rookes, Susan Swan, [cinema figure] Nancy Beatty, Peggy and Graeme.[2] [Publishing figure] Jim Polk is also there as it turned out. So is [poet] David Donnell. Later Peggy said to the hostess in the kitchen (as overheard by J), "Just how many old boyfriends of mine did you invite to this thing?" I realised at the end of the evening that now sometimes the temptation to social stress can be apprehended and viewed from above, much as a person might view his or her supine self on the hospital bed during an out-of-body experience. This cheers me no end.

TUESDAY, 15 JANUARY / KINGSTON

How I hear [Virginia Woolf's] *A Room of One's Own*. The use of £500 was way higher than necessary of course but the principle sound and applies equally to me; only now, with the capital saved up the past couple of years, am I free to some extent to write as I please, at least for a

1 George Galt (b. 1948), editor and author.
2 Leon Rooke (b. 1934), novelist and short story writer, author of *Shakespeare's Dog*; Constance Rooke (1942–2008).

time. This is quite separate from the fact that like all great manifestoes the book makes one feel that one is among the oppressed who should be rising up to its call.

THURSDAY, 24 JANUARY / TORONTO
Two long days in a Canada Council interdisciplinary jury. The only thing the panel can agree on is when to break for lunch. One of the members, an artist from Vancouver, expensively dressed, thin gold watch worth thousands, volunteers that he knows the best diner in Toronto. "And it's basically a gay place, so you know the food's terrific." Exactly what people used to say with respect to truck drivers.

FRIDAY, I FEBRUARY / VANCOUVER
J and I arrive on the early morning flight, and retreat to English Bay, where the cool water, I think, must be soothing to the rusty bellies of all the freighters anchored there (I count 10 of them, and try to sketch some). I have a dream about shopping with [a *Whig* colleague] and detectives working on the case of a murdered young woman. I'm shown a story about her on an old front page, which also reproduces the menu of her last meal (from her prom or some equivalent function). I feel useful to the investigation.

SATURDAY, 2 FEBRUARY / VANCOUVER
I rush to be within sight of both the Sun Tower and the Dominion Building and feel safe. We spend a long while at the poetry bookshop in the latter place. On Granville there's a [Charles] Manson lookalike doing a rap that both foretells the coming of the end of the world and protests against the GST.

MONDAY, 4 FEBRUARY / VICTORIA
We get away on an early ferry, and the Skeltons meet us at the other end, Sylvia looking patient, competent, and satisfied, and Robin, in his black felt Robert Graves hat, looking almost as befuddled as he is. J can only guess how the neighbours in Oak Bay must view the Skelton ménage, full of poets, witches, and other visitors, including on-again-off-again children. The house is huge (there are still old bells for ringing the servants) and stuffed with books and pictures and carvings and junk and all of it absolutely filthy. But then Robin puts no special store by cleanliness

(he smells most of the time). In the back garden is a circle of charred stones, indicating where his Wicca ceremonies are conducted. In the evening we go to Hawthorne Books to hear Susan Musgrave read, with Robin introducing her.[3] She wears a zip-front denim jacket, skirt and white bobby socks, and reads well, with polished patter between poems. I haven't seen her for years, not since northern Ontario somewhere. I'm surprised that she recognises me in the good-sized audience, but she does. Later she runs outside into the street to chat with me while I'm on my way to use the telephone at the corner grocery store to ring [an advisor] about the latest on the real estate problem. Red Lillard, the Alaskan, is there, and a number of us go out for drinks following the reading.[4] He and I agree that I will produce an auto-bibliography that he will publish as a pamphlet. This will strike at the heart of something in me: the need to document in order to forget. A long day when we climb into bed. I dream that I help [my father] GSF, a widower, to move [his mother] EF's body out of the house; she is wrapped in a shroud and is light as a sparrow, with a sparrow's bones perhaps.

TUESDAY, 5 FEBRUARY / VICTORIA
While J calls on the booksellers I read proof at the public library and get together with Ken Coates for coffee.[5] A historian who longs for a general audience but is hidebound by his academic prose; great ambition and industry though, rather like [a rival of his] in this regard but without any of [the rival's] toxicity of personality. I dream of Sandy Ross working at *Reader's Digest*.[6] Some *Whig* figures also seem to be involved with the publication somehow.

WEDNESDAY, 6 FEBRUARY / VANCOUVER
Up at 6:30 to scramble for the ferry back. We check into the Sylvia [Hotel] again, and while J sleeps I run into [an artist acquaintance] strolling along Denman. He holds up well but is as combative and pro-American as ever. Announces that he is earning little but making more

---

3 Susan Musgrave (b. 1951), poet and novelist, author of *The Charcoal Burners*.
4 Charles Lillard (1944–1997), historian and poet.
5 Kenneth Coates (b. 1956), historian and academic, author of *Canada's Colonies: A History of the Yukon and Northwest Territories*.
6 Alexander Ross (1935–1993), business columnist and editor of *Canadian Business* and *Toronto Life* magazines.

art. I recall [a mutual friend] saying how naïve he is about his decidedly naïve sculpture, thinking himself alone. He's no longer getting much local work as a musician, he says. I manage to have an acceptable conversation with him, but I keep my watch in my pocket, so to speak. In the evening we go to Kits and meet Thesen and her husband for dinner.[7] She is just as I imagined her – bright, a humanist to the core, startlingly feminine sometimes. They offer us their place on Galiano anytime. Her husband has to leave midway through for a meeting. Later she accompanies J and me back to the hotel for drinks. After we've called it a night and gone back to our room, J says to me, "So, are you in love or what?"

THURSDAY, 7 FEBRUARY / VANCOUVER

While J sees Dedora and attends to more book-fair business, I do an interview with Peter Wilson [book review editor] of the *Sun*.[8] At five we go to the Woodcocks' for drinks and end up staying for dinner – shepherd's pie, which George, in West Country fashion, calls cottage pie. He looks better than when last I saw him, with higher colour, but he is out of breath frequently and must shuffle rather than walk. He wears a handmade shirt but old trousers baggy in the seat, and he discourses as usual on an astounding array of topics. Says he is writing a history of historiography, a topic which Inge pronounces boring. She is hilarious this time, saying things like, "George and Al Purdy write to each other every week, like lovers, but it is only so that they can publish the correspondence." J buys some books from him to benefit the Woodcock Trust. He speaks often of death these days, but he is calm. Paula [Brook, a journalist and editor] told us the other evening that George would have liked to have a daughter but that Inge and he decided to put their work first. I wonder if they regret the decision now. A poignant moment when George tells over dinner how his family disowned him when he became a CO [conscientious objector] during the war – all except for one cousin, a bank vice-president, who resumed relations eventually, but only much later, once George's books began to get reviewed in *The Times* and the *Telegraph*. I venture that if he'd been reviewed in the *Express* and the *Evening Standard* the rift would have been total as well as permanent.

7   Sharon Thesen (b.1946), poet, author of *The Beginning of the Long Dash*.
8   Brian Dedora (b. 1946), gilder, picture-framer, and poet.

"Do you think your father would have come round to seeing your point of view if he had lived?" I ask. George is thoughtful and sad and takes a while to respond. "Yes, I suppose he would." But he sounds unsure.

FRIDAY, 8 FEBRUARY / VANCOUVER

Lunch with Bill New at the Hotel Vancouver, our first meeting, during which I warm to him and also think I make not too poor an impression for once.[9] He can be coaxed into candour. That evening we go to dinner with Don Stewart and Ann Webborn at a seafood house on Beach.[10] Ann has cut her hair, which makes her look even more Welsh by calling attention to her cheekbones and her dark eyes. Don a wonderful fellow in the best possible way, wise and shrewd but not cynical or corrupted. I like it that he likes J so much. Later the four of us go up to our hotel room to look at some books and to drink, and Ann unselfconsciously stretches out on the bed, where I join her. It is all rather exciting actually, for at one point all four of us are on the bed (looking at books!).

SATURDAY, 9 FEBRUARY / VANCOUVER

We spend the morning at Don's shop, browsing and packing for shipment back to Toronto all the books J has bought. Break for lunch with Don at a place in Gastown. Then J and I see a couple of movies and loaf before heading to the airport to await the all-nighter back to Toronto. I never visit Vancouver without wanting to move back. The problem is forever one of livelihood and also the fear (silly, isn't it?) that I will miss the reward that must one day attend my survival in Toronto if only I can hold on long enough (fat chance).

MONDAY, 1 APRIL / TORONTO

Much travelling the past month: to London again, also to the North and then finally back across to Boston. I conclude happily that New England is much more like England than New Mexico is like Mexico but differently so. That is, the architecture and the streets of Back Bay Boston are

---

9   W.H. New (b. 1938), critic and poet, editor of the journal *Canadian Literature* and, later, of the *Encyclopedia of Literature in Canada*.
10 Don Stewart (b. 1951), antiquarian bookseller; Ann Webborn (b. 1951), visual artist.

often quite lovely in their Englishness, just as New England villages often suggest English ones, but the people are American to the core. Walking about maintains the illusion that is shattered the first time you hear a resident open his mouth. Had dinner with Earle's eldest daughter and try to urge her to think kindly towards her father now that he's in difficulty. She's 26, intelligent, funny. Quite a young woman.

I have had to resume my practice of conducting a quiet little performance audit on my behaviour each day. I may have been a bit overbearing in Boston, for instance, when meeting with the film people – I always get into that corner. But I did quite well indeed at lunch yesterday with Christina McCall (dear woman).[11]

THURSDAY, 4 APRIL / TORONTO

J takes so ill with 'flu yesterday that she actually closes the shop. So I've slept on the sofa in the den, and while there have the following dream: I am in London with DSF, who has come over to attend a conference having to do with the fact that he has an employee with HIV. We visit Vanessa Bell's old studio, a high-ceilinged place in the West End somewhere, at once both Georgian and industrial. Anne Collins is using it as an office, and behind one of the tall bookcases we could see the top of an enormous old stretcher the previous occupant left behind.

FRIDAY, 5 APRIL / TORONTO

J works most of today and feels somewhat better this evening. A beautiful spring day, but I feel a bit disoriented. Haven't slept well the past week or so.

Among my errands today I stop into Writers and Co to pick up a book, and chat a bit with Irene [McGuire, the owner]. I could tell that I was speaking too quickly or running the words together in annoying groupings. What's more, a kindly reference I intended to make to George Galt came out sounding wrong. Otherwise my daily performance not memorably bad.

11 Christina McCall (1935–2005), political journalist and author.

SATURDAY, 6 APRIL / TORONTO

J somewhat better today, though she passed a bad night and is napping now as I write this (7:15 p.m.). Another spring day (two in a row) but with determined rain. Ring Brenda [Large] in Charlottetown to see how she's doing. I write the first couple of pages of the first draft of the *Whig* book. Determined to be orderly and productive; must be for months on end.

Why do I *insist* people take me with *precisely* the *right* degree of *seriousness*, which I don't in fact deserve and which of course they never do, and so naturally I am arch or impatient or at least appear hurt. It's all such a load of nonsense. I'm sick of myself.

TUESDAY, 16 APRIL / KINGSTON

A most strange visit to Kingston.

The paper in an uproar even more than usual the past two days over job changes etc. (Harvey to promotion and market research, Sheldon [MacNeil] to "HR" – already a complaint to the Human Rights Commission – Steve Lukits to the editorial page); Southam and the recession combine to give the place a depressing air. Yet I arrive in a calm state, and everyone is friendly to me there and in Kingston generally (the latter fact makes me suspicious). See [Bob] Hilderley, who's still a bit cold, though I do manage to get a few laughs from him, and he says he would in fact still publish my essays when I get the ms together one day. Later I initiate a coffee with [a writer], which was good to have done, for I realise now that he's simply crazy, no more no less; his insides always in a swirl, which causes him to speak in rhetorical extremity and gives him the appearance of a professional crank. Neil and I have coffee. As usual, it has taken me more than 24 hours to find out the subtle messages in what he says. The message in this case is that by asking how matters were at home he was telling me that I can extend my contract past December 1992 if I move back to Kingston but if not, not. Not, of course. It's time to move on, though I must say the money is good, and it would be well to still do a little column or something for a small stipend.

The brutal people who like to wound – who can't resist wounding – by passing on the cruel remarks of others about oneself, they are the most valuable sources of intelligence: absolutely compelled to give up the information they've gathered and requiring nothing in return for their service except maybe a hurt look.

THURSDAY, 18 APRIL / TORONTO
Lunch today with Don LePan at the Vikings. It is good to see him again
after so long a time. He's supportive. My speech flags a bit towards the
end, but isn't that bad: mainly loss of eye contact and increased speed
more than dysfluency per se. As his father has the same problem, I imagine that either he is inured to such speech or else deeply disturbed by it.
Yesterday I had a drink with [a colleague] and had to repeat myself
sometimes, as though I couldn't hear my own mumble (same experience
this week with Neil and someone else, can't recall who). How did I do
with her otherwise? I was collected, if maybe more aloof than I intended
or too cynical.

There are simply too many people everywhere. This is what seals off
the present from the past so unbridgeably and makes comparisons, even
references, worthless. This is what makes order, harmony and productive living so impossible for us as a society. The only response is for the
individual to live on the old scale, calmly. This I have tried to do.

The great fear: dying without having explained oneself properly.

TUESDAY, 23 APRIL / TORONTO
I ask Bob [Fulford] whom I should go see. He gives me two names. But
I learn on returning home that the promising-sounding one isn't in the
directory. I should move quickly on this (not that I expect a quick fix)
rather than allow events to flow uncontrollably, as last time. J not noticing this one, and I try to keep up a front. Poor Bob. He is really upset
when I tell him my story.

On my way home I stop at the bookshop and meet a man who tells me
about Two-Gun Cohen, getting all the facts wrong.[12] He then explains
that he is in showbiz, a magic-and-comedy act. "I did Letterman two
years ago, and just the other month Jack Nicholson had me down to
entertain at a party at his house. Old Jack!" He goes on to say that, in
addition, he is the owner of one of only two surviving flea circuses (the
other is in Germany) and that, before doing any of this, and before going
to the Far East where he became interested in Cohen, he was in sales –
and furthermore that in the '50s he was offered a job at the *Whig*. Why

12 Morris Cohen (1889–1970), Canadian adventurer, military adviser to the
Nationalist government of China.

does this last fact not surprise me in light of the ones before it? In antiquarian bookshops one is forever meeting people who used to be the
Archbishop of Canterbury or equivalent.

SATURDAY, 27 APRIL / TORONTO
When I do manage to reach him by phone, the doctor Bob recommends
tells me I don't sound depressed. So I must not be. He gives me an appointment for Monday, and I must keep it, but now I feel that I'll be
wasting his time.

TUESDAY, 30 APRIL / TORONTO
Saturday and Sunday were rather bad, beginning with the newspapers
and continuing on through a lunch with Roger [Buford Mason] during
which even *he* seems depressed; J is away in Ottawa at a book fair. Quite
a bit better today.

WEDNESDAY, 1 MAY / VANCOUVER
Flying over the mountains, a view of animal tracks on frozen lake-beds
far below. The city rather poor-looking and rundown compared to when
I last saw it not all that long ago. Some potential for screwing up simply
by following the path of least resistance – retreating into silence – but I
consciously fight against this and win. In the evening a drink with an
affectionate Paul Grescoe during which I correct past impressions.[13]
This is all to the good in view of the way that recently I have felt myself
under the crushing weight of all the accumulated social disasters down
through the years.

THURSDAY, 2 MAY / VANCOUVER
A[n arts council] jury all day and afternoon (the ostensible purpose of
the trip) followed by a cocktail party at which I commit one of the most
serious faux pas of recent years. What's more, I meet Keith Maillard.[14]
He is a smoker but I manage to steer him quickly out onto the balcony.
At it turns out, he has been instructed by George McWhirter (acting no

13 Paul Grescoe (b. 1939), journalist and editor.
14 Keith Maillard (b. 1942), novelist, author of *The Knife in My Hands, Gloria,*
and *The Clarinet Polka.*

doubt on the suggestion of Woodcock, to whom I spoke a couple of weeks ago) to feel me out about UBC; but alas they have no one-year appointment open for '93, merely one course on a sessional basis.[15] The day is also rough because of the *Sun*, but when I return to the hotel in the evening from a movie at the Stanley and I look at the clip, preparatory to throwing it out, it doesn't seem so bad (this is sometimes the way). How often have I gone to the movies, usually matinees, to brood in the dark and think about some crisis or other; a number of old films I see on television recall particular situations of this kind.

FRIDAY, 3 MAY / VANCOUVER

A phone call to J who tells me I've had a nice note from Leonard Cohen in Los Angeles. Otherwise a terrible rollercoaster of a day. Paula [Brook] stands me up for coffee (troubles with a new printer) and Don Stewart is down at lunch; he says he may have to leave the new building as a result of squabbles with the city and the landlords. Going to the Four Seasons with someone from the Asia Pacific Foundation for a drink, I see Murray Pezim walking along the street (carrying a football), and later I spot him again, in the bar, while I'm waiting.[16] I think that's a vivid comment on the condition of the market: the Pez drinking in the afternoon, before trading's ended.

SATURDAY, 4 MAY / VANCOUVER

As you get older, praise needs to be stronger in order to work, and insults hurt more.

FRIDAY, 10 MAY / KINGSTON

Taking a slightly earlier train home to Toronto after a tense week here. Taped interviews with Michael Davies for five straight mornings, and that was fine. Also, a positive and indeed upbeat meeting with [Bob] Hilderley who loved the *Some Day Soon* publicity (except for the attack on it in the *Whig*).

15 George McWhirter (b. 1939), academic and poet.
16 Murray Pezim (1921–1998), stock promoter and owner of the BC Lions football franchise.

With Southam, this is a dangerous period for the paper. The present much more complicated than I've put down here, but I'm tired and weary and have the strength to make only an *aide-mémoire*. Hear tell of a negative review by Abley in the *Gazette* and call Deborah Whiteman who reads it to me over the phone – it doesn't sound so bad as I'd been led to expect.[17] Still, a frustrating couple of weeks.

SATURDAY, 25 MAY / TORONTO

This past fortnight has been a dreadful time of one crisis or disaster after another. Irene McG[uire] started being terribly rude to both me and J: I fear this has to do with my views on America etc. Saw Rosemary S in an attempt to get the writer-in-rez job at the U of T for January 1993 when my Kingston contract expires.[18] For a couple of days, it looked promising, as they needed someone to fill in for one term only. But Audrey Thomas, who had expressed doubts earlier, decided to come around.[19]

J faints at the booksellers' party at Abelard [bookshop]. I have to go down and get her. The reason: she's resumed smoking.

TUESDAY, 4 JUNE / TORONTO

Lunch today with Don Bastian in one of the curtained confessionals at the Senator.[20] I am amused at my own uncertainty over how to relate to the fact that I occupy a senior's position, not in this instance perhaps, but with increasingly frequency. I'm at a loss to know how to respond with grandfatherly or at least avuncular pleasure at the continuation of the species. Afterwards, accepting a lift home, I am struck by how almost attractive the city is, under bright institutional sunlight.

I sense my bottoming out and fragile sense of getting better came when a review in the *Globe* seems to signal the end to the current run of bad luck – a real trough – and I am left to reflect that what I would miss most about not being alive would not be friendships or loved ones but stretches

17   Mark Abley (b. 1955), editor, journalist, and author.
18   Rosemary Sullivan (b. 1947), biographer of Gwendolyn MacEwen and Margaret Atwood.
19   Audrey Thomas (b. 1935), novelist and short story writer, author of *Blown Figures* and *Intertidal Life*.
20   Don Bastian (b. 1948), Stoddart Publishing editor.

of good luck, when I've covered a lot of ground quickly and far ahead of my pursuers – and never got caught. This is important. Of course, sometimes, in less fanciful terms, this entrepreneurial kind of creativity has limited me, tied me down, doomed me to small projects not requiring outside help.

Not quite so God-splattered as [D.H.] Lawrence, say.

THURSDAY, 6 JUNE / KINGSTON
Michael Ignatieff is in town to moderate some event at Queen's tomorrow, and I go to the Hochelaga Inn to pick him up for dinner. The old mansion house reminds him of the family home on Prince Arthur, he says. The floor of his room is a mess of papers and the detritus of travel, and his spare pair of underpants lies on the bed. He's not quite finished his column for the *Observer*, so I sit down to read some of the new Milan Kundera novel that happens to be lying open nearby. At Piggy he again proves himself to be a smart and most entertaining dinner companion. But he has moments of controlled melancholy – about how much he misses his father, about how the further decline of his mother's health affects him, about what it means to be the elder of the two brothers, about how it felt to see the family estate in Russia (the old house is now a school), of how he'll probably give up Britain in the next couple of years and return to Canada. I plant the seed about when [John] Fraser's contract at *Saturday Night* is likely to expire. He picks up when I tell him that John is getting $125,000. Afterwards we take a long stroll up Princess Street and through Sydenham Ward, still talking away. After saying good night I walk back to the *Whig* via Ontario Street. A beautiful clear, warm night. But I find a dead rat, 10 or 11 inches long, on the pavement outside the front steps of City Hall.

SUNDAY, 9 JUNE / TORONTO
Lately my quick judgements have improved, but I haven't always acted on them – to my sorrow. NB: I must bring my actions up to the level of my instincts.

MONDAY, 17 JUNE / KINGSTON
A day trip here that's not too bad by any means. Neil is solicitous, and I even manage to exchange a few pleasantries with the new publisher; the

antagonists simply stay away. The only unsettling part of the day was running into Don Swainson, and seeing the great toll the St George's [sexual abuse] scandal has taken on him; he says he's seeing a shrink. In general, I am quite satisfied that I can position myself in such a way – prepare myself, realistically rather than in a spirit of optimistic rationalising – for the time when I end my connection to the paper. I look forward.

TUESDAY, 18 JUNE / TORONTO

Things somewhat worse back here though. [The therapist], I've concluded, simply dislikes me greatly, even taking a couple of verbal pokes at me to see what I'd do (nothing of course). Thinks I'm a self-educated buffoon and is pretty condescending towards the end of the session. None of this augurs well.

Proof of inflation: recently saw some Portuguese boys pitching loonies. Proof of something far different, I'm not certain what: at the gym the other day, members of the women's self-defence course were flirting with their karate instructor.

SATURDAY, 29 JUNE / TORONTO

J comes home from the bookshop saying that she had to go down the street to look at some art books that one of her lesbian customers wanted to sell. "She lives with this large male transsexual. It was very weird. There were all these women walking in and out of the flat, and the one with the big tits turned out to have once been a man." Recently I overheard her explaining to someone how the video store on the street had reopened for business. "The psychotic woman with the boyfriend who's a heroin addict finally left, and this opened the way for the return of Eduardo."

TUESDAY, 2 JULY / TORONTO

Vera [Frenkel] comes for dinner (J is away) and gives genuinely helpful crits; after seeing the work of 10,000 students, she needs only a second on each picture. She also knows instinctively all the career problems and says some interesting stuff. "I didn't really know you then, but I remember when you were everybody's fair-haired boy." She has a *far* deeper understanding of *everything* than [the doctor].

The many study the few. The problem of history-and-the-present remains how to lead the necessarily good life as though the world were still small and underpopulated and the distances great. List benefits: self-education, organic relationships, sequential lives in a single biological span.

"Journalism is not really a literary profession. The journalist of today is obligated to hold himself ready to serve any cause – like the *condottieri* of feudal Italy, or the free captains of other countries. If he can enrich himself sufficiently to acquire comparative independence in this really *nefarious* profession, then, indeed, he is able freely to utter his heart's sentiments and indulge his tastes, like that aesthetic and wicked Giovanni Malatesta whose life Yriarte has written." Lafcadio Hearn[21]

"Of course, literature is the only spiritual and humane career. Even painting tends to dumbness, and music turns people erotic, whereas the more you write the nicer you become." Virginia Woolf to Katherine Arnold-Forster, 12 August 1919.

SATURDAY, 6 JULY / KINGSTON

I'm bound to lose when I get bogged down in the politics, because everyone else is better at these things than I am. But the chance to open a second front, or to extract a little sustenance before I get caught, is just too inviting and so necessary to survival.

SATURDAY, 20 JULY / TORONTO

Earle returns home today after a one-week stay. A productive visit and quite informal. I am delighted to see how well he's bearing up with the most recent divorce. J observes, when we drive to Stratford with him overnight (I break a tooth biting down on a hard sweet), that he has bought a pair of earrings for someone. One night we throw a barbecue for him with the Burford Masons, Val Ross, Landon, a lot of different people whom I thought he would enjoy for different reasons.[22] Hearing him talk with Landon at such a level about certain aspects of early

21 Lafcadio Hearn (1850–1904), Greco-American essayist on Japanese subjects, and exoticist.
22 Richard Landon (1942–2011), director of the Thomas Fisher Rare Book Library, University of Toronto.

bookmaking was pleasing. He and I are going to take a short trip together at the end of November when he's back from Italy and I from
Taiwan.

THURSDAY, 26 JULY / TORONTO
I breeze through a useful lunch with Judy Stoffman from the *Star* at Le
Select. Problems with [the therapist]. I tried to fire him but he wants one
more session, next week, to talk it over. He offers to have me keep checking in with him once a month, like a series of job interviews with a prospective employer who doesn't like my looks and has no intention of
hiring me.

SATURDAY, 17 AUGUST / TORONTO
People can be cursed with their fluency as I am with my dysfluency: I
shouldn't think ill of those with the gift of the gab, as I have tended to do.
Three Hail Marys and a bottle of rye.

THURSDAY, 5 SEPTEMBER / KINGSTON
This trip has laid me up with TMJ, sleeplessness, an overwhelming sense
of rejection, and tension, though I learn nothing new: was already aware
of [the new publisher's] aversion to serious journalism and his wish to
be *editor*-publisher. Reconfirm that he will honour the contract (though
he is alarmed to be reminded of its duration) but will not renew. So
what's wrong with any of that? Nothing. Strategy: write column for the
Magazine, mostly books with some travel; finish first draft of the book
by end of February; collect money (always phone first to make sure
cheque is waiting); and seek other fulfilment for '93. The truth be told,
the *Whig* lost half its appeal the moment Michael Davies sold and will
lose all the rest, of course, when Neil ceases to be even nominally in
charge of the editorial side. Besides – and I must not delude myself here
– I was already growing weary of the obligation. Remember Chinese
politics: I shall leave some people thinking they've won, while I depart
having gone round the world on assignments, having two books from
my *Whig* stuff already and with my current project, the book *on* the
Whig, well under way. Why then I am upset? [The therapist] tells me it's
a miracle that I'm not one of those people living alone in Parkdale eating
catfood. His exact words.

MONDAY, 8 JULY / TORONTO

A man comes into the shop after looking at a book entitled *Geek Love* in the window a few days ago. He asks J in heavily accented English for the book on Greece. She can't make him understand that it isn't about Greece or for that matter even about Greek love – but *geek* love. Also today she reports seeing a lesbian couple riding a bicycle-built-for-two: the one in the front wearing a tuxedo, the one at the back a floor-length evening gown, both apparently returning from some all-night function.

SUNDAY, 20 OCTOBER / TORONTO

Several strange arts events the past couple weeks. At a party for [Mel] Hurtig at George Brown House where I saw John Honderich talking to William Thorsell (whom I'd never met).[23] Went up and said hello to the former, was introduced to the latter but he wouldn't acknowledge me. Puzzling. Later that same evening, J and I walked into the posh party following the Toronto Arts Awards ceremony, and I was smothered in friendliness by [*Globe* arts editor] Katherine Ashenburg – accompanied as usual by Thorsell. Katherine introduced us, and this time he was hardly in a position to ignore me; it was easier to shake my hand (and no doubt wash his own at the first opportunity).

Fraser the other day in an uncharacteristic moment of public doubt and self-criticism: "Sometimes I feel like a Club of Rome statistic: 'Somewhere in the world every 13 minutes John Fraser is making an enemy.'"

MONDAY, 21 OCTOBER / TORONTO

The press centre at Harbourfront (a couple of rooms in that somehow despicable hotel, the Harbour Castle) is full of people and vibrating with nervousness, my own and everyone else's, when I go there to pick up Ignatieff. Over a drink I try to prosecute the thread of our last conversation, in Kingston, about why he should come back to Canada and take up some sort of public life. He knows I feel that he's one of the few who could not only elevate public discourse but actually rekindle liberalism. He tells me that Bob Rae has been asking him to take over TVO now that

23 John Honderich (b. 1946), editor and later publisher of the *Toronto Star*; William Thorsell (b. 1945), editor of the *Globe and Mail*, later director of the Royal Ontario Museum.

Ostry has been forced out of the job.[24] I urge him to accept but he has deep doubts – doubts about losing his writing time especially, doubts about how it would look to be given a position by his old friend, maybe also about enduring a dark period before establishing himself as a public figure here, doubts about starting over to be sure: "I'm not 30 anymore." I tell him we're both closer to 50 than we'd like and does he want to be 55, napping under a newspaper in a chair at the Reform Club in Pall Mall? More to the point, I go on, in England you'll only get bogged down in administration, the curse of the Left; in Mulroney's Canada, you could fight *evil*. He laughs but takes my point, I believe. Another factor: the reception given his novel over there has convinced him that he will never be accepted. Funny, he's sort of a Rex Mottram[25] in reverse: the Canadian aristo who's gone over *there* and intimidated *them* – but the same effect as if he had been a non-aristo with the identical Canadian accent.

The above discussion is interrupted by the arrival of Katherine Govier, who stays for only half a drink and is invited to come along to dinner but doesn't accept.[26]

I take Michael to the Pink Pearl on Avenue Road. Others present: Susan Walker, the Stoffmans; Eleanor Wachtel can't make it.[27] Michael holds everyone more or less spellbound with stories of his recent investigation of the food shortages in St Petersburg and also of the security implications of being friendly with Salman Rushdie – of having his assorted Special Branch shooters come to dinner with him etc.[28] Don't agree with him on every point (he believes ousting Saddam Hussein more important than not supporting America's attempt to do so) but one of the clearest thinkers I know. When the party breaks up, he asks somebody to drop him off at Baby Point Road.

24   Bob Rae (b. 1948), NDP premier of Ontario, 1990–95; Bernard Ostry (1927–2006), civil servant.
25   Rex Mottram, a character in Evelyn Waugh's novel *Brideshead Revisited*.
26   Katherine Govier (b. 1948), novelist, author of *Tales of Brunswick Avenue* and *Hearts of Flame*.
27   Susan Walker (b. 1947), *Toronto Star* arts reporter.
28   Salman Rushdie (b. 1947), British novelist, author of *The Satanic Verses* and *Midnight's Children*.

WEDNESDAY, 20 NOVEMBER / NEAR BALTIMORE, I THINK

Earle meets me at the Syracuse airport, and I can tell at once that he is doing okay despite his troubles – being left by another wife, difficulties at the university, and most recently the death of his younger brother while he, Earle, was in Europe, unable to return for the funeral. The reason becomes clear soon enough when I learn that he's in love again (Earle needs to be in love in order to be happy). The woman is only a few years younger than himself, the author of a book on Scots poetry and a professor of English in the Pacific Northwest. He spends much of the drive, and a good deal of the trip, telling me of her virtues – and of one difficulty that he pretends does not worry him. She has two personalities (she dubs them Amanda and Amanda T) and slips easily from one to the other.

Our goal this first night is the home of Earle's elder brother in Maryland. It's a desperately long drive through the slate hills of eastern Pennsylvania, which recall stories by [John] Updike and [John] O'Hara, with the beautiful arched spans crossing the river at Harrisburg and the infamous Three Mile Island cooling towers in the distance. It's mid-evening when we finally arrive. The brother is a self-educated genius who's made some real money inventing electronic medical equipment. He and his third wife live on a horse farm with two houses joined by a breezeway, the one serving as living quarters, the other as office for the electronics company's four or five employees. The house is filled with kitsch – in reaction against a genteel youth, says Earle. The brother has had a triple bypass but keeps himself well overweight, chain-smokes and eats enormous fatty meals – preferring to enjoy what time he has left, says Earle, rather than deliberately trying to lengthen it. He is also a book dealer (Alger, illustrated kids' books), an authority on the law, a computer expert, etc. Earle confesses he's always been in awe of him and asks me what I think. I reply that he seems like a cross between Mycroft Holmes and Davy Crockett. In fact, he reminds me most of the protagonist in Paul Theroux's *Mosquito Coast*. At dinner he discourses on the patent system and its weaknesses. I go to bed exhausted, having had only three hours' sleep last night.

TUESDAY, 3 DECEMBER / TORONTO

J and I to the Winter Garden this morning for the presentation of the Governor General's Awards. A crowd of a few hundred with many cameras and much hoopla. The fiction prize is as expected, but I am somewhat disappointed that Anne Michaels doesn't win for English poetry.[29] The only public disgrace and scandal is the English non-fiction winner. Harold Horwood must have overpowered Anne Collins on the jury (who would have thought Anne could be overpowered by anyone?) and not only kept David Macfarlane's book on Newfoundland off the shortlist (seeing it as poaching) but prevented Rosemary Sullivan's life of Elizabeth Smart from winning (he wouldn't go for what he doubtless considers all that feminist and belles-lettres stuff).[30] The result is that a stunningly poor but politically correct book by Robert Hunter is the winner.[31] After the ceremony with its speeches comes a reception spread over three floors of the theatre. There was a time when I would have listed here any of those I thought had been cool towards me, but I'm so awkward at parties myself that I must be more charitable in my interpretations of how others seem to be behaving. But some of the people I see: Katherine Ashenburg (coy and busy), Val Ross (coming down with the 'flu), Terry Kelly (all excited about the possibility of meeting Robert Hunter in the flesh), Geoff Hancock (cranky today), Avie Bennett (expensively tailored and quite charming in an easygoing way).[32]

Next I meet up with Wen Dong, who has defected from the People's Republic and has been living in Toronto on a visitor's visa, which he's naturally eager to exchange for resident status. I pick him up outside the King Edward [Hotel]. He is shivering in the snow and slush, though he seems to be wearing every layer of clothing he's brought with him. We have a coffee, then by prearrangement I take him up to *Saturday Night* to see John Fraser, who has agreed to advise on certain particulars of the situation. John is at his best: greets and chats with the guest in Chinese, asks pertinent questions, conveys all the recent intelligence from the world of the exiled Chinese democrats. Very knowledgeable and well-organized: not at all Fraser the editorial executive. At the end of the

29 Anne Michaels (b. 1958), novelist and poet, author of *Fugitive Pieces*.
30 Harold Horwood (1923–2006), journalist and author of *White Eskimo*; David Macfarlane (b. 1952), journalist and novelist, author of *The Danger Tree* and *Summer Gone*; Elizabeth Smart (1913–1986), novelist and poet, author of *By Grand Central Station I Sat Down and Wept*.
31 Robert Hunter (1941–2005), environmentalist, journalist, co-founder of Greenpeace, and author of *Occupied Canada*.
32 M.T. Kelly (b. 1946), novelist, author of *I Do Remember the Fall*.

meeting, he takes out his business card, copies out in Chinese, on the reverse, all the information, and puts in his home phone number. Going out of the magazine's offices we meet Anne C and I make introductions all round. She bows to Wen as she says hello.

WEDNESDAY, 4 DECEMBER / TORONTO

To celebrate J's forty-fifth birthday I take her, Robert [Wright, antiquarian bookseller], and Robert's girlfriend Lori to dinner in Harbord Street. The place must be chosen with care as J has been a vegetarian for five or six months now, a fact connected with her meditation classes and the way she is beginning to explore her resources in art and healing. She is influenced in these two areas by Jack Shadbolt and Robin Skelton respectively. Funny how much she and I refer to the West Coast. We have more friends there than here, she pointed out once, despite the fact that it's the seat of inhumanism, so to call it. Robert and Lori at first don't want to come, claiming extreme shyness, but I get them warmed up to the idea by proving that the act contains no social threat of any kind.

FRIDAY, 6 DECEMBER / KINGSTON

I always fret about the day trips to Kingston: the potential for political mishap is quite real in the kind of situation I'm in down here. But this one has gone smoothly. Neil and I have a good little chat, everyone is friendly (maybe it's the approach of Christmas), I get my work done, and flee to the six o'clock train, which is a half hour late. I am entering a year filled with peril. I must prepare for the expiry of my *Whig* contract in December 1992 while having something in place to replace it. All this is difficult during a severe recession and is full of psychological stumbling blocks as well. Planning. Thinking.

MONDAY, 9 DECEMBER / TORONTO

Bloor Street for photocopying etc. and on my way back up Albany I see Jane Jacobs walking along near her house. She is like an ancient cargo ship that wouldn't make any headway at all if the waves weren't there to pound it.

WEDNESDAY, 11 DECEMBER / TORONTO

I prepare myself for a meeting with [John] Fraser, who stops by for a drink on his way home from work. I always forget how smart he is or rather that he even listens or assesses – such is the volume of his talk. In fact he gives me some decent advice, based on close observation over the years. Cites my ability to quickly work up interest in a topic many would consider devoid of interest; balances this with my refusal to make the leap into being well known.

MONDAY, 16 DECEMBER / TORONTO
Bruce Whiteman and his sister, Nelson Ball and Ken Norris all here for dinner before we proceed to the ECW launch of our books at the U of T.[33] I am apprehensive, but I must say there is no need for anxiety. The affair well attended and mostly full of friends. Everyone charming. Susan Walker seems to be bearing up well – I think she's very strong. Curiously, she's stopped mumbling since leaving her husband. See Sam Solecki and am worried, as he's never had even a civil silence for me, but he is now effusive (in a way) or certainly friendly: amazing.[34] Jack David even sells a number of books.

TUESDAY, 17 DECEMBER / TORONTO
[The therapist] fires me as a patient, possibly, among other reasons, because I had wished to ditch him, though his official reason is that he cannot, despite his best efforts, get inside a dysphonic. The whole episode does little for the constant sense of rejection for which I had sought his help.

THURSDAY, 19 DECEMBER / TORONTO
News today that Roy Megarry will step down as publisher of the *Globe* effective the end of next year in order to do unspecified good works in some equally unspecified part of the Third World; this raises the constitutional question of whether a lame-duck publisher can govern Canada effectively.[35] I have a long talk with Val Ross, who comes by for a Christmas drink at five. She knows how the world works. I get her to give me the lowdown on how Katherine [Ashenburg] responded to my

33 Nelson Ball (b. 1942), poet and bookseller, author *The Pre-Linguistic Heights*; Ken Norris (b. 1951), poet, author of *Report on the Second Half of the Twentieth Century*.
34 Sam Solecki (b. 1946), academic and editor.
35 Roy Megarry (b. 1937), publisher of the *Globe and Mail* 1978–91.

suggestions for work. J sits in on the second half of the conversation, says afterward, "I don't see why all men aren't in love with Val."

SATURDAY, 21 DECEMBER / TORONTO
Earle's daughter and boyfriend Alf arrive last night late and Alf sleeps till noon (his custom, it appears). I organise a walking tour for them, and meet up with them in the late afternoon at the ROM. From there we go to Spadina, where she lived as a very little girl, in the days when I was working at Anansi. Then we meet up with J and Alf at the shop and go out for Indian food. Alf is, not to put too fine a point on it, a jerk: arrogant, rude, argumentative, part of a couple that quarrels a great deal, publicly and privately. I can't understand why a young woman with her brains and education and her interesting looks (somewhat like her mother's) should get into such a destructive relationship. Well, yes, I do understand; I simply regret that it is so. After dinner, she and Alf go out to listen to jazz, return at 2:00 a.m., play ball with the dog till three, then come upstairs and carry on loudly, forcing J to sleep downstairs in peace.

1992

I was researching what became *The Gentle Anarchist: A Life of George Woodcock*, working in the Woodcock papers at Queen's University and conducting interviews in Britain and British Columbia. I had also taken over publication of the journal *Canadian Notes and Queries*, as an interim measure, to keep it alive until another owner could be found.

SATURDAY, 11 JANUARY / VANCOUVER
See Maurice Yacowar, sounding him out about Emily Carr [Institute of Art + Design] (for I'm putting out all the bait I can these days in anticipation of what might happen in '93).[1] I'd forgotten that he used to live with [film industry figure] Eleanor Beattie and knew Bill Kimber at Brock.[2] Still faring pretty badly with my head cold but turn up at 5:30 at Don Stewart's store – the second one, which he's vacating soon: a farewell party for a departing employee, full of local booksellers and collectors, with the achingly nostalgic Vancouver light crashing through the big front windows.

TUESDAY, 14 JANUARY / TORONTO
Roy MacLaren calls to tell me a story about his son Malcolm who's in his third year reading history at Oxford. During a tutorial in imperial history, the tutor (English) told him he must read a book on the development of the press in Canada by Fetherling, published by Oxford U.P.

1 Maurice Yacowar (b. 1942), film critic and academic.
2 William Kimber (b. 1945), illustrator and visual artist.

I know him, Malcolm exclaimed, he's a friend of my father's. All the
more reason, said the tutor dryly.

TUESDAY, 21 JANUARY / KINGSTON
After two days in a bitter Canada Council jury I make a quick trip here
by bus to get my cheque and check the trapline. Three hours down, two
hours in town (enough to slip in and out and even have lunch with Mary
Anne Beaudette) [of the *Whig*'s editorial page], three hours back: a long
day when I'm already tired. I need to view these day trips to Kingston as
I would view a special op: to marvel at the clockwork, relish the hint of
danger, test my ability to think on my feet when the sands shift.

TUESDAY, 4 FEBRUARY / TORONTO
Early this morning the latest in a series of strange phone calls from
Edmund Carpenter in New York to discuss successive versions of his
Canadian Notes & Queries piece on Marshall McLuhan.[3] He falls to
reminiscing and at one point says: "Marshall always reminded me of
that passage in Boswell in which Boswell says that if you chanced to take
shelter from a rain storm for a few minutes in Dr Johnson's company,
you would come away convinced that you had just met the smartest man
in the world. Marshall was like that too. Of course, if you spent an *hour*
with Marshall, well, that was something quite different."

WEDNESDAY, 5 FEBRUARY / TORONTO
A sad yet highly charged call from Susan Musgrave in BC. She was to
have been here for dinner in a couple of days, but reports that she has had
to cancel her reading trip east owing to 'flu and laryngitis and assorted
personal problems. Something about her husband being on heroin again.

SUNDAY, 16 FEBRUARY / TORONTO
This evening the much anticipated dinner for Bob F's sixtieth birthday.
Moving or funny speeches – the most moving by Bob himself, surrounded
by his friends of different generations, choking a bit. Everyone on his or
her best behaviour. Geraldine looks smashing.[4] I tell her so. She is pleased.

3 Edmund Carpenter (1922–2011), anthropologist and Marshall McLuhan
collaborator.
4 Geraldine Sherman (b. 1944), CBC Radio producer and journalist.

MONDAY, 2 MARCH / TORONTO
I take J to Jake's for dinner to celebrate the arrival of my larger than expected PLR [Public Lending Right] cheque. In comes Jack Pollock, who's dying of AIDS, walking on a metal crutch.[5]

WEDNESDAY, 4 MARCH / TORONTO
An expensive Doubleday lunch today with Robin MacNeil of PBS.[6] To my knowledge, he is the only person I've ever encountered who was actually riding in JFK's Dallas motorcade and later met Lee Harvey Oswald. Later, a drink at the King Eddy with Dianne de F[enoyl] of *Saturday Night*, sussing out the circumstances surrounding her disapproval. I believe I put her in a better frame of mind about me, which is the point.

People are so americanised that they simply can't conceive of someone who would Uriah Heap his ego in the service of enquiry.

SATURDAY, 14 MARCH / TORONTO
Paul Stuewe wants to take me to lunch (perhaps a sign of some transparent design).[7] Seems he's still determined to move to Kingston but can't think how to make a living. I suggest the obvious, tell him how he can get Bob Hilderley, for whom the timing is perfect, to go in with him on the purchase of *Books in Canada*, so that he, Paul, can simply move his job, which he likes, to the place that he likes equally. I scratch out a whole business equation for him, and he's grateful. Later, as I promise, I call Bob at home and explain what I've done and generally bring the pair of them together. Frankly, I'm not without guile. It would be good for the magazine to downsize and refocus and recommit. Bob is the one person who can negotiate easy terms (since he would be negotiating with his brother after all) and who has the trust of all the granting agencies (particularly now, with the way he stepped in to solve the Geoff Hancock matter).

MONDAY, 16 MARCH / KINGSTON
The usual long gruelling day of terror and intrigue in Kingston. I set up lunch with Neil for next month. The place continues to deteriorate

5   Jack Pollock (1930–1992), innovative art dealer.
6   Robert MacNeil (b. 1931), television broadcaster.
7   Paul Stuewe (b. 1943), literary journalist, bookseller, and, later, professor.

apace. I'm certainly getting out just in time. Yet I mustn't let a certain amount of old flak near the beginning blind me to the fact that my timing has been quite lucky throughout, something for which I'm grateful to the gods.

FRIDAY, 20 MARCH / TORONTO

An exploratory get-acquainted meeting with Brian Henderson, the new editorial director at Oxford.[8] Certainly an improvement over [Bill] Toye in terms of personality. A poet. My generation. Things could be worse there. Later, at the gym, I see Rev. John Erb of St Michael's and All Angels, working out.[9] At one point he is spotting for a pro bodybuilder who's doing bench presses. Pastoral work among the thick-necked flock. In the evening, to Fraser's house to discuss the case of the Chinese exile. John is alone with the kids, one of whom (aged 10?) comes into the room and says, "Daddy, do you have a copy of *Frank*?" "No, no, darling," he says. "When there are guests, you say, 'Excuse me, Papa, have you seen Mother's copy of the *Church Times*?'" The child goes away looking perplexed. Later, John and I are having a drink downstairs, me stumbling orally. The girls are roughhousing upstairs. John goes to the foot of the stairs and yells up, "If you children don't quiet down, I'm going to send Mr Fetherling up to read a story to you." Utter silence thereafter.

TUESDAY, 31 MARCH / TORONTO

An upsetting day. J is ill in bed, as is so often the case, when Robert [Wright] phones from the bookshop to say that Dexter is unwell: panting uncontrollably, trembling, pacing, vacant expression. I rush him over to the vet. It seems he has canine epilepsy, which isn't life-shortening but still necessitates certain changes in routine. So what with one thing and another I am in no shape to go to M&S to interview Peter Dale Scott about the first Kennedy assassination but I do (I sound awful on the tape).[10] At one point, Scott, who has a crinkly smile like a reformed crocodile, is reminiscing about McLuhan, who was his thesis adviser.

8   Brian Henderson (b. 1948), scholarly publisher, poet.
9   Rev. John Erb (1933–2005), later, chair of the Anglican Foundation of Canada.
10 Peter Dale Scott (b. 1929), poet and assassination researcher.

"He kept me up until 3:00 a.m. arguing that the central subtext of *Finnegans Wake* concerns the cathode ray tube."

SATURDAY, 4 APRIL / TORONTO

I say goodbye to Robin Skelton, who has been staying with us for three days during a promotional tour. J says she has been disappointed by the visit: "Whatever special magic we had between us is gone," she remarks. But I think this is simply old age catching up with him. As J also points out, "He's not interested in books anymore." Only thrillers actually. His conversation bogs down in trivialities and he drinks too much scotch (despite his diabetes) and continues not to bathe. "My pedantry fails me when required," he says during a painful pause in one of our dinners, "only to reappear when no one desires it." This was uttered at the Indian restaurant up the street, where his strange costume puzzled the patrician Indian woman who runs the place (whom he proudly told of his military service on the subcontinent – one of his less adroit moments). On his second day he asked me whether or not we would prefer him to flush the loo after he pees in the middle of the night or to wait until morning "to pull the chain" lest he disturb us. I feigned polite indecision.

[D.H.] Lawrence in *The Plumed Serpent*: "There are only two great diseases in the world today – Bolshevism and Americanism; and Americanism is the worse of the two because Bolshevism only smashes your house or your business or your skull but Americanism smashes your soul." To which Harry Crosby replies in his diary: "Only he forgets the third disease, the English disease of stagnation. Better to smash than to stagnate."[11] To say the least Crosby didn't get the point. He killed himself soon afterwards.

SUNDAY, 5 APRIL / TORONTO

Sarah Lawley [journalist and editor] has sprained her back and so must cancel out of the Barbara Frum memorial service.[12] J is doing a one-day book fair at the north Market and at five I help her pack up. We have time to change and get out to High Park for a dinner party at Val Ross's with Katherine Ashenburg, [a male friend], and a lawyer friend of Val's,

11   Harry Crosby (1898–1929), US writer and avant-garde publisher, Paris expat.
12   Barbara Frum (1937–1992), CBC Radio broadcaster.

her old roommate (whose name I don't catch). The most extraordinary evening. Talk of nothing but sex from first to last. [The male] and Katherine drive us and the lawyer home, and all the way along Bloor he is badgering the aforesaid passenger to remind him whether they ever slept together.

MONDAY, 6 APRIL / TORONTO

A busy day relative to the World Poetry Festival at Harbourfront. Val Ross interviews me, Diane Keating, and Michael Schmidt and Peter Levi from Britain, and Tomas Salamun from Slovenia for a piece in the *Globe and Mail*.[13] Afterwards, while I'm having a drink with Schmidt in the Harbour Castle bar, I spot Jake [Doherty, publisher of the *Whig-Standard*], who's in town for CP meetings and the like. This puts me in a tightened mood at a time when I'm struggling to stay calm for my reading this week. In the evening, J and I make a brief appearance at the York Club for Christopher Ondaatje's book launch. Linda Spalding and Michael O seem to be attending under protest.[14] The few people I know are logically enough the few establishment types I know: [John] Fraser, Lownsbrough, [publisher and author] Anna Porter and Julian. Sarah Milroy [of *Canadian Art* magazine] there with her banker husband.

THURSDAY, 9 APRIL / TORONTO

After several days hanging about with the poets it's my turn to read. I'm preparing all day only to have two calamities befall me: Duffy and Los Angeles [unknown references]. Either one would be enough to turn me to jelly even on a normal day but somehow I struggle on, made stronger. I am not without appreciation of the irony here: I feel rather like the old prospector at the end of some western who must laugh at the gods when the gold dust he has fought and laboured for is blown away by a freak wind. Several hundred in the audience and I'm very nervous in the green room but in fact the reading goes quite well – much better than I or

13   Michael Schmidt (b. 1947), British poet, editor of the journal *Poetry Nation*, and publisher of Carcanet Press; Peter Levi (1933–2000), English poet and biographer, former professor of poetry at Oxford.
14   Linda Spalding (b. 1943), novelist, author of *Daughters of Captain Cook*.

anyone who knows me had a right to expect. I have bugged myself so that I can play back the tape with the text at hand and learn what I can.

SATURDAY, 18 APRIL / TORONTO

Lunch with A.F. Moritz whom I met at last during the poetry festival.[15] Roman Catholic, extremely bright, and supremely articulate in a slow-spoken and not terribly ironical way. He's now teaching at the U of T after a slow period during which both he and Theresa, having failed to make a living as a couple-of-letters, were reduced to working as secretarial temps. But this year he's on a Guggenheim. I rave on and on about favourite topics of the moment, no doubt giving Al a suggestion of deranged intensity, but I think we like each other.

TUESDAY, 21 APRIL / KINGSTON

It's late afternoon by the time I see Neil. He tells me of his Southam Network scheme for me, explaining that he's one of four on the committee to remake the old Southam News Service, but I'm sceptical and am growing weary of this Kingston connection. Of course I'll miss the money or rather the security but certainly not the tension of these trips (at the moment, until the book is drafted, only one a month).

THURSDAY, 23 APRIL / TORONTO

Two days in an OAC jury with Carolyn Smart who seems cool at first but warms up later, possibly the cumulative result of my overt attempts to befriend her over the years.[16] Other jurors: [poet] Karl Jirgens (like him: handsome Slavic face, quick smile), Dionne Brand (likewise meeting her for the first time, having praised her first collection in *Books in Canada* a decade ago).[17] Sprung from this to go home to find that Don Stewart and Ann Webborn have arrived. Booksellers' party down at Steve Temple's shop.

15   A.F. Moritz (b. 1947), poet, author of *Night Street Repairs* and *The Sentinel*; winner of the Griffin Prize.
16   Carolyn Smart (b. 1952), poet, author of *Stoning the Moon* and *The Way to Come Home*.
17   Dionne Brand (b. 1953), poet and novelist, author of *Land to Light On* and many other works.

FRIDAY, 24 APRIL / TORONTO

I spend the day with Ann, doing the Spadina galleries, looking at the architectural landmarks, lunching at Le Select, helping her pick up a small and absolutely smashing dress (how sexy her bare feet look under the swinging door of the changing room). She tells me how she is returning to painting now, having avoided it during all the years she was living with the painter (she once gave him a human skull as a present). We discuss her work as an occupational therapist etc. Her Welsh accent begins to return as she becomes more relaxed.

SUNDAY, 26 APRIL / TORONTO

I manage to stumble through an *Imprint* taping at TVO. Later, I leave Don and J to pack up at the conclusion of the antiquarian book fair today, then Ann and I (and Ann's brother-in-law) go to the AGO [Art Gallery of Ontario] and then to dinner. Then I scurry up to the Idler [Pub] to meet up with J and hear Bruce [Whiteman] do a reading. I've never heard him read before and am surprised at his skill and animation and poise at the mike. The Jewells are there too and Bruce's sister Lynda. Milt Jewell[18] is a nice fellow sober, which he is not at the moment. Dewdney and Gowdy at the next table.[19]

TUESDAY, 28 APRIL / TORONTO

Lunch with Bob F at Bofinger, which is becoming our usual place. Age catches up with him quickly now. The culture he once swam in threatens to submerge him.

WEDNESDAY, 20 MAY / MONTREAL

Meet with Tom Axworthy of the CRB Foundation, a pleasure not only for the possible financial result but for its mutual smoothness.[20] Axworthy has good intelligence sources: I admire that in a person. Then dinner at the Whitemans', where I stay the night. Ken Norris is there and Robert

18 Milt Jewell (b. 1939), painter.
19 Christopher Dewdney (b. 1951), poet, author of *The Immaculate Perception*; Barbara Gowdy (b. 1950), novelist, author of *Mister Sandman* and *The White Bone*.
20 Thomas Axworthy (b. 1947), principal private secretary to Pierre Trudeau, 1981–84; later, chair of the Centre for the Study of Democracy, Queen's University.

Lecker and his wife whose name I'm embarrassed to say I don't catch.[21]
Long and in the end somewhat drunken arguments about postmodern-
ism v. humanism, relatively good natured but with an edge.

SATURDAY, 30 MAY / TORONTO
The other shoe: Neil Reynolds resigned yesterday. I hear the news from
Judy Steed [of the *Toronto Star*] today before seeing it in the *Globe*, and
I call Donna [Jacobs, a journalist; spouse of Reynolds] who fills me in.
Then I have dinner at Shaul's with Dennis and Kog Reid.[22] J and I both
like the Reids a great deal.

SATURDAY, 6 JUNE / TORONTO
Someone comes into the bookstore and reports that [an acquaintance] is
getting married. I presume her pattern must be registered at the Clarke
Institute of Psychiatry.

SUNDAY, 7 JUNE / TORONTO
J is ill, so I go alone to a small but tense little garden party at Judy
Stoffman's in honour of Katherine Govier who has won another award.
I manage to avoid Pachter who's generally so rude to me, and spend
most of the time chatting with [another acquaintance] who's lost a tonne
of weight. Bob Rae is there too.

THURSDAY, 11 JUNE / TORONTO
Trying to get out with J more. Tonight, an auction at Waddington's of
works from Av Isaacs' personal collection.[23] J buys Mark Prent's infamous jar of kosher pickles that, on close inspection, is actually a jar of
green penises.[24] One is tempted to call this a seminal work. J and I are
standing in the street, holding an enormous jar of penises, trying to hail
a cab.

21   Robert Lecker (b. 1951), McGill University professor, publishing industry figure, author of *Dr Delicious*.
22   Dennis Reid (b. 1943), Art Gallery of Ontario chief curator, author of *A Concise
History of Canadian Painting*.
23   Avrom Isaacs (b. 1926), gallery owner and art patron.
24   Mark Prent (b. 1947), controversial Montreal visual artist.

MONDAY, 15 JUNE / KINGSTON

A beautiful spring day in Kingston, with the harbour full of sail (and the parks full of paedophiles no doubt). I limit my time at the office to some kitchen-cabinet stuff with Harvey, but Jake calls me in to say he's jake for me to be writer-in-residence at Queen's for half a year, as Michael Davies suggests, with the foundation picking up the other part. This would indeed be a neat solution to the problem, allowing me the time to digest the Woodcock papers, which are in the Queen's archives. Another year of money coming in, too, plus something to tell people I'm doing, something to announce.

WEDNESDAY, 17 JUNE / TORONTO

Going to the gym I run into Kildare Dobbs, who insists on buying me a coffee, all smiles and friendliness, full of forgiveness, some of it quite pointed and unsubtle, over having accused me of stuff at the *Star* all those years ago.[25] (What is it about me that makes people wish to make accusations. My awkwardness before and after – awkwardness of sound, awkwardness of silence.)

MONDAY, 22 JUNE / TORONTO

Earle arrives with his new love about whom I've heard so much. She has multiple personalities (well, only two actually), being not only Amanda, a 50-year-old professor of English and women's studies who met up with Earle through mutual classified ads in the *New York Review of Books,* but also Amanda T, her adolescent self, an aspiring poet who speaks with a lisp and a little-girl voice, with open-wide Orphan Annie eyes. She switches from one to the other many times an hour, sometimes in mid-sentence; but unlike so many other multiples, she is always totally conscious of whatever the other half is doing. She has (they have?) always taken a Reichean stand against therapy, believing that reunification would rob Amanda T of her creative powers. With all the good will and sympathy in the world, I can't help but feel sorry for Earle, whose life is complicated enough dealing with plain Amanda, a self-centred aggressive individual with far more education than brains and the usual

25 Kildare Dobbs (b. 1923), memoirist and man-of-letters, author of *Pride & Fall.*

social manners of someone operating with enormous handicaps: a person whose characteristic utterances are a harsh *What?* (for she doesn't listen to what others say and then must struggle to keep up) and a deafening cackle. What wretched luck to have two personalities and both of them bad.

TUESDAY, 23 JUNE / STRATFORD
With Earle and the two Amandas to see this year's production of *Romeo and Juliet*, with Megan Follows.[26] Earle explains sheepishly to J that this is Amanda's (or is it Amanda T's) choice: so touristy, he's sorry. In fact, it's thoroughly enjoyable, though set in the 1920s: Stratford always has had a weakness for modern dress. A wonderful dinner at the Old Prune. The Amandas slipping in and out like a manic ventriloquist.

THURSDAY, 8 OCTOBER / LONDON
I stumble jet-lagged down to Whitechapel to interview Vernon Richards at the Freedom Press to talk to him about Woodcock.[27] It's breakfast time but he has only beer in great quantity. He's a large garrulous fellow – hard to believe he's 77 – who still keeps a big market garden and comes into the press each Thursday. He's most derisive about George but then George, like so many others, was in love with his wife. Anyway he doesn't have much use for intellectuals, he explains.

SATURDAY, 10 OCTOBER / LONDON
Back from Corsham in Wiltshire seeing Lance Godwin, George's oldest friend (their correspondence dates to 1928). A retired teacher, he lives in a poorly heated little house where the electric fire does little or nothing to keep mould from destroying his books. Although he hasn't seen George in almost 45 years, he says that he sometimes finds himself thinking of him as though he were in the next room. He shows me the letter George sent him asking that he allow me to interview him. George called me "a youngish writer ... a modest decent fellow of distant Welsh ancestry."

26 Megan Follows (b. 1968), stage and television actor.
27 Vernon Richards (1915–2001), British anarchist.

SUNDAY, 11 OCTOBER / CORNWALL

A lovely and impossibly long trip from Paddington to St Austell. I peer into the woods: red soil, wind-sculpted rocks in an estuary; at one point, the broken hulk of an old wooden ship lying in shallow water. From St Austell to Mevagissey, where D.S. Savage and his wife Connie, both to one extent or another crippled with arthritis, live in what would be properly a stone cottage except that it's in the terrace in the village.[28] They generously have me to lunch, which consists of thin vegetable soup with its origins in the garden, a slice of brown bread, a potato the size of a lime and baked black, and two translucent slices of luncheon-meat ham. For the last item these poor people have obviously had to shell out precious cash. Derek and I talk upstairs. He tells me that in his view Inge must have put her foot down over [Woodcock's romantic friendship with] Marie-Louise and insisted that they move to Canada. He remembers stopping by the Woodcocks' flat on the eve of their departure. George had sold most of his books to help pay for their passage but there were some that the booksellers had rejected, and George told Derek to take any he might wish. "Those are the ones over there on the shelf," Savage says to me. After we finish taping we look at them: three Everyman's Library books. One of them has George's ownership signature in pencil on the flyleaf. Derek then makes me a present of this, inscribing it to me as a souvenir of my visit – a sort of passing on of the generations too.

MONDAY, 12 OCTOBER / LONDON

A morning interview in the room at the Russell [Hotel] with Colin Ward – such a kind and lovely soul – and a drink afterwards in the bar.[29] Then, to Cheam in Surrey, to see George's cousin Lewis Cooke. He is a retired vice-president of the Nat West bank, and secretly he must believe that George is the black sheep of the family (George feels the same about him – but openly). All very upper middle class. Oh won't you stay to tea? and Oh won't you please have another piece of sponge?

28 D.S. Savage (1917–2007), English poet, critic, and pacifist; author of *The Withered Branch: Six Studies in the Modern Novel.*
29 Colin Ward (1924–2010), English anarchist writer and town planner, author of *The Child in the City* and *Anarchism: A Very Short Introduction.*

TUESDAY, 13 OCTOBER / CHELTENHAM

Here to see Julian Symons who's come for the literary festival.[30] The town is as I had pictured it: boring lives led against a backdrop of pretty architectural vistas; the kind of place where the main social problem is Lucozade abuse. Symons just as in his photos, much younger-seeming than his 80 years despite a few ailments, including some deafness. Fond of George, whom he has visited in Vancouver (only Symons and Lewis Cooke wealthy enough to do so), less fond of Inge. Returning to London in the evening, drinks with Pat Treasures at Overseas House in St James's: two 18th-century mansions knocked together perhaps in the '20s, stuck in a cul-de-sac. The atmosphere very regimental. Am amused to learn that Gatenby is a member.

30   Julian Symons (1912–1994), English writer and critic of mystery fiction, author of *The Immaterial Murder Case* and *Bloody Murder*.

1993

The golden age of the *Whig-Standard* under Michael Davies's proprietorship is considered one of the high-water marks of Canadian journalism, but the institution was always a thicket of controversy. My book about it proved no less contentious. Difficulties surrounding its publication came at the same time as ones connected with *Travels by Night: A Memoir of the Sixties.*

SUNDAY, 21 FEBRUARY / TORONTO

Whenever I'm not full of gratitude for my health and general good fortune, I am fighting off waves of panic and sometimes, if the panic continues long enough, despair. Recently, I even had a patch screwing up meetings and conversations with people, not like that one in, when was it? 1985?, which took years to undo even partly; this was on nothing like that scale, yet it frightened me. I am 44. I feel my life dripping away but my creative life always round the corner.

The *Whig* book is finally at the printers: the sparks can begin. Happily, the summer break between terms at Queen's may be enough to absorb much of the damage: an air cushion against invisible shards of glass. At the end of the next year, I think I shall actually have a decent set of working files for Woodcock.

J is due back tonight from a week in Costa Rica with Dennis Lee and Susan [Perly] at their place there.

FRIDAY, 12 MARCH / TORONTO

A call from an angry Steve Lukits [a writer at the paper] "cancelling or postponing" our scheduled Monday interview for the *Whig Companion*: it seems Harvey has somehow circumvented the 30 March embargo and got a copy of the book (the same day I myself see an advance copy for the first time). So when Lukits virtually slams down the receiver, I call Harvey, who starts lashing out at me with threats etc. Of course, he's not accustomed to seeing his name in a book. I'm hopeful that he'll calm down in time when he reads the book as a whole and sees how well he's presented. Still, this does pose some interesting scenarios for the 30 March launch at the Grand. Either there will be ugly scenes or else a crowd consisting only of the poor benighted author and the few people from the Printed Passage [bookshop] list who will have come solely for the wine and cheese. I intend to split early and vary my routine Tuesday night, staying at the Royal Motel. Walkable to the train station for the first westbound of the morning. I just hope that my remaining trips to Kingston on my Queen's contract won't turn into the black bag jobs the last trips to the *Whig* building were – that whole dark era between Neil's resignation in May and my own slipping out of there for the final time in December.

MONDAY, 15 MARCH / KINGSTON
What was billed the Biggest Storm of the Century missed Toronto almost completely but struck Hamilton to the west and Kingston to the east, and I was optimistic that perhaps the trains to the latter place wouldn't be running. Alas. Getting into town I stop at Printed Passage to pick up some samples of the invitation to the launch and am flabbergasted to see that the booksellers have sent out hundreds of post cards calling me the former editor of the *Whig* and indicating that I will be giving a talk at the reception. This doesn't make my life easier; I must find a way of discussing all that when I'm introduced at the event. After cancelling out his appointment, Lukits turns up at my office to persuade me to do a telephone interview tomorrow evening for next Saturday's *Whig*. I also learn (no surprise) that Harvey got his copy of the book from Wayne at Printed Passage who got it from a brand new [publishers'] rep. Later, at dinner at [private-press printers] Fred and Margaret Lock's, I learn that my Queen's appointment was vigorously opposed by an American element in the English department, which Fred describes as spreading mischief unselfishly, without any thought of gain beyond a little devilish satisfaction. Just to make a wonderful day complete, I get a phone threat about the book – not, I'm certain, a death threat, but just one of generalised violence.

TUESDAY, 16 MARCH / KINGSTON

For my sins, I wake at 5:30 a.m. Can't get back to sleep. Decide to skip
a day's research at the Archives and take the 7:48 train back to Toronto.
Fax and phone call from Elizabeth Wilson, the PR person of the *Whig*, to
demand the return of the staff list she lent me for the launch and to send
her a letter testifying that I made no other use of it. Apparently, some
member of the staff, receiving her invitation at home, has phoned, certain that the company had sold her name as part of a commercial mailing list transaction. I also learn today (for I have my spy system too) that
Catherine McKercher of Carleton [University] is Harvey's choice to review the book in the *Whig*. She's another of his protégés. What a place.
Then, tonight, very much against my better judgement, I have a phone
interview with Lukits, whose drift is totally hostile. Tells me everyone
there dislikes the book, that the magazine even disliked the excerpts
offered.

The people at Stoddart [Publishing] are decent folks, quite likable, but
they're so straight as practically to be Mormons. I decide not to tell them
about the threat, as they would panic. Instead I meet with a former
member of the RCMP who once served in Trudeau's protection squad
and is now a private security consultant.

WEDNESDAY, 17 MARCH / TORONTO

Lunch today with [Elizabeth] Renzetti of the *Globe* (Val Ross, splendidly hatted, invites herself along as chaperone, as she likes to do whenever anyone mentions that they're lunching with me). As an exercise in
pulling my hand out of the fire, it goes rather well.

Some other bookseller or collector in Annex Books said he always assumed that J and I were sister and brother. Odd, considering all the present troubles, that I was pleased somehow.

I speak with [an acquaintance], whose wit falls in the grey area between Wayne's and Shuster's.

SUNDAY, 21 MARCH / TORONTO

The Saturday *Whig*s that arrive here for sale on Sunday lack the
Companion, so I have to call the newsroom and get Murray Hogben [a
reporter], who answered the phone, to fax me a copy of Lukits's piece
about the book. It's not *too* terribly hostile. Not much of a piece, but not

too terribly hostile. Another author might look at it and complain, "They spelled my name wrong half the time." But I, knowing the *Whig*, understand the effort necessary there to spell it correctly in the other half. A question of ullage, you see.

THURSDAY, 25 MARCH / TORONTO

Believing that Diane Turbide hasn't spoken to me for a few years nor responded to numerous invitations, I ask her to lunch and she accepts happily, enthusiastically, and we meet at some new place near *Maclean's*. She professes never to have been cross with me. A most enjoyable conversation, touching on such matters as the impending departure of the present editor. I come away quite pleased that I have taken the chance and made the effort. At the end of the day, to the big *Books in Canada* party at the Arts & Letters Club where the winner of the annual first-novel award is announced. Spend most of the time talking to Angel Guerra of Stoddart about Anansi. When it is time to retire, I politely slip downstairs and follow a strange series of ancient corridors to a door that leads to the alley in back.

MONDAY, 29 MARCH / KINGSTON

Penultimate week of the first term at Queen's, and the first time that I haven't any students wanting to see me. So I finish the work of copying out some research material for use in a later part of *Travels by Night*. This little labour, spread over several weeks, has been quite a trip through a strange part of the past. The feeling goes together oddly with the jumpiness caused by the suddenly on-again nature of the trip to South Africa for *Saturday Night*. But of course the real source of anxiety is the launch tomorrow night at the Grand Theatre for *A Little Bit of Thunder*.

TUESDAY, 30 MARCH / KINGSTON

The former Mountie is a half hour late meeting me in the bar. But he turns up and I pay him and we discuss the security implications. I buy him lunch. He promises to check out the room before the event. I have left the Ramada, where too many people know I stay, and book into the Royal Motel, surely the last place people would consider looking for me even if they were to propose calling every hotel and motel in the Yellow Pages. There are twin beds, with a mirror on the ceiling over only one of them. At the launch, I make my little speech, correcting the booksellers' stupid error in the invitation by making light of myself instead. Most of the time I am seated, signing books (they sell about 60), with the cop, looking not at all cop-like, mingling convincingly. He sees two people come in, and though he doesn't know either of them, hasn't heard them described or seen pictures of them, he instantly makes them as the troublemakers. By coming together, they are obviously trying to tell me that they are a united front. In a few minutes, I lock eyes with the first one, uneventfully. I think he leaves very soon afterwards. But the second stays and stays. At one point during a lull in the signing, he sidles over to me and snarls to indicate the exact nature of his displeasure with how he believes the book depicts him (altogether typical that he misses all the more subtle bits). I shake my head without answering, so as not to prolong the meeting even a few seconds longer to the point where my ex-policeman will have had to blow his cover and intercede. Neil's presence and especially that of Michael Davies no doubt help keep order too. A number of people from the *Whig* come, including one who brings her nasty husband. I see [another colleague] across the room for a moment but she soon disappears. Some community people, some friends like Swainson and the Locks. The problem is that Troublemaker 2, having retreated to the other side of the room, won't go home, even after all of the food and most all the other people are gone. It seems to me that he has simply decided to wait for the place to clear out before staging some violent confrontation. So after thanking the hosts I simply walk right past him to the vestibule and leave by the back stairs. The cop drops me off at the motel, where I watch some TV and tear up some old files, wrap up the bits and bury the bag deep in an already overflowing dumpster in the car park. What a strange evening and what a strange fate for the evidence of some of my past: a dumpster overlooking the swamp along Highway 2.

WEDNESDAY, 31 MARCH / KINGSTON–TORONTO
Leave the motel at 7:00 a.m., a short hike across old leaves stiff with frost to the train station where, as expected, Bob F's review of the book is on the front of the arts section of the *Globe*. I can only smile to myself at having left in my wake a perception of the book so absolutely contrary to the one held in Kingston.

THURSDAY, 1 APRIL / TORONTO

After days of frustration, the South Africa trip falls through because the travel expenses will come to $5,000 and Fraser, under constraints from above in these matters, will go only $3,500. It's just as well. I don't really have the time, the stamina or the clarity for a quick turnaround to Johannesburg at this point.

SUNDAY, 4 APRIL / TORONTO

I read tonight at the Idler with Daniel David Moses and Anne Michaels.[1] Anne reads some new stuff, including a poem referring to Marie Curie with such erotic and linguistic intensity that it sets the mood for the evening despite a poor sound system. The cigarette smoke is pretty thick by the end and I have to escape. Ride in the backseat while Anne and her boyfriend David Laurence (Margaret's son and Jocelyn's brother) drive me home.

WEDNESDAY, 7 APRIL / TORONTO

The Toronto launch for the book at Annex Books, a greatly more relaxed and likable affair. Although the date coincides for a dinner to celebrate Michael Ondaatje and the Trillium Award, we still get a crowd, including Val Ross, Ashenburg, the Fulfords et al. Vera sends flowers, as she always does, followed by herself. I like parties at Annex Books in general, and this is a pleasant one, with one or two people sloppily drunk and Debbie Viets [an editor] dressed to the nines. I dance with Turbide without benefit of music.

SATURDAY, 10 APRIL / TORONTO

No reviews of the book in the paper today, but soon, I think. In a way, I can't lose. Scathing reviews, while they'll still hurt, will cool things down in Kingston most likely by making it seem to the people there that the outside world (without the inexplicable exception of Bob F) agrees with them. Conversely, positive reviews, though they'll never be as positive as Bob's, will cast a bit more doubt in the Southam people's minds. I'm glad all this is happening after the end of term when, except for a half day's

---

1 Daniel David Moses (b. 1952), playwright and poet, author of *Two Women Talking* and other works.

visit, I'll be out of K until September. I remember Neil's remark on the phone after the Kingston launch: "I know you'll get your reward in Heaven for this book, maybe not on Earth but in Heaven."

WEDNESDAY, 14 APRIL / ORONO, MAINE
Wake up early at the motel and go sketching down by the river, which is in flood. Walk across an old railway bridge with the white water rushing right below. Down by the riverbank there is a sort of small white-trash section, but the rest of the village's residential areas are dotted with the evidence of 19th-century lumber fortunes. Go into Bangor, a city of wonderful angles and tricks of elevation. Downtown has three vacant department stores and of course all the cinemas gone. But the mall has by no means drained away business to the same extent as in many other places. Many bookstores and such can afford prime locations. Decent café and restaurants. No old-line downtown hotels left, alas. Odd how jewellery stores (usually a little row of them) are among the last survivors in downtown malled-out America. I suppose this is because the mark-up is so high that they need less store traffic to survive. In the afternoon, I speak for an hour to Ken Norris's creative writing class about the real world, then give a poetry reading to a group gathered from different classes and departments. One hour. Fairly successful, I think. In the evening, Ken, his wife Sue and the poet-manager of the local small press take me out for a Mexican dinner.

FRIDAY, 16 APRIL / TORONTO
This evening get a look at tomorrow's review in the *Star*. Anthony Westell.[2] Friendly but no ideas and poorly written. Lead position though.

WEDNESDAY, 21 APRIL / TORONTO
J's been stressed out for days and days. I think it's the book fair, she says it's the spill-over from the *Whig* book. I keep many of the details from her. See Stephen Smith, who's now m.e. at *Quill & Quire* but hopes to give London a try before the end of the year. No probing questions from him and I am guarded without the slightest trace of being so. I declare it

2   Anthony Westell (b. 1926), journalist, editorial executive, and educator.

a victory. Who does he still see at the *Whig*? I ask. He names three or four of the hostiles. My one bit of calculated candour is to tell him that though I too mourn the loss of the *Magazine*, I was never really welcome in its pages, and had to be blasted in by either Neil or Harvey. Why was that? he asks. I tell him of the *Magazine* people's reception of me on the very first day. It was a matter of some people there fearing an outsider with magazine experience and no natural sympathy for the folk trad. Smith is a nice fellow. I think his father must have spoken well of me to him in order to bring him round. Or perhaps he has learned how I helped to get him the Random House job that time. No matter.

WEDNESDAY, 28 APRIL / TORONTO
Talking on the phone tonight to John Metcalf who tells me of a call from Steve Heighton reporting the death of Tom Marshall in Kingston from a heart attack at 55.[3] The news chills me. Tom was a hypocrite in the *Whig* business (though less so than his friend who instigated it in the first instance) but he was never a leader of anything malicious, just a fellow who went along, head in the sand – the same ostrichism one saw so often in his reviewing. But he was a fine poet, in my view, and a firm friend of poetry. I always felt sad that he only ever came but partway out of the closet. To my knowledge, he always lived alone, never a stable relationship with another man. But then 20 years ago he no doubt would have been fired from Queen's no matter what George Whalley might have done on his behalf.[4] I remember what Ron Paulson, the Kingston bookseller, told me once of having some rough trade come into his shop in the morning to sell books obviously stolen from Tom's shelves while Tom slept.

TUESDAY, 4 MAY / TORONTO
Pasting up *Canadian Notes & Queries* here with Roger [Burford Mason], I am a bit edgy, because this morning Gzowski interviewed me on

3 John Metcalf (b. 1938), fiction writer, editor, memoirist, and controversialist; author of *General Ludd* and other works; Steven Heighton (b. 1961), fiction writer and poet, author of *Flight Paths of the Emperor*, *The Ad Men Move on Lhasa*, and other works.
4 George Whalley (1915–1983), poet, critic, and professor.

Morningside. Later several people who aren't flatterers told me that it went quite well. In the afternoon, I in turn interview Denise Levertov who's here for a Harbourfront poetry reading this evening, which I take in with J after we've dined at Le Fenace with a gaggle of the other poets, Gatenby, and the forever charming Val Ross.[5]

SATURDAY, 8 MAY / TORONTO

For J and me, this is our moveable anniversary (10th – moveable because we have house guests coming on the actual date), and so we check into the Four Seasons after looking at the Sotheby's Canadian art preview and browsing in C.C. Lai, the Chinese antique dealers. Tomorrow a graduate student is coming here to interview me for *Queen's Quarterly*.

MONDAY, 10 MAY / TORONTO

Dinner at our favourite Vietnamese organised crime place with Bill Kimber (who's looking chunkier but well) and Liz Woods.[6] This was ostensibly just a meeting to remember the old days, 1968–70, at various residences, but I drop the news about my memoir, tell them about it, ask them if they'll read it after I finish polishing it this winter. They seem eager and understanding.

MONDAY, 21 JUNE / TORONTO

The past month full of stress and strains, including some pleasant ones such as a few days' visit by Brenda Large, gives way to a calmer and certainly more productive period. J seems much happier since the book fair, for example, and the shop is perhaps limping a little less than previously. I now have two manuscripts – my memoir and the *Arthur Moss* metafiction – to rewrite during the autumn term, and in the meantime I'm writing poems again and also trying to fix up a book of essays. Sweet asylum. Mutual sanctuary not necessarily a function of diplomacy.

5   Denise Levertov (1923–1997), Anglo-American poet, author of *Here and Now* and numerous other collections.
6   Elizabeth Rhett Woods (b. 1940), novelist and poet, author of *The Yellow Volkswagen*, *Men*, and other works.

TUESDAY, 29 JUNE / TORONTO

Thinking about getting back to *Moss* on the second pass. The problem, or one of them, comes near the end. Writing fiction, I'm hit by fatigue at the same place as when reading much of it: all those multiple false endings.

THURSDAY, 1 JULY (DOMINION DAY) / TORONTO

Bob Hilderley here last night for dinner for the first time. He was in his gentle mode. A very pleasant evening of chat, and when J gave in to Dexter's insistent demands for a second walk, Bob and I had a few minutes to discuss some Quarry Press business. He owes money that I'm eager to collect.

MONDAY, 5 JULY / OTTAWA

The second day of a difficult Canada Council jury, difficult because of the usual ethnic, racial and gender sensitivities, as when a Métis writer storms out of the room in tears when other jurors question the fact that her tribal elders have given her instructions as to what does and does not constitute a valid application from people wishing to write on aboriginal subjects. The capital is hot and humid. I must stay through Thursday in order to tour the various official government residences, part of an article I'm writing.

TUESDAY, 13 JULY / TORONTO

Joan Murray from the McLaughlin Gallery was supposed to come for lunch at 1:30 but phones early in the morning to say she will be here at 11:30 and then in fact shows up at 10:30.[7] Doesn't care for any of the work I've been doing, but suggests a show from January through March 1995 for "portraits of friends, writers and so on," which I've not yet begun. At the end of the day, go to the Park Plaza roof for the book publicists' association presentation of the Jack award. The first one given to McClelland after whom it's named; in subsequent years, it will go to others. A nice party except for the guest of honour.

7 Joan Murray (b. 1943), curator and art historian, author of *Tom Thomson and the Group of Seven* and other works.

WEDNESDAY, 14 JULY / TORONTO

An Arts Foundation do at the home of Evelyn Huang, surely one of the most unusual and striking houses in Toronto. Basically deco (with a two-storey cataract in the living room) but with a generous degree of Chinese influence. Similarly, the art within. The mix much more organic-feeling than I would have imagined. Michael Huang's company developed Terminal Three at Pearson airport; so inevitably the house is called Terminal Four behind his back. Av Isaacs there (liked my Curnoe piece), Arthur Gelber (dressed like a bum or an ice cream man, but with his OC in the lapel).[8] Pachter is pleasant to me for the first time in his life when I meet him on the way out. See Vera too as I am leaving but don't get a chance to speak. Mrs Huang very Hongkong but with less perfect English than one might have expected. Interesting woman. When I tell her I collect books on China, she gives me one she has edited, with an elaborate flourish of the inscribing pen.

SATURDAY, 17 JULY / TORONTO

"He led a double life. Did that make him a liar? He did not feel a liar. He was a man of two truths." Iris Murdoch, *The Sacred and Profane Love Machine*

SUNDAY, 18 JULY / PITTSBURGH

Waking from a dream, I remember that she had a tattoo in Arabic – the first (and only) I'd ever seen – which, in answer to my question, she said could be translated as "The power of love is the strongest power." A touching sentiment for one's ass. She was from Red Deer but attracted to everything about the Middle East, in fact was part of some kind of ring.

THURSDAY, 22 JULY / ON THE ROAD WHO KNOWS WHERE EXACTLY

I speak to J on the phone. She has bought the late Tom Marshall's best books – Contact Press etc.: $2,000 worth – and is feeling much more chipper. I have a dream about Kingston stuff whose theme is mutual vulnerability leading to mutual respect.

8   Arthur Gelber (1915–1998), philanthropist.

FRIDAY, 23 JULY / STILL ON THE ROAD
Couple of hours to kill before the Greyhound at Pittsburgh, so I do library research, kick around, but sense that it's time to leave before anything bad happens: I have learned to trust my instinct on this. The bus station stinks of urine and vomit, so I bury myself in the book I've brought along – Sir Isaiah Berlin. Two cars burst into flames in the parking garage outside where I've stashed my bag in a locker, and the flames are so high in the sky and the smoke so thick that I fear the cops may close Greyhound, leaving me stuck. So I get out of there early and go to the airport, where I get an hour's sleep before the flight back to Toronto. J really pleased to see me. Mountains of chaos in the office.

TUESDAY, 27 JULY / TORONTO
All day in an interdisciplinary jury at the Ontario Arts Council. Touchy as always. When I suggest that we all seem to be sticking up for our respective fields and punishing the others, a South African woman of colour yells at me, "I deeply resent your use of the Christian metaphor of punishment." I explain that I am actually thinking more in terms of the board of education. Another juror, who sits on the board of *Fuse* and other journals, says of one applicant (I write this down for posterity): "I see his commitment to the past and this paradigm, but I'm not certain what his influences are or whether he's engaged critically with the paradigm or still cruising within it. He comes from a very Eurocentric position which he doesn't problematise. Of course, I came out of that tradition myself in the late 1970s. In fact, I fetishise it."

SUNDAY, 1 AUGUST / TORONTO
Having pushed ahead and finally finished my memoir *Travels by Night*, I am anxious – anxious is the word – for some reaction about whether it might actually be published, given the repressive climate today. So I have given a copy to Bob F, who returns it today with many helpful suggestions and a general statement that I move ahead with it. So I will show it to Jan Walter, who first suggested that I write it, and see whether she wishes to publish it. I fear the working-class stuff may be too much for her.

SUNDAY, 8 AUGUST / TORONTO
"Civilization belongs to cities,/Culture to the land." Elizabeth Brewster, *Wheel of Change* (1993)

SUNDAY, 15 AUGUST / TORONTO
The placement of *Travels by Night* is not going well. Jan Walter turns it down in no uncertain terms. This most diplomatic and tactful of people then goes on to add that she wouldn't publish it even if it came fully subsidised, then denies that she ever encouraged me in any way to write such a thing. Denise Bukowski, the agent, is positive about it – until she reads it. Then, offended by the manuscript's anti-Americanism, she fires me as a client, comes by at night and leaves the book on my porch like a foundling and sends me a middle-of-the-night fax telling me that it would ruin her standing in the profession if she were to circulate such a piece of crap to mainstream publishing houses.

WEDNESDAY, 25 AUGUST / TORONTO
So I get a different agent, Larry Hoffman, whom I knew in the late '60s and who hinted last year about wanting to represent me. He gives the manuscript an intelligent reading and makes simultaneous submissions to HarperCollins, Random House, Little Brown, Penguin, McClelland & Stewart, Douglas & McIntyre, Lester Publishing and others. The American-owned houses, predictably, have begun to turn it down angrily. The others, one feels, object to the presence of (just a little) sex and no doubt to other things as well. What an intolerant and truth-hating time we're living in now. I grow depressed already, and know that worse news is to come.

THURSDAY, 26 AUGUST / SAN FRANCISCO
A long tiring trip via Vancouver. But the city is alive. Still close enough to my modernist dream to be liveable.

FRIDAY, 27 AUGUST / SAN FRANCISCO
Interview people at City Lights. The store has declined along with the neighbourhood. More Asian than Italian now, and rougher. No old men playing boules as in Ferlinghetti's poems. Nearly get into a scrape in a dank restaurant where Vietnamese, pretending for some reason to be Thais, speak no English.

SATURDAY, 28 AUGUST / SAN FRANCISCO
Up early to take the ferry to Vallejo (1.5 hours) to interview David Koven, 76, a former electrician and a self-taught painter and writer who's

an old friend and colleague of the Woodcocks. The town of 100,000 or so was dependent on the US Navy repair facilities, now closed permanently; and so it is a place with Hispanic homeless sleeping under the messageless marquee of the old abandoned cinema in the high street. The temperature is 99 degrees F. Koven gives a good interview and shows me a cache of correspondence with George going back to 1949 when the Woodcocks were building at Sooke. This is priceless, but I know he won't lend it to me. He does, however, allow me to photocopy it. Armed with all the change I can carry, I go to the only nearby copying machine – in the neighbourhood gunshop. While I stand feeding dimes into this first-generation thermal copier, hoping to finish the job before the toner gives out, I can't help but overhear the talk of commerce. Three African-American fellows, either teenagers or in their early twenties, pull up out front, and one enters the shop while the other two remain outside with the motor running. The customer takes out an expensive linen serviette and unfolds it neatly, revealing a handgun, which he wishes to sell. The manager asks nothing about his age or name or the status of the piece. The only consideration is price. They settle on $65, the fellow takes his serviette with him as he jumps into the car out front and the trio speeds away. I finish the job, and barely catch the last ferry back to the city.

SUNDAY, 29 AUGUST / PORTLAND
Mallory Hotel, a big old once-gracious place, now pretty bare bones, too far from downtown and everything else. Needing bottled water, I walk a mile or so to a huge supermarket (owned, I suspect, by Loblaws – full of Loblaws products) and containing a laundry, a clothing department, an electronics department and so on. I am shocked to discover that a large number of the customers and some of the staff are highly inbred. It is in fact a store half full of mutants. I can only marvel at what I've stumbled into in darkest America. Portland, which I later explore more thoroughly, seems an uptight blue-collar town occupying approximately the same position in the Pacific Northwest as Houston does in Texas. Can't wait to get to Seattle.

MONDAY, 30 AUGUST / SEATTLE
This is more like it. A larger Vancouver (the old West End, I mean) minus the spectacular setting. I quickly accomplish my mission, but this trip is

not going smoothly. Trouble along the way and always a tangle of missed connections and the like.

TUESDAY, 31 AUGUST / VANCOUVER

I check in for a week to the Chinese-run apartment hotel near English Bay. Roaches, yes, but you certainly can't beat the view. Meet George W for lunch, same as last year, at a spot called Le Petit Genève, which I imagine he likes because of his tenacious loyalty to a decentralized Switzerland (he's blind to its flaws – both the country's and the restaurant's, I mean). For the next several days, I will be interviewing more of his old associates.

FRIDAY, 3 SEPTEMBER / VANCOUVER

Dinner at Cin-Cin with Sharon [Thesen], who looks great. Bright coppery red hair now, razor cut, and a little black dress with expensive lace-up half-boots. She is over her torrid affair with the thrice-married New York hairdresser who's building a stone cabin somewhere in the Interior (she shows me photos) and is going out in a desultory fashion with a property developer she doesn't seem to care for much. Problem is that instead of taking unpaid leave she actually quit her tenure-track job and now must reapply for it along with others – no way to avoid making enemies there. Meantime she is teaching a couple of her old courses on a sessional basis but pro-rated at her old salary. I spend much of the dinner telling her about my difficulties and she advises me to get a divorce at once. I tell her how it seems as though this memoir into which I've put my whole heart won't be published, and she advises me to stop writing for a couple of years. The trouble of course is that she has money and doesn't, cannot, realise that I do not.

SATURDAY, 4 SEPTEMBER / VICTORIA

Early morning seaplane to Victoria harbour where I'm met by Liz Woods, who reads the relevant chapter of the memoir and catches me in a few small errors of chronology. I'm relieved that she has no objection to having her younger self depicted as I have done from memory. She then goes on to kindly offer me writing tips. "You see, as a novelist, I'd know this and you wouldn't, but what I'd do here is …" Lunch with Charles Lillard and Jim Munro the bookseller. I stay the night at Charles and Rhonda's.[9] I like them ever-more. I read them part of the memoir (perhaps too much) and tell them of my troubles with the publishing establishment. Red, whose autodidactic smarts I respect more and more, posits some theories.

SUNDAY, 5 SEPTEMBER / VICTORIA–VANCOUVER
Fogged in for hours, am finally forced to take the helicopter to Vancouver. Coming over English Bay we pass so low over the ships always anchored there that I fancy we will almost touch their cranes. Later, I do something I've been meaning to do for a long time and briskly walk the five miles or so around the Stanley Park seawall. Find myself contemplating the underside of the Lions Gate Bridge.

MONDAY, 6 SEPTEMBER / VANCOUVER
Labour Day. Alan Twigg and I breakfast at the Sylvia.[10] He fills me in on some of the plans for the three-day Woodcockfest next May, with a conference, an 82nd birthday celebration, a rare-book display, an art exhibition. He has great energy, a mover who makes things happen; and these are all too rare at any time.

TUESDAY, 7 SEPTEMBER / VANCOUVER
Late morning meeting with Ann Cowan [university administrator] at SFU downtown, a plenary session for the Woodcockfest; I suggest some others for the committee, such as Paula Brook. In the later afternoon, a drink with Scotty McIntyre, one of two publishers still considering the manuscript – and I know he wants to do the Woodcock biography. I try to allay his fears. He does little to allay mine, but promises to make an offer by the deadline, 17 September.

---

9   Rhonda Batchelor (b. 1953), poet, author of *Weather Report* and other works; married to Charles Lillard.
10 Alan Twigg (b. 1952), editor of *BC BookWorld*, author of *Vancouver and Its Writers* and other works.

SUNDAY, 19 SEPTEMBER / TORONTO

Lori Wright helps me hang my little show at the Annex Art Centre. A small crowd, including two purchasers (Sandra Shaul and Carolyn Wood) help Joy, the proprietor, almost recoup the cost of the food.[11] Rough times for art patronage these days.

THURSDAY, 23 SEPTEMBER / OTTAWA

Following my reading at the National Library, I'm back in my room at the Lord Elgin having a nightcap with Lorna Knight from the library and John Metcalf. John has spent the day reading my manuscript and wants eagerly to publish it with Press Porcépic in the spring. During the nightcap talk, however, J calls with a message from Larry Hoffman, the agent, to say that Malcolm Lester has made an offer. At last.

MONDAY, 27 SEPTEMBER / KINGSTON

You've never been clinically depressed until you've been clinically depressed in Kingston, Ontario. All the more so after getting up at 6:00 a.m. to catch the train and then arriving to discover that one's first apprentice writer of the day is a non-blinking madwoman who writes very long religious poems of almost unbearable ineptness. "I only put in that third stanza there because my sister-in-law told me I should," she says. I nod sympathetically.

FRIDAY, 1 OCTOBER / TORONTO

Big party at Peggy A's Admiral Road place to launch *The Robber Bride*. I feel quite comfortable but we don't stay long.

SATURDAY, 2 OCTOBER / TORONTO

This morning after I leave the Apollo on Bathurst Street, where J and I usually have breakfast together, she stays behind to have coffee with [a neighbour] when a drunken taxi drives through the plate glass front of the restaurant. No one besides the driver is injured, but this is only because Paul, the owner, is away from the grill for a few seconds when the

---

11   Carolyn Wood (b. 1951) of the University of Toronto Press; later executive director of the Association of Canadian Publishers.

car strikes. Glass everywhere. J has her back to the window and is pulled across the table by [her companion], who sees what is coming.

I spend much of the day rearranging the studio upstairs, where an extractor fan and large skylight have now been installed.

SUNDAY, 10 OCTOBER / TORONTO

It's very late at night. Sharon Thesen telephoned yesterday to say that she would be arriving today between 3:30 and 5:30. The house was made immaculate, dinner planned. She has not shown up or called. Staying up for her after J finally goes to bed, I read *Life Work*, a sad and profound little volume by Donald Hall, who is suffering from cancer in his mid-sixties and uses the excuse of a book about the nature of work to give us his autobiography and his family history and some indication of what he wishes to leave behind.[12] The parts about the writing life as work ring quite true (am reminded of Woodcock and Skelton).

MONDAY, 11 OCTOBER / TORONTO

Thesen never showed up because it's *next* month she's due to arrive. I'm so confused these days. J smokes like a chimney to show her contempt and puts me down in public. Recently I learn by chance that she's transferred all her personal papers to another safety deposit box somewhere: much is in the wind. Anyone in whom I confide the situation, friend or professional, urges me to "change my life." Must get through the end of commuting to Kingston.

Bruce Whiteman arrives to stay through the weekend. J tells him a friend's story of losing someone's cat, which she was supposed to be babysitting, only to retrieve it after weeks of searching and advertising, then sending it by air to San Francisco at its owner's insistence – only to have it turn out to be the wrong cat. Says Bruce, "That sounds like a Beckett version of *Incredible Journey*."

THURSDAY, 14 OCTOBER / TORONTO

Go to Coach House today to borrow from Stan Bevington his 1968 photo of 671 Spadina, which I want to use in *Travels by Night*, and we

12 Donald Hall (b. 1928), US poet, appointed poet laureate 2006.

fall to reminiscing about the old days. He tells me that the owner of the bike shop up the lane is the son of a printer we used to know who ran a printing business in the cellar of a little rented house on the west side of Dovercourt, below College. He was the Movement printer. He always wore plaid flannel Jack Kerouac shirts. Whenever there was a note attached to a bomb scare in the city, the cops would descend on him and take samples of all his paper stocks. I first met Tim Inkster there one day.[13] Stan also mentions the fellow who printed Souster's *New Wave Canada*, a job Stan says he had to finish up himself. I'm not surprised. As I recall him, the individual was a surly fellow and too independent to be competent. I remember that he and Bob Serling, a poet from Detroit, had a place on the top floor of a building on the west side of Yonge at maybe Gloucester or Dundonald: in the summer of '69, they were up on the roof with their marijuana plants and their hammocks. Stan and I talk briefly about the special little printing jobs Coach House used to do for the Movement back in Vietnam War days. "We'd say, 'What state do you want it?'" he recalls.

FRIDAY, 15 OCTOBER / TORONTO
Lunch with Malcolm Lester to discuss the book he has now accepted, what it will look like and how much it will retail for, and so forth. Depressed or not, I bring two copies of an agenda to the restaurant. A productive meeting. Earle arrives to stay a few days, ostensibly to give me the benefit of his interpretation of my ms and also to listen to my woes when he drives me to Kingston on Monday morning.

SUNDAY, 17 OCTOBER / TORONTO
Earle disappoints me by being interested only in the page of the ms that refers to him. Goddamit, it's nice he's flattered but I need his help and he's no help this time. Oh well, maybe he'll be more critical and clear-headed at the page-proof stage. Tonight he, Bruce, J and I go to the big Harbourfront reception, opening the authors' festival. Disappointed not to see Peter Levi or Michael Ignatieff there, but many other familiar

13   Tim Inkster (b. 1949), printer, publisher of Porcupine's Quill books.

faces all the same: Robert Stone for example.[14] Earle makes an awkward conversational approach to Peggy A completely unaware that he's done so. (How often have I seen academic smarts devalued in world outside academia, and vice versa too of course.)

FRIDAY, 22 OCTOBER / TORONTO
Dave Mason [the rare book dealer] now believes that the thieves who cracked his safe and took the rare Hemingway/Callaghan material also took some Fetherling mss as well as some Ginsbergs and a Colin Wilson. Can this be true? If so, I'm flattered unreasonably. While there I view the crime scene. Peter Levi stops in, looking for Tennyson firsts. I go see the Wyndham Lewis show at the AGO, all the hack portraits of Jesuits he was kept busy with at Windsor. Nice to look again at the portrait of Mrs Paul Martin. Saw it once at the head of the staircase in the Martins' home in Windsor.[15]

14 Robert Stone (b. 1937), US novelist, author of *Dog Soldiers*, *A Flag for Sunrise*, and other works.
15 Paul Martin (Sr) (1903–1992), long-serving Liberal MP and cabinet minister; father of Paul Martin Jr, prime minister, 2003–06.

1994

A bumper year. After numerous difficulties, *Travels by Night: A Memoir of the Sixties* appeared in April, followed in the autumn by an experimental fiction, *The File on Arthur* Moss, and a 30-year *Selected Poems*. I also had two small art exhibitions. Also, I acquired a shack on a tiny parcel of land in the BC Interior for use as a writers' retreat; later I donated it to the Federation of BC Writers for that purpose.

TUESDAY, 14 JUNE / TORONTO

Just starting to get my strength back when a heat wave comes to zap it all. At the end of the day I go to the Park Plaza roof for a party in honour of Greg Gatenby. Not too frightening as these things go. Ellen Seligman [publisher] makes a big display of praising *Travels by Night*, as does Phyllis Bruce [publisher], though both their companies had rejected it. To bed early, instead of rearranging my schedule to take advantage of the (slightly) cooler night-time air.

WEDNESDAY, 15 JUNE / TORONTO

I struggle some more with the proofs of the novel and fiddle with some Latin translations I'm doing with outside help, as an experiment in col-laboration. But I'm having a hard time getting down to my bread-work. For the second time in my life, I have a wild and vivid erotic dream about Anne C. Perhaps I am thinking about her because the *Arthur Moss* is dedicated to her "in collegial friendship."

MONDAY, 20 JUNE / TORONTO

A lively publishing dinner in the back room of the Left Bank on Queen Street for Mikal Gilmore, the Mormon and *Rolling Stone* staff writer whose brother, Gary, was famously executed in 1977 by a Utah firing squad. He, I, Susan Walker, [broadcaster] Daniel Richler, and others tipsy. Gilmore wears *two* very large crosses. One is obviously a back-up.

TUESDAY, 12 JULY / TORONTO

Nervous the past couple of days because of a reading tonight at the back room of Longhouse. In fact, I read reasonably well, and for an hour and a quarter, and the crowd is quite large enough (19 books sold) despite the way the store manager has screwed up the publicity. Some friends have come to hear me, including Michael Holmes and a few other protégés of J (who stays away, at my request, as she does from all my public readings). Afterwards, I have a soda with Debbie Viets.

FRIDAY, 15 JULY / TORONTO

In the morning I work my trapline, in the afternoon read and rest, and in the evening meet Val Ross at her place for the purpose of attending a 1960s costume dance at the Pally to benefit Casey House, the AIDS hospice. I arrive somewhat in period style, with an identity badge reading: "Hello, my name is Kurt, the Beach Boy they never talk about, the one who wanted to be a threat to society." V says that in fact I look much like the Grateful Dead's lawyer ("Anything you have to say to Jerry Garcia, you can say to me"). So saying, she gives me a long black wig, which makes me look quite a bit like Charles II. We meet up with J there.

WEDNESDAY, 3 AUGUST / TORONTO

Animals always seem to like me. No doubt they sense I've never been to university.

THURSDAY, 4 AUGUST / TORONTO

Christina McCall and Stephen Clarkson have a kind of coming-out party to celebrate their completion, after so many years, of the second volume of their Trudeau book and their attendant return to socialising.[1] I'm coming to like Ken Whyte, the new editor of *Saturday Night*.[2] He keeps his extreme conservatism to himself and hasn't yet allowed it to

---

1   Stephen Clarkson (b. 1937), political journalist.
2   Kenneth Whyte (b. 1960), journalist; later, founding editor of the *National Post* and publisher of *Maclean's*.

interfere with the job he's been awarded because of it. He can't believe that he is standing in the middle of Old Rosedale. I know how he feels. He and I have a perfectly fractured conversation with Jane Jacobs, who looks like an ancient male in shapeless corduroy (ample) with all the labels hanging out. She keeps congratulating me on my new editorial appointment and Ken on the reception of *Travels by Night*, despite the continued efforts of her interlocutors and bystanders to straighten her out. Judith Skelton Grant here as well, mellifluously condescending.[3] So Val Ross and Eleanor Wachtel are two breaths of fresh air. Eleanor tells me of her difficulties working with one of her CBC colleagues.

SUNDAY, 11 SEPTEMBER / WHITBY

With John Fraser, who seems much calmer since leaving *Saturday Night*, to the annual corn roast at Anne C's family farm (I bring a copy of *Arthur Moss* with the dedication to her). J pointedly stays home. Not many people I know. [The journalist] Ian Pearson's golden lab, Lucy, keeps diving into the mucky pond and emerging to shake herself dry on Rosedale ladies, and later she gets her snout in the chili con carne. I retreat to the wooded hill at the west end of the cornfield and think. Returning later to the party below, I overhear Elizabeth MacCallum reminiscing with a fellow private school old girl about an absent third member of the tribe whose nickname was "Chubbs."

MONDAY, 12 SEPTEMBER / TORONTO

Just like old times. Meeting Neil Reynolds in a hotel room to receive an envelope of confidential documents (I'm wearing an old mac, of course). What a pleasure to see him again – genius, humanist, libertarian, freedom-fighter.

FRIDAY, 16 SEPTEMBER / TORONTO

Spend all day in an OAC jury with Anne Michaels (delightful as always), Frank Davey (polite this time) and Susan Swan (who suddenly looks very different, but then I haven't seen her in a while, to be sure).[4]

3 Judith Skelton Grant (b. 1947), society figure and biographer of Robertson Davies.
4 Frank Davey (b. 1940), poet and professor.

Advance copy of the Saturday *Star* review, a totally negative view of *Moss* by Marchand seemingly resulting from some red-white-and-blue issue.[5] Still, I know him and like him and know and like the book too and am glad to have published it. No one agrees with me so far, not even a little, as this type of metafiction is outside the boundary for most readers.

MONDAY, 19 SEPTEMBER / TORONTO
The annual McClelland & Stewart autumn party at Walker Court, AGO, a less populous and somewhat dowdy event compared to previous years, it seems to me. J and I stay an hour or so, hear Rob Davies speak. I meet either Wayne or Shuster – in any event, the one who is dead, I believe. Phil Marchand is coming in as we are leaving, and I make my disappointment known to him, saying that I believe he should cultivate more political tolerance at least in his professional persona, statements I of course instantly regret giving voice to – and probably always will.

TUESDAY, 20 SEPTEMBER / TORONTO
"She did not think about dying, which is disagreeable, even to young girls, but about death, which is luxurious, like a hot soak." William Gass
  "Only a dying civilisation neglects its dead." Chris Dewdney

SUNDAY, 25 SEPTEMBER / TORONTO
Yesterday I worked, with help, from early morning till dark and manage to install two of the three new floor joists on cement pylons. We're racing the change of seasons. Today I give a ten-minute reading ($100) from *Travels by Night* at Word on the Street. What a venue. Sudden odours from under the tent at John Street, lorries and lorry-drivers screeching outside, babies crying like murder, a sound system that keeps fading in and out, and a mariachi band across the way. No espresso machine, however, as at Yorkville readings of old. A wonderful street fair all the same, a sort of literary night market (though during the day). "Word on the Street always demands a little patience," J says to me patiently.

5   Philip Marchand (b. 1946), book critic and author.

MONDAY, 26 SEPTEMBER / TORONTO

While J attends, with understandable reluctance, a memorial reading for Daniel Jones,[6] I have Indian food with Arden Ford, now of McGill-Queen's (once of Anansi), who after reading my memoir has decided she was wrong about me all along, calls me courageous, humane, etc. (What had I done to make her think so little of me?) Her instincts, with which I concur, tell her the people who give out book prizes will *never* accept me. True of city book honours yesterday.

WEDNESDAY, 28 SEPTEMBER / TORONTO

Anne Michaels says to me, "This is where we must go in order to know that we are somewhere." I let her in, as I would few others, on my plans for BC. These days I'm putting my papers in order, just in case. I've always thought it was disgraceful and undignified of Tolstoy to die that way in the stationmaster's home, not having thought out a coherent plan for escape. I'm still feeling as though bad news or at least disappointment is round the corner – can't shake it on logical grounds. Last night I accidentally took two sleeping pills instead of one and have been groggy all day. Must be more careful.

THURSDAY, 29 SEPTEMBER / TORONTO

At the end of the day a launch for Katherine Govier's anthology of travel writing by women. The venue: a little restaurant, somewhat weather-beaten, at the Island airport, accessible by the ferry from the foot of Bathurst Street. Mel Hurtig in town, having dinner with [publisher and book distributor] Jack Stoddart. [A novelist] is there: a fellow always worth avoiding, because of his general crackpottery. I spend some time talking to Rosemary Sullivan, who brings Gwen's old friend, the artist Mac Reynolds.[7] Susan Walker coming in as I leave. Weather turning cold.

FRIDAY, 30 SEPTEMBER / TORONTO

Two events in my external life today. Lunch with the Taiwanese cultural liaison (he chose the King Eddy, as one would if struggling to learn about the host culture's older generation). Then in the evening a shared

---

6 Daniel Jones (1959–1994), poet and fiction writer; he committed suicide.
7 John McCombe Reynolds (1916–1999), sculptor and Spanish Civil War veteran.

reading with Roger Burford Mason at a gallery in Cabbagetown.[8] Read okay (blind drunk on vodka) but only one copy of *Year of the Horse* sold: cab fare.

THURSDAY, 6 OCTOBER / TORONTO

Breakfast with Val Ross so that I can give her the dedication copy of *Selected Poems*. I believe she fears she is becoming an old journalistic hag. Work hard on a project all day and then go to the launch for Brian Johnston's novel *Volcano Days* at the Squeeze Club on Queen, a bar with a slight air of New Orleans danger about it somehow and definitely the sort of place I'd hang out if I were a drunk. Susan Swan, who's easily charmed, I suppose, is terribly kind to me about *Travels* and other things.

WEDNESDAY, 12 OCTOBER / TORONTO

A day of risible social activity. Breakfast with the literary world's most improved bigot, who speaks of not being able to live as a writer any more (how common this statement is becoming as the old nationalist infrastructure breaks down) and is therefore studying to be both a masseur and a bartender. Then lunch with Katherine Govier, who I am coming to like a great deal. Then a black tie dinner (good grief) on the 68th floor of the Bank of Montreal (even better grief) in aid of the Writers' Development Trust. Govier again, Paul Quarrington, Daniel Richler, Sylvia Fraser, Christina McCall, and Stephen Clarkson are most of the other writers present.[9] I have a long talk with Christina in which she expresses her dismay and anger that I'm not on the Governor-General's shortlist for *Travels*. Later, I find myself mediating a weird conversation between the father of Garry Trudeau (a medical doctor in the Adirondacks) and General Lewis MacKenzie, who has more honours and decorations than I have ever seen in a democratic country on someone who was not actually lying in state at the time.[10] I have time to make the second half of an after-dinner speech across town by

8 Roger Burford Mason (1953–1998), private-press printer and short story writer.

9 Paul Quarrington (1953–2010), novelist and musician; Sylvia Fraser (b. 1935), journalist and novelist, author of *Pandora*, *The Candy Factory*, and other works.

10 Garry Trudeau (b. 1948), US cartoonist, creator of *Doonesbury*; Lewis MacKenzie (b. 1940), retired major general in the Canadian Forces.

Michael Sheldon, the biographer of Orwell and now of Graham Greene. Val Ross is covering this for the *Globe* and looks absolutely – literally, I swear – radiant.

MONDAY, 17 OCTOBER / TORONTO
I'm on *Morningside* at nine a.m., part of a panel of tired old white guys from Toronto talking about their novels. A friend says afterwards that I'm the country's most improved broadcaster. J says I am barely adequate. On Bathurst I overhear someone in a passing car scream about "junkie-sized mother death."

WEDNESDAY, 19 OCTOBER / TORONTO
Try to get into the *Canadian Art* anniversary party at 7:30 p.m. but the throng of people in expensive Japanese suits has already spilled out into John Street, drinks in hand, attracting the cops. Am unable to find Sarah Milroy and so leave at 11:00 without thanking the hostess. Will write note.

THURSDAY, 3 NOVEMBER / VANCOUVER
Dinner with Sharon Thesen at a little Klingon place she knows in her new neighbourhood (brownish fusilli in wild game sauce – extraordinarily tasty). Sharon, who was given the heave by [her previous companion] or he by her (I covered myself by predicting both outcomes), is dressed like a kinky Catholic schoolgirl. She buys my portrait of her on the basis of a Polaroid that I've brought along. She hasn't done any preparation to introduce me at the reading at Cap College (where, I see, she shares an office with Stan Persky, who is an American naval veteran and therefore is likely prejudiced against me).[11] The reading itself, however, goes fine, notwithstanding the Vancouver newspaper strike, which I fear might severely limit attendance at my various such events this week.

FRIDAY, 4 NOVEMBER / VICTORIA
With Lorna Crozier away at some conference in Oklahoma, Pat Lane meets me at the airport and takes me to the UVic campus and makes the

11 Stan Persky (b. 1941), political and sexual journalist, author of *Buddy's: Meditations on Desire* and numerous other works.

introduction, which he does with polish.[12] He has gained much in style and wisdom (and lost a lot of hair, like me) since our days in the late '60s, which we talk over. Hard to believe he's 56. He tells me that he once confronted George Bowering to ask why George had heaped so much abuse on him for the past 25 years; Bowering replied that it was because he had liked Pat's [poet] brother Red. Also tells me of Acorn threatening to kill Gwen if she came west (which she did anyway). Skelton and Lillard both out of town, so mostly strangers at the reading.

TUESDAY, 8 NOVEMBER / VANCOUVER

A small noontime reading at UBC, with Andreas Schroeder a consummate host, and lunch afterward with Keith Maillard who tells of his plans for his upcoming sabbatical year.[13] Later, the Arsenal crowd – Stephen Osborne, Brian Lam, and others – take me out for a Thai meal and then to a bar.[14] I like being part of Osborne's gang. He and I are hatching a plan to merge *Canadian Notes & Queries* into *Geist*.

MONDAY, 14 NOVEMBER / TORONTO

My good work for the day is encouraging Greg Cook to convert his proposed memoir of Alden Nowlan into a full biography.[15] I show him how to write a proposal. Also today I visit Milt Jewel's studio in Duncan Street and buy, as a combined birthday and Christmas present for J, his huge nude study of Bruce Whiteman, which she told me she admires. It is already hanging in the living room, where visitors' eyes are drawn to Bruce's seemingly enormous cock (I have no personal knowledge of the matter).

SATURDAY, 17 DECEMBER / TORONTO

This morning the *Globe*'s destructive review of *Arthur Moss*, which I have been expecting since the spring. It is written by a person who works in television; she begins by announcing that the book is a train wreck and that I can't write.

12 Lorna Crozier (b. 1948), poet, author of *The Garden Going on without Us* and numerous other collections.
13 Andreas Schroeder (b. 1946), poet and translator.
14 Stephen Osborne (b. 1947), publisher of *Geist* magazine and arts entrepreneur; Brian Lam (b. 1970), publisher of Arsenal Pulp Press.
15 Gregory Cook (b. 1942), poet; Alden Nowlan (1933–1983), poet, novelist, and playwright.

1995

Working both in Toronto and at the retreat in British Columbia, I produced a short travel narrative entitled *The Other China*, based on two earlier trips to Taiwan: one while it was under right-wing dictatorship, the other while under right-wing democracy. Once the book was safely published, I revisited Hongkong and went to Malaysia for the first time.

MONDAY, 30 JANUARY / TORONTO
A call last night from one of the producers at *Morningside* to say that George Woodcock had died and asking whether I could be in studio at 7:30 this morning to do an interview with Peter Gzowski. J and others who listen in say I was fine. Later in the morning I have to give blood. Wait anxiously for the doctor's office to phone telling me the results of this re-take. Earlier results had shown me losing platelets. At the end of the day comes word that I'm okay: the first blood test had been mishandled by the lab. An emotional day all round.

MONDAY, 6 FEBRUARY / TORONTO
Anne C here in the afternoon and buys the poster of herself; she's full of ideas about the fighting in Grozny, political matters in South Africa, her new readings in the Frankfurt School. I offer to go out to the farm in the autumn to help with their fruit harvest.

FRIDAY, 24 FEBRUARY / TORONTO
The first meeting of the antiauthoritarian study group I've formed to meet monthly at Albany Avenue for serious political talk. Present are the anarcho-feminist Susan Brown; Blaine Thomson, anarchist grad student and collector of anarchist material; Mark Conliffe, who speaks of

anarchism's attraction for many Russian literary figures in the period 1830–80; Al Moritz who seems to have elided his anarchism and his Catholicism in a way far more common in much hotter countries than Canada; and Bob Melcombe, who edits *Kick It Over* and lives completely off the grid, appearing in no one's database. A highly successful evening of talk, drink, food, talk, drink, talk talk talk. Three hours at least.

MONDAY, 3 APRIL / VANCOUVER
Coffee with Thesen who has a dreadful case of the 'flu. I deliver the portrait she has bought. She says she admires it, promises to give it a loving home, etc., but says she's surprised that her breasts seem so large. I paint 'em as I see 'em, I say. She breaks up, coughing.

TUESDAY, 2 MAY / WILLIAMS LAKE
From experience here, dreams benefit reality. Early, not later. Renovate your feelings. Buy some supplies, read, explore, wait for the truck. Not the pretty place Quesnel is, because Williams Lake lacks the natural setting and also because it long ago abandoned the town plat, so that it seems a suburb stuck out in the wilderness. Lugging more food in bulk up the hill, also an Ames No. 2 spade. Think of J and Sarah.

What you call limbo I call the place of the outlaw dead. I have a night in which I see my hand moving, writing down the description of GSF in a store but older than he is in 1955 perhaps, fairly thin and black-haired, triumphing over his imminent mortality, expected momentarily.

Fred and Maud turn up later, looking like sick pandas. On the trip they saw fox, bear (I hope the only one on this journey), deer, moose, even antelope. We decide to stay over here another night, so that they can recuperate.

FRIDAY, 5 MAY / QUESNEL LAKE
Make it to the cabin, barely. Make camp outside till cabin can be cleaned and repaired. Maud becoming very testy and condescending.

SATURDAY, 6 MAY / QUESNEL LAKE
Visits from neighbours, some sane, others less so, all very loquacious (non-stop in fact) due to lack of interlocutors. I don't mind. Not having to put any words in edgewise ensures my privacy. I try sleeping in cabin to give Fred and Maud the privacy of the tent but am awakened by a pack rat that wishes to share my sleeping bag and must be discouraged.

FRIDAY, 19 MAY / TORONTO

Dinner at Kim-bo with Anne C. What calm, intelligence, and philosophical integrity. We talk about South Africa and antiauthoritarian politics. I sometimes dream about her in the black-and-white 1920s. She could time-travel there.

SATURDAY, 10 JUNE / TORONTO

After two weeks of trying to get Fred and Maud to let me pay them what I owe, I finally receive a call from Maud, who won't tell me the amount over the phone ($4,611.33) but insists on coming round with her documentation (and her same frosty tone – even worse in fact). I cheerfully pay her off and turn the discussion to her sudden and apparently bottomless dislike of me. She calls me a liar, a fool, too stupid to even be on my own, incompetent, etc. *Stupid* of course is the ancient code word for dysfluency. I sit calmly while all this spews out (along with some remark about my hat, of all things, which I didn't comprehend at all – there's always one such nonsequitur to be found in a long string of accusations). I let her go on and then interject the hope of a resumption of friendship in the future, but she ignores this and storms off. J, too, has had her troubles with her in the past few weeks. Obviously she is going through a sticky patch, what with the job she hates and wants to quit but can't afford to, Fred going back to Europe in a few days' time. Sad. As for me specifically, I've always known that she was jealous of my friendship with him.

THURSDAY, 21 SEPTEMBER / TORONTO

To Harbourfront to see Their Imperial Highnesses Prince and Princess Takamado open the big Japanese exhibition. The Princess splits the fashion distance between Jackie Kennedy and one of the dowdier Windsors. Much Japanese media and much security representing both cultures. Ninja types in boxy suits on the balcony.

MONDAY, 25 SEPTEMBER / TORONTO

Bill Bryson, the transatlantic charmer, comes here for lunch.[1] I believe my fatigue problem is abating, but bad headaches too frequent. Yesterday I had to take enough codeine to knock over a mature quarterhorse.

---

1   Bill Bryson (b. 1951), Anglo-American travel writer, humourist, and author.

TUESDAY, 26 SEPTEMBER / TORONTO
A small private dinner for Bryson atop the Senator in Victoria Street. J and I are the only writer types there, aside from Phil Marchand, who doesn't seem aware that everyone else is boycotting the event because the naïve young publicist invited the Ogre. Even though the O sent her regrets (otherwise not even J and I would be here), the mere action of asking her offends Eleanor Wachtel, Val Ross, and everyone else she's ever attacked so callously, which is pretty much the entire literary community except for the Richler family. A fine meal all the same in surroundings intended to be decadent. Coming through the walls from the jazz club is the sound of Downtown Ray Brown. Perhaps one of his last Canadian concerts, given his age.

WEDNESDAY, 27 SEPTEMBER / TORONTO
A chilly night walking through Koreatown on Bloor to attend the *Blood & Aphorisms* launch at the Clinton (where one day 25 years ago I jammed with Zal Yanovsky). The party loud and yeasty. The guard is changing at the magazine, it seems. New blood for sure but what about some new aphorisms?

SUNDAY, 5 NOVEMBER / TORONTO
Earle and I get a chance to talk alone when we take Dexter for a walk after dinner. Speaking of his father (who died at 64), Earle says precisely the right thing necessary to lift my spirits: "I expect to live a decade longer than he did, because I like life more than he did by at least that margin."

FRIDAY, 10 NOVEMBER / TORONTO
Annual book tour lunch with Peter Newman who confesses the following: that he married the first time when he was 21 and divorced at 25. "This was in the 1950s when people married for sex. Well, the sex wasn't very good and neither was the marriage. And she had got me to foolishly sign an alimony agreement giving her a large percentage of my income for the rest of our lives, indexed to inflation. I've consulted the best lawyers over the years, who say they can get the agreement overturned – until they actually read the foolish document I signed. Meanwhile, she's married again but lives with a guy in luxury on all the alimony – 40 years' worth. Everyone thinks Newman must be rich because of the $500,000

advances and millions of books sold. If only they knew. The problem is that as I get older [he's 65] and sicker, I'll have less energy to write books, my audience will age and my income will drop off. Because of the alimony I haven't managed to save." I ask whether he shouldn't begin to store some funds offshore. "It would be the ultimate irony if she could drive me out of the country, my country, which is also the subject I write about. I've known a lot of expats like that, and I've never known one who was happy."

WEDNESDAY, 15 NOVEMBER / TORONTO

J lets drop a bomb in telling me that Bruce, who's been staying here, is likely to be offered the job at the Clark Library at UCLA. "I wonder how he will take it?" he asks her, referring to me. Well of course he doesn't need my blessing and I wish his career well. But I know that he and Deborah have no sense of social malevolence and are totally unprepared to resist what must be resisted in US life, especially in California of all places. If I were a parent I could never condemn my children to grow up there.

THURSDAY, 23 NOVEMBER / TORONTO

Lunch at Massey College with the master, John Fraser. Douglas LePan joins us at table, responding candidly to my enquiries about the "communications branch" spooks run by External Affairs independently of the rest of the intelligence community and responsible through the under-secretary to the minister.[2] But LePan, who used to *be* the under-secretary, says, "I know they never really told me the truth about what was going on, but what could I do?"

John tells me that Robertson Davies has been in hospital for three weeks with pneumonia.

In the evening, J and I to a party for Rosemary Sullivan at the Bamboo to celebrate her Governor General's Award. Ellen Seligman friendly. Henderson, no longer at Oxford UP, is now with HarperCollins. Long talk.

---

2   Douglas LePan (1914–1998), poet, novelist, and diplomat.

SUNDAY, 3 DECEMBER / TORONTO

A call from Craig Turner, the *Los Angeles Times* bureau chief, to tell me that Robertson Davies has died of a stroke at 82. I respond with what I hope is sensible and sensitive praise.

TUESDAY, 5 DECEMBER / VANCOUVER

I'm such a hopeless romantic, personal growth so slow: here I am in Sarah's and my old room at the Sylvia: I fancy I can almost smell her smell. Certainly I think of the gentle things she said to me in the night, for such moments are so few in life. I do my banking and shopping, which I always prefer to do here. "The school of night": *Love's Labour's Lost*.

SUNDAY, 17 DECEMBER / KUALA LUMPUR

The hotel rooms have metal triangles with KIBLAT on them, indicating the direction of Mecca. My window overlooks the spot where the two small rivers meet (Kuala Lumpur a "convergence" of "money"), the place where gold hunters found tin instead (largest producing country until supplanted by Brazil). A century later, independence from Britain was declared at the cricket pitch in the central park, where cricket is still played, under the shadow of what is purported to be the world's tallest flagpole (a queer flag – the crescent of Islam on red-and-white American stripes). Interesting how little the expats have changed but also how, and with what contortions, the language has survived first independence and then the break-up and later political upheavals. Taxi = teksi. Dutch words from DEI Company days are long lasting. Kope = hill. Komplex = shopping mall.

Walk an hour and a half to the Central Market where the bestselling tape and CD are those of Yusuf Islam, the former Cat Stevens, entitled *The Life of the Last Prophet*. Islam being the dominant but not the state religion is practised variously and to various extents. No apparent rhyme or reason in how the majority Muslim women do or do not follow strict dress codes. Certainly alcohol available everywhere. Beautiful Central Mosque. Newest landmarks, still abuilding, are two office towers with a Canadian-engineered permanent sliding skyway connecting them. When completed soon, these will be the tallest buildings in the world – but only for a few months perhaps, until a taller one underway in Shanghai is finished. (I point out that KL will never truly be world-class until it has a shoe museum like Toronto's. People mad with genuine concern.)

The Chinese are what makes KL as liveable as it is, which is somewhat more so than Bangkok. In any case, the same confusion everywhere: a new citywide elevated LRT project like Taipei's, with the train, tracks, and electrical work done by Bombardier.

I like the old colonial section. We settle in at a hotel (c$13 a night) with a teak-panelled taproom and adjoining dining room (steaks!) underused since opening, which was evidently in 1921, to judge by pages from an old newspaper on the wall: "What to do when your servant has malaria," the *Malay Mail* of 5 October 1921.

Many surviving buildings in this area from about 1915, but for how much longer? Even the Central Market, the hub of the city, had to be saved from planned demolition as long ago as 1936. A typical title in the bookstalls: "How to Stand Up to Your Broker." A graffito outside: "Where are the insane heroes?"

1996

While continuing to work on the biography of George Woodcock, I began the long process of writing *Jericho*, a novel set in Ontario and British Columbia, finally published in 2005. Another memoir, *Way Down Deep in the Belly of the Beast*, appeared in December.

SUNDAY, 21 JANUARY / TORONTO
In order to stay competitive in the global environment, I have had to lay off all my friends. Downsizing.

MONDAY, 26 FEBRUARY / TORONTO
Bruce W is indeed leaving his rare books position at McGill for a lucrative one of the same type at UCLA, and J organises a farewell dinner for him with some of her fellow booksellers, John Rush, Steve Temple, Hugh Anson-Cartwright, Asher Joram, and with Richard Landon and Marie Korey. J is furious with me for saying to Bruce, "So, have you decided if your kids are going to be Crips or Bloods?"

FRIDAY, 1 MARCH / TORONTO
Haven't slept in 20 hours when I meet Anne C for dinner at a small Vietnamese dump, "the sort of place," I joke, "where one can come heavily armed and not be made to feel uncomfortable." She's tired as well, and at one point verges on tears.

WEDNESDAY, 6 MARCH / TORONTO
I telephone Larry Hoffman on this his fifty-second birthday to wish him many happy returns. He replies: "Never say *returns* to someone in publishing."

WEDNESDAY, 27 MARCH / VANCOUVER

Get half way round the Seawall – Lions Gate Bridge at 6:00 a.m. – when dawn breaks rather suddenly and drastically. Tugs acting like sheep dogs, nosing a Filipino freighter out beyond the bay. Come back round to Robson and have to bum an extra quarter from a gentleman passerby to get a *Sun* out of a coin box and read the interview with me. Early breakfast with Don Stewart at the Hotel Vancouver. I tell him the story of J and Peter. He tells me that he admires the tenacity shown in *Travels by Night*. Spend day touching base with other friends and appearing on the appalling right-wing phone-in shows that dominate radio culture here. In the evening, reading at SFU Harbour Centre. Sell some books.

SUNDAY, 16 JUNE / TORONTO

J has been away in Orkney for two weeks and I have been full of resolve to advance on the Woodcock project, though I fail for the most part. Downcast (these days confined to the sofa) and worried about my physical health – right eye, general lack of energy, worrying about worrying itself. But I've put on a bit of muscle, as I must do if I'm going to be in shape for the month at the cabin beginning the first of August. *Beast* is now edited and I am awaiting the proofs; the first half of Woodcock is beginning its long protocol of readers; and I'm behind on the U of T project, yet filled with new ideas for *Jericho*. Relations with J much better the past couple of days: she's been calmer.

SATURDAY, 29 JUNE / TORONTO

Last night, dinner with Val Ross and Morton (and their three children) at an Italian restaurant of their fancy. How I always look forward to seeing Val but how sad I always become. Multicoloured melancholy. For example, it's always made me sad the way she's been attracted to right-wing men (Sandy Ross and many others – with obvious exceptions). Now I worry that she could fall into some trap with [an acquaintance], who's so clearly an American asset that he says prayers to Foggy Bottom every night. Anyway, Val and I talked through dinner about [journalist] Alan Walker, and this morning I find his obituary in the *Star*. Apparently he'd been dead for a couple of days when found. My memories of him began to seep up through the soil.

SUNDAY, 7 JULY / TORONTO

Bob F over coffee the other day: "I'm sixty-four. If I watch my intake of fatty acids, I hope to live long enough to see the city tear down that public art outside the new Metro Police headquarters." I say, "I hope to see them tear down police headquarters."

TUESDAY, 16 JULY / TORONTO

News about the closure of Coach House Press began to circulate on Friday. I tipped off Val Ross a couple of days ago but the *Globe* didn't respond until today, when the story goes big. Privately I wonder that the press survived this long under its management, but I'm a hypocrite in public and I take the customary tone when a crew comes here this afternoon to film me for the CBC news tonight.

FRIDAY, 6 SEPTEMBER / WINNIPEG

Back in the city of other people's ghosts for a poetry reading tomorrow. Same hotel as last time. Hard to conceive of the bustle that once obtained here. Old blind skyscrapers mute witness. Saw a 21-year-old red-headed girl, freckles, green eyes, and a ring in her nose. Winnipeg alleyway graffito: "God sucks." Classified ad in *Free Press*: "2 burial plots. Must sacrifice. Moving."

THURSDAY, 26 SEPTEMBER / TORONTO

J, who has been very sweet-tempered and loving these days, really knocks herself out in throwing a launch and signing for *Belly of the Beast* at Annex Books tonight. Good food and wine, a good crowd, a sale of maybe forty copies. Only unpleasant notes were Jim Bacque arriving (he begged) with some supposed journalist from the *Evening Standard* in London who deliberately insulted Bob F (whose party it is, too, because he is at the centre of the book). Also, [a colleague] turns up unannounced (she's writing a review for one of the weeklies) and this puts the zap on her ex. Unfortunately Lynn Crosbie isn't able to attend.[1] Someone from *Maclean's* turns up with two fellows who begin making out heavily in the Self-Help section. Numerous individuals become tipsy. These lines

---

1   Lynn Crosbie (b. 1963), controversial poet, novelist, and pop culture critic.

must make the event seem stressful, but it was rather the opposite. [A colleague's] douche lover Stephen stays late and helps J, Becky, and me clear up. Leftovers for days to come.

TUESDAY, 8 OCTOBER / TORONTO
A highly unusual evening performing with Howard Engel onstage at Harbourfront. Howard is nervous and awkward as he reads from his new book, getting his typescript pages out of order and flubbing. For once I am just the opposite. Interviewed by Gatenby for a half hour, I seem to be calm, nay poised. Afterwards I am approached by the Canada correspondent of the *Washington Post* who says he wants to do a piece on me; has approval from his editors. We set a date for two weeks hence to at least discuss the possibility. As I'm not published in the US, what's the point?

MONDAY, 14 OCTOBER / TORONTO
Pieces about *Beast* in both the Saturday and Sunday editions of the *Star*, neither mean-spirited. I await my fate in the all-important *Globe* one this coming Saturday (J will be away at the Ottawa book fair).

SUNDAY, 19 OCTOBER / TORONTO
My secret intervention seems to have worked, or at least done some good, because Neil Reynolds is taking over as editor of the *Citizen* in Ottawa next month and tells me I can move my book column there.

Devastating review of *Beast* in the *Globe* today as I feared, the kind that makes booksellers return their stock peremptorily.

THURSDAY, 31 OCTOBER / TORONTO
Lunch yesterday with the *Washington Post* fellow (I relented). But the point is moot. He ran my name past the consulate-general and took a lot of static and so edgily backs away. How naïve is it possible to be? He's 36, from Maryland, on his first foreign assignment, well scrubbed, orders steak and chips.

TUESDAY, 19 NOVEMBER / TORONTO
Neil and I catch each other's eye across the lobby of the hotel. We agree (I silently, he always with characteristic diplomacy) that we're looking

older. A long lunch full of possible projects relating to how to tap into his vast new budget at the *Citizen*, which Conrad Black is said to intend making the Southam mother paper. The conclusion: I will begin immediately to produce an underground weekly editorial at $150, soon will have my book column running at $200 a week, and then an add-on "biographical essay" column and then, finally, a special project (I mention five or six; the one he goes for is the going round the world on a tramp freighter). At the end of the day, a drink with Charles Gordon, the paper's book page editor, to be interviewed. Once we sit down, the very first words out of his mouth are: "Why does a little shit like you think he can write a book?" I carry on as though he were being civil.

Read George Grant's letters. What a fool he was capable of being sometimes, as I have long suspected. How he toadied to Diefenbaker (who we now know was *not* anti-American). A poorly edited book.

SUNDAY, 24 NOVEMBER / TORONTO
J in bed exhausted all yesterday and last night and so can't attend John Lownsbrough's dinner party, which therefore consists only of the host, myself, Anne C, and her husband Eric. John suddenly announces that he's gay. This is something all of us have known for as long as we've known him, but making the statement aloud seems to relax him in one way – while, in another sense, driving him in the direction of elaborate feyness: no doubt the temporary result of his utterance, of deep emotion suddenly released. Anne elegant as always and also the slightest bit tipsy. She tells of hauling bags of spuds, apples, etc. down to *Toronto Life* to sell to her colleagues. The sight of Anne in one of her stylish Bloor Street grey suits hawking fruits and veg in the antechamber is one for my personal image book.

Al Moritz recently at our study group, the Firm: "I look at Margaret Atwood and Michael Ondaatje and now Anne Michaels writing novels and making fortunes, and I know that I want only to be a poet, not a 'writer.'"

THURSDAY, 26 DECEMBER / TORONTO
Feeling much better for Peggy A's Boxing Day party, thank God. A big social event, with the host very much in charge of every detail. I am amused to see that Peggy orders the hats and coats segregated according

to their owners' gender, men's in the cellar, women's upstairs. Amused further that no one remarks on this. Neither Ron Graham nor John Saul is condescending to me, and David Young is actually oozing screenwriter's charm.[2] Talk also with Govier and John Honderich: uppercase *S* Society. Terry Kelly and his spouse the NDP-appointed judge looking very much as though they have wandered in from Ward Seven, as indeed must I; I talk with them and try to put them at ease. Ruth [Atwood], dressed up and coiffed, is the image of her sister at the same age – uncanny, almost eerie. J and I walk back home through the falling snow. How few blocks separate Peggy's place from our own, and yet …

2　Ron Graham (b. 1948), political writer, author of *One-Eyed Kings* and other works; David Young (b. 1946), dramatist and fiction writer.

1997

A year marked by difficulties and the deaths of several old friends. In the autumn I left for London to embark on a tramp freighter voyage across the South Pacific to the Middle East and Europe. The trip, lasting four months, later formed the basis of a travel narrative, *Running Away to Sea*.

MONDAY, 27 JANUARY / TORONTO

The subject at the monthly poker night is anarchism and Christianity. I am holding a straight flush.

Also, [an acquaintance] after more than a week of exhausting himself and also the city's patience, principally by his most pronounced inability to make or stick to a decision, has finally taken a place to live, a flat near St Clair, and will be camping there this evening, awaiting the arrival of books and other possessions from Montreal. I knew a good deal about him before his arrival yet didn't know about the private school background, for it is well hidden. Pondering this, I have reviewed in my mind all my old 12-code cases relating to trouble on that score.

I seem to be fighting a desire to write mystical prayers. J is away in Montreal and here all is quiet and lonely. Fragments of history constantly flying up on the screen of memory and reordering themselves: all part of the process of sorting out the past.

FRIDAY, 31 JANUARY / TORONTO

On my way to breakfast early this morning I see Paul the Cook, Mike the Letter-Carrier, and Wally the Convenience Store Guy huddled outside Barry's pharmacy. Barry is in a depressive state (severe) and hasn't been seen in two days. The cops come, break the glass in the door (rather clumsily, I find) and discover Barry in the cellar, a suicide. I can't gainsay him. Barry knew much sorrow. He served as a medic in the Israeli army, was divorced and estranged. J is taking the news harder than she lets on in front of me, having seen too many (Peter Day, Daniel Jones) go that route.

WEDNESDAY, 19 FEBRUARY / TORONTO
A call this afternoon from the president of St Mary's University in Halifax inviting me to accept an honorary degree (D.Litt.) at the May commencement. Peggy A and other loyalists wrote, I understand. Naturally I say yes, particularly as another recipient, the president of Ireland, will be doing the public speaking. I take this in the generous spirit in which it is offered, as a reward for longevity but not necessarily for good conduct. J says she will come to Halifax with me.

FRIDAY, 21 FEBRUARY / TORONTO
Today I finish the first draft of the Woodcock biography at 80,000 words. I now have a month in which to tinker with it. Long phone calls today about family matters and book-writing practices.

THURSDAY, 27 FEBRUARY / TORONTO
At the regular meeting of the Firm on Monday last, Fred announces that he and Maud have quit their jobs and are giving up their apartment over the barbershop and going north. This is precisely the conclusion to this mess that I foresaw. Frankly, I've felt as though he was her spy at these meetings. In any event, each remaining member must now bring in some new blood in order that the discussions not degenerate into mere conversations. I'll try a fellow I've heard about in Montreal, though I know that the practicalities argue against his coming up.

At the bank today, my teller, mid-twenties, decently dressed and coiffed, middle class, bears a terrible scar from having her throat slashed.

MONDAY, 10 MARCH / TORONTO
A morning set aside for shopping, and as I'm walking along Bloor West about 11:15 I encounter the aftermath of a big jewel robbery at Royal de Versailles. Three men and a woman with shotguns and a grenade scooped up diamonds and other gems while disarming a cop and holding the customers at bay.

WEDNESDAY, 12 MARCH / OTTAWA

No time this trip to go to the Archives or the bookstores or to see Neil or John Metcalf. Work nine to nine the first day of the [Canada Council for the Arts] Block Grant jury, with more and worse to come. A relatively happy day. Caroline Walker late of Fifth House Books (she slowly overcame her uncertainty about me); Marc Glassman, highly knowledgeable, all in black; a biker type whose name I miss; an Irish-Canadian academic from Newfoundland whose every other utterance is denouncing the Catholic Church on which he's turned his back; and Janice Bearg, who runs extension courses in writing at SFU and who's much more wonderful than I had ever imagined from talking to her over the phone in her other jobs. I hope for better progress and less kibitzing tomorrow.

THURSDAY, 13 MARCH / OTTAWA

A strange meeting where the teacher from Newfoundland keeps "voting strategically" (he loves the phrase) and giving double zeros to "big corporations" like M&S and Douglas & McIntyre, both of which have enormous accrued losses, of course, whereas some small literary presses end up with healthy surpluses after their grants come in (though of course this isn't the usual pattern). The man simply can't read a financial statement and won't permit himself to be instructed. Generally speaking, I refrain from making a fool of myself but come back to the hotel in the evening (after bowing out of dinner) and get roaring drunk in my room. The weather is bitterly cold, Siberian cold, and storms are imminent.

SATURDAY, 15 MARCH / OTTAWA

This evening wraps up the four-day jury at the Canada Council. Such a long bout of deliberation, in close quarters, has been enervating, of course. But I have gone to great lengths to leave a pleasant aftertaste. I daresay I face a mountain of work problems when I get back home tomorrow.

FRIDAY, 21 MARCH / TORONTO

The dinner party I thought Charles Taylor would never be well enough to have in fact takes place this evening. So horribly sad to see Charles in such decline, in such pain, and so near the end. He eats nothing, drinks some, looks like a natty clothes-wearing skeleton with a white

Col. Sanders goatee. Dennis Lee and Susan (who calls Dennis "Denny"), Noreen (worn-out from taking care of Charles), J and I. Much laughter and witty back-and-forth. The sheer injustice of the situation when my life is so good, especially since returning from Ottawa.

J is feeling better, and M&S have made an offer for the travel narrative.

SATURDAY, 22 MARCH / TORONTO

Still terribly moved by the sight of Charles, whose brother-in-law John Mappin calls today (coincidence) telling me that C is on a downward spiral. J ill in bed much of the day but she revives when Becky [Singleton] calls from the shop to say that a particular out-of-town dealer is on his way over and has asked if she will accept "a company cheque."

MONDAY, 24 MARCH / TORONTO

A day punctuated by other people's distress while I continue on happily for the most part except in my reactions to the news. I am to lunch with Fraser in his office at Massey. Just as we were to sit down, however, he takes a phone call, turns pale and then red in an instant and rushes out the door: their eldest daughter has been taken to hospital. (I will follow up in the morning to see if there's anything I can do.) Later a drink with Rosemary Sullivan, who wants my help with a book on Peggy A and her circle.

TUESDAY, 25 MARCH / TORONTO

With Al Moritz, at the coach house that is being revitalised by the young couple from Sichuan. Discuss the possibility that he and Theresa might write a Subway book on Emma Goldman's Toronto years. Late this evening as J and I are watching a video, Rhonda Batchelor calls from Victoria to say that Charles [Lillard] has died of cancer at home. Tears all round. I liked his frontier industry and his helpful good humour, and was so pleased that he got shortlisted for the poetry GG before he left. I have been thinking lately of a line from one of his poems, about "the last man down from the creeks" in the autumn. That was Red. My fondest memory of him was when he and I were among the panellists at the Woodcock tribute in Vancouver. Peggy A was moderating. At the end, she asked all the participants to say which of the classical Muses they thought George identified with most closely (my answer was Clio). I looked over at Red and could see him trying to remember what Sneezy and Grumpy were muses of.

SATURDAY, 5 APRIL / TORONTO
News tonight of the death of Allen Ginsberg, at 70, in New York at home, only a short time after being diagnosed with irreparable lung cancer. I hope he didn't suffer too much, but I fear that he must have. His death puts karma to the test, I suppose. I can't help but remember how kind he was in 1968 *et passim*. I got to bed at 7:30, sad, and dream that I have been invited to the Yale Divinity School, only to learn on arriving that there is no space for me there.

SUNDAY, 29 APRIL / TORONTO
Earle has gone after what I hope was a pleasant visit for him, though I was distracted emotionally and physically (a lightly twisted ankle) and sometimes had to be elsewhere – for example, at the Trillium Awards, where I was the only judge to turn up and where J and I had a long sweet talk with Anne Michaels, the winner, who was tipsy in the corner, wearing the dress she always seems to have on.

I am working at shortening my response time between perception of crisis and reversion to thoughtful rather than instinctive response. I now have it down to a few seconds in most cases.

THURSDAY, 1 MAY / TORONTO
An idiotic short list interview for the visiting position at the library. Evidently I am more impressive on paper than in person (surprise). The head of HR (HR is a scam) joins the director of operations (formerly called the librarian) and the head of the reference section. None of them knows a Canadian writer. "According to your c.v. here, you've written *quite a few* books," one of them says accusingly, using *written* to suggest *committed* or *perpetrated*. A perfect waste of time. Then to Harry Rosen for the final fitting for my tuxedo. (I have now joined the ranks of those sad and mysterious down-at-heels hangers-on at diplomatic cocktail parties. Dear friend: Three things about me you should know. I sometimes drink too much, I own my own tuxedo, I am a cyborg from the future.) With J this evening to a big 30th anniversary party for Anansi.

Dennis Lee makes a gracious speech in which he acknowledges me. I leave early, skittish. Stoddart people are like members of some particularly humourless sect of Protestant evangelicals.

FRIDAY, 9 MAY / TORONTO
Anne Michaels for lunch. Aside from a brief conversation at the Trilliums ceremony, this is the first time I've seen her since *Fugitive Pieces* changed her life by freeing her from teaching, giving her money for a home, and putting her in the front row overnight. I hope she gets the Booker.

MONDAY, 12 MAY / HALIFAX
J doesn't come with me after all. Spend the morning talking to Terry Whelan's poetry class, followed by a long disjointed walk back to the waterfront. So a couple of hours to rest before getting dressed for the convocation, which lasts two and a half hours. I *am* touched by the institution's sincerity and also by the hundreds of bright young faces: I do love pups, before the hardships of the canine life have worn them down. My heart goes out to the working-class kids whose relatives hoot and applaud when the family's name is called out. The audience can't see what we on the stage see: the absolute mortification on their children's faces. This is the point beyond which the family will be split along class lines, never to be the same again. I feel a bit foolish in my Beefeater-style cap, which looks like a hand-me-down from Erasmus of Rotterdam.

MONDAY, 30 JUNE / OTTAWA
Neil tells me of going last Sunday to the funeral of his first wife's mother, "the first woman I ever loved as a woman, not physically, of course, but in the heart." Fort Baxter, the *Citizen*'s building, is indeed a fearsome place. Walking the narrow green corridors with Neil, I keep expecting to hear a voice on the PA system say, "Security Unit to Sector 12, Security Unit to Sector 12!"

FRIDAY, 11 JULY / TORONTO
A week of discord with J. I *do* cancel the teaching gig in Wells because otherwise I fear what might be left standing when I return. This afternoon we attend Charles Taylor's funeral. Big Anglican church and quite

full, not because he was rich but because so many people knew and liked him. Afterwards, a kind of outdoor wake with writers, ex-jockeys, and lots and lots of straight people.

THURSDAY, 17 JULY / TORONTO
Lunch with Peggy A at Ave and Dav. Only as I get older do I realise how socially ill-at-ease she is and always has been, despite all her experience and intergalactic success. She looks great. No lines, moist skin, no sense at all of being 57. On this score, she tells me a funny story on herself about losing one of her meds while on tour in Europe and having to convince her publisher's doctor to write her an Rx on blind faith and nagging. She reminds me somewhat of the Queen, and vice versa. But such a heart and such a fine humour. Screwed up family of course (unlike the rest of us). Has the interrogative style of a really skilled Crown prosecutor. I believe she might have been worried about me.

SUNDAY, 27 JULY / TORONTO
Peggy and Graeme browsing in the shop when I stop in today. Peggy wearing khaki shorts and a safari shirt, for the temperature is past 30. Says she was robbed at knife point last week on Bernard Avenue in the middle of the afternoon by two young toughs. With the blade at her throat, she gave them her money (I didn't have the courage to ask the amount) but forced them to say polite thank-yous before letting her go. Called the cops, who took 1½ hours to arrive. Brave muggers indeed who would take on Margaret Atwood.

MONDAY, 4 AUGUST / TORONTO
News today of the death of William Burroughs at 84. Now there was an individual who knew that addictions are not spontaneous, that they must be cultivated and nurtured with tenderness and discrimination.

TUESDAY, 19 AUGUST / TORONTO
The dog climbs up on the bed and I put my ear to his chest and listen to his heartbeat: this has become a little ritual. Then I go to sleep thinking about whether I have any patrons and benefactors in the other world.

TUESDAY, 26 AUGUST / TORONTO

News in the paper this morning of Robin Skelton's death last Friday at 71. He was a good friend to me always and to J, especially since we've been together. A poet and a healer. I hated the way whole legions of other writers always treated him. J feeling somewhat better, but she must give up smoking.

TUESDAY, 2 SEPTEMBER / LONDON

Arrive at 6:30 a.m. in a London in mourning over the death of the Princess of Wales yesterday. Flags everywhere at half staff or half mast. Huge piles of flowers at the palaces and outside Harrods (owned by the father of the man killed with her – her lover). Harrods, however, open for business all the same. Travel onerous, the day hot and sticky. I look to be stuck for a week in this fleabag hotel room while waiting anxiously, eagerly, for news of my ship.

WEDNESDAY, 3 SEPTEMBER / LONDON

Still a bit groggy from the time difference, I struggle out to Canary Wharf to drop off my tribute to Robin Skelton at the *Daily Telegraph* and have lunch there with David Twiston Davies [the obituaries editor]. A handwritten note from Conrad Black to his minion "Charles Moore, Esq.," praising yesterday's coverage of the Princess Di tragedy, hangs in the newsroom. Later, stop but fail to shop at the Freedom Press Bookshop. Whitechapel even more run down than when I visited last. A little rest and then I travel by night through Camden (full of retro clothing shops, as Kensington was for the '60s generation) to Belsize Grove, former Woodcock territory, to talk with Elizabeth A.

THURSDAY, 4 SEPTEMBER / LONDON

So exhausted that I sleep until 11:00 a.m. The day hot and tacky. Other than going through the Chinese galleries at the Museum across the street, I keep to my room and to myself, reading and writing. Postcards to J, J. Bearg, and others.

FRIDAY, 5 SEPTEMBER / LONDON

The shipping line confirms 8:40 a.m. Tuesday for departure. Another day writing and reading: I am hoping this will be a most productive voyage that way. Every secondhand bookshop I enter seems to have a Robin Skelton title hidden away in the stacks. A votive moment at one of my favourite run-down churches, St Jerome's Bloomsbury. [Anthony] Trollope was baptised there, his sharp-tongued mother being a member of the parish. Cards to J, Bob Melcombe, Earle, Bruce Whiteman, Carolyn Wood, and others. I buy a bottle of my favourite Australian chardonnay.

SATURDAY, 6 SEPTEMBER / LONDON
Literally millions of people in London for Diana's funeral. Spectators 60 to 70 deep in the West End. It is as though all the blood in the circulatory system has rushed to one region of the heart, departing the rest of the body. Late afternoon I am way down in the East End where there is hardly a soul on the streets. Except for the palpable sense of danger in this now strict Muslim area, I feel as though I am walking a film set. Beneath the grime on a handful of old buildings are faint traces of the previous waves of inhabitants – e.g., "Soup Kitchen for the Jewish Poor" carved into the stone facing, above a set of doorways. Back to hotel to read, write and think.

SUNDAY, 7 SEPTEMBER / LONDON
This afternoon I telephone J. She is upset. She learned in Ottawa that she has to appraise the papers of Daniel Jones, including his suicide note. Hers was the final name in his datebook.

1998

I returned from the freighter voyage to find the house deserted and a telephone message informing me that I was being sued for divorce. Having taken ill on the last leg of the journey, I also learned that I required emergency surgery. Needing a helper, I invited a young writer friend – he went by his punk name, Dr Morose – to share the house. To pay the bills, I began work on *The Book of Assassins*, a study of political assassination in different ages and cultures.

FRIDAY, 30 JANUARY / TORONTO

Feeling some better today until I see the first review of the Woodcock book. It's by Joan Givner in *Quill & Quire* and it says that even though Woodcock was anti-academic and anti-American, he still deserves far better, as I have done him a great disservice. I had been hoping that I would be so shocked by recent matrimonial events that the knock in print wouldn't hurt me so much in my present condition. Not true.

FRIDAY, 6 FEBRUARY / TORONTO

Inge Woodcock got her copy of the biography yesterday and calls me this evening to say that she is enjoying it so far. I tell the news about J and she is philosophical. "Some women can stand the loneliness of being married to a writer. Others cannot."

SUNDAY, 22 FEBRUARY / TORONTO

Dinner with Katherine Govier on Bloor. We trade divorce stories. I find her very wise, sophisticated, funny, and well-grounded. Our divorces appear to be similarly unpleasant but mine, as I tell her, doesn't have all the noughts in the numbers.

TUESDAY, 21 APRIL / TORONTO

Up at six-thirty, ready at eight to be picked up by the Douglas & McIntyre rep and driven to Burlington for the Different Drummer Books authors' breakfast. We arrive to find no copies of the book for sale and none that can be fetched within the required time. What a screw-up. I count 215 book-buyers (extra folding chairs at the back) waving their Visa cards excitedly. Reluctantly, must leave the opportunity to Bob Fulford and Mark Kingwell whose respective publishers are more on the ball.[1] The day completely shot. Later, I phone the D&M publicist in Vancouver to ask what went wrong. She offers an astrological explanation, something about the position of Mercury affecting small business. Someone else tells me that the bookseller holds *me* responsible. "He thinks you're dissing him."

THURSDAY, 30 APRIL / TORONTO

Before the start of the PEN board meeting today, Ann Ireland takes me aside to say that while the board members like me personally they don't like my ideas: namely, to stop co-operating with the RCMP et al., to slowly expand the worldview beyond Massey College, to forge ties between the writing community here and the ones in Vancouver and other places: in short, to radicalise PEN and temper the public's perception that the organisation is the playground of rich white kids.[2] (As Ann says, "We don't care what anybody else thinks.") Accordingly, they don't want me to stand for chair next year – she, Ron Graham, and the others. So I tell her that I will back away and seek some other means of earning merit. Dinner this evening with Mark and Marilyn Seltzer.[3] Good talk of books. Mark shows me his Malaysian blow-gun and quiver of poisoned arrows.

THURSDAY, 11 JUNE / TORONTO

These days when so much goes on interiorly are precisely the ones when I lack the external strength to make these entries. The memorial service for Janet Hamilton today at Trinity-St Paul's United was packed with mourners. I wept copiously for Janet, dead of a brain tumour at only 47

---

1   Mark Kingwell (b. 1963), public intellectual and social critic.
2   Ann Ireland (b. 1953), novelist, author of *A Certain Mr. Takahashi*.
3   Mark Seltzer (1957–1998), dealer in rare travel literature.

and for Howard (67) and their son Jacob (who's 9 – what will become of him?). To bed with a heavy heart.

WEDNESDAY, 17 JUNE / TORONTO
Bruce Whiteman, in town for a Ray Souster tribute, looks awful, what with the stress of his daughter's difficulties and severe financial problems. Wish I weren't so powerless to help at this time.

SUNDAY, 27 SEPTEMBER / TORONTO
Much thunder and lightning and I'm awake at 4:30 a.m. instead of 6:00. Disturbing dream in which [an old friend] commits suicide and I attend his memorial service, which includes another friend who mimics the deceased's voice perfectly, much to the crowd's discomfort. All of this very disquieting, and the day is off to a rough start. So eerie so early. A large portion of the afternoon taken up with a visit by a Swedish academic in her 40s who's writing her thesis on Ondaatje and his Canadian circle. Her English is good enough to converse but not good enough to be polite: says she doesn't like the way the house is decorated, finds Toronto unbearably ugly, and Dexter a funny-looking dog. (Turns out she knows J, of course.) I heartily agree with her about Toronto.

SATURDAY, 3 OCTOBER / TORONTO
Dream about Janet Hamilton in which she warns me that the River Styx can take on the appearance of the Fraser or the Mekong or the Thames to lure one into the water on a ferry. She goes on to say that one believes that one will wake up from the dream, but one does not – and drowns instead. When she utters – reveals – this, I wake with a start.

WEDNESDAY, 7 OCTOBER / TORONTO
At lunch I remind Robert McCrumb, the literary editor of the *Observer*, how he almost published me at Faber and Faber (his stroke intervened). He limps now and one hand seems partly decorative, but his mind and speech are clear, though he says he has lost about a year's worth of memory on his hard drive, as it were.

SATURDAY, 12 OCTOBER / TORONTO
I see the first coin-boxes for the *National Post* put in place.
　　Words would not be my first choice to describe this place.

TUESDAY, 27 OCTOBER / TORONTO
First issue of the *National Post* looks good but naturally there are bugs in the system. Wrong email address printed, late delivery, voicemail not up: that sort of thing.

What a struggle to set down here in the daylight some of the feelings I encounter lying in the dark. I can certainly see with ever greater clarity the entire horrible extent to which I have failed to impress others as a viable personality down through the years. Even without the dysphonia, and associated problems, I would still, as Brenda L once pointed out, have had a struggle. The wonder really is that I did as well as I did, especially before I learned how to write somewhat acceptably or at least fluently. Of course I had the presumption of youth on my side part of the time. Rationally all I can do is to carry on, writing what I have to write so as to finish as much of the most necessary work as possible in whatever time remains. Necessary to me, that is, and no one else.

MONDAY, 2 NOVEMBER / TORONTO
I find myself kicking through the fallen leaves at Gwendolyn MacEwen Park. Now the city is naming parks after my old friends though most definitely not for that reason, of course. Were the practice to embrace mere acquaintances, the involvement of the federal government would be needed. "Arnold Edinborough National Forest. No shoes, no shirt, no service."[4]

WEDNESDAY, 4 NOVEMBER / OTTAWA AIRPORT
The local M&S contract publicist has three interviews lined up: one in a homemade radio studio in the one-bedroom apartment of the interviewer, a Carleton student; another on a two-bit TV noontime show whose other guest is a senior from Pembroke who makes ugly ceramic gnomes; and the third one over the phone to a radio fellow – a jock – who's never seen much less read the book and who begins by asking me where I went to school.

4 Arnold Edinborough (1922–2006), cultural gadfly and Anglican layman.

THURSDAY, 31 DECEMBER / TORONTO
Dr Morose off for New Year's Eve to a place called the Wrecking Yard, there to hear a band named the Texas Dirt-Fuckers. I manage to get through a good deal of non-strenuous publishing paperwork, and anticipate greeting the new year while asleep. Howard Engel kindly drives Morose to Canadian Tire so that we can buy a generator.

1999

A time for recuperation, ending with publication of a new poetry collection, *Madagascar: Poems & Translations*, a one-year appointment at the University of New Brunswick, and an extended trip to Burma that would become the basis of a travel narrative, *Three Pagodas Pass*.

FRIDAY, 1 JANUARY / TORONTO
Awake at 6:00 a.m. and linger in bed for two hours, finishing the novel I've been reading. I have had very little energy since the surgery, understandably enough. Kaleidoscopic frost patterns on all the windows. At approximately 10:00 a.m. I turn fifty, lucky and happy to be alive. Warm the office with a space heater and begin my bonus years by confronting paperwork.

SATURDAY, 2 JANUARY / TORONTO
Val Ross arrives bearing healthy goodies from Marks & Spencer and stays to talk about Coleridge. She has become interested in Utopian communities, so I give her all my files on the subject to keep. Forecast is for forty below tonight – the same in C as in F – and 30 cm of snow. By 5:00, as I write these words, the pipes in the basement bathroom have frozen.

SUNDAY, 3 JANUARY / TORONTO
Running Away to Sea gets a bad slam in the *Star* today. As far as I remember, the reviewer and I have never met or corresponded, but he's been attacking me this way since, I believe, 1969 or 1970, I don't know quite why, unless it is because he is a US veteran. I see why the *Star* book

editor has twice in succession stood me up for lunch. Still, this doesn't quite rival the time that the *Star* assigned my travel book in search of the newly democratic Taiwan to someone who had been a paid propagandist of the People's Republic. My server down today so no computer work. Snowdrifts against the window make the house dark.

FRIDAY, 15 JANUARY / TORONTO
Some headline such as "Fellatio Brings City to Its Knees" on the front pages this morning. Streets empty. Roofs creak under the accumulations of snow.

MONDAY, 25 JANUARY / TORONTO
Much relieved by an email from Neil saying that my column was reinstated the second week of the month and will be running weekly again. I am saved.

SATURDAY, 30 JANUARY / TORONTO
A visit from Malcolm Lester and then one from [an old friend], who tells me the story of her life up to the time we met (her first day in Toronto) in 1972. Rebelling against her parents' world, she took a job as a cook (she didn't know how to cook) for tree-planting crews and fell for one of the planters. She has a vivid memory of riding in his car, topless and on acid, when he said to her, "Babe, I'm taking you east." She thought he meant Central Canada. In fact, they went to Egypt where they maxed out two credit cards they had somehow got. She ended up broke in London and had to wire her parents for airfare back to Canada. She got as far as Toronto.

THURSDAY, 4 FEBRUARY / TORONTO
Susan Walker comes by and we talk about Robin Skelton. Although she did honours English at UVic, she never met him (I find this amazing) until she interviewed him for *Quill & Quire*. We have a long, somewhat personal talk. She's not smoking and is no longer a blonde.

FRIDAY, 5 FEBRUARY / TORONTO
Appear on the Pamela Wallin show on Newsworld with, among others, Sylvia Fraser, who I am relieved to see is more nervous of me than I of

her, and the ever charismatic Christopher Ondaatje, so thin and lanky that he folds himself up like a concertina when he sits. The subject is adventure travel narrative. Someone on the panel offers the bizarre opinion that travel writers should only write about places they resemble physically. In that case, I reply, Christopher should publish books about Chile and nowhere else. Feel good all day but of course tire easily.

WEDNESDAY, 17 FEBRUARY / TORONTO

Books arrive from Coach House. I finally complete the work I owe to W.H. New for his encyclopaedia. Feeling strong and productive all day. A dream in which Anne Collins is running some sort of event like the PEN benefit, and she and I both know that the host is a bore who will say all the wrong things. I follow immediately behind her down the left aisle of the theatre, part of a long procession heading for the stage, and I am transfixed by the muscles revealed by the low cut of the back of her gown.

MONDAY, 22 FEBRUARY / TORONTO

I live in strange times. Returning today from seeing the executive editor of the *National Post* (there's a possibility of their picking up the *Citizen* column, running it a week later) I happen on some excellent firewood in the Bathurst Street rubbish. So I return home, dressed to the nines, carrying an armful of forage fuel for the woodstove that's to be installed in two weeks' time. Dr Morose, who supplements his welfare payments through the barter system, is over at someone's house doing the person's income tax. I'm so tired I barely make it through teaching tonight. Bitterly and punitively cold.

FRIDAY, 26 FEBRUARY / TORONTO

The Knopf publicist who I had to call to get a review copy of the Matt Cohen novel tells Cohen I am doing the review and he hits the roof, getting her to phone the editor-in-chief of *Time* in New York to smear me. As the editor-in-chief is not in, she leaves a long vituperative message on his answering machine. I was in fact trying to do Matt a favour in accepting the assignment when asked but now withdraw. This prompts many long calls from the upset editor-in-chief, one as late as midnight, in which I try to dissuade him from making a big deal of this (for of course he doesn't know Matt, who always has been cross with me for a review of an early and ill-received book in 1972 – but have always tried to help since then in whatever small ways I could).

FRIDAY, 12 MARCH / TORONTO
Two yokels tear the office roof open to the sky, preparing to install the woodstove, a job that most likely won't be resumed until next week.

TUESDAY, 16 MARCH / TORONTO
Drinks yesterday with Noah Richler, literary editor of the *National Post*, sitting under a caricature of his father at the top of the Park Plaza. The younger Richler looks as dour as the figure in the picture just above his head. An odd sensation.

WEDNESDAY, 17 MARCH / TORONTO
Lunch with Elmore Leonard ("Call me Dutch"), who looks much as I might if I should somehow live to 70 and be in good health (what are the chances?). He tells me tales of Detroit when it was a real city, when streetcars waddled up and down Woodward Avenue and the ferry ride to Windsor cost a nickel.

MONDAY, 22 MARCH / TORONTO
The review of the Woodcock book I've been expecting from the *Freedom* crowd in London is as cruel as I imagined, but to me more than to GW. What a strange mob. Maybe my vulnerable state these days has impaired my perception of such matters. Difficulty teaching tonight. I feel I have returned from a visit to the culture of depression. My primary discipline has been survival. So few realise this.

SUNDAY, 4 APRIL / TORONTO
Sprained body and general sense of ill-being from yesterday's work on the woodpile, which the cold and wet on this Easter Sunday prevent me from repeating. A call from Vera Frenkel, who's feeling and sounding tired and mentions that today is Howard Engel's birthday; he's 68.

I finally find a copy of the first volume (I've only ever read the second) of Cocteau's diaries. He writes in 1951 that hard virtue set against soft virtue "was the misunderstood theme of [his 1926 play] *Lettre à*

Maritain. To restore to God the intelligence transferred to the devil's account, especially in the sixteenth century, when the devil took a leading role." I didn't know he had written about Maritain, once the leading Catholic intellectual of Toronto (and the West). There are no intellectuals in Toronto today. Later Cocteau writes: "The older I get, the more I realise that I am not read. My fame consists of rumours. Gossip."

THURSDAY, 15 APRIL / TORONTO
Up early and chopping, then some writing, then some work in the studio – a little bit of everything today, the kind of day I like. A quick dinner with Morose in Queen Street after a book launch for [a colleague] who coyly writes her phone number on cocktail serviettes and puts them in the books she signs.

WEDNESDAY, 21 APRIL / TORONTO
Being this depressed without being in Kingston or at least Vancouver feels wrong somehow.

I have always found self-destructive behaviour a valid form of self-expression.

SATURDAY, 24 APRIL / TORONTO
Bill Kimber and John Elmslie come by today for a glass of wine and to take some books in trade for two panels Bill has agreed to paint for the ground floor office. Bill was 54 yesterday.

MONDAY, 3 MAY / TORONTO
Come winter, when I see that Dr Morose is taken care of, I'll ship off, either with someone or alone, to Thailand and cross over into Burma through the Three Pagodas Pass. Let the people who hated the Vietnam War without hating the Americans who caused it work in support of NATO's errand in Kosovo. I see the future of political death on the other side of the world as well.

Long call this afternoon from Noreen Taylor who's organising a literary prize in Charles's name and on setting up a palliative care centre at Sunnybrook. "Charles was diagnosed with cancer two weeks after our wedding, so we had plenty of time to discuss these things," she says. Promises to phone when she's back from France in a few weeks' time (has horse-breeding business there). Has two upcoming exhibitions, one in aid of the ballet school.

TUESDAY, 4 MAY / TORONTO

Edgar Snow in his diaries: "What force is it, unseen by us, which urges men into voluntary withdrawal from crowd and kind? It must be some trace of atavism mixed with a driving pull toward the thrills of living that are found nearest the greatness of nature which despite all men's genius, still reduced his total accomplishments to nothingness in the great high spaces of time and perpetuity."[1]

Paintings were relatively small when patrons lived in palaces. Now, with educated people living in apartments, lofts and condos, paintings, when there are paintings at all, grow monstrous in size. Thin traces of the fact that they are completed to the dimensions of the museum, not those of the habitation. Art not a part of people's everyday environment but something they go to a big building (closed Mondays) and pay money to see.

WEDNESDAY, 5 MAY / TORONTO

Information from the shipping company begins to arrive. A day with only blessings so far, but I wonder if I'm bound to spend every day of the rest of my life worrying about my health? Dinner with Marcia McClung and one of her clients, Pat Ferns, at a Taiwanese hotel with great food and *dreadful* art.

MONDAY, 17 MAY / TORONTO

Some days (such as today) I think that the difference between me and a writer is the difference between a florist and a botanist.

TUESDAY, 18 MAY / TORONTO

My whole point in living is to prolong life so that I can write more. Yet today, for example, I write nothing, am capable of writing nothing. So existence seems meaningless at times, though seldom uninteresting.

---

1 Edgar Snow (1905–1972), US journalist in Asia, author of *Red Star over China* and other works.

WEDNESDAY, 19 MAY / TORONTO

Enshrined in the new office, at the ground floor rear with plenty of natural light, I am established in a new routine as well. Write this in the mornings, work on the woodpile from noon to one when no one phones or emails anyway, then nap, more exercise, and some different type of paperwork in the late afternoon. So far, fine. But freshness is the key to stability with me these days. I do not scruple to have things any other way. For me, nostalgia is largely a thing of the past.

THURSDAY, 27 MAY / TORONTO

Spring weather returning slowly, and me with it. Walking and shopping all day. Lunch with Judy Stoffman at the Coffee Mill, where, in the same phoney manner as the Park Plaza roof bar, a wall is now hung with literary portraits of some of the patrons – Peggy A (long inscription), Conrad Black (likewise), many I don't recognize because they are not inscribed. Pride of place is given to a huge photo of Greg Gatenby. Rest of the day rushing about with equal madness, ending up with a talk at the Arts and Letters Club, dreadful place however historic, where I see a couple of people who chat warmly as usual.

TUESDAY, 1 JUNE / TORONTO

Reading Richard Curle's affecting work on friendship, *The Last Twelve Years of Joseph Conrad* (1928). Page 29: "His temperament was not an equable one, and the charm of his natural manner made it all the more difficult to appreciate his liability to nervous storms. One learned to know him, more or less, as a pilot knows the intricate channels of an estuary, although, of course, one could never be quite certain whether the sands had not shifted in the night." Page 49: "Had he belonged to some Eastern race, he would have been the most famous figure of his generation."

Each morning I revisit the penmanship of the previous day's entry. Sometimes I cannot decipher all of it. But I continue to revisit, one day at a time.

WEDNESDAY, 2 JUNE / TORONTO

Keats: "twilight saints." Purpose every action. War-puppies. Yesterday at the preview of the Sotheby's jewellery auction I see Lord Thomson, looking thin, old, and cheap. Later stood up (publisher's fault) by Greg Gatenby, whom I was to interview. Of course he calls today to apologise and reschedule. Tells me disturbing news: Matt Cohen has been diagnosed with far-gone lung cancer at 55 (and Al Purdy at 80), and Carol Shields' case is even worse than I had believed: she's had a double mastectomy, and is recuperating in England.

SATURDAY, 12 JUNE / TORONTO
The nation is all atwitter over Stephen Reid, who has pulled a Red Ryan on the establishment. Formerly part of the so-called Stopwatch Gang credited with 140 bank robberies and the largest gold heist in Canadian history, he was converted to literature and domesticity by Susan Musgrave, who married him while he was still in prison – a famous incident. He's on the board of PEN for God's sake. But anyone with the least sensitivity to these matters knew that he was still in the life. You could see it in his eyes as easily as you could hear it in his talk. I've long had it in mind to go out to Vancouver Island again and see him. Something Susan said to me when she was writer-in-residence at the U of T suggested to me that she knew too, though she's forced to deny such knowledge in all the papers today, following his arrest after a bungled bank job and gun battle in Victoria. I admire his writing no less for this unfortunate business.

FRIDAY, 18 JUNE / TORONTO
The real anatomy of criticism: always ask yourself, "But who was taking the picture?"

SUNDAY, 20 JUNE / TORONTO
My self-interrogations these past few years have taught me much about myself and how I work and have explained many episodes remembered from a more distant past, but they've been less helpful in my dealings with the outside. The truth is that the examined life does not always assist one to understand the unexamined lives of others who respond only to ad hoc stimuli and conditions and possess not much in the way of a framework of ideas and who, in many cases, live without even motives: the morally dyslexic who live in Hell under assumed names. A change of cloud-cover, from outsider to outcast to outlaw.

FRIDAY, 2 JULY / TORONTO

About 13 hours spent at the [University of Toronto writers'] workshop, including an evening reading by all the instructors in the Hart House library. Privilege drips from the old walls there. I keep hoping that the grand piano will lift one of its stubby mahogany legs and pee on the expensive carpet. Bruce Meyer takes the instructors out to dinner beforehand, all but Terry Kelly and me, who beg off.[2] Bruce is naturally late returning – so much so that the audience begins to grow restless and I fear we will lose some. Therefore I take to the microphone, greet everyone as I believe Bruce would do, and give my 20-minute poetry reading. Just as I finish the others come barging in, apologising for their tardiness. Erin Mouré takes the microphone out among the audience and reads the way I would like to be able to read – funny, good-natured in her approach to very serious work from her new collection.[3] Cf Stephanie Bolster, whose style is very much that of the articulate, well-spoken honours academic that she is; I get much more out of her two books now from hearing her read selections from them.[4] Robert Sawyer has less ego in performance than he does on the page, which is pleasant to see, and Terry Kelly, with muscled biceps, speaks about the death of literary courtesy, on the occasion of the Hemingway centenary (an event that fills me with loathing – has it been *only* a hundred years).[5] Barry Callaghan reads effectively, but the star of the evening is Austin Clarke, who gives the world the first taste of his new novel: magnificent anger, nostalgia, rage, loss and humour.[6] He wears a tailored olive safari suit with highly expensive suede boots. Has the audience in the palm of his huge hands – hands as big as his heart. The library itself seems to have the most tiresome collection of books imaginable. Never have I seen so many copies of *Kon-Tiki*, real and imagined, all together in one room. I note with amusement that the only copy of one of my own books is among a dozen or so kept in a locked glass case, lest it fall into the wrong hands and warp impressionable young minds.

2   Bruce Meyer (b. 1957), poet and professor.
3   Erin Mouré (b. 1955), experimental poet.
4   Stephanie Bolster (b. 1969), poet and professor.
5   Robert J. Sawyer (b. 1960), science fiction author.
6   Barry Callaghan (b. 1937), novelist, poet, and publisher; Austin Clarke (b. 1934), novelist and short story writer.

THURSDAY, 5 AUGUST / TORONTO

Just returned from a drink at the Park Plaza with Cynthia Good from Penguin. Peggy A at the next table, talking condos with three or four developers. On her way out she stops to say that she's just back from the Coast, "visiting the sick" – Purdy, whom she describes as "vertical, which is amazing in the circumstances," Angela Bowering "who's in very poor shape indeed," and Jane Rule, whose arthritis is quite pronounced now.[7] I have my first alcohol in an age (a vodka martini) and am terribly drunk.

MONDAY, 16 AUGUST / TORONTO

A former student whom I'm helping with her book manuscript comes for a meeting today. She is supposed to have 400 pages by now but has produced only 78 and they are the wrong ones. I'm kindly but she suddenly bursts into tears at her failure to deliver what she said she had completed. Home later, she telephones, not making much sense.

MONDAY, 30 AUGUST / TORONTO

Reading Bacon, not someone one would like to have known personally (rare among the Elizabethans) but a soaring intellect, albeit with a Nixonian personality.

I feel that I am living in a society where the fire hoses shoot flames, not water.

WEDNESDAY, 1 SEPTEMBER / TORONTO

A splendid lunch with Peggy A, who is in fine humour and gives me health reports on all the other writers and gathers information for her medical file on me. We talk about the Jack McClelland biography, and she is full of little bits of information – that Person A probably got Person B fired because she (Person B) was getting too close to Pierre (just as she had to Mordecai): that kind of gossip and speculation. She also tells me that she was surprised to hear that Margaret Laurence hated her (I say: "Not hatred. Jealousy.") and that in her (Peggy's) opinion Jack convened the Calgary conference on the novel simply as an attack on *Survival*. This last one suggests to me that Peggy too is not without her moments

7   Jane Rule (1931–2007), novelist and short story writer, author of *Desert of the Heart* and other works.

of delusion, like the rest of us. She buys one of my portfolios [of prints] and is pleased with the gift of a copy of the Woodcock biography, which she hadn't seen. She says that she has high cholesterol, her diet is increasingly limited, and she sometimes passes out (most recently, flying to San Francisco). She'll outlive us all by at least one full generation. Tells a funny story about sharing a platform with Margaret Thatcher.

FRIDAY, 3 SEPTEMBER / TORONTO

Some more of what Peggy said on Wednesday. On sticking with me in the matter of the divorce despite overtures from J, whose two best female friends are P's sister and P's executive assistant: "I think we're all grown-ups here." On the divorce from my point of view: "Well, you certainly knew it was coming." For indeed, as I and so many others knew, she had been trying to get rid of me for years. Says she can't believe she's 60, and certainly looks a dozen years younger. Seems pleased to be asked for the second time to be a godmother, though she doesn't welcome the occasion: a friend who is seriously ill. Aside from a little professional paranoia (not a medical condition but a cultural one, and she's entitled) Peggy is the most level-headed person I know.

SUNDAY, 12 SEPTEMBER / TORONTO

I have no standing. I wish standing, but I know that such a desire contradicts my following the path of non-involvement (standing is so worldly). Have I been using (misusing) Taoism as a term to define my shortcomings?

WEDNESDAY, 22 SEPTEMBER / TORONTO

Anne C in long black jacket, black ass-hugging trousers and black lace-up boots, trudging back to the office as I watch her silhouette recede.

Unbelievably good news today in that I misread the signals from New Brunswick. Ross Leckie calls to offer me the writer-in-residency for the academic year commencing September 2000.[8] I suffer from the constant dilemma: having struggled through one year, wondering how I will or can make a living in the next. This appointment should tide me over.

8   Ross Leckie (b. 1953), poet and academic.

THURSDAY, 30 SEPTEMBER / TORONTO
Too much cheap informality keeps others at a distance without respect.
The mandatory use of nicknames is a poor substitute for friendship.

SATURDAY, 9 OCTOBER / TORONTO
Up early to do some exercise and house-cleaning. With Bernadette to dinner at Tim Brook and Fay Sims' on Howland.[9] Tim's best friend, another
sinologist whom Tim is trying to get hired at the U of T, also there, as are
all the children from Tim's and Fay's marriages (hers to George Galt).
Tim's daughter, still in high school (hard to believe), an actor and a
Marxist, full of intelligence and poise. Long discussion of Chinese painting. Tim keeps dragging out books, scrolls, votive wood-block prints
burned to honour the dead. Fay is sad-eyed, always dressed in denim, a
tiny voice and a big heart. I see why Bernadette likes their crowd.

FRIDAY, 15 OCTOBER / TORONTO
Butterflies not included in the price.

WEDNESDAY, 3 NOVEMBER / TORONTO
Read all the first hundred assassin files and get them ready for Cynthia
Brouse tomorrow.[10] Afternoon meeting with Anne C, who says it looks
like a go for the memoirs anthology.

SATURDAY, 6 NOVEMBER / TORONTO
Hoarse after a three-hour writing class.

WEDNESDAY, 10 NOVEMBER / TORONTO
Work all day revising the first hundred assassin entries, then at 8:30 to
Chapters where I run into Linda McKnight, wise but never wizened. We
share a destination – the U of T Press seasonal launch party, at the Royal
Yacht Club, where my job is to touch base with Bill Harnum and be supportive of Carolyn Wood. Talk a while to Michael Bliss.[11] Linda says of
[a friend]: "She writes as though she's wearing a lab coat."

  9   Timothy Brook (b. 1951), Sinologist and author.
 10   Cynthia Brouse (1957–2010), editor and journalism educator.
 11   Michael Bliss (b. 1941), historian specialising in medical history.

2000

Simply put, I carried on. *The Book of Assassins* was published towards the end of the year. So was a book by my friends Albert and Theresa Moritz that I published under my own small-press imprint – *The World's Most Dangerous Woman: A New Biography of Emma Goldman*. I taught writing courses in the continuing studies department of the University of Toronto, and passed part of the summer at the cabin in the Cariboo region of British Columbia. In the autumn I went to Fredericton to be writer-in-residence at the University of New Brunswick. There I worked on what became a travel narrative called *Three Pagodas Pass: A Roundabout Journey to Burma* and, more important, began a new novel, *Jericho*. Yet I was restless – until Opportunity not only knocked but grabbed me by the lapels and shouted my name.

WEDNESDAY, 12 APRIL / TORONTO
Snow on the ground the past couple of days. Significant snow. Anne C at lunch yesterday; just being with her calms me down. She says wearily that she needs eight more years of work and then, with the boys educated, she may consider moving west, where her younger sister lives. She looks tired. Tells me finally the story of the end of her friendship with the only person with whom she's ever been angry enough to hang up on, who she says has buried her East End insecurities in loads and loads of money. This came out during a period when I've been thinking that I no longer judge people but merely try to understand them.

Last night came home from the university in a taxi. I thought the driver was talking to someone in Creole on a mobile as we moved through the snow storm, as he was talking loudly and with animation. But he had no cell and no headset; he was having a conversation with himself.

FRIDAY, 21 APRIL / TORONTO
Paul Grescoe sends an overnight email to say that John Cruickshank [formerly of the *Whig-Standard* and the *Vancouver Sun*] is going to be editor of the *Chicago Sun-Times*, and be replaced at the *Vancouver Sun* by, ta-da, Neil Reynolds. I wonder if Neil will let me move my column with him when he goes. I'm sure the *Citizen* will kill it once he leaves on 15 May.

MONDAY, 24 APRIL / TORONTO
Al Purdy tributes and obituaries on this morning's front pages. Feeling better about the future after speaking with Neil on the phone. Very friendly, says there's much I can do for him at the *Sun*. I'll see him there in June when I go to meet [a friend]. Sleep-deprived. Up at four a.m. Pleasant conversation with Dr Morose today. We cook dinner together. I'm determined to master the cooking of fish.

MONDAY, 1 MAY / TORONTO
I have a long talk with Keith [Maillard], who's unhappy with HarperCollins and wants to go to Patrick Crean, has no agent, is generally all at sixes and sevens.[1] I'm able to prevent him from setting fire to any bridges and I give him my best and most expensive free advice, which is to put himself in Dean Cooke's hands.[2] Dean is to call me tomorrow.

WEDNESDAY, 3 MAY / TORONTO
Reading [Joseph] Conrad's letters in a lovely Nonesuch Edition. Such a big pile building up of books I want to read for pleasure. Maybe I can get some more such reading done on my two trips to Vancouver, next month and again in August. Working today with Theresa Moritz on the Subway Books catalogue, which should be in the mail before too long.[3] I'm actually quite optimistic of being able to sell 1,500 copies of the Goldman.

   Young woman, bare feet, playing her classical guitar on a broken-down porch while talking on the mobile cradled in her ear.

---

1   Patrick Crean (b. 1949), Toronto book publisher.
2   Dean Cooke (b. 1954), Toronto literary agent.
3   Theresa Moritz (b. 1948), scholar and writer.

THURSDAY, 4 MAY / TORONTO

An event this evening at the Victory Café in Markham Street for John Calder, publisher of 7,000 books, who gives a talk on Beckett, whom he published for years. Calder is in his high seventies, portly, with the disposition of someone who's tired all the time. I tell him the story about [literary agent] Anne McDermid taking Beckett to the strip clubs. "My office was not far away. No doubt he was seeing me, then going back to the club to be picked up." He thinks a moment. "But Ionesco now ... He used to like going to the strip clubs after a big lunch, to doze." Says Beckett gave up smoking only in the last few years of his life: emphysema is what finally killed him in 1989. "His body was failing, but his mind still sharp. But he was in an old-age home in Paris, couldn't eat most of the food. He never ate meat. So he just got thinner and thinner. People would bring him bottles of whisky. What he really needed was a person to bring him his books." Calder was born in Montreal and spent a few childhood years there, then returned soon afterwards when evacuated from England during the war. Still has many Canadian relatives. One of the last avant-garde publishers of the 1960s. Another (more mainstream) one, André Deutsch, died the other day. Calder wrote his obituary in the *Guardian*.

FRIDAY, 5 MAY / TORONTO

Run into Kildare Dobbs who tells me what happened aboard ship on the way from Tahiti back to Greece. The disturbed man who was forever detecting pests, agitating against the officers and otherwise causing trouble, was finally put ashore in Israel. With only a few days left before reaching Athens, the ship was in a Force 9 and one of the mature female passengers was lost at sea, though no one saw her go overboard.

SATURDAY, 6 MAY / TORONTO

Fine waking, with another travel piece today in the *Post*, but I grow progressively (wrong word) more downcast as the day moves ahead. I teach a dreadful three-hour class, then consider the nuances in recent unsatisfactory conversations. God I can't wait to blow this town and keep secret all my intimate knowledge of it. In general, I'm much less easily hurt than was the case a while ago, but still *too* easily all the same.

Go to the small-press book fair and buy a copy of a book by Blaise Moritz, Al and Theresa's son.

SUNDAY, 7 MAY / TORONTO
The first truly hot and humid day thus far. I launch a serious assault on the paperwork problem while Dr Morose (whose disposition is fine – he's bounced back) is doing laundry. Who should phone but Bernadette, asking if she might come by to give me my Christmas present (two pull-overs). Also to return the house key without being asked. News: her friend N died last week. About our voyage: She knows of one drowning, one suicide overboard, and one apparent overdose during the latter half of the circumnavigation.

MONDAY, 8 MAY / TORONTO
That which doesn't kill me pisses me off.

In the morning I attend the first awards benefit of the Charles Taylor Prize, partly to remember Charles. A dignified affair. I sit next to Penny Dickens (the first meeting for us) and tell her about the [Writers'] Union fiasco and my response to it. When I try to speak to Wayson Choy, one of the shortlisted (not the winner), he's incredibly rude.[4] I confront him on it, saying that he and I were becoming friends but he elected to go with J and has had no contact with me since the split. He denies seeing J, which I know from J's mouth isn't the case. Lunch with Kelly Hechler at McClelland and Stewart but I fear that I appear distant or distracted. Terrible heat today so I work at night. Writing this at 10:50 p.m. or so. Must not let my melancholy control my actions. Long talk this evening with Keith Maillard.

TUESDAY, 9 MAY / TORONTO
I lunch tomorrow with Bruce Meyer and have the following report to make to him: my lone remaining travel-writing student, the one who worked for two governors-general and brags of living in Rosedale, sud-denly flew off the handle with one half hour to go in the penultimate class, accusing me of rudeness, unprofessionalism, of not giving her

4   Wayson Choy, (b. 1939), novelist and memoirist, author of *The Jade Peony*.

money's worth, etc. In fact, she didn't like being in a class taught by a social inferior. I was apologetic, conciliatory. She went on again about the money (neither of us could recall the exact sum – I believe it was $325). I had no cheques or exact change and so offered her $350 in cash in return for a receipt. She took only $300, leaving me the receipt for the same, and stalked out of the room. I should probably turn up next week for the final class, in case anyone else shows, but dread the possibility of seeing her there, whether remorseful or not. This experience sours me on students, though rationally I know to expect at least one troublesome person each semester.

WEDNESDAY, 10 MAY / TORONTO
Get up and write the brief incident report for Bruce without agonising much over the matter. Bruce is a half hour late and as disorganised as ever. Return home not feeling well – lassitude, ennui, melancholy – and sleep most of the day and return to bed immediately after dinner. The good news is that Ross Leckie has found another $10K for me in Fredericton, which brightens my Vancouver first-year survival fund considerably. Dr Morose finally opens a bank account today, or another credit union account, ending, I hope, his reliance on the insecure and usurious cheque-cashing place on Bloor.

FRIDAY, 12 MAY / TORONTO
Finally decide to take the bull's horns regarding Raincoast in Vancouver and call Emi Morita, who's eager to see my fax c.v. and give me freelance work until I move.[5] (Mind you, I keep getting enthusiastic initial responses from people, then not hearing from them again.) A rescheduled lunch with Sarah Murdoch, new editor of the *Post*'s reviews section, who thinks the paper should be using me. I return to an email fuss with the *Citizen*. I'm so tired that I sleep most of the late afternoon.

MONDAY, 15 MAY / TORONTO
A party at the Capital Theatre relaunching the new *Saturday Night*. Speak for a moment to Diana Symonds, the fourteenth editor, until she

5   Emiko Morita (b. 1969), of the publishers Douglas & McIntyre.

gets busy with Anne McDermid. Mostly [ad] agency people I don't know who are all in black casual, drinking martinis, eating roast duck with hoi sin sauce. I recognise no one but David Cronenberg, the other old guy.[6] I buy a tweed jacket (for Fredericton) at Stollery's. Can't help but wonder if this is the last one I shall ever buy.

WEDNESDAY, 17 MAY / TORONTO
I sleep off most of the terror. My plan is to get the ms to Random before I leave for Vancouver, with enough columns in the bank to tide me over until my return. Looking at my penmanship the past few days I remember the spidery quality of Woodcock's when he got into his late 70s and early 80s and declined so rapidly. Am I declining rapidly? Or at a socially acceptable pace?

FRIDAY, 19 MAY / TORONTO
Cold wet day. [A colleague] working on the assassins drafts is all agog with her cover story in *Toronto Life*, a much-needed confidence-builder for her as she's full of working-class fears.

SATURDAY, 20 MAY / TORONTO
When the computer is checking for email, I see the names of the senders flash by as the programme scans the directory – just for a partial second in each case, just enough time for me to register the information. Similarly, when I'm deleting files, I have only an instant to say goodbye to them. So too it is with nights' worth of dreams on waking in the morning. Brief flashes, little dots of imagery, are all that remain.

A productive day of office work. [Lee Harvey] Oswald's is now the last assassin's biography to be written. My goal must be to get all the corrections keyed in and the ms printed out by the time I leave for Vancouver. Then I can turn in the work to Anne as I return from five days there, seeing Neil and picking up Midori.

6 David Cronenberg (b. 1943), director of such films as *Crash*, *Naked Lunch*, and *Scanners*.

WEDNESDAY, 24 MAY / TORONTO

I'm like Michael Corleone in reverse: I keep trying to turn crooked, but the mob keeps pushing me away. The tradition of immigration as a metaphor for rebirth, but it can also be a preview of death, learning how to survive without existing until one's existence is blown out like a candle. Tradition says emigration hurts, immigration heals. Little is imputed to internal migration. I say this: it can be and is either and both. Redrawing the circle of exile around one more tightly like a cloak, like a line of defence, like Squeaky (my head is full of history's demented assassins just now). Carry on and await opportunity.

FRIDAY, 26 MAY / TORONTO

Lunch with Marcia McClung, Nellie's granddaughter, at a "client" restaurant. A sweet person, smart, tends to gloss over difficulties to keep her cards close to her chest, but opens up occasionally. She says she used to be friends with Katherine Govier. At my suggestion, but through her own persistence, she has won the publicity and advertising contract for the continuing studies writing programme at U of T. Also, she's doing the new big show at the ROM. Pick up a job at Kate Murdoch's, the bookbinder. See a film. Now, set to get back to work on Saturday, when I teach my last class.

SATURDAY, 27 MAY / TORONTO

A warm but necessarily cryptic email from the captain in Rangoon telling me that he's said farewell to Midori and wishes her well. This suggests to me that she's in Bangkok now, awaiting her visa.

TUESDAY, 30 MAY / TORONTO

Deliver the assassins ms to Random. What a relief. Random is utter chaos because of the move from Yonge to Toronto Street, representing the bringing together of Random, Knopf, and Doubleday under one roof.

WEDNESDAY, 31 MAY / VANCOUVER

An easy flight, an earlier one than planned; then a room at the Sylvia. I call Neil, and set up coffee for tomorrow morning at a hotel where no one will see us, as is his custom. I survey my new/old neighbourhood

with new not old eyes. Many calls out. Confirmation fax from Bangkok.
I dream about some Jim Christy adventure caper.

THURSDAY, 1 JUNE / VANCOUVER
One of the best days of my life. I meet Neil at 9:30 a.m. and he offers me
a job at the *Sun* for next April and I accept. Many details remain to be
worked out, but this will make my transition to Vancouver possible –
indeed, make my retirement possible after a time. Will get me onto a
health plan, etc. I remember the feeling I had that day at the King Eddy
in Toronto when he hired me for the *Whig*.

FRIDAY, 2 JUNE / VANCOUVER
Walking the Seawall, I see a loon and a float plane take off together. Talk
to Mary Maillard after getting together with Keith and her. I've been
eating badly and am therefore out of shape.

The evidence itself conspires towards the conclusion: I meet Midori at
the airport but troubles commence soon afterwards. Her self is turned
inside out, so that her nerves and emotions are worn on the outside. She
unexpectedly breaks down in tears many times a day – judging by today
at least – and fully conforms to Dr Morose's diagnosis, based on some of
her stream-of-consciousness letters, that she is a teenager emotionally at
age 39. Like Kerouac's, the stream of a not very interesting consciousness. Much better humour than, say, Bernadette, but prone to angry out-
bursts. Reads me some letters her father wrote the family from prison
after the 1990 election, then announces – to my absolute astonishment
– that she supports the junta that imprisoned him and enslaves her people on the grounds that only a military government can make the country work and that one military government is very much like the next.
No political understanding whatever.

SATURDAY, 3 JUNE / VANCOUVER
Vancouver plays its part perfectly, looks like a Kodachrome advertise-
ment for itself. Midori shows me the small handful of rubies and emer-
alds that she has brought out of the country. Also, a few diamonds,
which her mother sells to the Chinese for gold. Her mother had 30 or so
private clients for gems, including Ne Win's wife, before China loosened
up economically. Her mother wanted her to take over the business,

which had been passed from great-grandmother to grandmother to mother. Midori of course refused.

We walk and talk for 10 or more miles spread throughout the day. Then return to the hotel about nine p.m. when she provokes a long argument about the junta. We visit the apartment and I get a full sense of her crying jags and what they represent, to say nothing of her racism, political naïveté, and temper that would make existence difficult. Because the Sylvia is full, we must move to the Hampton Inn on Robson.

My scheduled meeting with [a friend] at a café out on Commercial near her new apartment. She is much older-looking – face lined, etc. – and much heavier – by 30 pounds perhaps; hard to tell because she wears a kind of muumuu. So this is how she has dealt with her break-up. As always she hides her own thoughts and movements while invigilating me. So we revisit the past and I give a good account of myself. Certainly the meeting has been worthwhile. Return to one of Midori's crying sessions, lasting long into the night. Because of complications with her air tickets we cannot return to Toronto on the same flight or even the same day.

MONDAY, 5 JUNE / VANCOUVER

I set the alarm for 5:30 a.m. to accompany Midori to the airport for her seven o'clock flight, but she shuts off the alarm once I am asleep and she's long gone by eight when I awake. Instantly I know what has happened and begin searching the room for the inevitable long note. Find it in the bathroom. It says that I don't love her and that she doesn't want me. It is long, tearful, and emotionally overwrought for no reason. Says she'll stay two weeks in Toronto and then go to the UK or US. Dr Morose, good sport, will meet her at the airport. All of this is more or less what he has led me to expect. Now the problem remains, of how, when I return, to get rid of her without incident.

TUESDAY, 6 JUNE / VANCOUVER

Overcast. Business email. The Seawall. Feeling a dread, a slight dread, of Midori in Toronto and worry what Dr Morose might be going through. Otherwise a fine trip. Waiting to board the redeye, I phone Morose, who gives an epic account of his difficulties with her, taking me to task for taking up with highly strung women. The flight not relaxing. Hardly any sleep.

WEDNESDAY, 7 JUNE / TORONTO

Dr Morose has taken a telephone-survey job in order to lay aside money for the trip to Vancouver next April, when he and Victor will move my stuff. I began to consider putting together my change of address cards but right now I'm hard pressed to think of many people in the East who would wish to keep in touch. Strange call returned from the *Star*'s review editor, who then slams down the receiver in my ear. Curious.

FRIDAY, 9 JUNE / TORONTO

News this morning that the *Canadian Forum* may suspend publication (again); the editor and the entire 10-member board have resigned. I'm not unhappy about the loss of this particular board, but the loss of another voice worries me. In the chaos of the past few days I have neglected to note my sadness in reading, while in Vancouver, of H.S. Bhabra's death.[7] Apparently still depressed after being fired from a TV show that was his public identity (what a sick Toronto story), he leapt off the Bloor Viaduct, in the traditional manner. I remember his appearance on the scene years ago, when he launched two novels, under different names, on the same evening, following a witty introduction by John Pearce.[8]

SUNDAY, 11 JUNE / TORONTO

I'm pleased that I've been able to sell privately, with no sign, no ads, no photos in some estate agent's window, no open house. When the time comes, in April 2001, I can slip away unnoticed to Vancouver. Does this sound like burning bridges? Actually, the case is closer to the Swiss model of mining all the bridges, trestles and other approaches, not to foil invaders but rather to inhibit pursuers. A good feeling.

MONDAY, 12 JUNE / TORONTO

This evening, right before dinner, I pass Carl's barbershop on Bathurst and see Carl's terrier in the chair, getting a trim with the scissors.

7   H.S. Bhabra (1955–2000), novelist.
8   John Pearce (b. 1947), Toronto publisher; later, literary agent.

TUESDAY, 13 JUNE / TORONTO

I'll have this operation organised like a jail break. Dr Morose is out this evening, visiting the sick – specifically, a doper, who has a fractured collar bone and two broken ribs.

These events are, to a degree rare in life, mine to control, or I have back-up plans built into my back-up, almost to the point at which the whole affair begins to look like a maze. I exhort myself to be patient and relax. Again, Fredericton's pace may be beneficial to me in this regard.

Go to sleep thinking: I never spoke with an accent because I couldn't speak at all.

WEDNESDAY, 14 JUNE / TORONTO

Work on the Goldman ms – the first 100 pages to show the authors on Friday. Morose is working nights doing phone surveys – he's very good at it – which leaves me feeling lonely. A raging thunder and lightning storm from 8:00 p.m. on.

FRIDAY, 16 JUNE / TORONTO

A productive meeting with Al and Theresa at Dooney's regarding the Goldman editing. A lovely spring day, the nicest one so far this year. Earle's marked-up copy of assassins arrives by post.

SUNDAY, 18 JUNE / TORONTO

A terrible night, awake more hours than asleep. As often happens, I have the desire but not quite enough will or strength to turn on the light and write down thoughts and dreams before they fade and disappear. I imagine this must be something like what dying is like, when magnetic pull of ennui overpowers the desire to continue breathing. So a rough morning assured. I spend it at the CBA [Canadian Booksellers' Association] convention, which is surprisingly well attended and at which I commit no errors that I notice and indeed enjoy touching base with old friends. Home by one o'clock and just asleep when Midori calls from her brother's in London. My go-away-and-leave-me-alone email reply, so difficult to send but so necessary, has not been believed. She still wants to see me or even stay here when she has five days in Toronto in late July en route to Rangoon (thank God she's going home). I no sooner get back to sleep than she calls a second time – I know it's her – but I let it ring and ring and she doesn't leave a message.

Today Ellen Seligman tells me of going to Al Purdy's funeral in Ameliasburgh yesterday. Eurithe's brother spoke at the gravesite, then the mourners one by one tossed handfuls of earth into the grave. "Eurithe had a nice stone carved with the last few lines of the last poem Al wrote. The grave is by a tree near a small hill. Very beautiful and peaceful." This calls to mind the description of Alden Nowlan's grave (and funeral) in Fredericton, which I read about today in Patrick Toner's biography. David Adams Richards was present and uttered something mock-eloquent.[9] I see David today at the CBA, our first meeting in years. I wonder how productive I can make myself in Fredericton for eight months? On the example of Kingston, I believe I could be quite productive indeed if I build up my endurance and keep my focus. Staying organised is the key. Do one project until the draft is finished, put it aside while drafting the next. We'll see.

MONDAY, 19 JUNE / TORONTO
Bob F tells me what he believes is the real story behind the news reported in the *Globe* about [a common acquaintance] returning to Canada. According to Bob, he was arrested for murder and deported. The Canadian embassy had to lend him airfare. Bob in fine form. At the end of the day I gear up for the big Random–Knopf–Doubleday party, celebrating their new premises. I find the atmosphere terrifying. The place reeks of success – exactly the sort of situation from which I flee, but not before seeing Anne C for just long enough to say hello (I almost failed to recognise her because this is the first time I've seen her wearing light colours and heavily made up). Run into Susan Swan and her daughter Samantha Haywood. "The last time I saw you," I say to the latter, "you were in your crib. I spoke to you but you just gurgled." Coming home, I notice all the changes along, for example, Beverley Street, where I lived once with Bill Kimber and the others. Unlike open country, the city is constantly changing, constantly moving away from its own past and its own memories, constantly being rebuilt but only of course after first

9 David Adams Richards (b. 1950), author of *Road to the Stilt House*, *Nights below Station Street*, and other novels.

being torn down in pieces. In humans, we call this death but in cities it is life. On those, I hope, infrequent occasions when I must sneak into Toronto after settling in Vancouver, I expect to recognise very little of what I'll see.

FRIDAY, 23 JUNE / TORONTO
Run into Bill Davies and chat as I'm on my way to Massey College for a merging of new and old *Saturday Night* hands.[10] Gracious speeches, graciously short ones, Fulford, Fraser and Symonds. I see some people I haven't seen for years, such as Craig Allen. Spend time talking with Charlotte Gray about [William Lyon] Mackenzie.[11] Austin Clarke seems very happy to see me.

SATURDAY, 24 JUNE / TORONTO
This evening a call from Greg Gatenby (he dials me by mistake but we have a long conversation) who tells me more about Purdy's funeral. Says [another poet] was invited to speak. Reminds me of the funeral of a certain Toronto establishment gadfly, whose wife kindly invited her husband's mistress to the funeral. Like a wedding: wife's friends on one side of the aisle, mistress's on the other.

FRIDAY, 30 JUNE / TORONTO
Teach the first day of a tedious seminar at Hart House. I grow weary of these amateur writers, one of whom actually reads Sir Walter Scott for inspiration. Walking back I take some comfort in the fact that in two months' time I expect to get out of the Annex. Come home via Gwendolyn MacEwen Park, thinking that I must be patient, patient, patient.

MONDAY, 3 JULY / TORONTO
The reading at Hart House Library, the very room, Bruce Meyer reminds everyone, in which Morley Callaghan first read Hemingway (but I stay anyway). A flip through the card catalogue tells me that their most recent book of mine was acquired in 1971, so I bring a bundle of books to donate. The reading is hardly my most polished, but then this is the first

10   William Davies (b. 1950), physician, poet, and book collector.
11   Charlotte Gray (b. 1948), historian and biographer.

time I've read from *Madagascar*. After all the readings finish, I take Colleen Wagner to Bloor for coffee, to pump her for information about the UNB post, which she's held most recently.[12] She gives glowing reports of the programme and tells me how to live in Fredericton as a vegetarian but paints a disturbing picture of my future landlady, whose house is more or less unheated on principle; Colleen moved out after two months. C, in her facial features, mannerisms, and speech, suggests a dark-haired version of Susan Swan.

WEDNESDAY, 5 JULY / TORONTO
A sad lunch today with Bob F during which, throwing caution to the wind and swearing him to secrecy, I tell him of the Vancouver move.

SUNDAY, 23 JULY / TORONTO
Truly a day in which I accomplish a little bit under each category – the column, book work, housekeeping, exercise, cooking, correspondence, reducing possessions, study, leisure reading, relaxation. Indeed, a *peaceful* yet *productive* day is had by me.

SATURDAY, 29 JULY / TORONTO
Up at 5:00 a.m. in considerable discomfort from my back, which has worsened through the night. Walking like Groucho all day, but slowly. But for the permissions memo, I finish the Vintage anthology for delivery on Monday. Dr Morose gets lost for hours and hours trying to find Alpha Avenue to deliver a Goldman chapter to Theresa and Albert.

SUNDAY, 30 JULY / TORONTO
Being my own master, I am also my own slave.

MONDAY, 31 JULY / TORONTO
Start the day, post-paperwork, by delivering the memoirs anthology to Random House (see Anne briefly). While going to meet Rich Landon, I hear on the radio the news that CanWest Global has bought all of the Southam papers (and 50 per cent of the *National Post*) for $3.5 billion. I'm

12 Colleen Wagner (b. 1949), author of *The Monument* and other plays.

sure that Neil will resign in Vancouver and that I'll lose my *Citizen* column. I am left reeling for fear of my future in Vancouver (today the condo mortgage is discharged). But then I have been telling myself for weeks or months that I must not count on anything but healthy poverty in Vancouver and more energy for my serious writing. Anyway, I am inattentive during lunch with Rich (who following lunch joins a group of friends, including his ex-wife Ann, of whom I was always fond). Listlessness continues when I see Paul Copeland to discuss Burma.[13] To ensure confidentiality, we talk while taking a walk, because his office, he says, is not secure.

WEDNESDAY, 2 AUGUST / TORONTO

Get more than a third of the way through revisions (my own, not Random's) on the assassins book: one of the chores I must complete before leaving for Vancouver. Still I do nothing about Neil. Considering writing him an email over the weekend to see if he wants to have a coffee at the Waterfront when I'm in town. If he says no or doesn't respond, what have I lost? The news is full of Conrad Black's withdrawal from Canada.

THURSDAY, 3 AUGUST / TORONTO

I cannot biographise myself but only describe. But then revealing is always to be preferred to explaining. At one time I owned two tuxedos but I prefer police station coffee. If I must hold a meeting I do so in a hospital cafeteria – a public place but not too public – a place where no one asks you what you're doing. Favourite hymn: "Will There Be Any Boxcars in Heaven?" Have worked my way slowly to an assortment of belief systems and frames of mind.

SUNDAY, 6 AUGUST / TORONTO

The sea is death in liquid form.

MONDAY, 7 AUGUST / TORONTO

Toronto best viewed from afar, better remembered than still experienced.

13   Paul Copeland (b. 1940), civil rights lawyer and activist.

THURSDAY, 10 AUGUST / VANCOUVER
The car comes at 5:30 a.m. for the trip to the airport where confusion still reigns because of the Air Canada merger. A magnificent view of Mt Baker to the south as we come into Vancouver. As I leave early again tomorrow, for Williams Lake and beyond, I am hiding out in Richmond, evaluating it as a future holing-up place in an emergency. Seems like the Chinese version of Southern California urban sprawl. This is the day the house deal closes back in Toronto (I signed off on everything yesterday).

FRIDAY, 11 AUGUST / VANCOUVER TO WILLIAMS LAKE
Travelling provokes great confusion, exposes one to exasperation and Air Canada rage. Arrive at Williams Lake, drop off my gear at the home of a libertarian hypochondriac, and look up [his partner] when her shift ends at the diner in an alley off the main highway. Their truck has broken down and apparently cannot be fixed quickly. So I organise the rental of a car for the morning, to take the three of us out to Quesnel Lake.

SATURDAY, 12 AUGUST / QUESNEL LAKE
Stopping at Horsefly en route to Quesnel Lake, I check my email and am surprised to find a note from Neil telling me he's not sure "what the practical consequences of CanWest ownership will mean but [I] don't think any of this will impede our plans." Goes on to say that he'll know early next month and will keep me informed. I take this to mean he's secure about his own future as editor-in-chief of the *Sun* and wants to reassure me of my own future with him (great news to be received in Horsefly of all places on Earth). My qualified relief and joy are compromised somewhat when, at our arrival on the lake, the libertarian begins arguing with [his partner] as usual – the woman is a saint – and with me. A rough night ending in a stubborn migraine for me, from which I still suffer (I hope it's not one of the three-day variety). My cabin looks fine. Everything in place, just as I left it two years ago. Anything made of leather has gone mouldy – no surprise – but tools, provisions, etc. all in good shape, and vegetation has grown considerably, obscuring the shed from the road a bit more. This suits me fine, as of course the area is a bit more developed.

SUNDAY, 13 AUGUST / QUESNEL LAKE

I write this on the steps of the cabin, listening to the same woodpecker (I presume) that I hear each time. Late getting underway, of course, because of bickering by my companions (both of whom use reimagined names, by the way). We stop along the Horsefly Road to visit with Erik and Rose, who are prospering with extensive greenhouses at their new location. Return late. Of my two travelling companions: each prevents the socialisation of the other, with the result that they are both outcasts in any community where they reside.

TUESDAY, 15 AUGUST / VANCOUVER

Great to be alive and doing business in Vancouver. I spend much of the day copy-editing at the new library on Georgia. Later, I treat my hosts to dinner. Reread [Don] DeLillo before bed.

WEDNESDAY, 16 AUGUST / VANCOUVER

I check into the Sylvia. The ivy on the exterior walls is just beginning to turn red at this spot despite the sunniness of the location. Go to Richards, shop, do laundry, walk, walk, walk. [A friend], who's in her thirties now, says at dinner that she's got beyond seeing the culture in terms of gender roles.

FRIDAY, 18 AUGUST / VANCOUVER

Awake at 1:00 a.m. with the television on, then again at six with a sense that getting up requires all my reserves of resolve: a presentiment of winter in Fredericton no doubt. Sure enough it is cold and rainy and the street lamps are still on even though the sun has risen fully. Spend the morning walking, looking at shipping, returning about noon to find out Midori has called.

SUNDAY, 27 AUGUST / VANCOUVER

Only by living in Vancouver, where I'm despised as a Torontonian, can I be accepted as a Torontonian at all – in contrast to Toronto itself, where I'm despised as a foreigner. What's the solution to the paradox? Be a dropout from the karma circle of small hatreds altogether. Leave the literary life completely. Over the decades I've always come to Vancouver to heal.

FRIDAY, 1 SEPTEMBER / FREDERICTON

A surprisingly quick and easy flight here. I can see, however, the terrible
potential for getting the blues in the winter. I check in with Ross Leckie
at the English Department. He's as roly-poly and as bright and friendly
as everyone has led me to believe. I hope to begin working for myself
tomorrow. My room is a student's room, about 10 feet square and furnished with junk painted Chinese red, in a vast untidy old home close by
the campus, atop the hill with the steeple and the other downtown landmarks visible below through the tree tops. One other tenant I've met so
far is beginning the MA programme in creative writing after time off as
a line cook in Hope, BC, where she lived in a trailer park.

SATURDAY, 9 SEPTEMBER / FREDERICTON

Ross Leckie has been writing across the hall, but I hear his door close
and his footsteps recede. I wonder if I can throw myself into my wet
manuscript and lose the signal that at such times as these sends my mind
on tour. Unlike previous occasions, I have a fall-back plan in place on
which I actually *can* fall back. Get through the next eight or nine months
in a healthy state. Use the time to maximum effect in terms of having mss
to send round at the end. Slip away at the right time. Work now. Get
healthier. Save money. Disappear.

Later: whereas on the newspapers I had to keep all files and personal
items at home because the office environments were insecure, here the
opposite is the case. This household is a wobbly environment because of
the landlady. It is one that I might, just conceivably, have to walk away
from at some point, I'm not sure. So although I shipped files, books, etc.
to that address from Toronto, I'm now slowly transferring, one briefcase at a time, all this stuff to the office, which seems fairly secure, well
away from most of the department. When I finally get my ID card, I'll
be able to shower at the gym after working out every day, thus eliminat-
ing one more tie to this rooming house (I've already stopped getting
mail here). When the time comes when I have completed my assignment
successfully, I will sell off the books in office, the ones I don't need, and
destroy the papers I no longer require, and courier what remains to
Toronto. I've deliberately brought clothes that I won't be needing in
Vancouver, so these I can ditch too. Putting all this together with the

trips to Toronto in November, for an OAC [Ontario Arts Council] jury, and then again over Christmas, to pack up Albany Avenue, I should be able to smuggle myself out.

Later still: now I feel that this will be the loneliest period of my life if it does not become the most productive. I must not lose what few social skills I have managed to gather.

Jericho: perhaps I should write of Lonnie's loneliness in the Dexter Fireproof Hotel.

SUNDAY, 10 SEPTEMBER / FREDERICTON

The landlady has returned with yet more rules. The exact amount of seeds to be left in her bird-feeder and which species of birds are entitled to dine there, the direction in which both interior and exterior door-knobs must face when not in use. After only 10 days I have come to loathe this place, and I haven't really seen any students yet. Midnight: spent the past hour in a wonderful warm talk with Ross L about poetry and small presses.

MONDAY, 11 SEPTEMBER / FREDERICTON

The last straw with the landlady this morning. She left an interior light on for me last night that I, not knowing its function, had no way of knowing I was to turn off. Also, after earlier requesting that shoes not be worn in the house but left inside the front door, she tells me that she now limits people to one pair apiece – I am two pair over the limit. I tell her that hereafter I will keep my shoes in my office. Then I waste the entire morning and much of the afternoon trying to get my ID card so that I can use the library and the gym. The result is that even after a personal appeal to a vice-president, all I can get is a temporary library card and no access to the gym except as a special guest for a few days only – this despite the fact I am ready and willing to pay. The phones of all the relevant offices and bureaucrats simply ring and ring, without even voicemail. Mind you, this *is* the first day of classes. So I end up buying a membership in a down-town health club and then renting, for $700 a month, a place in the Lord Beaverbrook Hotel annex. Sounds pricey by local standards, it's true, but it comes with twice-a-week maid service and linen – and heat, and no landlady. I doubt I'll end up making or saving any money here after all.

WEDNESDAY, 13 SEPTEMBER / FREDERICTON
I lose the entire first chapter of the long back-story of *Jericho* in the computer and the experts at the computer lab can't undelete what I've done.

FRIDAY, 15 SEPTEMBER / FREDERICTON
I inherit Mark Jarman's old computer, slightly more powerful than the one I was first given, though slower, and the email programme is Pegasus, which is far inferior to Eudora.[14] So a frustrating day. But also a day of citizenship, in which I send flowers to the departmental secretary who's been helping me with the computer difficulties, and buy the books of all the poets who are coming to read. Get haircut, do laundry, cook two days' worth of chicken, etc. The barbershops in Fredericton still keep the personal shaving brushes of regular customers in a neat row. In Ontario, barbershop shaves are now illegal because of the contaminated-blood scandal.

TUESDAY, 19 SEPTEMBER / FREDERICTON
Jericho begins to take some rough shape, a front story and a back story, shuffled like a deck of cards. Lunch with a friend. We make plans to do a day trip to Saint John the first Friday of next month.

WEDNESDAY, 20 SEPTEMBER / FREDERICTON
Up at 7:00 a.m. waiting for the CBC's taxi to take me to the radio studio at 8:15. A long day, on the go until I return home at 10 p.m. Finally the net connection is made. Go to dinner with people from the department and tonight's three visiting poets: Anne Simpson writes in somewhat the same manner as, for example, Stephanie Bolster.[15] Jan Zwicky is deeply committed, diverse, reeking of excellence, stylishly nondescript, and of imprecise age, a talented reader if a bit too fast, one hand in a pocket sometimes, hands clasped behind her other times.[16] Some of Zwicky's mannerisms apply to her mate, Don McKay, working class from Cornwall, Ontario (I can see its railyards in his face).[17] Writes funny

14   Mark Jarman (b. 1955), author of *Salvage King, Ya!* and other works of fiction.
15   Anne Simpson (b. 1956), poet, author of *Loop* and many other works.
16   Jan Zwicky (b. 1955), poet and philosopher.
17   Don McKay (b. 1942), poet, author of *Night Field, Another Gravity*, etc.

poems. Scrawny guy, a floppy mop of bushy hair, somewhat like Matt Cohen in manner but devoid of the underlying anger. Good-humoured and unaffected, in fact. I am interested to see how Ross Leckie presides over the evening. Ross has his hands in most literary activity in town (which is maybe why he detests [a Toronto poet] – same ambition to make it big in the poetry scene, a desire I associate with people in the 1960s). Between times an interview with Joe Blades at his apartment at York and George.[18] The former landlady sits next to me during the first half of dinner, until Ross switches places with her to rescue me, using the excuse of wanting to give him a chance to chat with his old friend McKay. She is condescending, but that's all.

THURSDAY, 21 SEPTEMBER / FREDERICTON

Try to sleep in, then go to the gym and over to the *Telegraph-Journal* bureau to have my photo taken for Eric Marks' interview with me in the *Reader* on Saturday.[19] Receive the Random House catalogue listing *George* Fetherling's first book, with a March publication date. So it *is* coming out after all.

See Fred Cogswell in the corridor today. He is retired but still uses the department as a mail drop. He looks precisely the same as when I saw him a dozen years ago except that his hair is silvered (finally, in his eighties). I am told he has a new younger wife – in her 50s. Several little chats with Ross during the day. At one of them I tell him the plot of Kent Thompson's new novel – a nude murderer captured by a sightless detective – and this occasions great hilarity in the departmental corridor, as Kent apparently enjoyed notoriety as a nudist and a streaker.[20]

FRIDAY, 22 SEPTEMBER / FREDERICTON

I do about 2,000 words on *Jericho* today, making that my priority once the email is dealt with, as should and shall be my pattern except on Mondays and Tuesdays – student days – when I will work on *Three Pagodas Pass* between appointments with them, and on one day of the

---

18   Joe Blades (b. 1961), experimental poet, visual artist, and small-press publisher.
19   Eric Marks (b. 1970), poet and journalist.
20   Kent Thompson (b. 1936), short story writer and poet.

weekends, when I shall draft my column and attend to sumptuary matters. This is the plan at any rate, now that I have my computer problems solved for the moment. I have a nap in the afternoon, before heading over to the gym.

SATURDAY, 23 SEPTEMBER / FREDERICTON

Up at five a.m. to be the first at the Boyce Market at six where I get decent fresh fish and some chicken and fruit. Then back for a nap, after scaring up a *Telegraph-Journal* containing the interview promoting the Tuesday reading. Then to the quiet of the office for dealing with the mail and working on *Jericho*. Important with the latter that I carry no deadline in my head but just work along, a thousand words of draft each working day if I possibly can, and allow the characters to develop by themselves, as they are just about to begin doing now. I'm reading a great deal of poetry every day while writing my own prose. Maybe the process will be reversed or perhaps I'll do both at once. J said that just after her mother died I entered a period of trying to create everything at once. I may be atop another such period now.

SUNDAY, 24 SEPTEMBER / FREDERICTON

Thinking about Jan Zwicky (still reading her other books) – poet of philosophy and music, an original intelligence. I consider trying to strike up a correspondence but lose the resolve, believing that I would be condescended to. Still, I am enjoying the books. Work at the office in the evening. Distressed to learn that the university rents out classrooms at night as rehearsal space for rock bands.

MONDAY, 25 SEPTEMBER / FREDERICTON

Better sleep, up at 7:00 a.m. for this, a long day of students with mss. My routine is falling into place now, laundry and shopping on the weekend, cooking at home more adventurously than before, drafting out *Three Pagodas* on Mondays and Tuesdays between and among students, working on *Jericho* the other days. Little or no social life except that which the university obliges. Predictably, the English Department is like the officers' mess, but this comparison must hold for all English departments everywhere and every officers' mess.

TUESDAY, 26 SEPTEMBER / FREDERICTON

Anticipating the worst later on in the day, I carefully make the bed this morning. But the poetry reading comes at 4:00 p.m. and I give a decent performance, one or two or several small missteps but speaking slowly, clearly, and in a well-modulated voice. I am preceded by Sharon McCartney, the mate of Mark Jarman, who reads poems about her three c-sections. She is pale, with thick tightly curled hair like J's. Turnout about 55 people. Sell some books. The principals return to Mark and Sharon's large lovely house afterwards.

WEDNESDAY, 27 SEPTEMBER / FREDERICTON

I return to the city in time to hear the aged Robert Hawkes, a former editor of *Fiddlehead* (who has not been the editor of *Fiddlehead*?) reading his poems about Archbishop Cranmer. Afterwards I ask him to sign two books. He can't figure out how to depress the top of the ballpoint pen. "I have difficulty with technology," he says. I begin to spell my surname for him, but he says, "Spelling and time are two subjects with which I am greatly concerned." As I walk home diagonally across the military compound, I hear nearby church bells peal eight times.

THURSDAY, 28 SEPTEMBER / FREDERICTON

Up at 6:00 a.m. and off to the gym – what discipline – then work all day on the two mss. After a 12-hour day, I'm walking towards the Atlantic Superstore in Smythe Street and notice when passing the Legion that the flag is at half staff. I suspect why. Getting home with my fish and groceries, I turn on CBC to hear that, indeed, Pierre Trudeau has died. I think back to seeing him at the *Globe* in King Street, of conversing with him when at the GGs with Gwen MacEwen. He leaves pygmies crawling over the political landscape.

FRIDAY, 29 SEPTEMBER / FREDERICTON

Late this afternoon I go to hear Al Moritz read with John Riebetanz.[21] The latter is badly outshone by Al, who by the way has lost weight and

21 John Riebetanz (b. 1944), poet and professor, author of *Near Relations* and other works.

more hair, and is impeccably dressed in a new green turtleneck, a Windsor check suit, expensive shoes. Al is one of the most remarkable poets I know or know of. Riebetanz, a perfectly nice fellow, was Ross's thesis adviser. Along with Joe Blades and one of the grad students, we all go out for Chinese food afterwards. I treat because I don't want Joe, who can't afford a cup of restaurant coffee (seriously), to be embarrassed. Many ideas for *Jericho* today.

TUESDAY, 3 OCTOBER / FREDERICTON
Recalculation shows my bank balance not quite so bad as I feared. Work on *Pagodas* at the office (no students today) and on *Jericho* (planning) at home, where I cook myself a decent pineapple chicken stir-fry. All the ivy and the appropriate maples have turned deep red, but the temperature today remains warm.

WEDNESDAY, 4 OCTOBER / FREDERICTON
Try a new barbershop that's full of old hockey pictures and an enormous gold-framed portrait of the Queen. The barber is the taciturn, inarticulate type from the New Brunswick back country rather than the somewhat garrulous kind that's closer to old oral traditions and storytelling. Work on *Pagodas,* then supply-teach a poetry class for Ross at the Ice House. Then back to the office for more work.

SATURDAY, 7 OCTOBER / FREDERICTON
Up fairly early to get the papers, as I have several pieces and mentions today. At first all I can find is the *Gleaner.* I'm reading it in Tim Hortons (the only place open) when I see Joe Blades. We sit talking for an hour about publishing, journal-keeping and how we're going to fill an hour of airtime on the radio on Tuesday night. He has a system of note-taking not unlike my own, with pocket-sized spiral-bound notebooks, picked up one year, then laid aside, only to be written in again years later. Also, he carries round a bound sketchbook, seven by nine, in which he makes notes on everything (not in the calligraphic penmanship of the former art student that he is). He dates the entries with a revolving rubber stamp: clever idea. Back here for breakfast and lunch, read a book I have to review, then rearrange all the furniture in this dump to give myself some light and better flow.

TUESDAY, 10 OCTOBER / FREDERICTON

See only one student today and so spend most of the time on *Pagodas*. I reach the point in the story where writing becomes emotionally draining. Work until dinnertime, when it's time to do the interview with Joe Blades for his writing programme on campus radio. He's not much of an interviewer, has no journalistic background; but he has more important qualities and the tape may have some stuff I can salvage in the transcription. We walk downtown together afterwards, and I buy him a sandwich (Joe is always grateful for food but never lets on). He kindly lends me two books. I ask his expert advice about living in Vancouver on $1,250 a month, and frankly he is sceptical that the goal can be achieved. In bed, I spend a lot of time thinking about Peggy, rumoured to be a possible Nobel Prize winner late this week or next. Remember an offhand remark of Joe's: "When my father was this age [Joe's 39] he'd been on heart pills for two years."

WEDNESDAY, 11 OCTOBER / FREDERICTON

Off to the university where there is a big (actually, small) flap about my sending out so much mail the other day. I resolve to do my mailing at the post office downtown, outside the confines (and I mean confines) of the university, just as I have had to do with a gym, office supplies, library services card, and, so I would guess, photocopying. In his absence, I take over a mandatory first-year composition class for Mark Jarman. A pretty unsophisticated bunch of kids – passing notes, giggling, staring blankly, in one case falling asleep. There should be a remedial course. I pity Mark having to teach this section. Then today a fairly successful reading from *Madagascar* at Westminster Books. I am in pretty decent form, good questions after. Small but attentive crowd and I sell some books.

THURSDAY, 12 OCTOBER / FREDERICTON

Ross is back from his readings on the West Coast, saying several people tell him about my moving there but he can't remember who. I work on *Pagodas*. Will soon face the dilemma of making the whole first draft into a whole second. Spend far too much time on the Net – an odd phase I'm going through, related no doubt to lack of human communication in Fredericton. Resolve to accomplish tomorrow (full morning) all the chores I failed to do today.

MONDAY, 16 OCTOBER / FREDERICTON
The curiosities of this tiny apartment. The bathroom lights often go out, because of a problem in the ancient breaker, although the switch doesn't trip. Takes me weeks to figure out that I must reset the switch anyway before using the loo. Likewise, the television, once turned off, will come on again, of its own accord, at two or three in the morning, wrecking any hope of a decent night's sleep. So I unplug it. If it still comes on without visible power, I'm moving or seeking out an exorcist.

TUESDAY, 17 OCTOBER / FREDERICTON
Sleep poorly so up for a healthy breakfast at 5:00 a.m. and at the gym when it opens at six. More discipline, that's what I need. Do one small writing job, making my day's expenses: that's my plan. Then return emails, work on *Pagodas* and *Jericho*. This is the first truly cold morning, with heavy frost on the ground until late.

FRIDAY, 20 OCTOBER / FREDERICTON
The copy-edited ms of *Assassins* arrives from Random House. This and the GST will consume my weekend. I drink some wine at the Lord Beaverbrook Hotel with Walter Learning.[22] Seems a splendid fellow. Promises to introduce me to his local circle.

SUNDAY, 22 OCTOBER / FREDERTICTON
I'm awake at 4:30 or so and go to the campus at 6:00 a.m. and work at rewriting the *Assassins* introduction for Anne C. Ross Leckie turns up about 2 p.m. He seems less fond of me today, but still genial. Before returning to the Lamonte Building I find a Friday message saying that Tim Brook and Fay are in town and staying at the Lord Beaverbrook. I'm not surprised, as I read last week of a conference of China scholars to be held on campus this weekend. But by the time I get the message, they have checked out.

A graffito over the urinal in the English Department: "Jesus is watching you pee!" I suspect that the writer is affiliated with the sister institution, St Thomas's.

22 Walter Learning (b. 1938), actor, playwright, and theatre director.

MONDAY, 23 OCTOBER / FREDERICTON

At the office today from about 8:30 to 4:30. Main accomplishments are getting a long letter and the revised introduction off to Anne at Random by fax and writing an extra backup column for when I'm away in Toronto early next month. See two students – or rather, people from the community – and lead a busy electronic life. Manage to stick to my schedule. Positively Old Testament in my resolve.

WEDNESDAY, 25 OCTOBER / FREDERICTON

A sound night's sleep despite word from Vancouver that the tenant absolutely refuses to pay and is being evicted on 1 November, a financial setback to me of perhaps $7,000 (though the half of that representing his uncollectible arrears is presumably a tax deduction). A big hit when I'm financially the most vulnerable. Yet it doesn't appear to worry me much, for I'm feeling pretty upright these days, all things considered, as though spring and not winter were round the corner. Later: I take the bull by the horns and call Neil in Vancouver. He assures me that all is well, though the paper may not legally change hands until December. "The most that can happen is that I hire you on contract," he says, "but I think we'll be able to proceed with you on staff," as we both wish.

THURSDAY, 26 OCTOBER / FREDERICTON

Awake about 7:30 feeling rested. Still calm and optimistic following yesterday's talk with Neil. The sight of fog on the river is so subtle, dramatic, and mysterious that I believe Turner would have liked to paint it. Work steadily (get the first half of the manuscript back to Random) but get a bit frazzled and testy by the end of the day: too few calories, I'm betting. Get fresh ingredients and cook up a large pot of vegetable soup.

SATURDAY, 28 OCTOBER / FREDERICTON

Sleep soundly and unvexed. Arise to see the first day of bad weather of this Fredericton stay – extraordinary that we have made it nearly to November unscathed. The big sky is leaden, the river rough, large trees bending this way and that, sizable pieces of rubbish being blown round and round, as high as birds fly. Looks cold, but I've not been out yet for the newspapers, and from the window I see no one on the street. I usually look east to the federal building and the Lord Beaverbrook Hotel to see how people are decked out before going outdoors in the morning, but the practice is not always reliable, because the citizens here are a hardy breed and don't necessarily dress warmly when it's cold.

MONDAY, 30 OCTOBER / FREDERICTON
Spend the morning fixing the second chapter of *Jericho*, which I then lose in the computer, far beyond retrieval. So I begin to re-keyboard it from my hard copy. Hope to finish this chore tomorrow. Need to get parts of both *Jericho* and *Three Pagodas* in shape to give to Rhona Lawlor for editing if I am to have clean copy (if needed) in Toronto. One should always have clean copy in case of ill fortune in the same way one requires clean underwear in case accident strikes. A cold, wet, blustery night.

WEDNESDAY, I NOVEMBER / FREDERICTON
The end of my first two months here, and although I haven't accomplished as much as I would have liked, I have accomplished something and gone some way towards figuring out how I'm going to live in Vancouver. I've regained many survival skills I had feared were lost, have begun to write poems and stories again, have whittled away at *Three Pagodas Pass* and *Jericho*, and along the way have tried to live in a healthy fashion.

THURSDAY, 2 NOVEMBER / TORONTO
Up at five in the morning for the flight here. Very strange but I'm prepared emotionally to see this city, my home for the past 34 years, as a stranger. Dr Morose has lost maybe 60 pounds (he won't tell me the figure) and has worked out how he can move my stuff to Vancouver round January first rather than in April. This is the news I needed. Life will be so much smoother this way. He will get out of Toronto during the two worst months of weather, returning in March to clean out his place here, with me arriving from New Brunswick in April, staying in the empty house for a while, making sure the transition to the buyer (and the buyer's cheque) goes smoothly. But the first chore I do in Toronto is stop at Random and deliver the rest of the ms to Pam Robertson who looks different every time I see her and is always gracious and charming. This evening I relax in the cheap hotel in Avenue Road. Can see Casa Loma from the window – just like a tourist.

FRIDAY, 3 NOVEMBER / TORONTO

The streets full of very rich strangers. I can honestly see that this place will soon be unknown and unknowable to me. I can barely restrain my anticipation, while continuing, of course, to pursue the virtue of patience, in which I have always been weak. Lorraine Filyer at the OAC always has run a tight, efficient jury. This time, Michael Holmes, Leanne Chow, Veronica Ross, and I.[23] Michael bumps into me at Starbucks a half hour before, and I tell him again how much I miss his friendship. He apologises, says everything is okay, that he hasn't seen J in the shop in more than a year. "I wasn't as good a friend to you as I should have been," he says. Veronica Ross, who I've never met before, is a down-to-earth professional fictioneer.

SATURDAY, 4 NOVEMBER / TORONTO

Being in Toronto makes me tense. Perhaps it's done so for the past three and a half decades. But seeing Morose in such good form was a pleasure. He and I go to a movie in the afternoon. I retreat to the hotel, heavy with mail, invoices, etc.

TUESDAY, 7 NOVEMBER / FREDERICTON

An excellent meeting this morning with Rhona, who seems to be the editor I've been seeking and can afford. Having tried her out on a couple of stories, I've now given her portions of *Three Pagodas* and *Jericho*, the ones I need to get in shape for Anne C. I'm curious to see her memo on the fiction especially, as she used to read fiction for Goose Lane [publishers].

Another month and I'll be back in Toronto for Christmas, packing all my books and stuff for Morose and Victor to take to Vancouver.

WEDNESDAY, 8 NOVEMBER / FREDERICTON

"Still we were grateful to him, for ... he showed an example of contentment to us slaves of unnecessary appetite ..." Lawrence in *Seven Pillars of Wisdom*.

---

23   Michael Holmes (b. 1966), poet and publisher; Veronica Ross (b. 1946), poet and novelist.

FRIDAY, 10 NOVEMBER / FREDERICTON
Next week looks like a light one for official duties, so I'm hopeful of extending *Jericho* a bit.

Read a book by John Braine, of all people, in which I find these words: "the only acceptable system of government for the writer is one which allows people to drop out, to huddle together in dusty, seedy, cosy corners and make a mess of their lives in their own way."

SATURDAY, 11 NOVEMBER / FREDERICTON
Remembrance Day is a big affair here, like Halloween, and I pass an honour guard, marching in close order, as I walk along Charlotte Street this morning, taking more architectural photos. I go to the Boyce Market and attend to other Saturday morning rituals.

SUNDAY, 12 NOVEMBER / FREDERICTON
Do not accomplish half the work at the office that I wish, but some. In the afternoon must attend a party at Mark Jarman and Sharon McCartney's place along Waterloo. Meet the university president and the guest of honour, Catherine Bush, who reads from her novel tomorrow night.[24] She's pale, forty-something perhaps, compelling. Educated at Yale, taught at Concordia for a couple of years, and now back in Toronto. Of the age where she considers herself sophisticated for having spent a few years in New York. Certainly bright, well-travelled, a skilled conversationalist as they say. A talker of sense. We end up having dinner at the Lord Beaverbrook, the only place open on Sunday evening for dinner in this part of town, until the scandalously late hour of 10 p.m. I like her. We exchange email addresses.

THURSDAY, 16 NOVEMBER / FREDERICTON
I am testing all my weakest spots, confronting my fears of early death, my lack of patience, my habit of wearing my heart on my sleeve. How, looking at the situation as objectively as I can, have I survived the divorce, the Vancouver fiascos, the assorted clashes, flare-ups, disasters of the past two years? Rather better than I would have done previously, though some of the negative effects have been remarkable for their duration.

24 Catherine Bush (b. 1961), author of *The Rules of Engagement* and other novels.

I must keep steady until the situation with Neil is resolved one way or another; must be prepared to adopt the new life as George Fetherling in Vancouver no matter which way the tree falls. Meanwhile, have faith that the cycle of bad luck will end. I begin to sound like Sun Tzu.

SATURDAY, 18 NOVEMBER / FREDERICTON
The post office in King's Place is open 9:00 a.m. to 1:00 p.m. on Saturday, so I am able to get the ms off to Random House. Then walk for more than an hour, eastwards, along the trail, out beyond Point Anne, but find the wind chill pretty rough. Still not quite warmed up. Having thus acquitted my walking requirement, I do stretches and weights at the gym and return to read, rest, and work. Reading a new life of Ho. Thinking of the situation at the *Vancouver Sun*, I realise that I must treat it as I do the endless electoral melodrama between Bush and Gore in the States – keep a casual eye on what the headlines tell me each day but not obsess or even become too interested. This is essential to stress reduction. Matters I cannot control should be treated with the respectful dispassion they deserve.

SUNDAY, 19 NOVEMBER / FREDERICTON
Dinner at Mei's with Eric Marks, who's come up from Saint John for the evening. He's thirty, balding, a Rhodes scholar from a small rural New Brunswick community – very thin, very literary, very easy to talk to – and such a martyr to severe allergies that he lives mostly on potatoes and carries a puffer for when he gets a little wheat or egg by mistake and goes into shock. I eat chicken sparingly, he abstains, but later, during intermission at the Holly Cole concert for which I have got us good seats, he excuses himself to run across to the Lord Beaverbrook to grab some potatoes he's stashed in his room.

Eric and I have a good evening, with a nightcap at the Beaver afterwards. I put him up there on my tab and he kindly gives me a copy (one of 300) of some of Æ's letters to Yeats, printed by Yeats' daughter (Cuala Press, Dublin, 1936). We are to meet in the LBB lobby at 8:30 a.m. so I can hitch a ride with him back to Saint John.

MONDAY, 20 NOVEMBER / SAINT JOHN
Eric and I set off in the early morning frost ("I'll just go out and warm up the car") and talk all the way to Saint John about our respective

works in progress. He tells me in considerable detail about his David-Adams-Richard-novel type of family, its various murder victims and suicides. When I read the *Globe* along the way I'm saddened and distressed to read the obituary of Libby Scheier, dead of breast cancer at fifty-four, a remarkable poet I tried to befriend for years but her hurt and anger, the sources of her two strongest books of poetry, were just too great. Eric drops me off in Prince William Street, near where he lives, before continuing on to the newspaper office. This is one of my favourite Saint John streets, with its almost unbroken row of Victorian counting-houses and godowns near the waterfront. I wander the bitterly cold streets, ducking into bookshops as I can, and turn up at Leslie J's political science seminar at 1:30 to speak on the current military and political situation in Burma. Everyone seems pleased with my performance, which ends with my urging the students to consider ways that rebels might harry the *western* frontier to cause the junta to divert troops from exterminating refugees on the eastern one. Then the department takes Leslie, another of the profs and his wife, and me out to Harry's in the market for dinner: the leading seafood place. Leslie and I then go to her and Greg's place and yak until 1:30 about poetry and politics. They have a sunny apartment near Queen's Square, an area with the houses built by shipping fortunes next to frame cottages. Greg is in much better form – thinner, healthier looking, no longer drinking, clear-eyed and rosy of cheek. Leslie sits on the sofa with her long legs curled under her. I sleep over. Their hospitality is perfect.

2001

Using a publicity tour for *The Book of Assassins* as my cover, I went cross-country and resettled in Vancouver, where I continued work on the novel *Jericho*.

MONDAY, 1 JANUARY / TORONTO

I awake fifty-two years old, astonished, resolved. A cold, sad day ahead. Virtually all of the packing is now complete – Morose and I work together happily all day – waiting only the arrival of the container and the crew on Thursday. I've determined to spend Friday and Saturday nights in an inexpensive downtown hotel rather than face the echo in this dark empty house.

Some thoughts on my name change. It indicates that I am still mutating. And every time anyone calls me "George" I am reminded of GSF and then of my own mortality as well and so am encouraged to use the day more fully.

THURSDAY, 4 JANUARY / TORONTO

A day I won't forget, the day I escape Toronto and the Annex. Everything is packed, but Dr Morose is a nervous wreck. The twenty-foot container is dropped off about 1:00 p.m. and the doors on it close at about 4:00 p.m., thanks to a good crew, led by Victor, the Australian archaeologist who, until recently, worked at the beer store stacking cartons and really knows how to pack. His mother, a scientist, is a White Russian from Harbin, where his grandfather designed many of the buildings in the Russian sector (which I remember seeing while on the trans-Siberian trip); his other grandfather was the last White general killed by the

Bolsheviks, in 1923. Periodically, and paradoxically, Victor looks a great deal like Lenin. He speaks with a bit of Strine and is strong as a sinewy bull. Twilight [his girlfriend] helps as well, thus earning some merit. We end up using the full container, not the seven feet Morose at first thought might suffice. An emotional moment for me, so I don't linger when the work is done but check into the little hotel in Charles Street. I can't say that I will miss my life here as it has been the past few years, though I will remember it. I'm not starting over, but carrying on, continually. This morning I stopped at the bagel place in Bathurst Street and ran into Marty Ahvenus, the genial old bookseller. How fitting that I should have a good long pleasant talk with him, one of the first people to befriend me in Toronto, many decades ago.

THURSDAY, 11 JANUARY / FREDERICTON

Neil emails from the *Sun* to say that I should fly out in early March to talk turkey. As feared, CanWest has imposed a hiring freeze across the board, so he will have to pay me on contract. Not the perfect solution but I am happy – overjoyed in fact, as only an hour ago I poured out my deep-seated financial anxiety in a message to Anne C.

FRIDAY, 26 JANUARY / HALIFAX

I check into the Waverley (1876), where Oscar Wilde stayed on his 1882 tour, visit some bookshops as I take exercise in moderate cold. Halifax, like Saint John, is truly urban. I love the steep streets lined with both frame dwellings and stone houses, the former wholly vernacular, the latter perhaps architect-designed at a low level. One can always sense if not see in which direction the harbour lies. Today it is full of naval vessels receiving maintenance. I spend the evening working frantically on various sets of chores: bills, manuscript evaluations, and the like. I check my email but find nothing important – happily. Later: I don't care for this room, the former front parlour of the house or part of it. In fact, I don't care for this hotel, which in its feel and administration is too much like a B&B. I despise B&Bs as their professed hominess is actually unbearably intrusive. Give me the anonymity of a genuine hotel over the surveillance of a jail-house or a B&B. (I remember having to flee that horrible place in Los Angeles that DSF had recommended so highly. No locks on the doors, no taxis, guards with homespun folksy smiles all round – it was like being trapped inside a PBS pledge drive. I ended up at the old Ambassador of blessed memory, saw the kitchen where Robert Kennedy was shot.)

WEDNESDAY, 31 JANUARY / FREDERICTON

From [Somerset] Maugham's "Masterson" (a Burma story): "He was a tall, dark fellow with the aloofness of manner you often find in those who have lived much alone in unfrequented places. Men like this are a little restless in the company of others and though in the smoking-room of a ship or at the club bar they may be talkative and convivial, telling their story with the rest, joking and glad sometimes to narrate their unusual experiences, they seem always to hold everything back. They have a life in themselves that they keep apart, and there is a look in their eyes, as it were turned inwards, that informs you that this hidden life is the only one that signifies to them. And now and then their eyes betray their wariness with the social round into which hazard or the fear of seeming odd has for a moment forced them. They seem to long for the monotonous solitude of some place of their predilection where they can be once more alone with the reality they have found." Instantly recognisable as Maugham but so much subtler and more soundly constructed than his usual.

FRIDAY, 2 FEBRUARY / SAINT JOHN

Writing this in Greg [Cook] and Leslie's bedroom (to my embarrassment, they give me the good room again) after a long night of talking about Thai politics, counter-intelligence, Alden Nowlan – everything – in their living room. I arrive on the early bus, kick round town, admiring it all the more in more moderate weather this time, then meet Eric Marks for lunch at Billy's Seafood in the City Market. Eric has chosen the restaurant, unaware that I am booked to return there at 6 p.m. to meet with the vice-president of UNBSJ who is head of the international programme to discuss the possibility of teaching Canadian literature for a term in China at the university level. This is one of the ideas I have up my sleeve in case Neil won't let me do the *Sun* books column after all. An exhausting day and evening.

SATURDAY, 3 FEBRUARY / FREDERICTON
Greg and Leslie drop me off for the 9:30 a.m. bus. The ride passes quickly with the novel I'm reading. Nap on arrival, then to the campus to prepare for tomorrow and Monday. Greg's unusual manner of speech – so many ellipses and curlicue hand gestures, so much pointed circumlocution used to such generous ends. His beard grows ever greyer and still more biblical.

SUNDAY, 4 FEBRUARY / FREDERICTON
A productive time at the office, where I see the graffito "Why Theory?" written above the English Department urinal. Below the question, someone has answered: "Scholasticism." Beneath that a further rebuttal: "A matter of degree."

MONDAY, 12 FEBRUARY / FREDERICTON
Dark days but that's the youth we were given.

FRIDAY, 16 FEBRUARY / FREDERICTON
The old sense of the word *vivacity* – surviving winter. That's what I'm doing here, tucked out of harm's way.

Exchange email today with Chris Moore in Bangkok.[1] One could disappear there quite easily and finally if necessary.

SATURDAY, 17 FEBRUARY / FREDERICTON
Browsing one of the antiquarian book sites on the Web, I come on the copy of a book of mine I inscribed for [the poet] Stanley Cooperman when I spoke to his class at SFU in June 1969. I remember walking across Lions Gate Bridge to get to his hillside house, trekking through woods part way. So long ago and yet how clearly I recall sounds, sensations, and encounters of that spring and summer. I felt bad when Stanley killed himself a few years later and have often wondered what became of Jennifer. Remarried perhaps, possibly living in the US; but I don't l know why I think this. I scribble these words in the quiet time of the evening, when all I hear is the scratching of the pen's nib on this paper

1   Christopher G. Moore (b. 1952), expat Canadian thriller writer and novelist.

– that is, until the space heater kicks in for a few minutes. Morose sends a last transmission from Vancouver today, having done his job admirably well, I think; he boards the bus back east tomorrow. Suddenly I am conscious of being in Fredericton reading the poem about Greece that Karen Connelly wrote while in Fredericton.[2]

SATURDAY, 3 MARCH / FREDERICTON

The other day, I found myself confessing to Bill Cameron that if BC doesn't work out I can always disappear into Asia.[3] People assume that this would be an impossibility for a European, but in fact the sheer worthlessness of a European makes the goal practical and relatively easy to achieve. Big fuss in the weekend papers about Canada Customs intercepting foreign mail and turning over the contents to various other government agencies for input into databases of a sinister or suspicious nature. But Jesus! I've known this for years, and the villains aren't limited to Customs or the targets to mail from outside the country. More and more activities, associations, relationships in Canada become illegal daily, monthly, yearly. This growing authoritarianism is one of the major triggers of my feelings.

WEDNESDAY, 7 MARCH / VANCOUVER

Up at 4:00 a.m. to catch a six o'clock flight to Toronto, where I make an easy connection to Vancouver. I swear that Toronto is the only ugly place in Canada. Flying over the Prairies at 39,000 feet, inspecting the frozen coulees, like crystal rivers, and then, in the mountains, the actual river valleys frozen solid, of course, but with fog down there taking the place of liquid. I feel better about my existence the moment I get into Vancouver. Morose has done an even more superb job on the flat than I had imagined, unpacking, arranging, writing manuals and treatises on how to work this and that. The place is small but the bedroom quite large. First order of business tomorrow, once I've met with the banker at 10:00, is to get a handyman to work attaching and refitting bookshelves. That's the key to the problem of the unpacked boxes, which in turn prevent

2 Karen Connelly (b. 1969), novelist and poet, author of *Burmese Lessons* and *The Lizard Cage*.
3 Bill Cameron (1943–2005), journalist, broadcaster, and documentarian.

painting or decorating. Still, I feel I'm under way. Staying tonight only at the Sylvia Hotel.

FRIDAY, 9 MARCH / VANCOUVER
Walk the Seawall circuit so early that I see the full moon replaced by the sun like two numerals descending and disappearing mechanically on an old-fashioned manual cash register.

TUESDAY, 13 MARCH / TORONTO
Pearson Airport is as far as the weather in Atlantic Canada has permitted me to venture. I show virtually no signs of stress during the flight cancellation and ensuing chaos all round. Spend the night in an airport Sheraton reading Henry James. The last time I read Henry James in a hotel room was in Newfoundland in the early or mid-1980s.

FRIDAY, 23 MARCH / SAINT JOHN
Feeling much better after a proper sleep and Anne Carson's new book.[4] Do some work on another of the sketches, walk the old Uptown streets, where so many of the buildings bear the dates 1877 or 1878, chilling evidence still of the Great Fire of '77. A little cold, a little snowy, but in no way extreme. Locate the military surplus store I discovered when I was here many years ago and delight to find they still stock used Canadian Forces black leather work gloves, the best I've ever owned for chores such as wood-chopping; I buy two pair. Saint John is one of those cities where one can still see how the money is made. Shipping in the harbour, smoke rising like cartoon balloons from tall stacks and chimneys. Of course, the commercial heart pushes out even further from Uptown, leaving hollow buildings such as the magnificent Dominion Custom House and the old Bank of New Brunswick next to it. But then this leaves the shipping business, the antique trade, the bars and pubs and strip joints close to the harbour, as of old, I have no doubt.

4 Anne Carson (b. 1950), poet and classicist, author of *Short Talks* and other works.

SATURDAY, 24 MARCH / SAINT JOHN

A brief notice in the papers this morning of Louis Dudek's death in Montreal.[5] I've always felt that George Bowering nailed him correctly in *Curious* as a bitter, hateful conservative who especially despised the young without showing a great deal of sympathy for his own generation either. (Yet the Bowering axis later warmed to him, as there was a special Dudek issue of *Open Letter*.) That entire generation of Canadian poets, who came of literary age in the 1950s and were the dominant mature voices of the late 1960s, had severe personality disorders, whether as mild as Purdy's incessant lechery or Ray Souster's Mittyesque fantasy life lived unrestrained – and so on, down to Birney's general careerism, the ego of Layton, Waddington's sheer meanness of spirit.[6] The near-hermits such as Avison survive the best in memory simply because they *were* near-hermits, unknown, unknowable.[7]

SUNDAY, 25 MARCH / SAINT JOHN

Much to my surprise (for I didn't send a copy of the book to the review editor) the weekend *National Post* carries what seems to me an enormous and entirely positive review of Subway's Emma Goldman book. I suspect the benevolent hand of Gerald Owen, to whom I *did* send a set of proofs, hoping, vainly, to provoke a piece on the Discovery page, which he edits. So far, the book is two for two, a fact I hope to see reflected in sales when the new figures come from the U of T warehouse.

MONDAY, 26 MARCH / SAINT JOHN

Anne Compton picks me up shortly after 6:00 p.m. and drives me to the Lorenzo Society reading, where she gives me the most gracious introduction I've ever had.[8] A good-sized audience, and I read rather fluently and am asked intelligent questions. Everyone seems pleased. Afterwards, the society takes a few of the students out to dinner Uptown along with Pat

5   Louis Dudek (1918–2001), prolific poet and critic.
6   Miriam Waddington (1917–2004), poet, author of *Say Yes* and other works.
7   Margaret Avison (1918–2007), poet, author of *Winter Sun* and other collections.
8   Anne Compton (b. 1947), poet and essayist.

Joas, the bookseller, Greg (Leslie arrives in time for dessert after a four-teen-hour day) and Eric. Long vivid conversations. Very late when I walk back to the hotel from the restaurant in Canterbury Street.

SATURDAY, 31 MARCH / FREDERICTON
Awake in Saint John to see a huge Norwegian (I think) container ship in the harbour and considerable snow on the ground. From the window of the bus back here I see the woods as an enormous wicker basket steadily filling with snow.

WEDNESDAY, 4 APRIL / FREDERICTON
I am nervous about being interviewed by Bill Cameron for the *National Post* profile. Bill calls at 9:00 a.m. to announce that he is in Saint John, where he has flown in error, but we arrange to meet at noon. He still looks remarkably like the young journalist at whose coach house apartment Sarah and I attended a party in 1968 or '69. He picks up some of my books at the campus bookstore, and we lunch at the Lord Beaverbrook (adequate), with Bill asking penetrating questions – he's no amateur, though he seems a bit uncomfortable in literary waters. We then try to put each other at ease. We discuss old lovers, people we've both known as friends. I wonder if, after filling the last leaf of this journal, I will, on rereading the thing, find that I've been stalking myself.

SUNDAY, 8 APRIL / FREDERICTON
A devastating review of *Assassins* in the Sunday *Star* in Toronto sends me into a frightening downward spiral.

TUESDAY, 10 APRIL / FREDERICTON
I know that danger has passed and contentment has returned as I lie in bed in a state of resumed consciousness but before knowing quite where I am. The totally new aspect of these periods, such as the one occasioned by the *Star* on Sunday, is how they attack my concentration, making me unfit to think about anything else or to do anything else. Concentration without benefit, for I am in no better position to think a problem through.

Spend all day ducking email from the author-bashing gossip writer who also peddles trash to *Frank*. (Spent some of yesterday avoiding him too.) Early this evening he calls me at the hotel, having got the number from an unwary publicist at Random House. I refuse the interview and tell him why. He admits who put him up to calling. I tell him he will have to proceed without my co-operation. I won't give evidence against myself at my own show trial.

WEDNESDAY, 11 APRIL / FREDERICTON
The Random publicist tells me that CBC *This Morning* has declined to have me on because the show is "not comfortable with the material" in the *Assassins* book. I should hope not. Why *Canada AM* on CTV wants me is a mystery. The book has absolutely nothing to say to their audience.

SUNDAY, 15 APRIL / FREDERICTON
Not his feast day, but a day to consider Paul, who took the simple teachings of Jesus and seeing an opportunity turned them into the first truly multinational megacorp, selling superstition on a global basis. Paul was the first American.

FRIDAY, 20 APRIL / TORONTO
Day ends when the Calgary publicist tells me that the book editor of the *Herald*, Charles Mandel, is Eli's son and is "deeply offended" by something I wrote about his father and for that reason won't see me. In fact, I always tried to be fair with Eli who – this is embarrassing but absolutely correct – despised me for my dysphonia, hanging up on me when I had lapsed on the phone, once telling [a mutual friend] that my handicap showed I was evil. Good grief. Otherwise a tiring but not too terrible day of television and some print interviews: Phil Marchand of the *Star* and Brian Bethune of *Maclean's*. The latter I meet for the first time: a former mediaevalist fallen to journalism. Plans some little squib. Phil takes shorthand as usual but doesn't know when the piece might run, also as usual. He is friendly, though. The itinerary for Calgary looks positively hellish: twelve hours of solid radio and TV of the worst sort. Tomorrow morning I expect to see a bad review in the *Globe*, making my agony complete. How I hate this whole author business. I'm tired of being hurt.

SATURDAY, 21 APRIL / CALGARY
In a perfectly friendly email from the *Sun*'s book editor, Rebecca Wigod, I learn that my first column is in today's paper. Also today, a perfectly

fine "New and Noteworthy" capsule review in the *Post*, which is precisely the way that Andy Lamey [the book review editor] should have
handled the matter, given the coverage of the author in last Saturday's
edition. So I am prepared to move on to Calgary with a lighter heart if
also with heavy luggage. I realise only late in the morning that part of my
problem today is that I'm a tiny bit hungover. An Advil makes me think
more clearly about what I was playing with in my mind yesterday: how
the self-destructive imagination is closely related to contemplation and
for some people even to prayer and that, for me at least, it both cleans
and focuses the mind.

SUNDAY, 22 APRIL / CALGARY

A terrible time getting here from Toronto after I was temporarily banned
from Air Canada following an argument with them at the ticket counter
during which I contrasted them unfavourably with Aeroflot in terms
of friendliness and efficiency. Today I have the concierge scrambling
all over town trying to find yesterday's *Vancouver Sun* while I attend
to paperwork and steel myself for tomorrow's twelve-hour promotion
schedule, all or very nearly all of it worthless. No point at all, just five
minutes of radio or TV here and there, mixed with signing store stock at
Chapter's and Indigo. This kind of activity is the sign of a publicist without contacts, pull, or ideas.

To dinner this evening at Don LePan's in Sunnyside, where I meet his
g.f. Michelle. Excellent conversation until about 11:30 when I must return to the Palliser to get *some* sleep. Don's Broadview Press offices, as it
happens, are in the old Grain Exchange, virtually next door.

MONDAY, 23 APRIL / VANCOUVER

Finally I arrive in my new home and collect all the accumulated mail and
banter with [my new neighbours] Bev and Marty. This after a long hard
day in Calgary, from *Breakfast Television* (I am on immediately after the
leg-waxing demonstration) to a phone-in show with a host whose first
question is, "Is your name pronounced the way it sounds?" Still, the
publicist and I get along quite well throughout the day. Then problems
at the airport – arrogant thugs at Air Canada again. Partly because I have
overweight hand luggage, they at first refuse me seating, but I manage to

get aboard in the end, though not without insults from them. I'll soon have 100,000 points, enough for another trip to Asia, possibly in the autumn, but I'll use one of their partner airlines if I can. Exhausted, I go early to bed and sleep long, and have no dreams that I recall.

FRIDAY, 27 APRIL / VANCOUVER

Some frustration today, some ups and downs (I retreat to bed in the afternoon), but I rise as the day progresses, write a book column in the nick of time, and by evening I feel quite mellow, partly in the hope of good news in tomorrow's newspapers. I feel that I am beginning to priorise my life. I should so like to be content in my last phase of life. I browse local shops. In the local bookstore I see *Thirty Days to a More Spiritual You*, a title that seems to me to have enormous stress potential.

How much supposed secrecy is merely forgetfulness.

SUNDAY, 29 APRIL / VANCOUVER

Spend the morning on Peter Newman's tugboat, asking him about his heart problems, his divorces, his late rediscovery of his Judaism. He is extremely forthcoming. A really moving interview if only I can recapture some of its honesty on the page. It is sad to see Peter at 72, short of breath, dappled with liver spots, slightly stooped. Others have always mocked him; I've always admired him.

MONDAY, 30 APRIL / VANCOUVER

A day when about everything goes well and I am wonderfully happy to be alive and in this beautiful city. I straighten out my banking mess, move on to a brief exchange with Neil (I drop him off a signed set of my books to replace those he lost in the fire), then lunch with Jim Sutherland, the *Mix* editor, and Rebecca Wigod, the books editor. Sutherland is smart and knows that he knows a lot and is quite agreeable to all my suggestions; I like them both.

FRIDAY, 11 MAY / VANCOUVER

An even more handsome day, marred only by the sad news from Theresa Greenwood in Kingston that Barry Hill-Tout has died of cancer. Jen

Williams here at noon. She weeps in joy at her wedding presents. We drive out to a nursery somewhere in Point Grey to buy flowers for her picnic on Sunday (but she can't decide). I return here to receive a Toronto closing-time call from Anne C, who has come round to agreeing to contract the completion of *Jericho*. She is a skilled chess player.

WEDNESDAY, 23 MAY / VANCOUVER

A phone call from Sharon Thesen, who's married yet again, this time to an Australian, and has converted to Catholicism, which doesn't surprise me in the least. Also, she's taken on the editorship of the *Capilano Review*.

THURSDAY, 24 MAY / VANCOUVER

The past week or so I've been struggling with a difficult decision: whether to make the trip east and do the two writers' workshops, in Toronto and Fredericton, for $2,400 – and three weeks of my time. On the one hand, I could use the money. On the other, the Toronto workshop has no students for me and I hesitate to be away from Vancouver for that long, especially when I'm so newly arrived and enjoying it so and not yet firmly established at the *Sun*. So this morning, I achieve a final decision, and inform both parties that I won't be able to attend. Everyone seems very understanding once I explain in detail. Also this a.m., I register for the beginning Chinese reading course I've been wanting to take, which I would have missed by being in Fredericton. I feel good about these decisions and the ways I have arrived at them. Another, more nebulous reason: I'm just not ready yet to see the East again.

A very moving lunch today with Peter Newman at his really quite splendid house (built by a late architect friend of Peter's as his own home). The highlight is a Klimt, one of the few artworks his father was able to ship to his London office when the Nazis invaded Prague – a painting one sees reproduced often but assumes isn't in private hands, certainly not in Vancouver. Even more so than on his tug a couple of weeks ago, Peter is showing his years and talking of his death even as he plots and plans for future living and works. When he leaves the office to take a phone call from *Maclean's*, I move my eyes round the room and cannot help but see the instructions for his funeral lying in a wooden tray on his desk. Downstairs, his famous fire-resistant filing cabinets in a long row, such as one might imagine J. Edgar Hoover to have had. Above them, copies of all the Canadian, US, and overseas editions of his many books. He enlists me in a plan to begin a luncheon club of off-the-record chat for Vancouver writers. Peter, it turns out, is a great founder of dinner clubs and the like, somewhat in the eighteenth-century manner (though I doubt that's a comparison he would click to). He plays me a bit of Stan Kenton and shows me a letter from his old friend Izzy Asper, who is himself a maniacal Kenton fan (imagine, two of them in a country Canada's size).[9]

SATURDAY, 2 JUNE / VANCOUVER

I have a weird dream in which P.K. Page in Victoria suddenly says of one of George Woodcock's friends, "I hate her. I suspect that she's a compulsive journal-keeper."

SUNDAY, 10 JUNE / VANCOUVER

By the close of office hours I have piled a lot of envelopes in the Out basket and am reading my bootlegged photocopy of George Woodcock's private diaries. How the poor man suffered under Inge's stinging temper. (That's what my life might have been like.) How he hid his daily troubles from the world, financial ones especially, and also the deep underlying uncertainty he felt about his decision to live in Canada: a matter he had to keep to himself in order to enjoy the fleeting and, in retrospect, superficial respect of his peers and contemporaries.

THURSDAY, 14 JUNE / VANCOUVER

A drink at the Sylvia with John Burns of the *Straight*. He brings up the past, saying, "There was one sentence in the piece I did on you at the time of the Woodcock book that I want to apologise for." I say, waving the matter aside: "Oh, the remark about my speech." "Well, it was wrong of me, and I want you to know that I've grown up a lot since then." I reply: "That's gracious of you to say but entirely unnecessary."

9   Israel Asper (1932–2003), television and newspaper mogul.

SATURDAY, 23 JUNE / VANCOUVER

Curiously but happily, I find that I'm about to resume work on *Jericho* after so many months away. I attribute my absence to ambient tension, what I mistook for a lack of the support I'd hoped for from Anne (who came through eventually), and my own natural indolence. The trick, it turns out, I believe, taking a cue from this journal, is writing in pen and ink – specifically at the now-cleared kitchen table, a fortress of solitude in early morning and late evening, where I have been jotting these lines the past couple of weeks. That is, at the far end of the flat from the desk and the computer, which I now associate with journalism and correspondence. In preparation, I'm going through the *Jericho* files, trying to pick up the thread. Is this a sign that I've priorised my task at last, signalling a respite in this building's condo wars and the end of the settling period? I certainly hope so.

TUESDAY, 26 JUNE / VANCOUVER

Finally connect with Dennis Duffy for a drink at the Sylvia. He's been resident here only since last August, and is doing a good bit of travelling. He's younger-looking than his sixty-two or so years, red-haired and be-freckled and still a bit golly-gee in his diction. Always a friendly figure in my life (though I could never get him to read anything I've ever written). We talk about death and such.

SATURDAY, 30 JUNE / VANCOUVER

Exiles are settled. I'm still a refugee, wandering from spot to spot, hoping always to find a place where I will be accepted. Haven't found it yet. So many writers are this way. Sometimes I believe that mistrust, conde-scension, and even hatred of outsiders are all that have held society to-gether all these years. People are simply hypocritical and two-faced in not acknowledging publicly what they make socially obvious everyday: that there are three levels of citizenship, rather as there are levels of the Order of Canada, depending on place of birth. People in the first-class lounge never accept me and never will. Second-class passengers are more likely to treat me with normal human respect. I speak when spoken to and keep my eyes averted, trying to strengthen my self-sufficient non-involvement in the Daoist and antiauthoritarian sense.

TUESDAY, 3 JULY / VANCOUVER

A reporter calls me looking for a comment on Mordecai Richler's death. I have been hearing for a few months that he was perilously ill, but wasn't aware that he had passed, as the end came after today's *Globe*, *Post*, and *Sun* had been put to bed and I don't often watch news on television. I hope I said helpful words, as I'm always careful to be kind to young reporters as I was one myself and remember everyone who has been decent to me or not decent to me since 1965. My first meeting with Richler was an informal evening with him and Brian Moore with four or five of us young writers at Massey College in 1969.[10]

WEDNESDAY, 4 JULY / VANCOUVER

Extraordinary coverage of Richler's death and life in all the papers, not simply in the *Post* where he was the mascot and where so many of his family members are employed. The entire front page of the *Globe*, for example. Obits, outside articles by Peggy A and others, a special supplement, editorials, time-lines, the life in pictures, and so on. Bob F supplies the only real perspective, and I send him a note.

THURSDAY, 5 JULY / VANCOUVER

A new bout of condo politics today after [a fellow owner] tells me in the lift (in response to the word *Hello*) that he launched another lawsuit earlier this morning. Number five.

SUNDAY, 8 JULY / VANCOUVER

Thinking about the entire period surrounding this transition from East to West: the final year at the Albany Avenue house, the *Assassins* book, the Fredericton interlude, the initial attempts to establish myself here. I notice my skilled use of feint and diversion in controlling the speed of messages and information. Previously I could use coloured smoke only to mask a retreat; this time I used it to obscure forward motion, advancing under the confusion I created. Now the diversion is over, and I must begin to assess and plan.

10 Brian Moore (1921–1999), author of *The Luck of Ginger Coffey* and other novels.

TUESDAY, 10 JULY / VANCOUVER

Finish first draft of the third chapter of *Jericho* (having finished one and two in New Brunswick). A challenge to tell it not only in a female voice but also in conversational tone. Good thing I've read so much Defoe in my time. The other challenge is to keep the story qua story always on the move. This is easier with the parts that actually describe travel of course. Two more chapters of the same length need to follow – about fifty or fifty-five notebook pages each. This will be a short novel but not a novella, for the structure is completely novelistic. I'm eager to complete the draft so that I can start fixing it, preparatory to putting it aside to age a bit (not too much), whereupon I can solicit advice from outside readers, fix some more, then put it in the drawer for more curing. I always worry that Anne C won't get back to me. This book is something I'm writing both in search of a certain technique and for inventory purposes, you might say.

SUNDAY, 15 JULY / VANCOUVER

Hermiticism cannot be escaped but a change of hermitage every now and then does a body good. I'm quickly getting rid of the East and its people. The isolation and indifference here to the East is almost perfect and will be my salvation. People outside these circumstances must believe that emigration is running away from problems – Bernadette, for example, told me as much flatly – but rather the reverse is true. The beneficial effects of rejuvenation here may delay my physical decline. I hope so (though it's hard to believe this on such a day).

WEDNESDAY, 25 JULY / VANCOUVER

First go to see the small-press printer Tom Snyders, who lives and works in an industrial space in Franklin Street, across the hall from a sweatshop full of poor Asian women and upstairs, he explains, from BC's largest porn studio. He is a young fellow full of ideas if somewhat weak on the necessary follow-through techniques. Then to New Star [publishers] to see Rolf. We have a bite and a drink at the Havana, then he drives me to the Sylvia where he's meeting some visiting author. Get back to find an email saying that Anne has offered a $6,000 advance for the novel. Dean wonders if I'm insulted. I'm delighted: that's $5,000 more than I expected.

SUNDAY, 29 JULY / VANCOUVER

A call from Peter Newman, back from European research for his memoirs; he found a former inmate who led him through the Nazi camp where most of the Newman family perished. In a short while he begins cruising on the tug until Labour Day, to get the experience out of his mind. He volunteers to speak again to Donna Logan [at the University of British Columbia] when he lunches with her next week. Always so helpful, Peter. He's never treated me like a foreigner (being one himself), and pretends never to have noticed my speech. He says his health was fine on the trip, but tells real horror stories of health care here. His cardiologist, the head of the department at St Paul's, has told him to go to Seattle in an emergency. We agree that Vancouver and BC are places without a normal political culture, which is why things such as health care and transit cannot be fixed when they are broken.

TUESDAY, 31 JULY / VANCOUVER

I return from the Seawall to find an email from the *Sun* requesting a tribute to [the poet] Eldon Grier, who has died.

SATURDAY, 4 AUGUST / VANCOUVER

More vicious personal abuse in the *Sun* this morning, as well as my Grier obit with my name wrong. I grow disillusioned. A long walk with Mary [Maillard] round the Seawall in the rain; she's a good sport to put up with me when I'm feeling down. With one portion of my mind, I still consider going to Thailand, where health care is plentiful, of high quality, and cheap. Shortly before closing, I meet up with Don Stewart at MacLeod's, where he's done a $3,700 day, and we take the Skytrain to his place near Clark Park where Ann (why does a Catholic not spell it Anne?) is full of bonhomie. Don is a remarkable fellow. He's just turned fifty and has had the bookshop since shortly after coming to Vancouver at twenty-one. He's amazingly well read, often coming up with unexpected insights or bits of accurate information no matter what topic is in the air. He shows me some of the highlights of his truly outstanding anarchism collection. The house is – the only word for it – funky. Vernacular, old, eccentric, well cared for, slightly redolent of the late '60s, full of art, books, posters, cats, and good feelings. Booksellers' folk tales exchanged freely. I am full of wine and feeling much brighter by the end of the evening. At midnight I walk home down Davie, which the cops have closed off to accommodate the throngs of holiday-makers returning from the fireworks on English Bay. Oh yes, Don tells me stories – finally – of being bugged and spied on by the Vancouver police intelligence squad for a couple of years in the early 1980s. He doesn't elaborate overmuch and I don't ask.

MONDAY, 6 AUGUST / VANCOUVER

I conspire with myself to get several hours' work done before leaving to have lunch with Max Wyman and his wife, Susan Mertens, at the Hotel Vancouver, one of the few lunch spots open on the holiday and not one I would select otherwise.[11] Susan, who I meet for the first time, is delightfully bright and charming, and Max, whose leave from the *Sun* expires in October, looks well for someone who's undergone the health problems he has had. Such a decent man and humanist; lately he's occupied himself with Canada Council and UNESCO labour and work on the 1848 novel he's been writing for twenty years. An hour's work after lunch before meeting a friend of Mary's at the Sylvia for a drink (Mary's idea – she's a matchmaker). She (the friend) is an Asiaphile with an interest in erotica.

SUNDAY, 12 AUGUST / VANCOUVER

In the evening, I return to work on the *Jericho* manuscript, moving from the desk to the sofa to the kitchen table as I scribble pages in the notebook I'm using.

MONDAY, 13 AUGUST / VANCOUVER

Dream in either a hotel suite or the first-class lounge at Heathrow where Chris Moore from Bangkok is being quizzed by journalists as to why his first book, the one that established the format, was published by a mysteriously rich businessman in Mississauga or some other Toronto suburb.

Come home and begin the editing of *Three Pagodas Pass*.

TUESDAY, 14 AUGUST / VANCOUVER

Wake up rested, determined to overcome all of yesterday's frustrations. Not successful. The day is full of rejection and general callowness and

11   Max Wyman (b. 1939), dance critic and wide-ranging arts commentator.

stupidity from orgs as different (or as similar) as the Writers' Union and Word on the Street. So far the local literary world has not exactly been welcoming. Considerable hostility actually. But then, true, I've been here only a few months. So I turn to *Jericho* for relief, and find it.

WEDNESDAY, 15 AUGUST / VANCOUVER
Early today in the lift I say good morning to a woman with short dark hair, a resident with mail; she would not respond. Late in the day I enter the lift again and there's Chucky; once more I say hello, but no response. Yet while not responding he seems to seethe with rage. Fascinating to stand apart, a bystander at one's own crash site, as I was yesterday and more so today, watching as everything is crumpled. The spectacle is always mesmerising even as it hurts.

SUNDAY, 26 AUGUST / VANCOUVER
Lying in bed at 7:00 a.m. (what a layabout) I recall my circumstances a) five years ago and b) ten. Five years: I was still married, though barely, J having ceased any meaningful communication a year or two earlier, and I was awaiting publication of *Beast* any day and would soon start writing about books for the *Citizen*. Ten years: I was still at the *Whig* writing about books, *Year of the Horse* had come out in the spring, I was working on the book about the paper, and worrying mightily about my future – which is now. Obviously the future has worked out far better than I had feared or expected.

TUESDAY, 28 AUGUST / VANCOUVER
Mary picks me up at 6:30 with Michelle, a charming and down-to-earth young Welsh woman, in the car, and we go to Capers for dinner, then to Mary and Keith's, where I'm writing this, to spend the night, so that Mary, Michelle, and I can get an early start to Quesnel Lake in the morning, intending to stay over tomorrow night at Williams Lake.

SATURDAY, 1 SEPTEMBER / QUESNEL LAKE
Both Mary and Michelle have had less sleep than they need when I get them up at 6:15. I clean the cabin and pack the contents into the boot and the back seat while the pair of them powerwalk and sunbathe. I oil the hinge on the squeaking door as though I were coming back, but of

course I know I'm not. One year ago today, I turned up at UNB determined to save some money to effect my removal to BC.

WEDNESDAY, 5 SEPTEMBER / VANCOUVER

Writing fiction is like raising a crop: the benefits are unknown but likely small and, in any event, a long time in the future, yet the rewards along the way are deep though the labour backbreaking. In the evening, a condo meeting at which, despite the always disruptive presence of Chucky, a little headway is made regarding the terrible mess that is this building's affairs.

SUNDAY, 9 SEPTEMBER / VANCOUVER

Wake early to finish drafting the [Salman] Rushdie interview. Such a charming man and such a pro that the task is a pleasure. A long morning call from Peter Newman. His news is that he feels the *National Post* is going to shake down in a month or so. I am in good cheer as I rush round the Seawall, where an east wind, strong and unusual, kicks up a pretty good sea. That's what I like. I paid two bits, damn it, I demand surf. Return home to other chores. I feel fine and healthy today. How often do you hear me say that?

TUESDAY, 11 SEPTEMBER / VANCOUVER

I sleep only six hours, and find myself awake at 5:00 a.m., as I sometimes do. I worry about the *Sun* interview with Rushdie. When the papers arrive at 5:45, I read it first, with satisfaction that the desk, while inserting its usual wobbly grasp of punctuation, etc., has eliminated my own excesses. The front of the *Globe*, however, has a story that neither the *Post* nor the *Sun* has: that Air Canada has banned Rushdie, as have airlines in the US. This makes us look faintly ridiculous, though Rushdie might be in Seattle by now and could actually take a taxi to Vancouver for Monday's reading if necessary. Shortly afterward, while having a coffee on Denman, I hear the first report of a suicide pilot striking the World Trade Center in New York. By the time I return to the flat, it is clear that this is the opening salvo in some sort of concerted terrorist attack on New York, Washington, and perhaps [early reports proved incorrect] Chicago. The Pentagon is on fire. Thousands are probably dead or injured in New York. The White House has been evacuated. And all flights in the US and Canada have been cancelled. These events are unfolding as I write these words. My initial reaction is sympathy for those poor people – that, and the suspicion that Washington will use the chaos as an excuse for harsh authoritarian wartime measures. My fear is that there will be some Canadian spillover. At about 9:15 a.m., CNN identifies Afghanistan as the source of the attack, a country that of course was America's friend and pet when at war with the Soviet Union (Sylvester Stallone even made a pro-Afghan movie). This came very shortly after Tom Clancy, of all people, appealed for calm understanding of Islam rather than blanket recrimination. So even the hawks are frightened. Americans generally turn even more sentimental in such moments. I happen to be passing by a sex site on the Web and see this message: "In view of the events this morning let us put fantasy aside to address the real obscenity of terrorism. God will exact a terrible vengeance upon the perpetrators, but let us support one another. God Bless America!" Exclamation point indeed. I marvel at how Americans trying to ape the diction of the Old Testament – "God will [should be *shall*] exact a terrible vengeance upon [not *on*]" – end up sounding so Islamic. But I keep all my true feelings to myself in case these pages should fall into the wrong hands. Calm may not return for several days, and then, in time, the US will destroy Afghanistan, or Palestine, or Iran, or Iraq – some "little" society they know nothing about. What amazes me is the successful attack on the Pentagon. Not even in '68 was the Pentagon *seriously* threatened. The World Trade Center has of course been a target in the past. Putting World in the name ensured that it would become a focus of antiglobalisation forces.

WEDNESDAY, 12 SEPTEMBER / VANCOUVER
Wake up with the CBC still on. The papers almost entirely given over to the events in New York and Washington. I'm hopeful that, though the discourse will of course continue loudly, some steps towards normalcy may begin today. Still, one knows that America is taking all this very seriously indeed (major league baseball suspended, Disneyland and Disney World closed).

THURSDAY, 13 SEPTEMBER / VANCOUVER
After days of struggle, I manage to contain my grief. The newspapers are full of bellicose twaddle. One of the worst offenders is [Margaret] Wente

of the *Globe*, to whom readers turn for comfort, knowing precisely what
she will say in any situation and the exact words she will use.

THURSDAY, 14 SEPTEMBER / VANCOUVER
Chaos much of the day. Gertrude, the most loquacious person I know
(and one of the kindest), arrives to cook for cash, filling the freezer with
container after container – perhaps as much as two months' worth of
entrees, by my rough count. I tell her to please do so again anytime she's
down from Williams Lake and looking for a bit of extra money. A pleasure to watch a properly trained cook at work and see the ease with
which she has a different recipe going at the same time on each of the
four rings. In the middle of this comes the unsurprising news that
Rushdie has cancelled both Vancouver and Toronto and indeed the remainder of his US tour as well. I suspect that the RCMP and others put
pressure on him. More's the pity as nothing would have done so much
good as to have him, this Muslim-reared figure who has suffered more at
the hands of the Muslim extremists than anyone still living perhaps,
stand on stage and urge tolerance. Tolerance is in very short supply,
though some counter-reaction to the mutant American patriotism is beginning to appear – hesitantly, tentatively – in the press (but none of
course in the other media). Bush is an imbecile. Business people predict
a serious economic trauma, though in fact war has always been a boon
to the economy (only to lead to recession when the fighting stops and the
bills come due). My history would suggest that I should be bewildered
and depressed by events, but I am not, not yet.

SATURDAY, 15 SEPTEMBER / VANCOUVER
Everyone is already speaking of "the war" that hasn't yet begun. [A
friend] is representative of a strain of dissent I am just beginning to hear;
her understanding and fear of the intelligence states is growing rapidly.
This promises to be an interesting autumn.

SUNDAY, 16 SEPTEMBER / VANCOUVER
Very difficult time getting started today (a brief computer problem
doesn't help) but I manage to come round in the afternoon. Weather
much cooler and wet. The airwaves full of idiotic war talk and of spooks
pitching for more budget and sweeping new powers. I get back to *Jericho*.

I am impatient to complete the ms yet I shall miss such an outlet when I finish. I cannot, however, lose myself completely, because the nonsense of the news keeps intruding. Agh! I'm sick of a war that hasn't begun yet. There's a graffito on the Denman Street pavement that reads: "Do you suffer from bad dancing? Eat sea monkey."

MONDAY, 17 SEPTEMBER / VANCOUVER
In a dream, I sit in on a Random House editorial meeting in what looks like the *Toronto Life* coop in Front Street; Anne presides, wearing a long flannel nightgown, as apparently she is working so hard that she now sleeps at the office.

I wake to the morning ration of war news. Madonna has appealed for calm (as Bush appeals for chaos). The last US soldier to leave Saigon in 1975 is reported, erroneously, I suspect, to be among those killed at the Pentagon. Washington announces that it wishes to nullify the Ford administration's executive order forbidding the assassination of foreign leaders by the US government, and a poll reveals that sixty-five percent of Americans surveyed support the proposal. Why has no one written of how Bush is probably declaring war so as to free the mind of his father's crushing stalemate in the Persian Gulf a decade ago? But then America has an extraordinary need for war every ten years or so. Some point to the remarkable twenty-year peace between the world wars, but which countries did the US invade during that time? Several in the Hispanic world certainly.

All morning I stumble, drop things, lose my ability to put keys into their locks, have difficulty recalling names. I fear the worst until I work out that in fact I've had only four and a half hours' sleep. Except for one very brief nap, perhaps fifteen minutes, I manage to stay awake all day and even do the Seawall, which is deserted on this cold cloudy day. Near the end of the circuit I see a man carrying a large cross on his back, as though in re-enactment of the Crucifixion; the horizontal portion of the cross is covered, front and back, in Arabic writing. I return home to learn that the *National Post* has killed *Saturday Night* and that I must write an 1,800 word obituary for the *Sun*.

TUESDAY, 18 SEPTEMBER / VANCOUVER
Comforting images in the dream traffic. In the papers, more war news but still no war. A great deal of belligerent talk. Air travel now seems

downright impossible, and I fear it will remain so for so long that I shall have to forget about going to Asia in November. As last week's hijackers used X-acto knives as weapons, there is now an official crackdown on office supplies, as airport security in Canada has started to confiscate paper clips from passengers, lest they be straightened and used as weapons. One appreciates the light absurdity amid the spreading fear and stern self-censorship all round. Hard-working today rather than working hard: poor concentration and stamina.

THURSDAY, 20 SEPTEMBER / VANCOUVER
I awake to find the *Globe* is reporting Woody Allen's analysis of the war, which by the way seems poised to begin, as the US dispatches aircraft and such. No one's truly certain if they know whom they're fighting. News from Random House that they have sold Japanese rights to *Assassins* for US$5,000, the translation to appear in the next twenty-four months. John Burns calls with the offer of two reviews for the *Straight*. I begin to weed out stuffed filing cabinets for next year, partly to make space for files now stored in the closet, partly in recognition of the fact that my future will be leaner than my past and my files should match.

FRIDAY, 21 SEPTEMBER / VANCOUVER
A busy, busy day – happy and productive. Much of it spent seeing people at the *Sun*, including Neil, who must feel he doesn't have anyone there with whom to discuss politics seriously because he does so for a long time with me, to my delight. I always feel respected and warm after seeing him. Then I wander the alleys of downtown Vancouver, my mind far from both the war news and my own purely personal concerns.

TUESDAY, 25 SEPTEMBER / VANCOUVER
Foreign Affairs has advised Canadians to leave Malacca and North Malacca, not simply Aceh and Timor. This appears to nail shut the coffin lid on Indonesia, at least for now. I'll still make the Thai trip. A night of broken sleep. At midday I go round the Seawall in the cold and a surprising fog that gives the ships at anchor a ghostly appearance.

WEDNESDAY, 26 SEPTEMBER / VANCOUVER
I take a sleeping pill about 10:00 and get an additional 1.5 hours' sleep. Not enough to bring my total into the black but enough to do some

good. War news in all directions, all of it missing the essential points –
why states make war on non-states, why there is no moral justification
for the tacit assumption that an American's life is naturally worth more
than anyone else's. As day turns to evening, my sleep deprivation drives
me to an edgy suspicion of myself, of others, and of my surroundings. An
end-of-day drink at the Sylvia with Trevor Carolan, a teaching colleague
of Jennifer W's. He's a fifty-year-old Yorkshireman in BC since childhood
or adolescence, looks somewhat like the old-time Toronto hair stylist
Mister Ivan (same goatee, same manner). Has been a rock promoter
and a city politician, a poet-writer, and a Buddhist teacher. Worships
Bob Hunter and June Callwood and is publishing a memoir of Allen
Ginsberg.[12] I would have been more hospitable if I'd had more sleep. On
parting, he bows deeply with his palms pressed together before his chest.

Receive a delightful chapbook from George Elliott Clarke. What a
talent.

SATURDAY, 29 SEPTEMBER / VANCOUVER
The electric heater kicks in during the night for the first time. Nearly
every evening now I hear sirens close by where I used to hear dogs. I
can't see how this might relate to world events; just coincidence surely,
though the US now has rangers on the ground in Afghanistan. The opening gambit in their war on economic recession.

Reading Woodcock's unpublished journals and letters, I am coming to
understand how much, right up to his final illness, he worried about his
heart, damaged in the major coronary of 1966.

SUNDAY, 30 SEPTEMBER / VANCOUVER
Go off to my first Writers' Union meeting in Harrison Street and finally
meet Mona Fertig: an instant bond, as I had imagined.[13] Spend time
making the acquaintance of Michael Slade (Jay Clarke), the thriller writer and former law partner of Bill Deverell. He looks, sounds, and acts
rather like a younger Tiff Findley. He kindly answers a legal question in
connection with *Jericho*. Andy Schroeder also there. So are a number of
snooty amateurs. By prearrangement, I leave early and sidestepping

12   June Callwood (1924–2007), journalist and social activist.
13   Mona Fertig (b. 1954), poet and small-press publisher.

Word on the Street have a talk with Ralph Maud [the biographer of Charles Olson], a lonely man despite his young family.

Have a phone interview with Jamie Reid for a piece I'm to do for the *Straight* about the fortieth anniversary of *Tish*.[14] He says: "George Fetherling? I once met another Fetherling at George Bowering's place in Montreal in 1969." I think of saying but don't: "Must have been somebody else."

Discovering my resentment of America for the way it has now made all of us in the West unwelcome in the rest of the world. Yet I find also that the contraction of geography is oddly comforting. Find as well that, contrary to all expectations, this crisis is heightening the cultural distinctions between Canada and the States. I await the rapid growth of the protest movement. If the USA keeps up its mission, the reaction will grow louder, some allies will defect, Americans themselves will become sick of their casualties (but not of their own exceptionalism).

THURSDAY, 4 OCTOBER / VANCOUVER

The papers are full of such nonsense as patriotic attacks on the owners of Afghan hounds. George Bowering is quoted in the *Globe* saying that "Canadian writing is almost hopelessly humanist and anecdotal." I work away at home and worry about money and my health. Autumnal leaves litter the Seawall like little Indian flatbreads.

FRIDAY, 5 OCTOBER / VANCOUVER

Little to report these days, as people wait patiently for the US to begin invading Afghanistan and resume the cycle of violence. President Bush has urged his people to return to their normal lives "and take the kids to Disney World."

SUNDAY, 7 OCTOBER / VANCOUVER

I go out for echinacea at about 3:00 p.m., returning to hear from Bill and Peggy New over the phone that the Americans have begun bombing Kabul a few hours ago. I called it exactly right the other day when I predicted the strike would be this weekend in view of the fact that

14 Jamie Reid (b. 1941), poet, author of *Mad Boys* and other collections.

Washington has insisted that their retaliation was way off in the future. The republic is taking this seriously: the Emmy broadcast is being postponed.

TUESDAY, 9 OCTOBER / VANCOUVER
I resolve not to watch television news coverage of the war except for truly major developments such as Islamic retaliation for US retaliation or what naturally comes up during the eleven o'clock broadcast. Pledge to get my daily dose from the newspapers only, except as noted. The papers are a fount of priceless information, such as the fact that the Americans are dropping leaflets on the illiterate in Afghanistan. The serious news is that Chrétien, who until now has been cagey with the Yanks while pledging support, has committed two thousand troops, a half dozen ships, and assorted aircraft to the war.[15] A sad day.

WEDNESDAY, 10 OCTOBER / VANCOUVER
The problems are like Windows – one pops up in the foreground of the screen, obscuring the others in the background, as when, for example, the war news makes me forget my medical worries for a day – but only for a day. The constant popping up or recession of such screens is taking its toll.

THURSDAY, 11 OCTOBER / VANCOUVER
Today I realise that my desire to downsize and generally simplify my living quarters followed the period when I had achieved my youthful goal of a house in the Annex full of books and pictures. Then came the tiny place in Kingston, the cabin at Quesnel Lake, the hotel room in Fredericton – and now the Vancouver condo: the most sophisticated of these but no more complicated an operation than the others. This desire to simplify was undoubtedly tied to J's emotional retreat. To maintain, and maintain an interest in, a big home, I (we) needed a homelife. After 1986 or 1987 we really didn't have one. My only other morning thought is just how much I resent this all-powerful intrusion of news into my life. A long late lunch with Michael Carroll, who's been running Beach

15   Jean Chrétien (b. 1934), Liberal prime minister, 1993–2003.

Holme.[16] He's suddenly taken a strong interest in my work. I don't quibble but, alas, like the other few people whose loyalty I arouse, he of course has no money for acquisition. Still, he and I might be able to find ways of working together. Return home to find yet more condo trouble, even more stressful, lurking in the email. Then off to the Vancouver Club to seek strategic advice from Max Wyman and Susan concerning the *Sun* and other financial matters. Such decent and civilised people. Susan is embarrassed about belonging to the VC, of which she became a member by accident, when her women's club merged with it. I was amused to see that there is an old-fashioned set of scales in the gents' loo (off the men's cloakroom) and that three black notebooks rest on top in which members record their weight at each visit: a curious custom indeed.

FRIDAY, 12 OCTOBER / VANCOUVER

The television news and the morning papers make me tense, and of course I'm not the only one. How few appear to understand that the Americans are inserting themselves into a civil war (a civil war among Islamic factions world-wide) somewhat as they did in Vietnam. One should not take sides in a divorce.

In the early evening, an informal meeting about the once-again-looming condo crisis (new lawsuits, new attempts to stack the board with people in league with the developers and others); I give a rousing talk aimed at bringing two of the newcomers to a more active role in the struggle, to relieve some of the people who are burnt out. I find it difficult to fight on two or three fronts at once.

SUNDAY, 14 OCTOBER / VANCOUVER

War news: more widely scattered anthrax cases; anecdotal evidence that US policy is full of contradictions, with Colin Powell, the only grown-up in the group, being cut out of some key decisions.[17] Everyone still expecting both a new attack from the East (though some feel that the anthrax may be it – so they are hoping) and the US ground offensive in support of the anti-Taliban movement within Afghanistan; said movement seems timid and disorganised. Shades of South Vietnam in the days of the advisers.

---

16   Michael Carroll (b. 1953), publisher and editor.
17   Colin Powell (b. 1937), US secretary of state (2001–05), former general.

MONDAY, 15 OCTOBER / VANCOUVER

More anthrax reports, conflict renewed between India and Pakistan, illustrating the fragility of the alliance. Ottawa introduces police-state-style legislation. How Americans attach themselves to these long-drawn-out melodramas (remember the Iran hostage crisis – "Day one hundred and two"?); odd that war, when suddenly they are forced to consider foreign countries and alien peoples, should ultimately make Americans more insular rather than less. Myself, I have never been certain in which I take less comfort, isolationist America or *engagé* America.

WEDNESDAY, 17 OCTOBER / VANCOUVER

Yesterday received an invitation to a black tie event in support of the Writers' Festival to be held the same night – too late for my batman to fumigate my evening wear.

A dream in which Al Moritz and I are among those invited to a phoney arts conference in a terribly rich and snobbish Swiss town that looks a bit like Whistler. I contemplate the theft of a valuable painting, plotting all the details, but in the end decide against the crime as the hotel staff and local shopkeepers are all suspicious of me to begin with, because I betray my socio-economic origins by expressing my feelings. I interpret this as advice from my sleeping self about how to handle a security matter that has been troubling me. The final answer I have been seeking comes to me this evening on the Granville Street Bridge as I'm walking back from the launch, on West Broadway, of Trevor Carolan's book on Allen Ginsberg, feeling a bit poorly. As for war news, there is none, simply people waiting for more shoes to drop. Panic about anthrax may have peaked for the moment. Hard to say. I am reminded of the way I and others who had shoulder-length hair were barred from the Colonnade on Bloor Street in the '60s on the grounds that our hair was a hepatitis carrier. Similarly, of course, I recall an age when the word *communist* could be substituted for *terrorist* in all of today's rhetoric.

THURSDAY, 18 OCTOBER / VANCOUVER

An early morning call from Anne, here for the Writers' Festival, to arrange breakfast on Sunday. A dark, wet morning indeed, but I feel quite optimistic and healthy. The news, however, is dramatically grim: the Palestinians have assassinated a sitting Israeli cabinet minister. Well, that's done it, as restarting the Israeli-Palestinian peace talks is of course the key to settling any of the underlying causes of the US-Afghan war. By late afternoon, following a day of work at the computer and of rain without stop, anxiety reasserts itself because of war news on the one hand and worry about tonight's contested condo meeting on the other.

FRIDAY, 19 OCTOBER / VANCOUVER

My stress level is quite high. I meet Ronald Wright for breakfast at the Sylvia and can barely manage coherence; he must think me a terrible dolt.[18] His bearing suggests someone who is nicely divorced from the world (I envy him), though he is a committed leftist. Looking at him over coffee, with his broad shoulders, slender frame, and lantern jaw, I remember his friendship with George Galt and am struck by how much writers admire fellow writers who look like they do.

SATURDAY, 20 OCTOBER / VANCOUVER

Thinking about Inge Woodcock after learning from Ronald Wright, who sits on the Woodcock Trust board, that she is so ill that she says she wishes her suffering would end and is refusing to see visitors.

My homeliness is becoming quite distinctive but not distinguished in the least.

A few days ago, one big publishing problem seemed to solve itself, though the reality is that a third party intervened most helpfully. When I fail to navigate successfully when things are going badly for me all round, I resort to labelling the experience as simply a minor illustration of my almost Elizabethan belief in fortune, the strong invisible currents of good and bad luck in which one is swept along.

The Americans confirm their first ground fight with the Afghans, a two-hour skirmish.

A good wind today: spinnaker weather. I count twenty freighters (a record?), and see two warships, stationary but not at anchor, between the First Narrows and the Second: frigates. I've seen nothing about this in print, but the government is obviously concerned about port security. Choppers on constant patrol for well over a month now.

18   Ronald Wright (b. 1948), historian, novelist, and writer of travel narratives.

SUNDAY, 21 OCTOBER / VANCOUVER

Sleep all right with one interruption – I flatter myself that I am learning how to cope with these – and have a productive three-hour lunch with Anne (and, for the first hour, her older sister Marsha, a law-firm worker in Victoria) at the Wedgewood. Anne wears a wool pullover and plaid woollen trousers. As monsoon-like rains come down in Hornby Street, we discuss the novel, I give her another sample chapter, and she promises the contract in two weeks. Her tone is very warm and supportive. Carol Shields visits our table for a few minutes, and it heartens me to see her looking so well, though she still wears a head scarf to hide the hair loss resulting from chemotherapy.[19]

MONDAY, 22 OCTOBER / VANCOUVER

Condo chaos all day and all night, preparatory to what could well be a decisive meeting tomorrow. I spend an hour or so this morning walking downtown in a machine-gun rain, picking up a book contract from U of T Press at Purolator and going to see Don Stewart. Don is in good humour, even complimenting me on last week's column, an action that runs counter to not expressing one's feelings. I like being in his shop when it's wet out and really empty inside. Then home to write a column, which takes me some hours this time. A pleasant phone conversation with Jim Christy in Gibsons. Stress over war news is hardly unique to me but actually seems pandemic and not only in North America.

TUESDAY, 23 OCTOBER / VANCOUVER

The biggest surf I've ever seen in the Bay, bringing the concept of the primal sea quite close for once. I dress and hurry down to the Seawall and applaud the spectacle as the spray revives my face. When I return to the flat after standing on the beach I feel relaxed as well as invigorated, with the bright sun streaming in as well as the howl of the wind and the crash of the waves. In fact, I feel quite fine all day. An email circular from one of the owners in the building telling us to beware of possible violence from [another resident] who is being served with a subpoena today.

19 Carol Shields (1935–2003), novelist, author of *Small Ceremonies* and other works.

WEDNESDAY, 24 OCTOBER / VANCOUVER
I have managed to put together everything for a trip to Vietnam, Cambodia, and Laos in three months' time.

FRIDAY, 26 OCTOBER / VANCOUVER
A *Sun* photographer picks me up at 8:45 a.m. and we drive to the Hotel Vancouver to snag Pierre Berton for a tour of the three old newspaper buildings from his days in the 1940s, the era of highly competitive newspaper publishing in this city – indeed, a long drawn-out newspaper war in the Toronto manner. We bluff our way into the old Sun Tower and the *Province* building and then the former home of Berton's first paper, the *News-Herald*. It is now a massage parlour. We talk our way in and are shooting photos of Berton against paintings of bulbous nudes when a young woman in a black satin teddy says to him, "I guess this place has changed a lot since *you* worked here." Berton looks round and says, "Well, it retains certain characteristics. You see, this room was the publisher's office." He was a good sport throughout. He is still imposingly tall, and his voice retains much of its strength, but he walks with difficulty (and of course a cane) because of congestive heart failure and several other diseases. He is eighty-one. He says: "The doctors have told me I can have only four ounces of liquid a day. That being the case, I prefer mine in the form of a martini."

The war against civil liberties reaches the point that this morning in the *Globe*, Christie Blatchford, historically the voice of the cops local and federal, expresses concern about people searched without warrant, detained without hearing, and locked away without trial or prospect of bail.

SUNDAY, 28 OCTOBER / VANCOUVER
I have a high-voltage erotic dream about Anne. It rates very high on the Richter scale but of course to describe it is to make it seem ridiculous. In short, Anne, wearing one of her ass-hugging but otherwise sedate and somehow asexual outfits, is dashing in and out of her Random House office, which is partly outdoors, in a setting reminiscent of Stanley Park. Waiting for her to return at the end of the day, I do some touch-up painting; later, we leave together. Such a dream, which of course in no way reflects or comments on the real-life Anne, is an unearned gift to the dreamer.

This is the first day back on standard time and the effects on the spirit can be noticed, as Theresa in *Jericho* would say.

America's war strategy is already showing its faults, and a commitment of US ground forces seems even more likely. Seeing one of Bush's performances is like watching a bad ventriloquist.

MONDAY, 29 OCTOBER / VANCOUVER
After weeks of emergency, the US military effort has begun to sputter and Americans have learned a new word, *cutaneous*, bringing the average vocabulary to about 650.

WEDNESDAY, 31 OCTOBER / VANCOUVER
Except for grey hair, Jim Christy at fifty-six shows little sign of ageing, but he does evidence a new maturity, speaking eloquently of the war, giving voice to what I, too, feel: "I never thought I'd have to live through this stupidity a second time. The shame is that Canadians let themselves be suckered into taking part." He's right; the US has actually been using the loaded phrase "hearts and minds." I predict that when their spring offensive begins they will start lying about the body count. Jim is accompanied by his present g.f., a retail copywriter who drinks rather more than she can safely hold.

FRIDAY, 2 NOVEMBER / VANCOUVER
These days I get most of my news through dreams.

SUNDAY, 4 NOVEMBER / VANCOUVER
The war news dribbles along. Like some eighteenth-century conflict, this one seems likely to go into hibernation soon, then erupt in a ground offensive in the spring. How recently we saw the future in terms of huge trading blocs – the North American, the European, the East Asian. How quickly a new template has been imposed – the post-Christian liberal West (though, of course, never as liberal as people like me wish), the Islamic world, and the Confucian world (which so far has managed to stay on the sidelines of others' conflicts). I believe that more and more this will come to be seen as America's war. A hopeful note: the dreadful rise in patriotism in Canada has not led to muzzling of the press. In fact, quite the opposite. I wonder what the effect of the war will be on the political landscape here. Will the dire atmosphere prompt the people to swallow this weariness and keep the Liberals in power? Or will the country rush to the ridiculous and of course totally unprepared opposition – totally unprepared for

responsibility of any kind whatsoever, much less for wartime governance, and totally undeserving, too. And the NDP? Normally it would stand to benefit from the inevitable rise in antiwar sentiment, but any antiwar feeling here must be expressed carefully. The situation calls to mind Australia in the late '60s when Canberra had so stupidly and recklessly committed itself to participation in Vietnam. Technically, Canada is now creeping towards being a police state. Opposition will be dangerous and difficult, though of course not to the same extent as will be the case in the US – assuming that the will to appeal even exists on the other side of the border.

MONDAY, 5 NOVEMBER / VANCOUVER
I wake up to find a long round-robin email from Dennis Duffy's son with the alarming news that his mother is dying in Mount Sinai in Toronto after a med-evac flight from Spain following a diagnosis of terminal cancer. Such a wonderful woman. Poor Dennis, losing his soulmate in such a way, a tragic and terrifying lack of fortune.

Talking on the phone today with Michael Carroll I suddenly become acutely aware of all my ers and ahs and struggle to suppress them. This happens to me frequently of late.

WEDNESDAY, 7 NOVEMBER / VANCOUVER
I go to the Sylvia to have a drink with Michael Carroll and see George Bowering enter the bar with another man (Jamie Reid?). George is grey and limps a bit from surgery but is still majestically slim. He has a bald spot and is wearing white socks with leather shoes.

THURSDAY, 8 NOVEMBER / VANCOUVER
See Don Stewart this morning. He is hale. I like the quality of light in his shop. Then to the Federation of BC Writers office a block to the west, in a splendidly down-at-the-heels 1913 office building, all bright work and hardwoods, with mail chutes and frosted glass, to see M, the self-proclaimed debutante-in-rebellion (borrowing the phrase from my Woodcock book).

FRIDAY, 9 NOVEMBER / VANCOUVER
A drink at the end of the day with Scott McIntyre at the Sylvia. In him I sometimes see myself as others see me: he's so insecure yet such a rugged survivor, can never find the proper balance between talking and

listening, candour and caution, revelation and reserve. I'm remembering how I used to plead with and curse Toronto, demanding acceptance and equality. The impulse seems so far away now in time, geography, and temperament. I was never sure whether I was better off airing my personality or keeping it in the dark, where logically it seemed to belong. It flourished only in hotels: the natural meeting-places in modernist urban civilisations – public but not public sector.

MONDAY, 12 NOVEMBER / VANCOUVER
A plane crashes in New York and the hysterical Americans immediately suspect terrorists. Oh Lord.

THURSDAY, 15 NOVEMBER / VANCOUVER
The war – at least the Afghanistan phase – may have made a turn in the Americans' favour, as the Northern Alliance rebels have taken Kabul. But I am disgusted by the hypocritical writers who have become pro-war patriots, in one case, parading on the Orpheum stage in support of the US. I am sad to see [a friend] side with them, but one looks to her for her heart and her prose, not for even the most basic understanding of politics.

SATURDAY, 17 NOVEMBER / VANCOUVER
I live in a state of quietly heightened awareness about everything. I awake again wondering which windows I have propped up while I slept and I think "My God, what if I'm never in better circumstances than I am now?" A long phone conversation or two from M – all her conversations are long – and a coffee with Mary. I marvel at how ill-suited my personality is to avoiding worry while I also routinely make momentous decisions without much thought or review, based solely on instinct. Why is my writing life stalled? When Alan Twigg had his successful brain surgery he experienced quite a boom in energy and a burst of creativity. I must make my own progress happen rather than wait disappointedly for an unsolicited donation.

SUNDAY, 18 NOVEMBER / VANCOUVER
The day begins, I learn from the news, with a gay man murdered in Stanley Park and ends with a meteor shower.

MONDAY, 19 NOVEMBER / VANCOUVER
The day is a waste except for when I pick up Alan Twigg and [the book publisher] Ron Hatch and we go to the old Main Library at UBC where we meet up with Tony Phillips and Bill New for a productive meeting with the head librarian aimed at getting the permanent Woodcock display reinstated. Alan wears one half of a black suit with clogs.

SATURDAY, 24 NOVEMBER / VANCOUVER
Quite by chance, and in some alarm, I come on the following in Gide's *Journals*, written in 1942: "Doubtless I no longer cling much to life, but I have this fixed idea. To make myself and my dependencies last a little while longer: linen, clothing, shoes, hope, confidence, smile, graciousness; make them last until the farewell. In view of this I am becoming economical, parsimonious of everything in order that none of this should give out ahead of time …"

MONDAY, 26 NOVEMBER / VANCOUVER
A failure of expectations or a triumph of motives? We all live in hotels. This state of mind helps, but of course does not actually achieve the elimination of desire.

TUESDAY, 27 NOVEMBER / VANCOUVER
Finally! I get back to work on *Jericho*. How eager I am to be done with the draft so that I might begin the next.

WEDNESDAY, 28 NOVEMBER / VANCOUVER
Decent progress on *Jericho* today, and the kind of tranquil, well-rounded day I most enjoy.

FRIDAY, 30 NOVEMBER / VANCOUVER
The day goes well, as when I have a coffee with Don Stewart, who sees me on my best days as well as my worst. George Harrison [of the Beatles] dies.

FRIDAY, 7 DECEMBER / VANCOUVER
At my urging, M has been pursuing the idea of buying a condo in this building, and she's got a nibble on a one-bedroom on the fourth floor.

I've offered to lend her most of the down payment. She looks at the place tonight. I write all day but am distracted, sad, easily vexed. Go to the Kate Walker [book distributor] sales conference to present the Burma book.

SUNDAY, 9 DECEMBER / VANCOUVER

A dream about someone wearing a wig and playing a harp (two forms of disguise) and one of Anne who has an attic office with a great deal of light coming in.

I am so demoralised at this point in the novel that I fall back on the essence of my own Daoism: the world is an institution (the biggest one of all) from which we must disengage. My present plan calls for me to withdraw my cash savings when the certificate comes due in a few months and live on that for several years, assuming both the money and I last that long. Of course this is an impractical thought, easily over-turned when I feel better.

WEDNESDAY, 12 DECEMBER / VANCOUVER

Thinking about Anne C. Her remark, like those of Fraser, say, or Bruce W, has been very useful as an insight from the other side of the mirror, setting in motion a mechanism for self-understanding. (Looking at the past few months, I must admit that I've not always been getting stupider – consider my growing ease in expressing myself in correspondence and in this journal.) If one were to convey this in a poem, the lines would read: "I do not deserve your insults/because they are so fine a gift." Sounds like one of Martial's epigrams.[20] I feel somewhat better today during daylight hours, though I fade quickly thereafter and with a thud. My voice, however, is actually worse than yesterday. In the evening, while watching television of all things, I have a visitation and see the plot of the novel clearly. Soon afterwards, a call from M to say that her offer on Suite 404 has been accepted, closing 14 January.

20 Martial or Marcus Valerius Martialis, Roman poet of the first century CE.

WEDNESDAY, 19 DECEMBER / VANCOUVER
A card from Jen Williams telling me how pleased she is to have me in Vancouver and quoting from "Paradise Lost": "The mind is its own place, and in itself/Can make a Heaven of Hell, a Hell of Heaven."

FRIDAY, 21 DECEMBER / VANCOUVER
The day is bright and dry but very cold. Breakfast with Michael Carroll at the White Spot at Georgia and Seymour. Whenever a publisher elects to take one to a meal at the White Spot, one can assume that the advance offered will be paltry. So indeed it proves to be – $3K to reprint *Year of the Horse* and *The Other China* in one volume under a new title, but of course I get to correct the text and add to it.

MONDAY, 24 DECEMBER / VANCOUVER
A productive morning's work, after returning from the nearly deserted Bread Garden where a Chinese-Canadian server is wearing a Santa hat at six in the morning. Max Wyman picks me up in the late afternoon for his Christmas get-together at Lions Bay, where he and Susan have a designer-style house on the water. There I meet Timothy Porteous, the former director of the Canada Council who resigned on a point of principle under the Tories. He tells of writing Trudeau's nomination speech in '68; later he plays a private one-off CD of Leonard Cohen reading a Frank Scott poem to music, complete with back-up singers.[21] Also present is one of those people who doesn't drink but constantly appears to be drunk; she smells as well. Chris Dafoe of the *Free Press* Dafoes, former BC arts correspondent of the *Globe*, is an intelligent and easygoing man who suggests a chubby version of the actor John Cusack; his wife Gloria is a film publicist, and indeed there are numerous film people there. I spend time talking to Eldon Grier's widow Sylvia, a painter who lives nearby and is one of those charming people of indeterminate age. She was once Grier's student; they were married for forty-six years, yet she scarcely looks old enough to have been an adult for forty-six years. With these people I find myself down on the beach singing carols round a bonfire. Max and Susan are the soul of tact and hospitality. Max is an

21   F.R. Scott (1899–1985), poet and constitutional lawyer.

interesting character: a soft English voice but rapid speech, now poised to become head of UNESCO in Canada after easing himself out of journalism and, via the Canada Council, into arts consulting and arts diplomacy. In Vancouver since the '60s when he got out of Fleet Street, he has an encyclopaedic knowledge of the local personalities. Susan, who left the *Sun* once chronic fatigue syndrome overtook her, is strikingly thin and young-looking for almost fifty – in fact, for an adult of any age. A bit nervous perhaps (is it I who make her nervous? I don't believe so), but so cool that you never see her mind working so quickly and efficiently as it obviously does. Home late and sleep soundly.

TUESDAY, 25 DECEMBER / VANCOUVER
Christmas dinner with [a neighbour] and her daughter, a casino waitress, who makes everyone hush so that she can turn up the radio to full volume to hear a Christmas novelty tune in which the singer stutters badly.

THURSDAY, 27 DECEMBER / VANCOUVER
Up about 5:30 to calmly drink coffee and read the papers in the morning darkness. I'm shocked to learn of [the Toronto theatre critic] Urjo Kareda's death from cancer at fifty-seven. I remember how he shared certain prejudices of Nathan Cohen whom he succeeded as drama critic of the *Star*: a distaste for revue, for example, with the result that years later Dan Ackroyd used "Urjo Kareda" as the name of a pretentious character on *Saturday Night Live*, doubtless remembering some old review or column in which Toronto's Second City was slighted. How much reading his obit, as well as a list of who's died in the past year, makes me feel vis-à-vis Toronto like one of those exiled former Montrealers one saw in Toronto so commonly. Or perhaps my situation more closely resembles that of a Shanghailander after the communist revolution, full of surprising nostalgia for the former place of exile from which it has become necessary to ask to be excused.

Get some of my discipline back today, but only some.

2002

Having completed *Three Pagodas Pass: A Roundabout Journey to Burma*, a sort of travel novella, I returned to Asia in the summer but otherwise laboured away on the novel *Jericho* and the affairs of the Federation of BC Writers.

FRIDAY, 11 JANUARY / VANCOUVER
Often I feel that Canada is a private club and that I am standing at the Members Only door, fighting with the sergeant-at-arms who is charged with keeping out riff-raff like me.

TUESDAY, 15 JANUARY / VANCOUVER
This is M's day. At noon she goes to her new home, on the fourth floor of this building, and formally takes possession, getting the keys from the estate agent. I tag along, as I have not been inside the place. It has attractive northern exposure, with the mountains in the distance, and generally far more light than I had imagined. Considering that it has been rented out to an endless succession of transient tenants over the years, it is in quite good nick, with only the customary yellow staining from cigarette smoke and one damaged interior door (where someone, in a moment of dis-ease, put his or her fist through it). M is happy, figuring out her decorating scheme, plotting which furniture will go where, and so on. I'm so pleased that in my small way I could help bring this about.

FRIDAY, 18 JANUARY / VANCOUVER
An early dinner at Tojo's on West Broadway with John Ralston Saul, who's in the city for media appearances and lectures. We chat about

Burma and much else, and he is full of charm and energy. When we finish I ask for a lift downtown as it's pissing rain and I know I won't be able to get a taxi. He says, "Of course. I'm sure the Mounties won't mind." When we get outside and he relays the request to one of his two body-guards, I say, "This is exciting. I haven't been in the back seat of an RCMP vehicle for several decades." John laughs appreciatively; the cop struggles to remain expressionless.

TUESDAY, 22 JANUARY / VANCOUVER

This evening, as I sit in the green chair reading and writing as I always do, I will perform an audit on the day, asking whether I have lived more than I have died in the past twenty-four hours, whether my account is in surplus or in deficit, and most importantly what the exact balance is.

WEDNESDAY, 23 JANUARY / VANCOUVER

The snow returns, accompanied by sleet and by hailstones the size of clichés. The morning begins badly when a near idiot is playing with power tools in the corridor and fills it with dust to the point where my throat closes and my lungs are impaired. At length, he creates enough hot dust to trigger the fire alarm. The noise is deafening. I check the other floors just to make absolutely certain that there is in fact no fire. When I return, he says, "I end noise," and wanders off, but he doesn't really know how to stop it and the racket continues a considerable time until firefighters arrive armed with axes and wearing respirators. They make noise go way.

THURSDAY, 24 JANUARY / VANCOUVER

My mood is blackened by news of Peter Gzowski's death from cigarettes at sixty-seven.

FRIDAY, 25 JANUARY / VANCOUVER

Bob F writes a particularly fine appreciation of Peter G in this morning's *Post*, a paper I don't read any longer, except the Saturday edition, as I can't really afford all the papers I subscribed to previously; I send him an email about his piece. Aside from going to the gym, I spend the day reading Flaubert for next week's column.

SUNDAY, 27 JANUARY / VANCOUVER
M is upstairs, painting away madly, wearing gold earrings and a
Home Depot cap and tattered trousers that are the property of some
old boyfriend. I spend two and a half hours at the gym before realising that too much yoga makes me tense. In the evening [an old
Toronto acquaintance] calls and invites me for a drink at the Sylvia.
"Back east, everybody took me for a beatnik," he says. "Here they all
think I'm a tough guy." I reply: "Why must the two be mutually ex-
clusive?" I admire his personal economy but he remains a spiv, though
a somewhat mellower one these days. He always tries to make me
feel bad and tonight he succeeds once again, this time with more of
Peter Trower's remarks about me. I come away from him death-weary
and wary.

MONDAY, 28 JANUARY / VANCOUVER
Morning coffee with Neil Reynolds, who begins by telling me that
Conrad Black told him three times, via [his wife] Barbara, to get rid of
me. He implied that I'm lucky that the ownership changed when it did,
as he wasn't sure how long he could hold off on the proprietor's wishes.
All of this is highly ironic, of course, in view of how I went to Barbara
and planted the idea that she hire N for Ottawa when he was down on
his luck in Saint John. I imagine she wishes a conservative in the post.
Anyway, the matter to hand. I tell Neil that I've thought long and hard
about whether to have this conversation, for I don't want to engage in
self-pity, guilt, or special pleading; but I must confide in him my primal
fear, which is that I will be ill again and needful of further surgery just
about the time he retires. I go into considerable medical and financial
detail, saying that I hope he can find some way – I make a few suggestions – to restore the other part of my *Sun* fee before too long, once the
economy improves. He is a good soul, listens attentively and with concern, and promises to be mindful of the issue, which I have no doubt he
will be. We then speak about the fiction I'm at work on – he seems delighted – and I say how grateful I will always be to have had him as my
only literary patron. And these are exactly the terms in which he has seen
our long association, always finding ways to keep me fed while leaving
me time for the other type of writing.

TUESDAY, 5 FEBRUARY / VANCOUVER

Dinner with Steve Osborne at the Snow Garden on Richards, opposite MacLeod's, and I remember at once what I like about him: his warmth and his voice. We then walk over to SFU where I give a mini reading to his writing class and talk and answer questions for two hours. This goes surprisingly well, in fact very well. The students come by afterward to thank me one by one. Stephen says that [one of the university administrators] always attends these sessions but this time her absence is conspicuous. I'm frankly surprised that she even permitted my being asked.

WEDNESDAY, 6 FEBRUARY / VICTORIA

On the ferry to Victoria, up near the prow, a group of high school kids are down on all fours, making placards for a protest against budget-slashing affecting their school. Two of the posters say STOP THE HIPOCRASY. I gently point out the spelling error to a girl with red hair. She thanks me and promptly turns the cardboard over and prints on the other side the words RESTORE FUNDING FOR ENGLISH! Ah! the pragmatism of youth. In Victoria I go to see Richard Olafson of Ekstasis Editions, who turns out to be a genial eccentric with strong opinions on every subject. A most curious literary publisher in all ways except the important ones. M and I have dinner with Rhonda Batchelor and her new partner Alex, the printer and engraver from Prague, who seems like a Czech printer from a play or film. He and Rhonda are collaborators in Poppy Press. Rhonda seems sad. She's not writing at the moment, and I suspect that she is still mourning Red [Lillard].

MONDAY, 11 FEBRUARY / VANCOUVER

I find the following in Simone Weil: "We must be rooted in the absence of place." Reading this I naturally and inevitably feel as though she was writing to me directly, one individual to another. Then I come on this in Derek Walcott: "O Christ my craft and the long time it is taking!" Which seems a pretty pale and no doubt unintentional paraphrase of Chaucer's line about "The crafte so long to learne" and a distressing illustration of the impoverishment of the language in our age.

TUESDAY, 12 FEBRUARY / VANCOUVER

I settle down for the day's editorial chores and then get in a good lick at *Jericho*, motivated by panic, for the Random House contract arrives today, with the stark deadline of 15 August now set out in unrelenting, unforgiving black and white.

THURSDAY, 14 FEBRUARY / VANCOUVER

A sweet letter today from Peggy A on the letterhead of the Hotel California in Berlin.

TUESDAY, 26 FEBRUARY / VANCOUVER

In the late afternoon M and I go to UBC to hear Bill New lecture, brilliantly, I believe, on irony. (The Greeks had no word for irony. I find this ironic.) Later there's a reception at which I meet Jean Wilson, the associate head of UBC Press, whom M once knew. Turns out that she is a buddy of Carolyn Wood in Toronto.

SATURDAY, 9 MARCH / VANCOUVER

The morning promises computer problems, but they resolve themselves in the afternoon. I use the time between to do some editorial work on *Three Pagodas Pass*, with which I am very late.

I have been thinking about Pierre's (so to call it) career path, how he has virtually no characteristics of the artist or the person of ideas but rather publishes all these books to prove to himself how interesting he is, such range, such a polymath. He writes in order to disguise himself, to hide.

MONDAY, 18 MARCH / VANCOUVER

Lately I have been thinking about how *Travels by Night* has changed me. It has certainly contributed to my departing from, withdrawing from, Upper Canada, knowing that I will never be accepted. (Other factors, of course, include getting divorced, being ill, not wishing to sit round waiting for my own and other people's obituaries as I sensed I was doing.) *Travels* also made me see more clearly than ever before my hopeless position vis-à-vis other Canadian writers. Suddenly chance remarks by Bruce Whiteman (speaking aloud, casually, unaware of how significant I will find his words) and Michael Ondaatje made perfect sense. The book or rather the clarity its reception brought has caused me to feel disillusioned by English Canada, the subject to which I've devoted so much energy all my adult life; I now must face the reality that these people won't have me, are offended by my interest in them, wish only to be flattered, are always seeking someone – even the lowliest of them – on whom they can look down (and I of course am the default setting). Yet the book has also fired my desire to struggle to write better and differently in the remaining minutes of play.

SATURDAY, 30 MARCH / VANCOUVER

A dream in which I pay a call on Michael Ignatieff and his present wife in Boston. They have invited me yet are surprised to see me, and having nothing to eat in the house, or perhaps not wishing me to linger there, suggest we go to a neighbourhood place (which turns out to be in London). They are very fretful about who will pick up the bill, and of course I volunteer as graciously as I can. What's wrong here? Well, it turns out that Michael doesn't recall who I am.

Thinking about Pierre, how he does in fact seem to be growing up a bit, albeit at the price of increasing social conservatism, which of course he does not recognise. Perhaps one day he'll be able to lift the façade a bit and admit who he really used to be. Maybe a part of the problem is that he always has used his writing to market his self-myth rather than to question it or even understand it somewhat.

My existence until now has followed this pattern: I am judged and found wanting (on superficial grounds, I believe – even the bigots are rarely so hard on me as I am on myself) and then I go into exile somewhere. One exile after another, leaving messes behind each time. The sequence may be approaching its conclusion. How sad.

SUNDAY, 31 MARCH / VANCOUVER

The Queen Mum has died, at 101, a model of longevity.

TUESDAY, 2 APRIL / VANCOUVER

A pleasant in-store and out-for-coffee meeting with Don Stewart in the morning. He is in an upbeat mood and tells me about his Highland family, especially his paternal grandfather who served in the South African War and then came to western Canada, working in an insurance office

just down the street, in present-day Gastown. Don has a truly astonishing memory for books. He is in such a fine mood that he shakes my
hand goodbye and extends an undated invitation for lunch. Then I stop
in at the *Sun*. The place always makes me tense in the extreme, though
Rebecca is relaxed this early in the week and goes to great lengths to be
welcoming. Any newspaper I've ever been involved with, whether as a
freelance or a staff member or something in between, has made me cautious and defensive, so thick have been the internal politics. After the *Sun*
call, I move on to a reasonably productive day.

MONDAY, 8 APRIL / VANCOUVER

I now believe that one's talent for expression, if that's what it is, changes
constantly just as the make-up and shape of one's body changes, and
that in the one case as in the other, the wise person is alert to the changes
and divorced from simple notions of good or bad.

SUNDAY, 21 APRIL 2001 / VANCOUVER

I spend the day writing my appreciation of Carol Shields, then go down
to the Sylvia at five to meet Rhea Tregebov and her Vancouver friend
Billie Livingston.[1] Rhea is the absolute salt of the earth: such warmth and
humanity; I am humbled. Arrive home about 7:30, slightly plastered.

SATURDAY, 27 APRIL / VANCOUVER

Dean Cook at lunch. He's here for the BC Book Awards (M is going but
I stay home to work). He seems full of confidence about *Jericho* at
Random; he is a fine fellow for believing that it's part of his function to
represent people such as me, who make him no money whatsoever.

MONDAY, 29 APRIL / VANCOUVER

This morning while I'm waiting in the doctor's crowded waiting room, a
large fellow opposite me with shades and a black goatee gives me the evil
eye. When his name is called, he stops on his way into the examination
room and throws the magazine in or at least at my face, shouting "Read

---

1   Rhea Tregebov (b. 1953), poet and professor, author of *The Strength of Materials*
and other collections; Billie Livingston (b. 1965), novelist, author of *Going Down
Swinging* and other works.

this, you fucker." When I get out, I'm talking on the mobile at Burrard Street and he approaches me and curses from about two feet away: "You're lucky you're still alive, you fucking shithead." My guess is that he was having his dosage adjusted.

WEDNESDAY, 1 MAY / VANCOUVER
More of the same. I virtually have *Three Pagodas Pass* ready to go to Michael Carroll for production. That should free up things, allowing me to knock off other overdue projects one after another. Such is my hope, wish, and expectation at least.

SATURDAY, 4 MAY / NELSON
At the Fed AGM, I am elected president by acclamation. Later, M and I tour the town. I'm sad about its economic future (the hospital has been closed, for example) but I love 1910 mining towns: the old industrial culture in which I grew up. M is melancholy, for thirty years of her life were bound up with this area, particularly the Slocan Valley. The workshops are far more professional than I had expected, though one woman reads a decline-of-Canada poem containing the lines "We are travelling on the *Titanic* / while Rome burns ..." The entire atmosphere is collegial and positive.

SUNDAY, 12 MAY / VANCOUVER
I compare how Jane Rule was received by Marian Engel and the others with how Audrey Thomas fared a decade later when she came into her own and how Carol Shields was lionised all during the '90s. Now one would not be far wrong in noting that the degree of these American-born women's acceptance by Canadian-born women has been in accord with the extent of their talent. I also sense, however, that the trend-line has to do with cultural politics (rock breaks scissors, paper covers rock, feminism beats nationalism) and that its effect has been cumulative. One cannot write anything worthwhile if one is writing in order to be admired or even accepted as an equal. Such is my experience at least.

SATURDAY, 18 MAY / VANCOUVER
A day gone splendidly wrong. I am quite up and breezy at breakfast until I am put down with cracks about my upbringing. I am tossed into a

gloomy state, illustrating once again, as though illustrations were required, the close connection – especially close with me – between the blues and anger, with humiliation the middle ground. Because I need food and fresh air, I then keep my commitment to go shopping with M, but relations deteriorate when she speaks highly of the blackmail press and even wishes naïvely to buy a copy of the current issue containing a mention of someone she knows. Later I experience a bubbling up of the infection that lies doggo for long periods. Other problems, mainly financial, have weakened my resistance, and I retreat into solitude, thus puzzling M, who keeps sending what I mistakenly presume to be unintentionally rude emails and messages. I stay alone in the dark – alone and furious – plotting escape, disappearance, reinvention: the usual. At this late stage in my life, I'm not going to cure this behaviour, but I do claim to understand it more than in the past. These episodes relate specifically to sudden failure beyond my control, following some modest success that is my own doing – Michelangelo's scaffold crashing down, that sort of thing.

TUESDAY, 21 MAY / VANCOUVER
A strange call indeed from some alleged PR guy with a Chinese accent and a Middle Eastern name who wants me to meet him for an early breakfast one day next month at some remote White Spot. I fear my life may be entering its baroque period.

FRIDAY, 24 MAY / VANCOUVER
Lunch at Zefferelli's with John Burns of the *Straight*, a youngish and somewhat introverted literary person with an elite education. I've grown fond of him and respect his approach. I was at the Fed office earlier where everything seemed quite disorganised. Still, some work accomplished there and in Pendrell Street.

SATURDAY, 25 MAY / VANCOUVER
A dream in which the Woodcocks are living in a big place – different from their homes in earlier dreams – with tall bookcases, and looking over the shelves I recognize many familiar texts. Set high up in the centre case is a television. I express surprise, but George says that he has been curious about this Johnny Carson chap and wished to see for himself.

TUESDAY, 28 MAY / VANCOUVER

At some point during the day I realise that the storied personality of the "explorer" – unable to be satisfied with the civilised present, always striking out into the unknown future, restless (and reckless) to a fault – is rather like my own except that work on self-schooling takes the place of geography or topography. This is strange in one so interested in the past, but true.

MONDAY, 3 JUNE / VANCOUVER

At 4:00 p.m. or so, Rhonda Batchelor arrives from Victoria, for I am taking her to the Alcuin Society awards dinner – her Poppy Press has received a well-deserved prize for the P.K. Page book and I am her escort as Alex is away, attending his daughter's graduation from Princeton. Jim Rainer gives us a ride. While I'm standing at the bar, a woman comes up to me suddenly and kisses me on the lips: Margaret Reynolds, wearing a man's pinstripe suit, and very well, too. So at the table I have Rhonda on my left – smart working-class – and Margaret on my right – elegant, sophisticated middle class, always at ease, only now going after more education. An eventful evening, at the conclusion of which Margaret drives Rhonda and me back to Pendrell (she's sleeping over in order to take an early morning ferry).

WEDNESDAY, 5 JUNE / VANCOUVER

Peter Newman, a half hour late for breakfast, owing to a nosebleed, looks quite pale and frail, which is alarming. He says he is leaving Barbados for the German-speaking part of Switzerland. He seems not to have made much progress on his memoirs.

THURSDAY, 6 JUNE / VANCOUVER

A big mess today with Random House. They cancelled the planned Vintage paperback of *Assassins* six months ago without telling me, which means that the British hardcover probably won't have any of the many connections. When I become angry when such matters go wrong, at whom I am angry? The persons whose fault it is or myself for not being in control, of being a pawn of fortune, whether good or ill? I'm honestly unsure, though I hate to think the former is the answer, for that would contradict my principles and generally Daoist attitudes (as I understand Daoism at least). So, a trying day.

FRIDAY, 7 JUNE / VANCOUVER
Better today. I may have solved the Random problem without having to bother Anne. Also, I get the better part of an advance column done – after this one, only two more to go.

THURSDAY, 20 JUNE / VANCOUVER
A generally satisfying lunch today with Bill New at Zeff's. Bill is floating towards retirement while on a big wave in his career; books of all kinds appearing constantly, lectures, awards, and the like. He's a bit wily really, as long experience in the literary world teaches people to be, but perfectly amiable – and kind.

FRIDAY, 21 JUNE / VANCOUVER
Don Stewart this morning confirms something that Bill New had mentioned: Inge Woodcock is in a special-care home and the McCleery Street house, now empty except for the dregs of the library which Don is buying, is being sold, apparently to help defray the cost of her upkeep in the facility. Don is upset, reporting how she had been falling and how she became addicted to painkillers and was drinking a great deal. Seems she was in two other such places previously but was so obstreperous that she had to leave. Also, she's quite deaf now. Don tells me that the house is likely to be torn down by new owners. "We're all going to end up the same way," he says to me when conversation has carried us out onto the pavement: a day of Mediterranean brightness, the official start of summer.

Also, news today of Tiff Findley's death, at seventy-one, of congestive heart failure. I remember his Macmillan launch at Nora Clark's flat for his second novel and comeback book: my first meeting with him. How he grew towards *The Wars*, never to reach that height again. His acceptance into the *Maclean's* middle-class pantheon of the mundane exactly tracked the mainstream's long-delayed acceptance of him as a gay man. But he was capable of being more than a Stratford veteran interviewed by Gzowski.

SATURDAY, 29 JUNE / VANCOUVER
Having plugged as many holes in the dike as possible, I go to the airport, courtesy of M, for the long tiring flight to Bangkok via Taiwan. The

airport at the latter place, surely among the world's most poorly designed and most confusing, is even more itself than I remember from the early and mid-90s. Yet when travelling I am always more relaxed than I am when stationary, showing greater patience and more ability to absorb frustration, which is all to the good on a trip such as this, if experience is any judge.

SUNDAY, 30 JUNE / BANGKOK

Same day but different date. I arrive about 1:00 a.m. All flights to Bangkok, in my experience, arrive at one in the morning, regardless of their origin or eventual destination. I breeze through the formalities and check into the hotel in Soi 8 that Chris Moore recommends: basic and clean, Indian-owned. Then to a massage place to remove the travel grime and restore circulation. Then I stock the fridge for M's arrival in two days' time by way of Tokyo. I have been in transit about twenty hours and sleep the sleep of the righteous.

MONDAY, 1 JULY / BANGKOK

Dominion Day in Bangkok starts with the *Post* and the *Nation* in the incompetent little restaurant, quite deserted except for me, on the top storey of this place. I explore the district. Bangkok is dirty, polluted, and overcrowded and of course this is why we enjoy it so much. The air is stifling until mid-afternoon when – surprise – there is no monsoon rain but rather a pleasant wind. Dusk: I look out over the ugly rear ends of buildings and see palms poking up above the slums. Then night, with the sound of stray dogs (many of them evidently are rabid) barking at something in the darkness or perhaps just feeling sorry for themselves.

TUESDAY, 2 JULY / BANGKOK

Enough sleep for once, though it develops that my watch hasn't been set quite correctly and I'm in the lobby at 5:30 a.m. wondering why no one is about and why there's no food to be had. So I sit and read the newspapers, treat myself to a gourmet breakfast at one of the toffs' hotels, and then walk for a couple of hours in Sukhumvit Road in both directions. In Nana Plaza nearby, the bars and strip palaces are stuck thirty years in the past, like so much of expat Bangkok. Some of the courtesans, I observe, have lower rates during this the wet season. M is to arrive tonight – at about 1:00 a.m. I'll warrant – and will certainly be justified in being exhausted. In the afternoon I work on the piece of fiction that I have to hand and turn to the book I carry, Susan Cheevers' memoir of her father, *Home Before Dark*, in which I find these beautiful words: "My father noticed too well that the comfortable lives his friends and neighbors had so painstakingly fashioned for themselves were an ineffectual bulwark against the ancient lusts and expectations that pick up men and women and dash them screaming on the rocks of their own desires." Less musical but of greater concern to me is her statement that John Cheever "never quite trusted medicine. On the one hand, he always knew he was dying. His perception of physical reality was tenuous at best." The author's personality reminds me a bit of Carolyn Wood's: so tolerant and insightful, absolutely secure in her social position but never taking all that too seriously.

M arrives as expected at about one o'clock but is full of energy, too zoned out on her own surroundings to concentrate on conversation.

WEDNESDAY, 3 JULY / BANGKOK

Lunch with Chris Moore at one of his favourite restaurants, Les Chevaliers in Soi 3 Sukhumvit, whose curmudgeonly expat proprietor has appeared in thin disguise in a couple of Chris's books. Chris is fifty-two but looks to be in his mid-forties; I ask because he has lived here for twenty years following four years in New York and teaching law at UBC. His thick black hair and general youthful appearance fool people. Everything about him a bit mysterious, attractively so. He is well connected to say the least, in the expat community but in the host one as well. I question him about Heaven Lake Press and he says that it is owned by, and run for the benefit of, its six Thai partners; but clearly Chris is the person who makes all the decisions as well as the author of all its English-language titles (for there are also a few Thai books on the list). What's more, he knows that entire region well, speaking learnedly of Burma, for example (having only recently returned from Mon State). In short, an intriguing and congenial character whom I am happy to meet at last after a long email relationship. Like everyone else in Bangkok of whatever description, he works hard.

M and I have wine at lunch, too much of it, and this combined with the heat sends us to bed quite early and for a long time. The heat finally breaks for a few hours when lightning zaps a distant high-rise and monsoon rains come forth. We watch from the roof then return to bed.

THURSDAY, 4 JULY / BANGKOK

M is not always so happy-go-lucky a travelling companion as I had hoped. Today I return from a walk to find her working in the lobby on her fisheries project and she suddenly tells me of the latest skulduggery at the Fed – a long and anguished conversation. Later we go to the Wireless Road where I order three more shirts from the fellow I've been going to since 1990, when he was a young chap starting out, newly arrived from the Middle East.

MONDAY, 26 AUGUST / VANCOUVER

Once yesterday and twice today vexing situations have arisen that I have more or less walked right through, and I am pleased and relieved at my performance, an indication that my spirit is in good health. How little success is required to give me some confidence, how little failure can send me sprawling.

THURSDAY, 29 AUGUST / VANCOUVER

Jane Eaton Hamilton and I have been emailing each other for a few years and this morning we finally meet for breakfast at the Sylvia. On the surface level, the meeting is not successful as I am dysfluent slightly (as I was yesterday – I'm simply not seeing enough of people these days), and she, having just left her dentist, is distracted to the point of being conversationally absent. On another level, though, we connect. She talks of having lived all over Canada and coming here twenty-some years ago, where she came out, and of the same-sex marriage lawsuit she and her partner, an MD, are helping to fight, of her new story collection for Oberon [Press] after a long absence from bookshops, of her struggles with a novel (fifth or sixth draft). She is from a farm background and a bit unpolished but absolutely genuine.

MONDAY, 2 SEPTEMBER / VANCOUVER

I awake to rain on the windows: the annual monsoon has begun: the dark season. Hard work to get this place sufficiently cleaned up and organised to do the work I must do this week.

SATURDAY, 14 SEPTEMBER / VANCOUVER
To Sechelt to see M's uncle, the retired naval officer. Gibsons sparkles but Sechelt is a wretched place, poorly planned if planned at all and badly misdeveloped. [A friend of M's] lives, fittingly, next to the mountain of sand and gravel in the middle of town where the real mountain used to be.

TUESDAY, 17 SEPTEMBER / VANCOUVER
The miracle of Neil Reynolds, which used to so enrage J: today, like yesterday, I am chain-kicking angry and low-down until, after a brief meeting with him, I suddenly turn sunny. This following an interview with James King, the biographer, at the Hotel Vancouver. Later: sometimes I worry that I am too much consumed in each day, to the exclusion of contemplating the larger uncertainties. (Other days, of course, I worry just the opposite.)

THURSDAY, 19 SEPTEMBER / VANCOUVER
In the afternoon, feeling confident and lucky, I phone Anne about *Jericho*, which she promises to read and report on during June. The conversation goes well – long, friendly, and full of promises that she will in fact publish the book in late spring, based solely, so far, on the report by her editor, suggesting a new opening etc., which document she pledges to send to me. She continues to be charming (as well as exasperating, though less so to me, I fear, than I am to her). What always has struck me has been her way of introducing – with no embarrassment whatever – the most embarrassing details of her personal life into serious conversations, in order to – do what exactly? reconnect with her listener and prove the non-middle-class roots she otherwise hides so obscurely? This time she appends a paragraph of conversation to the end of a long discourse on death and public necessity. It concerns the way she has managed, by discipline and Pilates, to shed twenty pounds and thus restore her original ass-line, "as I was getting so that I didn't want to wear jackets."

SUNDAY, 29 SEPTEMBER / VANCOUVER
As I usually analyse what goes wrong, so now I analyse what goes right. What promises to be a day of frustration turns into one of assured calm, the kind of lack of apparent nervousness that other people like. I go to

Word on the Street reluctantly and meet with Mona Fertig at Rosie's, the nearby pub. She is on good behaviour and so am I, and the meeting is pleasant, if also sad and alarming when she tells me that Peter Such had a heart episode yesterday. Pierre sits down at the next table with – can't remember his name, a friend of Stuewe's from Toronto who is trying to be a writer. Compared with some of my other meetings with Pierre, this one goes quite well; I do not let myself feel bad. At the next table over to the right of Pierre's evident g.f. (he likes women with thick eyebrows but doesn't introduce them) sits Peter Trower, who's precisely as I imagined: a short, stocky, taciturn fellow, drinking beer, as befits a retired logger and folk writer.[2] For as long as I've been in Vancouver, I've been hearing his derogatory remarks about me and my column, which he now has the hypocrisy to tell me he enjoys. Later, out in the street again, Ron Hatch introduces me to George Payerle (who tells me that I am Douglas Fetherling's brother) and Daphne Marlatt (who is not fierce and humourless as I have always imagined her, but on the contrary is warm and open).[3]

TUESDAY, 1 OCTOBER / VANCOUVER

A drink today with [a colleague]. How sad that I can't really get to know such a talented and warm person simply because of the lesbian gap. I fancy that her lesbianism is the comfortable Boston marriage kind of old, a version of self-sufficiency based on calm and monogamy. But of course I don't really know. In any case, sexuality is just another screen by which I feel excluded from so much. An untouchable in youth, like me, remains an untouchable late in life. Subtracting A from B, what I find is a certain lessening of the outward manifestations of my dysfluency making me less offputting to people than I was then – the process aided perhaps by the school kid remaining in many of the Anglo middle class that makes them still pay lip service to writing (anything but actually reading, which is work).

2   Peter Trower (b. 1930), poet and novelist.
3   George Payerle (b. 1945), poet and fiction writer, author of *The Afterpeople*; Daphne Marlatt (b. 1942), poet and novelist, author of *Ana Historic* and other works.

THURSDAY, 3 OCTOBER / VANCOUVER
Dream about being "subversive inside the monastery" – specifically, "at
the buffet."

FRIDAY, 4 OCTOBER / VANCOUVER
Those who can talk, do.

MONDAY, 7 OCTOBER / VANCOUVER
This flat is an unqualified mess, especially now that a big leak has ruined
the carpet in the front hall. So I begin by clearing one small corner of the
place. At the end of the day, M and I are off to the UBC bookstore for the
launch of Bill New's Can lit encyclopaedia. Rebecca is there and I finally
meet up with John O'Brian, the art critic. As launching parties go, it is a
pleasant one.

SUNDAY, 20 OCTOBER / VANCOUVER
The day begins with promise, though I soon tense up. Still, I finish a
column (the pressure is really on to write write write), and M and I go in
the afternoon to Keith Maillard's launch at a restaurant in Ambleside,
which I'm sure has been selected by Mary. A good turnout and many
copies of the novel sold. Looking at Keith I realise that many people
must view him as they view me at their most charitable: someone who is
shy and quiet but occasionally able to rise for short periods. So thinking,
I consider how fortunate I was to have been young and awkward in the
'60s and '70s when outcasts were better understood and even in some
cases respected; I should be at an even greater disadvantage if I were
young today.

MONDAY, 21 OCTOBER / VANCOUVER
To the Granville Island Hotel in the late afternoon to interview Wayne
Johnston, who's slightly jet-lagged from flying in for the Writers' Festival
and for some reason can't make eye contact at all.[4] He seems quite like
his novels: smoothly male, polite, maybe somewhat intriguing, driven by
narrative. A friendly encounter.

4 Wayne Johnston (b. 1958), author of *The Colony of Unrequited Dreams* and
other novels.

THURSDAY, 24 OCTOBER / VANCOUVER
More and worse mutterings.

FRIDAY, 25 OCTOBER / VANCOUVER
Lunch with Eric McCormack, who plays the raging Scots loon to the hilt, skilfully.[5] The day ends with a drink at the Sylvia with Nancy Duxbury of the city arts branch to inquire about a small emergency grant to the Fed. She replies: "I can't think of a precedent except when the Vancouver East Cultural Centre had a disastrous fire." To which I then reply: "I'd be prepared to start a fire if necessary." But of course there is no hope. Nancy is a young, pale ultrafemme person, born with earrings, unable to speak without using both hands to gesture yet when she does, speaking very softly indeed.

SUNDAY, 27 OCTOBER / VANCOUVER
Breakfast with Patrick Crean before he departs for the airport. He's talking of a desire to quit Toronto and move here: I know the symptoms. He is precisely what Keith so innocently said he is: an Upper Canadian gentleman, a type Keith knows only from other people's novels but among whom I moved for decade after decade. He's an amiable but rather unobservant representative of the type. Evidently thinks I'm a sports writer or reporter or something of that sort.

MONDAY, 11 NOVEMBER / VANCOUVER
When I return here there's a message from a *Sun* reporter asking me to comment on George Bowering's appointment as Canada's first poet laureate. I find the message too late to be helpful.

FRIDAY, 29 NOVEMBER / VANCOUVER
A meeting with Scott McIntyre who, I realise with some horror, acts the way he does round me not because he's so generally insecure perhaps but rather because I intimidate him as someone who's a few years younger yet a professional contemporary and have become (so I believe he feels)

5 Eric McCormack, (b. 1938), short story writer and novelist, author of *The Paradise Hotel* and other works.

a notorious artist/rebel figure. Sounds absurd, I know, but this is the impression my instinct dictates.

TUESDAY, 17 DECEMBER / VANCOUVER
News in the national papers the past few days about Howard Engel's stroke (itself news to me, though a few years ago) having left him without the ability to read. One day, I hope, someone will write Howard's story – the deeply troubled and troubling first wife, the saintly second one who is differently troubled and dies young, a few years after giving birth – the thwarted, tangled literary ambitions of the three people.

TUESDAY, 24 DECEMBER / VANCOUVER
As she suggests I do, I phone Anne to discuss the maddeningly unspecific editorial memo she has sent regarding *Jericho*. I get her in the middle of mopping the farmhouse kitchen's floor in preparation for cooking a feast tomorrow; at one point, she accidentally drops the phone into the bucket. A long talk from which I come away mildly reassured, though she still refuses to commit herself on timing. Later, though, a courier delivers her marked-up copy of the ms, and I am plunged back into despair. She has read it so hastily that she has misunderstood more often than not, or so it seems to me, and the thrust of her remarks is towards non-fictionalising the language and simplification of an almost journalistic sort. (Later: I am overreacting to say the least. Anne is right, as usual.)

THURSDAY, 26 DECEMBER / VANCOUVER
I cling to the liberal humanist tradition because it is what I know but also because it is the measure by which I can state that my life has not been a failure, because, whatever else I've done, I've grown.

TUESDAY, 31 DECEMBER / VANCOUVER
New Year's Eve. I slide into 2003 and my fifty-fourth year while working at my desk. M promises a wild party for me this time after I passed the holiday in silence a year ago, but having only twelve months to get organised she of course has failed to plan anything at all, as I expected. I say this only with comic insight, not bitterness.

2003

While still struggling with successive versions of the novel *Jericho*, I also began work in earnest on two other projects, a book-length poem entitled *Singer, An Elegy* and the main body of what became *Tales of Two Cities: A Novella Plus Stories*. I completed much of this labour in Yukon while writer-in-residence at Pierre Berton's childhood home in Dawson City.

FRIDAY, 3 JANUARY / VANCOUVER

I find myself making the rounds, selectively at least, of people I have trespassed against or otherwise have been in messes with, including messes of silence, like some person in AA. This has something to do with being by no means assured of the longevity required for the recognition of ability, for none of us is guaranteed anything.

THURSDAY, 9 JANUARY / VANCOUVER

Lonely for Bangkok. Also, telling myself that I must realise that these intellectual games I play with regard to messes are for my benefit alone, that such messes as get solved do so through the passage of time and opportunity for correction – and then only given a deeply liberal spirit on the other person's part. By my intensely focused reaction, however, I do help to draft emotional policy.

SATURDAY, 11 JANUARY / VANCOUVER

A wildly disturbing dream merely to process anxiety that has built up, as so many of my dreams do. Neil is involved. It contains these lines: "I left before I even knew to live without" and "I *was* with part of the attack, I am hearing." Yes, dreams are neuropsychological experiences (yet

Freud was hardly without merit in believing they are also attempts by the subconscious to gain the chair's attention and be recognised). The middle ground, to which I subscribe, is that dreams are the trash bin of the mind but nonetheless highlight or priorise – certainly clarify – the inner agenda.

SUNDAY, 12 JANUARY / VANCOUVER

A youngish addict with a long thin English face – looking a bit like Richard Landon – sits on the concrete lamp-standard base in the Shell station's car park, injecting himself in the back of his left hand.

FRIDAY, 24 JANUARY / VANCOUVER

Nancy Richler accepts an invitation to lunch at the Banana Leaf, unaware that I don't know that she keeps kosher.[1] Of course none of the food there is prepared under rabbinical supervision. I don't think there are hallal dishes either. Anyway, most everything on the bill of fare contains shrimp or shrimp paste. She refuses my offer to go somewhere else and makes do with bread. This leads to talk of her background: how she grew up in an Orthodox household, had to keep even her collarbones covered all through school, and when married could not shake hands with her husband's male friends. Then she became a lesbian and moved to East Vancouver! Such a highly intelligent and humane person. She shows me snapshots of one of her dogs and her two donkeys. I meet the other dog in person. The day is springlike and the dog is taking inventory, sniffing the entire landscape all over again, an inch at a time, the way dogs believe it their devoir to do. Humans don't understand the labour involved.

MONDAY, 27 JANUARY / VANCOUVER

Odd how the past is usually seen as less sophisticated than the present (part of the liberal idea of progress, which perforce is directed forward, not back). Yet when talking of cities, the past is often perceived as a golden age. Thinking also of how the middle-class readership always

---

1 Nancy Richler (b. 1957), novelist, author of *Throwaway Angels* and *Your Mouth is Lovely*.

looks on writers of other backgrounds as somehow broken, damaged, both on the page and off. Examples I have known from past generations: [Hugh] Garner, Acorn, Marian Engel. Now all of those were difficult personalities, the result of (in order of appearance) alcoholism, psychosis, and just nasty awkwardness, and they did not fulfil their potential as writers (who does?); but this perception that their outsider status makes them unworthy to be read bothers me. Of course, the perception is not spread evenly. Garner isn't read at all, Acorn has a regional and leftist following, Engel is propped up by her gender appeal and her surviving followers from the original pack. Thinking also of all the acquaintances who died younger than I will (much healthier than dwelling on those who outlive me): H, Brud Delaney, Sandy Ross, Matt Cohen, many others – all dead in their fifties.

TUESDAY, 18 FEBRUARY / VANCOUVER
How often have small messes been resolved after years of avoidance when the other party has died. Of course the partner in the mess was usually – almost always – a member of an older generation. Now it's my turn. Others wait for *me* to die, it seems.

MONDAY, 24 FEBRUARY / VANCOUVER
Erotic dreams always sound ridiculous even when only alluded to, much less described, yet they are sometimes the most vivid; I once had an exquisitely erotic dream that depended on the fact that Anne C was wearing red when everyone else was in black-and-white; I am reminded of Eisenstein's *Battleship Potemkin*, in which one scene featured the red flag hand coloured on copies of the print: audiences gasped.[2]

THURSDAY, 6 MARCH / VANCOUVER
Broken sleep appears to have set me up for a frustrating day, though the gloom is relieved when Deborah Campbell comes by, allowing me to try getting a better fix on her.[3] She is bright and confident, and has begun studying Arabic to go with her Hebrew. Has stories of living in Israel

---

2 Sergei Eisenstein (1898–1948), Russian filmmaker.
3 Deborah Campbell (b. 1970), political journalist, author of *This Heated Place*.

during the Gulf War. Is restless. Of course I can't help but recall what and how I was at her age (thirty-three). I was nearing the absolute professional bottom in 1982, unable to pull myself up until the latter part of the decade; I was getting involved with J. I had nowhere near Deborah's ability at anything. Yet I am sad somehow to discover just how thoroughly a non-fiction person she is, actively distrusting the imagination.

THURSDAY, 20 MARCH / VANCOUVER

A drink at the Sylvia with [a colleague], so tremulous, so full of himself yet empty of himself at the same time, as he tries unsuccessfully to mask or at least acknowledge his low self-esteem with puffery and name-dropping. I fear he may never be the artist he wishes so desperately to be, because he wastes his time worrying about his stature while making the same piece of art over and over. There's so much more he could do.

FRIDAY, 28 MARCH / VANCOUVER

In the afternoon, riding along Burrard, I see a man crossing the street carrying a large ornamental planter containing an enormous pot plant, quite a healthy specimen.

SUNDAY, 6 APRIL / VANCOUVER

Still trying to fix *Jericho*, a task I have returned to. Lonnie [a character in the novel] talks the conversation I never had with GSF, about whom I continue to think with respect to *Singer*. In the absence of knowing him better, in the absence of having had the opportunity, I am drawn to the people with whom I risk being the target of the condescension that lurks beneath their humanity; to the famous no one but me has ever heard of; and sometimes to established men, far more successful than I am, whose other acknowledged contemporaries are of the same kind.

WEDNESDAY, 16 APRIL / VANCOUVER

Deborah C and I talk politics for an hour or so. She basically adheres to the popular view of the three large forces at work in the world: the multilateralists, mostly European, who see the threat of concerted military and economic action as the only means of holding chaos at bay; the American fundamentalist unilateralists, bent on world domination if only by proxy in some cases (as even they know they can't occupy the entire world) and hostile to all international bodies, treaties and courts they do not control; and of course the Islamic fundamentalists, accounting for perhaps twenty per cent of the faith and feeling that a radical return to their own past as they perceive it is the sole means of reclaiming some of what the West has pilfered. She is full of knowledge and dedication to the craft, meaning of course that she is a reader first. Strangely, she seems to have no major gender issues informing her actions, leastwise none I am permitted to see. But then I get the sense that she views me as an elder colleague.

THURSDAY, 24 APRIL / VANCOUVER

Peggy A is in town as part of a three-month tour to promote her new novel, and she and I have a touching breakfast at the Wedgewood. Touching because she feels she must be mindful of my welfare as she is of the welfare of all the other human detritus from her past. Have I planned my gym regimen (I guess the results are visible) in consultation with my doctor? Have I kept my money out of the equities markets? GICs, yes that's good, but there are bonds I might have considered as well. Do I have enough to see me through the ten years until my Canada Pension kicks in? I take care to lie and say yes, lest the dear woman write me a cheque by way of a small contribution. Conversation between us has seldom been easy in terms of the mechanics, yet we have meaningful meetings and this is one. She tells me of her successful legal action against [a newspaper columnist], whom she loathes. The subject of Michael Ignatieff's flip-flop on the Iraqi war comes up, and she surprises me by citing his bloodline: "They're White Russians, loyal to the empire. A different empire now but the loyalty is the same." Her size always surprises me. So tiny. She laughs when I reaffirm my faith in her magical powers. Two sometimes-friends from the old days sharing breakfast, one so successful, the other not in the least. Then I'm off to the library to take part in a mass book signing. I arrive sufficiently early to swipe place cards so that I can share a table with Nancy Richler and Deborah Campbell in order to introduce them to each other, knowing they will get along well. The big surprise is that [a somewhat volatile writer] does not attack but rather the opposite, possibly with some encouragement from her friend. She confirms that she is giving up her apartment here. Afterwards Nancy and I go for a bite on Pender. We seem to hit upon the same thought simultaneously: "I've never met an extrovert who's smart."

SATURDAY, 26 APRIL / VANCOUVER

Bill Cameron, in town to see his parents and promote his first novel, a
satire on the media, comes round in late afternoon, and we reminisce
about Sarah and her crazy friend. That he's sixty is astonishing: the part of
him that is show biz, as distinct from the part that writes, has taken care
of himself well and expensively. M comes down, all dolled up, and the
three of us go off to the BC Book Awards. The host is Bill Richardson (he's
the host of all such events).[4] He wears a kilt, sporran, and tam o'shanter
as well as high heels (with rolled-down bobby socks) and a double strand
of droopy pearls, and minces for the audience, making jokes about picking
up hockey players. Carol Shields wins the fiction prize, collected by her
daughter who whips out a mobile at the podium and calls the sickroom to
convey the news. Such sympathy awards are always a judgement call.
Otherwise the awards tonight go to: a mediocre commissioned corporate
history as best non-fiction, a picture book about tugboats as book of the
year, one of bill bissett's latest collections as best poetry. Long tedious
speeches. Nonetheless, an enjoyable evening of talking at the reception
before and after to John Burns, Peter Milroy [of UBC Press], Jean Wilson,
and Bill New, not to mention [a colleague] who turns out to be a slicker
character than I had imagined. This is the attraction of such events.

MONDAY, 28 APRIL / VANCOUVER

I deliver back orders to various downtown bookshops, inevitably recalling the similar chores I did at Anansi in 1967–68. Thinking more about
Peggy: how she always had taken the sharpest interest in, for want of
a more dignified term, Canadian literary gossip. Her knowledge of
Canadian writers' lives is wide and deep and of course of no interest
whatsoever to her foreign colleagues, much less her foreign audience:
rather, it is what she carries round privately, as one does family news.

FRIDAY, 9 MAY / VANCOUVER

Coffee in the morning with Taras Grescoe, Paul's son, who in his late
thirties looks like a much younger fellow, full of bushy-tailed innocence.[5]

4   Bill Richardson (b. 1955), humourist, broadcaster, and writer.
5   Taras Grescoe (b. 1967), non-fiction writer, author of *Sacré Blues* and *The End
of Elsewhere*.

In fact, his mind is far more mature than his visage. A good chat. Then to lunch at the Templeton in Granville Street, among the sex shops, with Kate Taylor, whose novel about Proust's mother is most well done of its sort, though the sort is the usual: two narratives, one historical and the other modern, crisscrossing, with some of the latter carefully set in Canada to forestall criticism at home – but not enough to encourage other criticism abroad.[6] Kate, born in France to diplomat parents and reared variously, is nobody's fool and proves to be funny as well once I get her warmed up a bit. She is small, green-eyed, looks only vaguely like her thumbnail in the *Globe*. We spend quite a while talking about the paper. She says offhandedly that [a particular colleague] has "no human warmth whatever."

SATURDAY, 10 MAY / VANCOUVER

The *Globe* this morning has a positive paragraph about the paperback of my Woodcock book, though Woodcock is called Woodstock. M and I go to the wine-making place up Davie Street to bottle my latest batch of cab sauv. Such a generous spring day, full of shipping and dogs, that I remember how I have planned to use such weather to break my horrible cycle: when I remain at home, I feel frail, falling into a role; when I go out, I sense mortality in imagined overexertion. All this far worse in dark wet weather.

TUESDAY, 13 MAY / VANCOUVER

Thinking more about Peggy, possibly because I read that Dennis Lee is coming to town for a reading. Those two old university friends share the same awkwardness of speech, which I can characterise only as a tendency to talk of the rarefied and the commonplace as though they were exactly the same weight, telling you stuff that's fascinating and stuff everybody knows in the same sentence, with no distinction between the categories. In Peggy, I find this charming; in Dennis it's simply frustrating, preventing real communication of even the non-verbal kind. Peggy is, of course, different. I find her full of humanity, sometimes archly expressed, but mostly not.

6   Kate Taylor (b. 1962), newspaper journalist and novelist, author of *Mme Proust and the Kosher Kitchen*.

THURSDAY, 15 MAY / VANCOUVER

Eleanor Wachtel, in town for the Jewish Film Festival, swings by here for morning coffee. Her hair, black when I last saw her in Toronto, is now various beiges, buffs, and browns. Her sterling qualities are always so obvious, yet one suspects that there are even better ones she keeps hidden. I like her company to be sure. Her new book has a heavy glam shot of her on the jacket, a *Vogue*-style shot.

FRIDAY, 16 MAY / VANCOUVER

Proofing day. Also, I begin to see the end of the last version of *Jericho*, which cheers me, as I may then be able to get on with other work. In the evening, M and I go to a play at the CBC on Georgia, a work whose description in the listings intrigued us, because it is set in a short-time hotel in Bangkok. A two-hander: a young Vancouver woman who's been teaching English and a Cambodian refugee (and, it turns out, a former Khmer Rouge guerrilla as well as Khmer Rouge victim), now a Patpong prostitute who wants to flee to Canada. Patches of effective writing and one polished performance. Preachy, however, and the Cambodian part is played by a woman with what sounds like a Caribbean accent. We were one-quarter of the audience.

SATURDAY, 17 MAY / VANCOUVER

Finish the draft – the fourth – of *Jericho*. The manuscript is much improved by Anne's suggestions. Not wasting time, I turn back to work on *Singer*, and doing so I realise once again that I must tackle the long-neglected memoir.

MONDAY, 19 MAY / VANCOUVER

Spend much of the day reading for the column, but a day of writing as well. It is spring. Is the deafening report I hear the ice jam breaking up in this office? How I hope.

WEDNESDAY, 21 MAY / VANCOUVER

A surprisingly enjoyable all-day breakfast today with George Bowering at my favourite Granville Street diner (est. 1934), which I hope might suggest his beloved Helen's or the east side while leaving him close to his next appointment downtown. He looks ruggedly well. More importantly he seems now like someone who has been mellowed and evened out by age and unfortunate sorrow (his health the past few years, Angela's death), though on the surface he usually seems as of old – as when, for example, he terrorises the wait staff with non-stop banter, badgers them with banter in fact, like a boyish Groucho. He is a person whose just-a-guy openness of manner does nothing to obscure a system of defences that the Marquis de Vauban [the 17th-century French military engineer] might have admired. He tells me that eight or nine months ago he made an approach to Annex Books about wanting to sell some good books, including a copy of *Double Persephones* given him by Peggy. When he returned to the subject in another email only recently, J replied curtly, he felt, hinting at some change in circumstances that she acted as though he should be aware of. Later: thinking more about Bowering as one of those people I met in the late '60s. We have mostly avoided each other since that time. Thus there is certain awkwardness in his conversation with me as a result of the gaping informational chasm caused by my speech today – the gaping gap, so to say. But he does his best to give a successful interview despite having me as the interviewer. I find the attempt interesting as it requires some of the new seriousness he has acquired through age and misfortune and lately has had cause to exercise in his role as poet laureate.

WEDNESDAY, 28 MAY / VANCOUVER
Opening the email this morning I see Neil's name on a message and know even before opening the text that he's quit the *Sun* to settle back in his beloved eastern Ontario. Since the paper was sold, he's never had the budget to maintain the paper at the level he wants, much less improve it. I feared he was going to quit last summer while I was away, and tried to dissuade him. Still, I was hoping and frankly expecting that he would stay another two years until his sixty-fifth birthday. His decision otherwise of course puts me in peril, because his successor, whoever it may be, will get rid of me at once; such is the pattern; Neil is the only one who's approved of my work.

THURSDAY, 29 MAY / VANCOUVER
Neil has been such a catalyst for me the past, let me see, sixteen years that I'm still in shock. Yet when I take realistic stock of income and

expenses without any money from the *Sun* I realise that I can probably make do until I die or reach sixty, barring large unforeseen expenses, such as might arise from legal bills related to the condo mess.

SATURDAY, 7 JUNE / VANCOUVER

An important date, the day of the Fed's annual conference and AGM, at which I hand over the presidency to Margaret Thompson, thank God. To prepare, M must rise at 3:00 a.m. on only three or so hours sleep. I have the luxury of her driving back to pick me up at 11:30 and taking me to Douglas College in New Westminster, where the festivities unfold. Attendance is actually not bad. As always, the spectacle of someone such as me trying to run a meeting according to Robert's Rules is bizarre. My little speech on stepping down, I hear, actually does animate the members, as intended. Being organised by two New West patriots, the conference itself suggests intellectual hillbillyism, though frankly not to the extent I feared. The so-called banquet, however, is dreadful, with the mayor, the MLA, and the editor of the local weekly and other mindless worthies munching chicken pot pie in the student pub while a woman does her impression of Emily Carr: a one-woman show of sorts, I'm told. I contrive to miss this by going to the theatre early with Susan Musgrave. I think she and I shock each other by how steadily and rapidly we have aged. Seeing her now fills me with sadness for what the years (and personal tragedy) have done to one of the central beauties of her generation. She is, however, unfazed by this to all appearances and in fact rather unflappable generally, except when, as the result of an organiser's foul-up, the comp hotel suite for her, her younger daughter, and the daughter's boyfriend does not appear to exist. No doubt there is an element of racism involved, as the boyfriend is Native. Also, Susan is strangely dressed, as usual. The Fed finally straightens out the mess. Susan is wonderful as the host of the big reading from the *Fed Anthology* – funny, relaxed, candid, gracious. The readers in the audience respond well to her. David Watmough, now almost unable to walk, is a sorry sight, as too his companion Floyd, who's beaten bowel cancer but at a big price and now is recovering from deep vein thrombosis, using a walking frame; I spend as much time with them as I can.[7] Alan Twigg, although

---

7   David Watmough (b. 1926), novelist, author of the "Davey Bryant" cycle.

a contributor, does not read but comes anyway, to support the organisation, wearing one of his trademark second-hand tropical shirts. We have a few minutes' meeting in the corridor to discuss the BC Book Prize Society, Woodcock and Skelton, the BC Arts Council, and his paper. I may be beginning to win him over to the view, so rarely held by anyone as to be worth remarking on, that there is in fact more to me than meets the ear – a bit more anyway. This fills me with hope. M and I get back to Pendrell Street shortly before midnight.

THURSDAY, 12 JUNE / VANCOUVER

The drug dealers being pushed off Hastings Street by the cops have taken up residence elsewhere, including a tiny park on Thurlow where you can watch them making crack deals with hand signals not unlike those used by stock traders in the old days: touching one nostril furtively means $12, for example, while touching the other means $15. Don Stewart and I pass a school of these fellows as we leave his shop and go out for what's becoming our usual chicken biryani lunch (actually lamb in Don's case); they are shirtless on a hot day, and quick of hand like so many stage conjurers. A split second and the deal is done.

FRIDAY, 13 JUNE / VANCOUVER

I rouse myself to interview [a novelist] on her new book. She despised me actively though discontinuously for thirty years or so, writing vile things about me (I recall a letter to Fulford in particular) and once refusing my financial donation to a literary charity she was involved with. The publicist, who is innocent of much historical knowledge about Can lit, tells me she was told to expect trouble. In the event, though, she is fine at dinner, even charming, a change I attribute to a) many overtures on my part, and b) age. Knowing how much she has had difficulty with my speech (for she told Bob F I was "pathetic"), I work as hard as I possibly can. I'm far from perfect, of course, but evidently good enough.

SUNDAY, 29 JUNE / WHITEHORSE

I sleep with the left hand elevated, and sleep surprisingly well considering. In the morning light, the [broken] finger looks even more awful, swollen like a fat German sausage with blue and crimson casing. I have difficulty carrying the heaviest bag – books, of course – that I have to get to Dawson. With M's help, however, I catch the Air North flight and arrive here to be met by the proprietor of the *Yukon News*, a young fellow who has bought out the other members of his family. The town is pretty much as I remember it.

MONDAY, 30 JUNE / DAWSON CITY
During the seven-hour trip to Dawson I talk with a gold miner, late forties, who must go to Dawson to fly back to Pelly where he's to take up a new job with a company that's been mining in the region for the past eleven years. An amiable fellow, not too overly talkative, like so many in the North, or so I've often found. Dawson is hardly abuzz with tourists, as SARS, a strong Canadian dollar, and of course the ever-present threat of militant Muslims keep the Americans away. I do, however, see some Japanese. The Berton House is most pleasant: a well-renovated cottage or bungalow, comfortably furnished.

WEDNESDAY, 2 JULY / DAWSON CITY
I come back and make another stab at trying to read Bruce Chatwin but still cannot take his prose or the structure of his books seriously. I do redeem myself, however, by finally settling down to work after dinner and writing ten pages of the *Tales*, which looks now to be a novella of between fifteen thousand and twenty thousand words. I finish the session before midnight and fall into bed joyfully.

THURSDAY, 3 JULY / DAWSON CITY
Off to some errands in the morning, such as buying a backpack at the self-styled outfitters – the one I have been using, bought on the pavement in Sukhumvit Road, Bangkok, having lasted longer than I imagined a counterfeit would, which was not long. Sloth and poor habits all afternoon, but now I prepare to go back into the novella or whatever it is. Sometimes the act of writing euthanizes a piece of one's personality, under cover of disinfecting a particular experience, permitting something else to replace it. Such was certainly the case with *Travels by Night* and to a lesser extent *Jericho*. Perhaps this fiction will do something similar.

FRIDAY, 4 JULY / DAWSON CITY
At the market in Front Street, where I've gone for milk and juice, I see a man in his sixties wearing a large pin in the shape of an American flag

that lights up and blinks – first one stripe, then the next; similarly with the stars; the lights are themselves red, white, and blue. The pin is affixed to his T-shirt, which bears the legend OPERATION IRAQI FREEDOM. His cap proclaims the same message. I hope that these items are intended only for this American holiday. I am reminded of the often reproduced archival photos of the American crowds clogging this very stretch of Front Street on 4 July 1898, even sitting on the roofs, tangled in flags and bunting.

TUESDAY, 8 JULY / DAWSON CITY
Stepping even a short distance outside the town grid reveals wild flowers – blue, yellow, and burnt orange. There's something of the saprophyte about this town, living off its dead past to the extent it does. But then it also honours something truly remarkable that took place from June 1897 to say July 1899, when the wowsers and scissorbills killed it.

FRIDAY, 11 JULY / DAWSON CITY
Busloads of mostly US tourists, brought here from Skagway as part of their cruise ship tours up the Inside Passage, troop to the Robert W. Service cabin directly across the street and the Jack London one a few doors down. The Canadian holiday-makers want to see the Berton House as well. I see them studying the interpretive material placed round the lawn. Today, as I'm coming out of the bathroom, fully dressed, I find two couples videotaping the living room and fingering papers on the desk. I draw their attention to the notices outside asking zoo visitors not to feed the writers-in-residence, as it were. Then I shoo them away and lock the doors.

I have reached the hundred-page level of the novella draft, right on schedule, but find that the story needs more telling, and so I will continue with it even while I move on to another task, namely the draft of *Singer*. At the post office this morning, I find the proofs of the Bangkok edition of *Three Pagodas Pass*, so these must be tended to as well. Happy and productive.

SATURDAY, 19 JULY / DAWSON CITY
Check my email at the saloon to find someone praising my tribute to Shields, which evidently the *Sun* ran on Friday. I have been worried

– stupidly, of course – about what's going on in Vancouver in my absence. But that's always the way: anxious about Toronto when in Kingston and vice versa, etc. I hereby renounce this behaviour. I come back to Eighth Avenue to resume work on the poem, which continues to secrete words.

WEDNESDAY, 30 JULY / WHITEHORSE

I return to the Horse by means of the nine-hour bus trip through alder, poplar, and spruce, through swamps and enormous bald mountains far and near, with short stops every hour or two at places like Stewart Crossing or Pelly where an occasional RV stirs the dust. We see two young elk, a porcupine, and a glumly curious and inquisitive male moose standing in water past his knees. Arrive in the city to find a Native guy playing the tenor banjo in Main Street while actually nodding off to sleep. Also find out today's *Yukon News* displays me on the front page: treatment to which I am accustomed only when being indicted.

WEDNESDAY, 27 AUGUST / VANCOUVER

Dream about Michael Ignatieff allowing me to use his house – near Harvard? – a big white frame house, smelling like a cabin – as a hideout. I'm on the run. Michael gives me a track suit to take in my bag when, the danger over for the moment, I move on.

THURSDAY, 28 AUGUST / VANCOUVER

The day begins tensely and ends bizarrely even by the loose standards that now prevail. Trouble, or what looks like trouble, in Bangkok at 6:00 a.m., but in fact it is simply an interim more-later message. And no doubt there *will* be more later. The question is forced to the background by an expected attack from Ottawa. The fact that I expected it does not of course lessen the impact, the hurt, the anger, or the damage. At this stage, the day has begun to play havoc with the very notion of stress abatement, which begins to grow urgent (thereby naturally causing more stress). These concerns in turn are pushed aside by a phone conversation, more than an hour, with Earle. He says the reason he hasn't been in touch or answered my letters, returned my calls, or acknowledged the books I've been sending is that I have affronted, no assaulted, his "moral centre" both by using irony and by using my middle name. The latter act, he says, has convinced him that I have changed my personality as well and obviously not for the better: "You are no longer the person I knew all those years. You've become a complete stranger to me" and this both frightens and angers him (my words here). When he then accuses me of actually having crossed over into madness, I must resist the temptation to introduce the pot to the kettle. By repeatedly accepting blame for whatever I am charged with, I manage to get him calmed down, but this is hard work, especially when he is lashing out at me, interrogating me about my "motives" and snarling odd accusations. By the end, calm is restored and he offers hope that we can repair all this damage of which I have been completely unaware – for all this is factually nonsense, of course, though not therefore nonsense in his own mind. I put no stock in the name-change business but put quite a bit in the irony matter. At some point in the ageing process he has burned out or otherwise lost the ironic function, at least as it relates to speech. He now requires unnuanced speech, direct and unadorned by the mastery of expression he always exhibited in his own conversation. Now he sees danger in such talk: trickery, deceit, traps ready to spring. Insofar as I myself am concerned, he doubtless had considerable prodding from his present wife, whose sarcasm about me has been evident from the start. In any case, I'm left uncertain about how to respond if he does indeed ever resume contact: write him very carefully (I don't know to what extent his reading is affected as well as his listening). That would be tiresome though I would have to do so and keep at it if I believed it would help somehow. It's tempting to consider this as being akin to the Cabbagetown problem which resolved itself in my mind once contact was made, rendering further communication unnecessary when I learned that the other party was all right. In any case, a strange and powerful addition to my bestiary of monsters. No doubt I'll be making more notes on this in the future. Stay tuned.

TUESDAY, 2 SEPTEMBER / VANCOUVER
A promising start to the day when I go out for the *Sunday Times* of London and find Frederick Forsyth's positive review of *The Book of Assassins*, then return here and discover a cheque for the Czech-language edition of the same.

SATURDAY, 6 SEPTEMBER / VANCOUVER

A catch-up reading day, deep in the new autumn books, and it strikes me that there is one element in mainstream Canadian fiction that resembles Flemish painting. Individuals or small groups of figures find comfort in all the detail of middle-class life that fills their lives and the square rooms in which their lives are played out. Allegory stands out boldly, even at times absurdly, against a background of observed realism. Light and darkness do battle, and shade is the result. The characters live in cities and suburbs but yearn for the lost past and a simple, romantic, or easily romanticised existence in a rural world they never knew. The Prairie grain elevators in such writing are indistinguishable from the windmills in Dutch cigar-box art.

MONDAY, 8 SEPTEMBER / VANCOUVER

Nancy Richler comes by. She's recently returned from yet another trip to Italy, where she's evidently becoming as popular as her father's cousin Mordecai was. She shows me a photo of the place in the Fraser Valley that she and Vicki have bought; I'd had the impression it was a simple country dwelling but in fact it's an expensive brick ranch house that the two of them are having gutted and rebuilt to their specs. Also, they're adding an outbuilding for the donkeys and a kind of tree house over-looking the river for N to write in. I enjoy her company, and I find I have no jealousy whatever concerning her good fortune – an inheritance fol-lowed the last novel; she wears her money lightly and uses it well not only on herself but also on people and causes she believes in. A nervously sincere and amusing conversationalist, she surprises me by saying that one of the reasons she enjoys going to Italy is that the Catholic masses there are so elaborate and grand.

THURSDAY, 11 SEPTEMBER / VANCOUVER

A true autumnal day (and the first few are always so invigorating). I work away at the tottering stack of books that must be read urgently, then at day's end go to the City Hall spill-over office space on the north-west corner of 10th and Cambie for the city book awards meeting. Nancy Duxbury, who's been overseeing the prize programme for Cultural Services, is leaving her position on Monday to join the na-tional association of municipal culture planners she's become involved with, and seems distracted. She is short and slightly *embonpoint* with fine pale skin and a raspberry mouth. She's always dressed stylishly (a little unusually so for Vancouver) but rather conservatively (ditto), and she speaks in luxurious whispers. She's somehow suggestive of the 1940s, though I would place her age in the low thirties at most. I manage to get an honourable mention for Fiona Lam's poetry collection and to steer the jury to splitting the prize between two similar and equally excellent books, *Heroines* and *Every Building on 100 West Pender*. I'm asked to stay on as a juror for next year, as the prize has now adopted the Canada Council practice of having a continuity person. I return home dreadfully tired and get into bed, listening to the winds blow rain against the north side of the building. Thus do I avoid the orgy of patriotism on American television this day, which has become a holy one to cowboys and rednecks.

SUNDAY, 14 SEPTEMBER / VANCOUVER

Eating Indian food with G, who's talking about the effects of Timothy Taylor's novel *Stanley Park* on the actual park when who walks past the window but Timothy Taylor wearing a raincoat and heading purposefully in the direction of the Granville Mall. We watch his red hair disappear in the distance.

WEDNESDAY, 17 SEPTEMBER / VANCOUVER

At 6:30, out of loyalty to the publicist, I go to the Hotel Vancouver for HarperCollins' big launch of the shall-we-say Micheneresque novel about Vancouver (in fact, called *Vancouver*). A jazz singer, a Chinese lion dance, and Native drummers, but far fewer people than I had expected, certainly not enough to make much of a dent in the big space that is (I believe) the Panorama Room. A rare event for Vancouver in that everyone is dressed up. This fact provides a tiny observation of the sort writers put in their notebooks for future use: when women of my generation don gowns that show large portions of skin, they also reveal the tattoos they acquired on West 4th in such years as 1972. "I'll just get this butterfly on my right breast here, and no one will ever see it except Stan." I end up having a long talk with David Kent, the HarperCollins president, who graciously pretends we've never met when he was the president of Random and didn't seem to care for me. I get the impression, no doubt the one I am expected to get, that he is well connected and culturally sophisticated, as he doubtless is. In any case, I like him.

FRIDAY, 19 SEPTEMBER / VANCOUVER
Linda Rogers from Victoria comes by.[8] I enjoy her poetry and her private-school bearing. Yesterday Spider Robinson was here.[9] He is a folksinger literally as well as figuratively, and most amiable as well.

THURSDAY, 25 SEPTEMBER / VANCOUVER
One of the neighbours is especially volatile today, and when I return home at 2:30 after lunching with Don Stewart I hear him yelling – for that is the correct verb – at two people in the parkade, only to enter the lift and begin berating me when I get in at the lobby level. Were he not carrying grocery bags in both hands, I believe he would have swung his fists. Both M and Hilary have been accosted or screamed at by him in the past week (this in addition to the three legal writs he's served in the same period). Both women say they intend to add new paperwork to his file at the community policing office.

SUNDAY, 28 SEPTEMBER / VANCOUVER
File my column in the morning, work on a review due for the *Straight*, and then troop off to Word on the Street. First I encounter Joy Kogawa looking serene. (Those last four words are like a line from a haiku.) Later [a colleague] makes an expected condescending crack, though of course this may well be her way of dealing with nervousness. Yet I doubt she wishes she had kept quiet, because I doubt she does self-criticism. (I of course have rather the opposite inclination, always assessing and reassessing, atoning but also seeking to learn from the events just ended, as though every day were Yom Kippur; I mean this with no sarcasm of myself or others; it is simply that I tend to contextualise and criticise daily, especially in the periods immediately before falling asleep and immediately after waking, creating a monologue, some of which finds its way into these pages.) As I'm leaving Library Square I run into Brad [Cran] and Gillian. I get a hug from Gillian, perhaps brought on by joy,

8 Linda Rogers (b. 1944), poet and novelist.
9 Spider Robinson (b. 1948), science-fiction author.

as she announces that she's three and a half months pregnant with their first. Brad is affable as always. I wonder what will change in their lives. For one thing, I doubt they'll be leaving Vancouver now. Gillian says something about returning to teaching in a year but only part-time. Given that Brad is determined to live as a freelance magazine writer, I presume they are looking towards inheriting capital; they're the right age and class. When one is old like me, one can view such matters dispassionately.

Then in the evening, M and I go to the [Maritime] Museum for a reception laid on by the Swiss consul-general, and attended by diplomats from six or eight other countries as well, on the occasion of the rededication of the museum's new submersible. Nice to see Robyn Woodward [heiress and marine archaeologist] enjoying herself in a mauve pants suit, the only person present who seems to be dressed for fun. Jim D at his smoothest, which is smooth indeed.[10] The party spills outside.

MONDAY, 29 SEPTEMBER / VANCOUVER

Day begins at 8:00 at breakfast with David S from the Canada Council who has been in town for Word on the Street. The highlight is a long noontime chat on Pendrell with Micha from Lost Moose and John from the other Whitehorse publisher, Wolf Creek Books. Promises of mutual support. I work on a friend's manuscript, an exercise in the pointless and the endless, rivalling the marking of student papers.

TUESDAY, 30 SEPTEMBER / VANCOUVER

In the evening to Genni Gunn's imposing home in Shaughnessy for the first meeting of her and Aislinn Hunter's literary salon.[11] The topic, new British writing, turns into an intense and once or twice simply tense discussion of the class system in Canada. Aislinn is charming, and most friendly to me, to my mild surprise. Patrick Friesen, too, is charming, suggesting, in my mind's revisionist function, that he was merely ill at ease when I sat across from him at one of Greg Gatenby's big Harbourfront

---

10 James Delgado (b. 1958), marine archaeologist and museum director, author of *Across the Top of the World: The Quest for the Northwest Passage* and other works.
11 Genni Gunn (b. 1949), poet and novelist, author of *Solitaria* and other works; Aislinn Hunter (b. 1969), poet, author of *The Possible Past*.

dinners in Toronto.[12] The poet George Stanley present also, as is Ryan Knighton.[13] Perhaps fifteen people in all. I come home late with the sense of having completed another social encounter with no particular mess-making. Whether one grew up in the middle class or not, a small dose of middle-class entitlement (or something similar) comes with age.

THURSDAY, 2 OCTOBER / VANCOUVER

In the afternoon I go to the Metropolitan for a drink with Ann-Marie MacDonald, whose new novel is on the Giller shortlist announced this morning.[14] Long experience, especially from Toronto journalism days, teaches me that determining whether an actor is smart is always difficult, for even an actor who's only slightly competent can play smart, and presumably the ability to do so rises with the level of talent. A-M, I believe, is in fact very smart indeed (despite an evident interest in astrology). I can see that she's been on the book-plugging routine, following the Silk Road of the media, for she's perspiring a bit under the pancake make-up from some TV studio and her hair – the standard lesbian cut – has cowlicks. A very resilient and polished interviewee. After the extraordinary if not extreme commercial success of the first one, the publishers are now frightened, and indulgent towards her. Good for her.

FRIDAY, 3 OCTOBER / VANCOUVER

Dinner with Lloyd Axworthy at the Teahouse in Stanley Park, a pleasant occasion even to the extent that I feel relaxed and confident afterwards.[15] We talk for an hour and a half about his book, then spend an equal amount of time in general getting-to-know-each-other conversation. He looks younger than he is and he is certainly frank and sincere. He also seems in despair about the US, as those with knowledge always are. The travel involved in his Liu job [at UBC] is rapidly becoming too much for him, he says. He also confides that he thinks that Conrad Black may be

12   Patrick Friesen (b. 1946), poet, author of *The Shunning*.
13   George Stanley (b. 1930), author of *Vancouver: A Poem*; Ryan Knighton (b. 1972), memoirist, author of *Cockeyed*.
14   Ann-Marie MacDonald (b. 1958), actor, playwright, and novelist, author of *Fall on Your Knees* and other works.
15   Lloyd Axworthy (b. 1939), Liberal foreign affairs minister (1996–2000) and later university president.

struck down in the present scandal. A foggy night, with the chill that fog always brings this time of year.

SUNDAY, 5 OCTOBER / VANCOUVER

I'm in the shower and so fail to hear gunshots in the alley, which M must come down and report to me. We go outside to investigate and find the lane crowded with bystanders and of course cops – cops everywhere. From what we can piece together, two fellows nabbed at the Safeway up Davie Street ended up in a high-speed chase, driving right through the triangular Morton Street park, crashing into a couple of other cars, and ending up on foot behind our building. One of them sits dazed and wounded with his back against the rear wall of the hotel next door; the other is at large but, judging by the yelps of the police dogs, may have been found hiding at the Sylvia. Details no doubt in the papers tomorrow.

MONDAY, 6 OCTOBER / VANCOUVER

Anne C promises to read *Jericho* this week and says she still feels it should be published in January or February 2005. I am resigned to this now if she is equally resigned to actually publishing the damn thing. She visits Vancouver in December.

MONDAY, 13 OCTOBER / VANCOUVER

Ken McGoogan, here for a lecture at the library, comes for dinner, just the two of us: the traditional Thanksgiving chicken curry, highly spiced. A fine fellow in my view. Less polished a writer than he still needs to become but far more sophisticated in style and content than when he was a tyro novelist of the Kerouac sort. I'm happy that he's landed so well. I think we can become true friends.

TUESDAY, 14 OCTOBER / VANCOUVER

I am reading the books of my panellists for the [Vancouver Writers'] Festival, an enormous amount of work all round for a hundred dollars but of course a worthwhile cultural public service. The Festival is riotously disorganised. I'd known this already, of course, but only from the standpoint of someone looking in. As I find myself having to explain to Chris Moore in an email, "It's not after all the *Zurich* Writers' Festival.

It's the *Vancouver* Writers' Festival. It's bound to be a bit goofy. Expect that when you arrive."

FRIDAY, 17 OCTOBER / VANCOUVER
In anticipation of entertaining Chris Moore and [his wife] Od next week, I go shopping at the liquor store up Davie and also have the suite thoroughly cleaned by Evan, the former Christian bookseller turned massage therapist/personal trainer/male cleaning lady, who always works in the nude. The place is so dirty that he's here the entire afternoon, his cock swinging musically as he hoovers and scrubs. He finishes just in time for me to run up the street to have a hurried dinner with George Elliott Clarke – hurried because he has to rush to the Van East Cultural Centre to see his opera performed. What a pleasure to spend time with such a charming fellow at the height of his powers as a writer – probably the height of his popularity, too, for he is the fashion now and fashion is nowhere more fickle than in Can lit as it's now constructed. George is a conservative personality (he speaks of himself as a baroque writer, a fact that has presented difficulty with respect to the libretto form, he says). Both liberals and conservatives like him because he's full of joy, gusto, bonhomie, and good humour, but always in the service of a serious outlook. "You've got to keep fighting for acceptance." He says this without being so obvious as to indicate that he's giving one advice. "If you stop, you lose the gain. Never give up." He tells me he's teaching *Travels by Night* at the U of Toronto this term. I say: "Presumably as an example of the cautionary tale."

TUESDAY, 21 OCTOBER / VANCOUVER
In late afternoon I go with M to City Hall for the mayor's announcement of the city book awards. While a crowd of us await our turn to enter the chambers, a group from the Industrial Workers of the World push past us and begin playing guitar, singing and unfurling banners to protest the treatment of squeegee kids. Their song calls listeners to rally round the black flag and rise up against their oppressors. A spirited confrontation with two beefy security men with walkie-talkies looms, but the threat of serious disruption fades with the last chorus of the song, and I applaud them (the protesters) as they leave. Then it's our turn to enter the small panelled chamber (the city's population was

comparatively small in 1930). The room looks like the den of a rich man with retrograde tastes and little imagination. At the reception afterwards, there is general agreement with our choices and with our decision to split the prize between two strikingly similar visual-art-influenced monographs on the Downtown Eastside.

WEDNESDAY, 22 OCTOBER / VANCOUVER

I quite enjoy being abroad at 5:00 a.m., the streets deserted, wet leaves underfoot. Later I scurry to complete a day's work by noon, when a volunteer driver, carrying her ten-week-old baby girl, arrives to take me to Granville Island for the Festival. Waiting in the lounge of the G.I. Hotel, I see Chris looking relaxed and smiling. A long talk ensues. Finally, M.A.C. Farrant, Isabel Huggan, and the young Australian novelist James Bradley and I are led to the green room and then to the stage for the panel I'm to moderate on the topic "Short Fiction: The Silent Killer" – or something like that.[16] I had assumed that the audience would be made up of adults for the most part. When I step on stage, however, I see that all but a few patrons are Catholic schoolgirls; the room is a trackless expanse of kneesocks, cotton blouses, and burgundy pullovers. Farrant and Bradley nonetheless push on with their sexually forthright readings. Afterwards, the accompanying teacher looks a bit sour. My guess is that the required number of Hail Marys will be multiplied considerably. In the evening, at the opening party (very much like last year's), I avoid those people who resemble lizards looking to pick a fight in the desert.

THURSDAY, 23 OCTOBER / VANCOUVER

Little voice left today, and my throat is sore. I'm moderating a panel on war and family in fiction with Chris Moore, Frances Itani, and Joan London.[17] Itani, who seems quite unaffected, is a remarkable novelist, judging from *Deafening*. I worry whether such instant universal success will silence her, as I fear it might be doing with Anne Michaels, for example. London, from Fremantle, has written by contrast a perfectly

16 M.A.C. Farrant (b. 1947), Isabel Huggan (b. 1943), and James Bradley (b. 1967): short story writers.
17 Frances Itani (b. 1942), novelist and poet; Joan London (b. 1948), Australian novelist.

turned if rather familiar-sounding work that smacks of creative writing programmes. The event draws, I would guess, about five hundred people to Performance Works. Waiting in the lounge for the summons to begin, I introduce myself to Lynn Crosbie, whom I almost fail to recognise because her hair, now worn long, is electric fuchsia. She is jetlagged and so her voice is even less modulated than usual, and she introduces me to her mother, a small blonde woman. Lynn talks a bit, bitterly, about her split with Michael [Holmes], whom I once painted as a decomposing Christ. "I hated leaving that wonderful painting," she says.

FRIDAY, 24 OCTOBER / VANCOUVER

A long pleasant lunch with Chris in Davie Street. He more or less agrees with my assessment that while BKK has provided him with rich material it's not provided him with literary or intellectual stimulation of the type he deserves, as its English-language community consists mostly of macho writer-adventurers. I advance the idea that he and Od should live here at Pendrell for free while M and I go to the Yukon next July and August, as a way for him to put down a renewed root or two in Canada. We talk at length about the transition he must make from crime novelist to novelist without the adjective. At the end of the day I go back to Granville Island to have a drink with Anna Porter: our first successful long conversation the whole time I've known her (and I believe I met her the very week she arrived in Canada in 1969). We talk of Bob Fulford and Peter Newman, two versions of how to survive into one's seventies, the former wonderfully successful; of Malcolm Lester and other publishers who've gone by the wayside; of my divorce, renaming, and transplantation to the West. While we're talking, another publisher interrupts and, not recognizing me, says "Oh you must be one of Anna's authors." I say: "No, I'm one of yours actually" and give my name. I should have kept my trap shut, of course.

SATURDAY, 25 OCTOBER / VANCOUVER

Brian [Busby] finishes up here about 1:00 p.m. and he and I go over to Granville Island to hear Chris and others on a creative writing panel at the Arts Club Revue Theatre. Chris speaks well and reads the wonderful passage from *Waiting for the Lady* about the drug interdiction museum, but he reads it poorly, which surprises me as he read so well the other day. In fact, the event, moderated by a local TV personality who has done no evident preparation, is a bit of a shambles. At 6:30, Chris and Od come here for drinks with M and me. He's naturally pleased by the feature on him in today's *Globe*, and we talk some business. Then the four of us have dinner at M's. Both C and O are easy, charming, with intelligent things to say and the eloquence with which to say them. The result: a pleasant and relaxed yet also stimulating evening. After brandy at the end of it all, we put them in a taxi at Denman Street. They're off to Toronto and New York.

MONDAY, 27 OCTOBER / VANCOUVER
Continued fog, to the extent that the West End seems without tall buildings. I wake thinking of a story Chris told us about his friend the gem dealer who's the factual basis for the main character in *Waiting for the Lady*. A Thai "houseboy" recently attacked his wife with a claw hammer, almost killing her (as he intended to do, so he could then scoop up the inventory of rubies and religious art brought over the border from Burma). He told the Thai police: "I want one of this guy's ears before you kill him, so I can tan it and make it into a sack [for gems?]." The cops replied: "This can be accomplished," indicating by their tone that a discussion about the fee should take place.

SATURDAY, 1 NOVEMBER / VANCOUVER
I feel slightly better after getting rid of some phlegm at last, and work on *Singer* until quite late. Feels good to return to this project after a few months, but terrifying as well.

TUESDAY, 4 NOVEMBER / VANCOUVER
Jennifer Duncan, whose book about women of the Klondike gold rush I enjoyed, turns out to have grown up in the Annex with a hippie mum and a hippie dad and to have been the employee of the housepainting business run by Anne C's husband, Eric. In fact, she once painted the place on Albany Avenue. She enumerates her family's friends until I finally have to ask: "Did I ever *sleep* with your parents?"

Later, over lunch at the Wedgewood (the Random House hotel) with Jonathan Raban, who I had expected to be a different sort of English expat entirely.[18] He looks laid back, fiercely so, but is actually rather intense in the extremity of his articulation, especially as regards his vapid middle-middle-middle origins, his return to fiction after so long a time, and the Iraq war. Not a warm fellow, I find, but sharp, a wandering exile whose home base or point of origin has been destroyed by the passage of time if nothing else. He dresses well but wears a baseball cap to cover his baldness. He is embarrassed today because he's come to lunch still wearing make-up from his appearance on Vicki Gabereau's show. Hates television (we do have something in common); he's a talker, not a performer.

WEDNESDAY, 5 NOVEMBER / VANCOUVER

Last night I missed going to Genni Gunn's salon but today I have lunch in Davie Street with Aislinn Hunter to catch up. She sounds distracted. Keeps saying such things as that she's bored with her success and may do a second MA, maybe at Cambridge now that she doesn't have to quarantine her dog to take it to Britain with her. I've seen her with her charm turned on, but today she acts a different part. I come home and do more cleaning up and then read Rushdie: "the partisan simplifications beamed down to us from satellites."

THURSDAY, 6 NOVEMBER / VANCOUVER

I'm at the gym where a Chinese Canadian fellow is trying to pick up an anorexic young woman on the next treadmill. She has a huge bandage on one knee. He's saying to her: "Every native speaker of English should be required to learn German to learn about the heritage of their language." And she, pant pant, agrees.

Kenneth Rexroth: "You don't have to read Toynbee or Hegel to know that there is a systole and diastole of history."

SATURDAY, 8 NOVEMBER / VANCOUVER

I've been on Vancouver Island. Now, going home to the West End from the ferry terminal, I must take the #250 local. At the first stop, sixteen teenagers, drunk or drugged, or in some cases both, raise hell – screaming, pushing, etc. Fifteen of them begin chanting for the sixteenth to take off

18   Jonathan Raban (b. 1942), travel writer and novelist.

her top, which she does. Two more stops and another group, all of them male, enter. They claim to be Mexicans. Tension rises. Finally a third bunch, bringing the total to thirty-two by my count. A number of them begin yelling "dead baby blowjob" and I have no idea what variety of blowjob this might be. One guy falls on me violently and I throw him into the aisle. As we're nearing the bridge, a fellow – slender, bearded, looks a bit like a down-and-out Gordon Lightfoot – boards the bus and sits next to me, carefully balancing an upright roll of carpeting. I mouth pleasant-ries and he replies softly: "I'm not permitted to carry a weapon. It's a condition of my parole."

WEDNESDAY, 12 NOVEMBER / VANCOUVER
A late breakfast at the Wedgewood with Bill Bryson. We're to talk about his new book but other topics dominate. After five years or more – more, yes, that's right – he and his family have returned to Britain (where, de-spite the handicap of being from Iowa, he once worked as a subeditor on *The Times*). When I last saw him, he had a US accent softened with ac-quired British vowels; now he has an English accent enlivened by a few American inflections. He looks good, though his face has gone patchy. At fifty-one, he says he aspires to write the sort of books he can do while "wearing my carpet slippers all day" – though he wouldn't mind doing another travel narrative (on Canada this time). "I'm not building any more, I'm simply trying to keep going with what I have, until I reach my dotage." Am I the same? Shudder.

SATURDAY, 15 NOVEMBER / VANCOUVER
I see Don Stewart and others waiting patiently out front when I turn up this morning at a Yaletown antique shop for the sale of George and Inge Woodcock's pictures, primitive art and Third World knicknacks to benefit their charity, Canada India Village Aid. Quite sad to see well-heeled folk-singers pawing over George's equally sorry collection of travel souvenirs. Depressed, I go for vegetarian chilli at the Templeton in Granville Street and walk home in the rain to work quietly – M being away for the weekend.

FRIDAY, 28 NOVEMBER / VANCOUVER
Talking this evening with Linda Rogers who tells me that Red Lillard was in denial about his cancer, always saying he had 'flu whenever

launching into a coughing jag. But I posit that he was merely being polite. L also says that he "could be very difficult." I daresay.

TUESDAY, 2 DECEMBER / VANCOUVER
Dinner at the Raincity Grill with Anne C. She looks wonderfully healthy.
Her few middle-aged facial pleats become her. In everything she says
about writing and publishing she shows herself as smart and perceptive
as always, but seeing her again reminds me of her impatience as well as
of all her established tricks, such as tossing out some unrevealing bit of
candour to fulfil the candour requirement imposed by friendship and so
in that way remain totally private. Also, I wonder sometimes whether
her tiny feminine voice isn't used to cushion gratuitous insult or hurt. In
any event, she wants another version of *Jericho* – number five, if I agree
to it. I must decide what to do. Begin, I suppose, by crafting a letter.

FRIDAY, 19 DECEMBER / VANCOUVER
Go to MacLeod's Books and Don and I have a coffee at the café on the
corner as he keeps a lookout for some drug dealers who sometimes ply
their trade outside his shop. We talk of deaths – of Inge Woodcock who's
passed at eighty-seven and I suppose is now sternly reprimanding whatever God there is for wasting her time and ignoring her wishes.

MONDAY, 22 DECEMBER / VANCOUVER
Trying to accommodate some of the hundreds of changes Anne C wants
in the ms of the novel but I realise finally that the task may be hopeless.
By a strange coincidence Peter Newman writes today from London ask-
ing about Anne's abilities. "She was the best section editor I had at
Maclean's," he says, "when she got everything her own way."

WEDNESDAY, 24 DECEMBER / VANCOUVER
I dive into Anne C's marginalia once again but come up with nothing but
the blackest despair. The situation is so bad that I take the risk of calling
her at home the day before Christmas to express my feelings. The end-
of-conversation compromise plan is that I will fly to Toronto at my own
expense in a month's time and go over the ms with her page by page in
a hotel room, remote from telephone and other interruptions. In the
meantime, I'm going to write a bit of linkage about Bishop [a character
in the novel].

THURSDAY, 25 DECEMBER / VANCOUVER
Reading quite an interesting article about [Ezra] Pound who the author says "was at his most ingenious when he pretended to be someone else." This points to a quality that I almost always admire most in writers (the exception being Pound for whom I carry no brief). The essay also quotes Hugh Kenner on Pound's pseudo-Chinese poetry to the effect that it uses "the *vers-libre* principle, that the single line is the unit of composition; the Imagist principle, that a poem may build its effects out of things it sets before the mind's eye by naming them; and the lyrical principle, that words or names, being ordered in time, are bound together and recalled into each other's presence by recurring sounds." Kenner was never more incisively brilliant.

FRIDAY, 26 DECEMBER / VANCOUVER
I wake to pluck the *Globe* from under the front door and find that [John] Newlove has died at sixty-five. A fine poet indeed in his prime in the '60s and '70s, but odd that he should have been so popular with the rulers of literature when he frequently wrote about the lower order. Odder still that they continued to ply him with praise after he lapsed into silence and went to work for the government: hardly their usual tactic. There is always a gentle dialogue underway between those who simply need someone to look down on and those only slightly more complex people who seek somebody to feel sorry for.

SATURDAY, 27 DECEMBER / VANCOUVER
I work on the *Jericho* insert, writing a thousand words according to plan.

SUNDAY, 28 DECEMBER / VANCOUVER
A leisurely morning, then resumption of work on the first *Jericho* insert, followed by a job I usually avoid until the last moment: transcribing an interview tape. I often find derision and even anger in the interviewee's voices that was not always apparent face to face. At such times I'm also aware, as increasingly I'm generally more aware, of the additional burden of having a deep voice – so deep that the modulation that opens people up to an interlocutor is simply not there – so deep many people cannot make me out (though if asked why, they always respond with a comment about "mumbling," though of course that isn't really the difficulty).

TUESDAY, 30 DECEMBER / VANCOUVER
A few hours after rereading Jung's remarkable chapter on the afterlife in *Memories, Dreams, Reflections*, I have a dream in which George Woodcock is aboard a ship, about to depart for Hongkong. He is apprehensive about the voyage, uncharacteristically so, and sitting in his cabin, which is quite well appointed, confesses his unease to me and I suppose also to J, who hovers nearby.

2004

A busy year in which I published *Singer, An Elegy* (poetry) and *One Russia, Two Chinas* (a travel narrative). While writer-in-residence at Massey College, University of Toronto, I finished *Tales of Two Cities: A Novella Plus Stories. Jericho* finally emerged from the editorial process, and I broke ground on another novel, *Walt Whitman's Secret*.

SUNDAY, 4 JANUARY / VANCOUVER

I stay inside all day, getting the *Singer* draft (looked publishable yesterday but not today: this is always the way) in shape to send to Rhea T for her crits.

MONDAY, 5 JANUARY / VANCOUVER

I have a series of emails from Anne C, including one saying that she has to write the catalogue copy for *Jericho* and wants suggestions. Which tells me that she is indeed going to publish the thing after all.

THURSDAY, 8 JANUARY / VANCOUVER

No heat last night, as there is a leak in the gas main. I write this, trying to block out the sound of the jackhammer, while sitting in the kitchen next to M's space heater, with a blanket nailed over the doorway to keep in as much heat as possible. Must write a review today.

SUNDAY, 11 JANUARY / VANCOUVER

On Denman Street I see a homeless man, as scraggly as Saddam Hussein at the time of his capture, looking into the window of a temporarily vacant shop and, seeing his reflection, cursing himself as someone else, some motherfucker as he says, and finally spitting at his own image.

MONDAY, 26 JANUARY / TORONTO
This is the day of the meeting with Anne about *Jericho*. She's about ninety minutes late because of the snowstorm, a fierce one indeed, but the editorial meeting once under way moves along splendidly and all questions are resolved in only about three hours. At one point she grabs a manuscript chapter and goes to the bed and gets under the coverlet. "After thirty years," I joke, "I finally get you into my bed, but you're alone there and your teeth are chattering." She laughs.

TUESDAY, 3 FEBRUARY / VANCOUVER
Another go at lunch with Rita, the first having been unsuccessful. She is dressed provocatively, though whether on purpose I cannot say, and seems to have a slightly higher opinion of me this time, possibly because I have agreed to be the host-moderator of a Literary Press Group reading at the VPL. Since our previous meeting, she says, she has read *Travels by Night*. "You write like a Catholic," she says. "Thank you," I reply, having little idea what she might mean except in the broadest possible terms – all modern autobiography descends from St Augustine.

THURSDAY, 5 FEBRUARY / VANCOUVER
I have lunch on Davie Street with [the blues singer and actor] Jim Byrnes, who has a new CD – the first work he's been able to complete, he says, since falling ill the past two months with a serious infection in one leg. At one point, he says, doctors were talking of amputating another section. We talk together easily like the two middle-aged men we are – no pensions, health concerns, ex-wives, the integrity of work – and in his case, "a fifteen-year-old daughter I'll soon have to put through university." For the first time, he talks about his Catholicism, how he always carries his late father's rosary.

SATURDAY, 14 FEBRUARY / VANCOUVER
I spend most of the day working on a long round-up for Olga [Stein] at *Books in Canada* and doing more of the tucking and nipping on *Jericho* that Anne needs by the end of the month. More rain, which does

wonders for my dry and now badly scratched skin but occasions the return of my arthritis (though not seriously).

MONDAY, 16 FEBRUARY / VANCOUVER
In the evening, reading in bed, I find this in a piece by Ursula K. Le Guin: "Essays are in the head. They don't have bodies the way stories do; that's why essays can't satisfy in the long run." Dinner with Janice Kulyk Keefer.

TUESDAY, 17 FEBRUARY / VANCOUVER
Thinking about J.K. Keefer, someone whose work I've long admired and who I've always hoped to meet. She was reared in the West End of Toronto – her father was a dentist, son of Ukrainian immigrants – and she considers herself a more or less active Slav, though she has achieved absolutely high-end WASP speech and manners: a real pro. Smart, and well-informed about more than just writing and academic life. One could hardly ask for a more comfortable dinner companion.

FRIDAY, 27 FEBRUARY / VANCOUVER
I rush to meet Rita at Granville Books where she's dropping off stuff for a window display. As we stroll down to the library to pick up posters and handbills for the reading I am moderating there next week, she tells me that Ron Hatch has rejected *Singer* out of hand, refusing even to glance at the ms, and making disparaging references to me – to the extent of refusing my offer of putting his URL on my website links page. Odd behaviour. I'll try Brian Kaufman at Anvil who might actually enjoy designing such a book.

SATURDAY, 28 FEBRUARY / VANCOUVER
A dream about George Woodcock telling me that contrary to common belief elephants "are full of humanity and have soft skin." I come awake feeling this is a comforting dream image from the other side of consciousness if not actually from the Other Side.

MONDAY, 1 MARCH / VANCOUVER
A long conversation today with Brian Kaufman at Anvil Press about the possibility of publishing *Singer*, which I email to him. What I propose,

assuming he responds well to the work, is that he produce the book and I'll produce the CD to go with it. I admire his design skills.

WEDNESDAY, 3 MARCH / VANCOUVER

I wake to find Kate Taylor's picture on the front page of the *Globe*: she's won the Commonwealth Writers' Prize in the first book category. I shoot off my congratulations. I must categorise, as Woodcock did, the tone of my responses in professional matters when dealing with a) elders, b) contemporaries, and c) the young. In time, the need for the first state of diction will grow very infrequent and that for the third will become the normal one in most communication. George, I see now, was the master of the third – and much else.

SATURDAY, 6 MARCH / VANCOUVER

In the morning's *Globe* I see the death notice for Miriam Waddington, 86, an interesting poet actually but by general agreement a most disagreeable person. I met her but once. One summer night in the '70s I was at a party at Howard and Marian Engel's place at 338 Brunswick. The night was warm, and I was standing on the porch, drink in hand, chatting to some other writer, I forget who. MW came out the front door and preparing to pass down the steps said to me, "Get out of my way, whatever your name is." Need I mention that, like the equally charming Dorothy Livesay, she had been a social worker.

TUESDAY, 9 MARCH / VANCOUVER

I open the postbox in the lobby this morning to an envelope from the Canada Council. I tear it open, intending to glance at it quickly and then put it in the shredder, to prevent myself from getting up in the night to read over it. My eyes, however, catch on the word *pleased*. Astonishingly, I have been successful in my application for a senior writing grant – my first application to the Council since 1969. The cheque for twenty thousand should arrive more or less when the money from the *Sun* stops. Not a terribly large windfall but a substantial one, and the timing is propitious. I tell M when we are out together on the Seawall, walking the neighbour's black lab. I feel so relieved as the three of us prowl along the water. A stiff wind has been causing sizeable surf all morning and the dog's ears are flopping about as though in sympathetic joy.

TUESDAY, 16 MARCH / VANCOUVER
I have lunch with Nancy Richler at a student diner. Being there gives me
the feeling that I'm cutting class. She looks and sounds terrific, is working seriously now on her new novel, which she expects will occupy her
for three years or more.

FRIDAY, 19 MARCH / VANCOUVER
At the first Vancouver Arts Awards presentation in the atrium of the library, 300 people who've paid $125 to sip champagne are down below,
on the lower level, until the ceremony begins, leaving the rest of us chatting in the cold under heavy security. Steve Osborne, who wins in the
writing and publishing category, is never in better form, while Arthur
Erickson, the winner for lifetime achievement in design, looks frail without the thinness usually associated with frailty and makes sly reference
to his declaration of bankruptcy.[1] Following (without admitting it, of
course) the Toronto Arts Awards model, these VAAs are constructed so
that each winner selects a younger artist in his or her discipline to receive
$5,000 to complete a creative project. The lifetime achiever in "culinary
arts" misunderstands and awards his five Gs to fellow chefs to put towards the cost of a trip to Paris. Steve gives his to his long-time protégé
Brad Cran. Erickson chooses a young architecture student but cannot
remember her last name at the crucial moment [for, as became known
later, he was suffering from Alzheimer's disease]. As at all such events in
Vancouver, the range of dress is quite wonderful, from smoking suit and
classic evening gown to Day-Glo toga and circus garb.

TUESDAY, 23 MARCH / VANCOUVER
All through the morning, beginning about 6:00 a.m., a kind of running
skirmish with Random by email, which is resolved by Anne's patient
understanding. She is unusual that way – sometimes difficult to work
with because of her desire for control and refusal to delegate detail
(truly a dangerous combination) but wonderful by virtue of her desire
to give sanctuary and harbour strays (the only reason I'm able to be
published by Random House). I devote the evening to finishing Don

1   Arthur Erickson (1924–2009), architect and urban planner.

Coles' novel. Trying to stay awake long enough to get back on a normal sleep schedule.[2]

THURSDAY, 25 MARCH / VANCOUVER

This evening I moderate the first of a new reading series at the library for the Literary Press Group. Crystal Hurdle from Cap College reads her book of poems about Hughes and Plath; she seems to be developing an obsession about romantic obsessions, for her new work centres on Nabokov's *Lolita*. Then Lorna Jackson reads from her novel a passage about the bar circuit in the Interior: a rich book that seems to be full of steel guitars and second-hand smoke. I notice that she has a tattoo of a star immediately behind her right ear. Then the star, Marilyn Bowering, a wonderful poet, whose smile seems a bit forced this evening; perhaps she's tired or merely bored. About 65 people show up. A successful evening in its own terms. Rebecca Wigod sits next to M, knitting furiously as she listens.

MONDAY, 29 MARCH / VANCOUVER

George Clarke writes with praise – understanding praise – for *Singer*. Then John Fraser emails and then phones from the U of Toronto to say that I'm indeed to be writer-in-residence beginning January 2005. What timing!

WEDNESDAY, 31 MARCH / VANCOUVER

John Fraser emails in a panic to say that I've not in fact yet been selected to be the 2005 writer-in-residence; I'm to stay tuned until next month sometime and see what happens. An ex-president of the absurd CAA [Canadian Authors Association] apparently has written a long letter to the *Sun* complaining about my speech handicap.

FRIDAY, 16 APRIL / VANCOUVER

I have lunch on Davie Street with Bill New, who's just returned from the Galapagos Islands. Such a dear man and so supportive of me. I always feel that I can be candid with him, and am. He tells me of an experience

---

2 Don Coles (b. 1928), poet, author of *Forests of the Medieval World* and other works.

that so far has eluded capture in his poetry. When he was about five, he fell into a flooded foundation – a quarry-like body of water – and his two companions, rather than trying to save him by running for help, returned to their homes and said nothing, obviously fearing to catch hell. Bill somehow managed to get out but can't recall just how. Such an experience foreshadows a literary life.

TUESDAY, 20 APRIL / VANCOUVER

I am marginally better today, by dint of meditation, and despite a sub-migraine I finish the first proofs of *Jericho*.

SATURDAY, 1 MAY / VICTORIA

Linda Rogers picks me up at 11:30 for lunch and a long long talk, during which she says, "I've had guests for dinner every night this week except when I went to prison." She means the evening she visited Stephen Reid, to whom she brought a big flat of strawberries, which she covered in chocolate that she melted in the visitors' area microwave. He enjoyed them with his many aboriginal friends. Later she tells me of having had an affair with an Armani-clad publisher. "It was ridiculous, like a tiny opera. He's in such an oratorical tradition." She's a delight. She reappears, resplendently, at 5:30 and we go to Government House for the BC Book Prizes in a lovely room with an even lovelier view. Many of the usual suspects and some new ones. Pat Lane, Marilyn Bowering, Robert Wiersema limping and I believe scowling, and Scott McIntyre who is apologising to everyone near him without remembering what exactly he's apologising for.[3] Everyone beautifully dressed for a change. Linda and I actually slip away tactfully before predictable awards themselves.

SUNDAY, 2 MAY / VICTORIA

I meet John Gould at Munro's in Government Street and we go to a place by Bastion Square.[4] He is smooth and friendly enough but goes down a couple of degrees when my speech falters and also when I ask about the possibility of doing something at the Victoria School of

---

3   Robert Wiersema (b. 1970), author of *Before I Wake* and other novels.
4   John Gould (b. 1959), writer of short fiction, author of *The Kingdom of Heaven: 88 Palm-of-the-Hand Stories*.

Writing. But to be fair, though, both of us have headaches, his apparently quite severe. I ask him about his relationship to his uncle, Bob F. He comments more than once on Bob's "generosity with his anecdotes and stories."

MONDAY, 3 MAY / VICTORIA

A visit with Jim Munro at his bookstore, where I do some Subway business. Victoria is so blessed with bookstores, showing the extreme poverty of Vancouver in this regard. I'm relaxed here, in this city. And this fine old cheap hotel, which in spirit at least is rather like the Sylvia but unfortunately it's to be razed soon, I'm told. I read Wang Wei much of the night.

SUNDAY, 9 MAY / VANCOUVER

En route to the gym, I witness a most interesting drug transaction. A screaming psychotic type, wearing a parka despite the twenty-degree weather, pushes the crosswalk button violently, repeatedly. When the light changes and he crosses to the middle of the street, he accepts money from a woman wearing a sweatshirt whose extra-long sleeves, hanging perhaps four or five inches below her fingers, prevent me, and everyone else, from getting a good look. At the same moment, using her other hand, she passes a packet of something to him. Neither breaks stride. The two of them disappear into the crowds on their respective sides of Denman Street long before the lights change again. Neatly executed if not quite subtle.

MONDAY, 10 MAY / VANCOUVER

Heidi Greco, a Fed member who's Brian K's poetry editor at Anvil, is here for five hours working with me on the *Singer* ms.[5] She has a good eye for small errors but I'm not sure we agree about enjambment, line breaks, punctuation, and indeed poetic diction. I believe she wishes to edit in such a way as to emphasise what prose would emphasise. But I'm lucky to have her.

---

5   Heidi Greco (b. 1947), poet, author of *Rattlesnake Plantain*.

THURSDAY, 13 MAY / VANCOUVER

I meet Dan Francis for the first time, over a drink at the Sylvia, and try to talk him into writing a history of prostitution in Vancouver, for I must begin to get some longer-term Subway projects under way.[6]

TUESDAY, 18 MAY / VANCOUVER

A manic call from John Fraser, made from Windsor Station in Montreal, saying that I do in fact have the Toronto appointment, that he will see I have the official letter before the end of next week and that delay and silence are not his fault but rather the fault of the English Department people, who he says are uniformly and notoriously hopeless in such matters, oops don't tell anyone I said that, must run, here's my train, gotta go. Time elapsed: five to eight seconds.

WEDNESDAY, 19 MAY / VANCOUVER

Up at 6:00 to prepare for the museum's second annual fundraising breakfast at the Bayshore where I sit next to Dan Francis, who tells me he agrees to write the prostitution book for Subway, and Michael Carroll, to whom I hand off the travel-book proofs.

THURSDAY, 20 MAY / VANCOUVER

At the Hotel Vancouver to have a drink with someone who has led me to believe (or I have inferred, as his English is anguished) that he is a small-press publisher in Korea who's translated a number of Canadian poets and wishes to do the same for me. In fact, he's a Korean Canadian from Willowdale who has printed a thousand copies of a strange bilingual journal of which he admits having sold only seven so far.

SUNDAY, 23 MAY / VANCOUVER

I finish up the work on the *Singer* corrections and get the file to Brian at Anvil. Such literary chores make me feel as though I'm turning the long holiday weekend to good account, but I'm still woefully behind, as always.

---

6 Daniel Francis (b. 1947), historian and author, editor of *The Encyclopedia of British Columbia*.

SATURDAY, 5 JUNE / VANCOUVER

I hear the news that Ronald Reagan has died at ninety-three, struck down in mid-career. Odd how the stupidest people live longest; I think of this as the Ringo Factor. Finally, news today from the U of Toronto, officially offering me the position for January. I officially accept it, much relieved.

THURSDAY, 10 JUNE / VANCOUVER

An invigorating conversation with Anne C about final details of *Jericho* and what I hope to accomplish at the U of T, which is to complete a full draft of *Tales*. Sure, she sometimes seems to manipulate my great affection for her but this may be partly because it might frighten her if she did not. In any case, she always has been so supportive of me.

I spend the day on bread-work, resolved not to get in a rut.

MONDAY, 14 JUNE / VANCOUVER

A morning conference call with the Manitoba Arts Council. Soon afterward I learn of Jack McClelland's death at 81. Now the accolades will begin, comparing him to Alfred Knopf and so on. In truth, no one knows whether Jack had any taste in books or not. The law of averages being what it is, he sometimes found a Margaret Laurence. His ballyhoo was so monotonic that it precluded a clear sense of discrimination: to him, Layton was always the "greatest" Canadian poet of all time. Significantly, though, the writers he chose to hang out with were his fellow Anglos and Scots: Mowat, Berton, Harold Town, and the like.[7] Birney while an Anglo wasn't a public school boy whereas Peter Newman, who went to UCC, was kept at a distance as a Jew, even while making Jack millions. He liked boisterous personalities. Going on wild binges was as much a part of his business style as it was of his personal style. That the company has survived his management of it is remarkable. The most significant conversation I ever had with him, driving down the Don Valley Parkway, concerned my haircut, of which he disapproved. But of course this was in my mute adolescence. I was totally awkward and he was totally tolerant. We never quite got comfortable together. My fault needless to say.

7   Farley Mowat (b. 1921), writer and environmentalist, author of such works as *People of the Deer* and *Never Cry Wolf*.

THURSDAY, 17 JUNE / VANCOUVER

Thinking more about Jack McClelland. A proto-Trudeauian figure, charismatic, but still a poor businessman, a promoter, far more a Liveright than a Knopf. I see him now as an upper-middle-class kid to say the least, growing up in Russell Hill Road and ending up in Dunvegan Road – not much of a progression really. His worldview, I think, dealt largely with his own pleasure and thirst for success. At the time, however, he seemed unspeakably sophisticated. Certainly he seemed so to me. Intimidating. Today I am embarrassed by how small the world was back then.

TUESDAY, 22 JUNE / VANCOUVER

At the end of the workday I go to the boardroom of the VPL to see P.K. Page inducted into the city's literary walk of fame. She looks and sounds very well indeed, and I ask her if she's lonely. "No, not lonely," she says. "I have my work, though I don't think it's very good. I'm writing a bad long poem. Everybody needs one." She reminds me that I interviewed her about Woodcock perhaps ten years ago. "I was so angry when he died. It was as though a big hole was torn in the sky. He was such an extraordinary man. We weren't that close, because of the distance, but when we were together we really clicked." Then the ceremony began with Alan Twigg, all besuited and at his most charming, but with the guest of honour of course outcharming everyone, for she has few rivals when she turns on the fountain. What a diplomatic hostess she must have been when she was posted abroad with Arthur. She speaks with easy eloquence of the importance of poetry to learning, then unveils the flagstone plaque that will be fitted into the pavement (it looks distressingly like a tombstone). The award comes with $5,000 from the company formerly known as BC Gas. P.K. concludes by saying she will think of them kindly whenever she turns on her gas fireplace, "now that I can no longer manage wood."

SUNDAY, 27 JUNE / VANCOUVER

At breakfast I postulate that a certain type of spirit – ghost – will pester the living not because its body died violently or in order to warn those left behind, but rather because broken-off conversations – and their relationships – prevent the spirit from being at rest. I sometimes fancy I

shall be an unsettled, frustrated spirit owing to such truncated relationships as those with [two colleagues]. I find myself wishing now, while
still in a viable corporeal format, to redress old awkwardnesses of this
sort. Is this process not like the first baby-steps in a twelve-step programme? I have had some success with some of these ancient puzzles but
a great number of seemingly insoluble ones remain. They prey on me.

SATURDAY, 10 JULY / VANCOUVER
Dream in which Inge and George Woodcock are cleaning up or possibly even cleaning out their house: a different place this time but high-
ceilinged like the last one. In two or three months they are to close it up
(for good!); the location is either Dublin or Amsterdam.

My back goes into spasm while I'm returning a DVD that M and I have
hired. I barely make it home, as I've gone abroad without the stick.

SUNDAY, 11 JULY / VANCOUVER
Another dream about George W. This time he asks me, seeing as how
I'm in Belgium (probably Antwerp), to go to a military and naval club
and retrieve something that Graham Greene, an acquaintance from the
'30s, has left there for him. I arrive at an old narrow house with a re-
dented roof and find an official sergeant who acts as a kind of gate-
keeper and porter. He reluctantly agrees to go upstairs to the clubroom,
where I, as a non-member, am not permitted, to look for the parcel.
Meanwhile I see three books I'd like at the gift kiosk in the lobby. When
the sergeant returns I purchase them for reading on my travels but he
gives them to me individually wrapped as gifts. I request unwrapped
ones but he tells me with bureaucratic delight that such a request is out
of the question. Later I'm somewhere else, a party or a launch perhaps,
and see Michael Ondaatje and also, in the corner of the room, Vera
Frenkel. Vera is cool to me, indeed cross with me, presumably because I
no longer live in Toronto or, more precisely, because of the stealthy manner of my leaving it.

MONDAY, 12 JULY / VANCOUVER
Another Woodcock dream. What's going on here? Chinese coins worth
a thousand dollars – old cash, cast bronze, with holes in the centre.
He extracts them for me in a room lined with bookcases in which a

disproportionate number of the spines are a brownish yellow. His English (rather than Welsh) relatives are there.

WEDNESDAY, 14 JULY / VANCOUVER

Careless, I propel myself up Davie for lunch with Dean Cooke at Stepho's. Easily the most successful lunch we have ever had, because it is the one at which my speech is more fluent than at any other time in his presence. We spend three hours talking about the prospects for *Jericho* (dismal in my view) and the problem with publishing *Tales* once completed (not unsolvable says Dean). Then we fall to discussing Anne C of whom we are both so fond.

THURSDAY, 29 JULY / VANCOUVER

Visit Michael Carroll in the Beach Holme offices, where at last I take possession of the second proofs. Later I also manage to advance the Anvil book to the second-proof stage. At present I'm involved in four titles: Beach Holme travel, Anvil poetry, John Wiley a reprint, Random House novel. All of these should be appearing between late September and mid-January, a detonated log jam of Woodcockian proportions. Plus at the moment I'm reading two stacks of novels for two competitions I'm helping to judge. So the days are full with stuff that matters moderately.

TUESDAY, 24 AUGUST / VANCOUVER

Don [Stewart] and I are sitting at the café across from his shop. As we talk, he points out Robin Blaser crossing at the light: thin elderly man, grey of skin and white of hair, wearing a beret and a long coat, carrying a portfolio of papers.[8]

THURSDAY, 2 SEPTEMBER / MONTREAL

I see even more clearly than ever before the need to check into hotels now and then to clear my head and refresh my spirit, rather as the religious will go on retreat occasionally. In a hotel close to St Catherine Street I'm like a Trappist in Babylon. The Trappist comparison is even more apt, of course, because I hear the French language all round me but

8   Robin Blaser (1925–2009), poet, author of *The Holy Forest* and other works.

do not let on, being barely able to converse in English. Before going to bed, somewhat worse for the great deal of wear, I catch sight of myself in the mirror while cleaning my teeth and hope that I now appear less frightening to people as a much older person. The equation is a delicate one, I realise.

SUNDAY, 12 SEPTEMBER / VANCOUVER

Fully recovered late morning, I go with M to the Chan Centre where I'm to read a poem or two as part of a fundraiser for Canada India Village Aid, the charity founded by the Woodcocks. Chat a bit with Bill Richardson, who reads beautifully from a novel in progress – comic, of course – and see Lynne Van Luven and Sharon Thesen. The latter says she is leaving Cap College as soon as she can land a job in Kelowna where she now lives most of the time. As M reminds me, I must withdraw from at least some of these public obligations, saving my meagre bursts of ability for those of most benefit to my books.

MONDAY, 13 SEPTEMBER / VANCOUVER

A dream about Woodcock speaking about India, obviously a result of my taking part in the event at the Chan. No such prompt is necessary, but I nevertheless take the hint and phone Keath Fraser, the organiser, to thank him.[9] We end up having quite a long conversation. He tells me that when the McCleery Street house was being cleaned out, he bought the ugly old easy chair from George's office – and is sitting in it as we speak. He gives me a description of Inge's last days in the seniors' facility, which were even grimmer than I had imagined. She had bowel cancer and refused all chemo and other treatment. She suffered dementia as well and towards the end was very childlike. Sarah McAlpine would take her out for an ice lolly, Keath says, and this would be the highlight of her week as far as anyone could tell.

FRIDAY, 24 SEPTEMBER / VANCOUVER

With M over to the Rowing Club in Stanley Park for the Association of Book Publishers of BC thirtieth anniversary party. Not a large affair (the

9 Keath Fraser (b. 1944), short story writer and novelist, author of *Popular Anatomy* and other works.

room is too big for the occasion, as it is for nearly all occasions) but some congenial people are there, including Bill New with whom I have more than one pleasant chat, including one about learning Chinese from flash cards. Steve Osborne gives a witty po-mo speech while Scott McIntyre speaks parenthetically, interrupting each sentence in the middle to begin the next, the way he does. The whole evening is presided over effortlessly by Margaret Reynolds.

TUESDAY, 12 OCTOBER / TORONTO
Feeling somewhat punk all morning, but I get myself together for required attendance at the *Books in Canada* first-novel award at the Much Music Building, which I of course remember visiting when it was the home and printing plant of the Ryerson Press. An interesting event. Olga Stein, whom I meet for the first time after five years of email and telephone contact, turns out to be young and blonde, dressed in a pink suit in the Jackie Kennedy manner. She gives a solid speech under the MCship of Daniel Richler, who's quite skilled in such situations, neither too formal nor too breezy. Olga introduces me as an "urban legend," which I suppose is better than an urban myth, and I see many old Toronto publishing acquaintances including a few I'd forgotten about and some I'd been trying not to recall.

MONDAY, 18 OCTOBER / VANCOUVER
I go to the Anvil Press/Talon office to pick up the first copies of *Singer, An Elegy*. The book looks quite all right despite the Brechtian photo on the front.

TUESDAY, 19 OCTOBER / VANCOUVER
M and I go to City Hall to watch [Mayor] Larry Campbell give out the city book awards. I'm the only judge present. Dan Francis looks extremely happy to have won and Annabel Lyon a bit downcast, so I take her aside later and comfort her, telling her how difficult the decision was and how she has many awards ahead of her yet, which is certainly true.[10]

10   Annabel Lyon (b. 1971), novelist, author of *The Golden Mean*.

THURSDAY, 21 OCTOBER / VANCOUVER

Susan Swan is here for the Writers' Festival and we meet for lunch at Stepho's. She astounds me by pointing out that her next birthday will be her sixtieth. We fall naturally to talking about matters long ago, about how for example we let the fire in the fireplace get out of control and later we ran out of gas on a country road somewhere. Her blue eyes are bluer than those of most blonde blue-eyed people.

THURSDAY, 4 NOVEMBER / VANCOUVER

At 6:00 p.m. I meet Yosef [Wosk, Vancouver rabbi and cultural philanthropist] at the Dan George Centre, the former Canadian Crafts Museum, near the cathedral in Hornby Street, and we go across the street for a sandwich once we've had a private word. All this is preparatory to the monthly meeting of the Academy of Independent Scholars. The speaker is Michael Cahén, son of the late Oscar Cahén, one of the Painters Eleven, talking in great detail about his plan for marketing the works held by the estate. He seems to have no aesthetic sense whatever and is concerned only with riches. I can't keep from jotting down some of his characteristic utterances. One: "I want to use synthesis as the control surface for what I'm saying." Two: "The key to art is to make a decision statement – if only a decision statement stating that it is difficult." Three: "On the index there are thirteen screens to determine whether an artist is competent. Paul Kane scored seventy-three per cent." Robert Reid, the book designer and craft printer, walks out, muttering. Yosef is as usual philosophical, saying that the speaker is obviously still in mourning for his father, who was killed in a car crash in 1956.

SATURDAY, 6 NOVEMBER / VANCOUVER

A third dream in which both J and M appear and there is a big bird in a cage.

To dinner with Charlotte Gray, who's here promoting her new book. What a charmer. "You are by way of being my favourite dinner companion," I tell her, "now that Jodi Foster is no longer speaking to me." She laughs. We speak about novelists (she's a Giller judge this year) and historians for three hours. Her judgement of books is usually sharp but her judgement of individuals even sharper. We're both quite tipsy at the end, having knocked off a bottle of Yellow Tail shiraz, my favourite, and I struggle to find her a taxi in the punitive rain.

SUNDAY, 14 NOVEMBER / VANCOUVER
I'm quite moved today reading the selection of Al Purdy's letters. Sam Solecki's apparatus is frequently incomplete or inaccurate as to who has died and when etc. and full of his own extra-editorial prejudices, but the cumulative effect of the letters is to show Al to have been what the truly intuitive people such as Peggy and Dennis always understood him to be, underneath: kind and philosophical, if given to what seems like hypocrisy but is merely a desire to be civil face to face, if more candid behind people's backs. There's a touching final note to Dennis near the end, the night before his surgery. A man who was an unknowable loner who was nevertheless quite public. (Not a role model I would have selected consciously, but the similarity – in essence, not in importance – is one I cannot gainsay.)

THURSDAY, 25 NOVEMBER / VANCOUVER
At noon I go to Villa del Lupa, an Italian restaurant in Hamilton Street, perfectly pleasant but unknown to me previously, to be the host of a luncheon for the independent booksellers and talk to them about *Jericho*, giving them tools they might need in handselling it. A smaller turnout than I had hoped and Random had expected, but several of the important ones come, including Gary Crompton from Book Warehouse. Because I have rehearsed myself, I am quite relaxed and reasonably articulate. To check these assertions later, I tape my performance. What's more I feel that I have come up with some additional things to say when the time comes for promotional activity in the media.

SATURDAY, 27 NOVEMBER / VANCOUVER
Dream in which Michael Ignatieff does a walk-on.

WEDNESDAY, 1 DECEMBER / VANCOUVER
I'm part of a panel on anarchism at the VPL. I speak on Woodcock, Mark Leier speaks on Bakunin, and another, Jerry Zaslove speaks, incomprehensibly, on the role of anarchism in the establishment of the SFU English

Department in 1965. Zaslove seems to use the term anarchist as an honorific for people of whom he approves – Bowering (who's in the audience), Warren Tallman, Robin Blaser, Lionel Kearns – none of whom, as far as I know, fits the category politically.[11] He's a dreadful speaker, far worse than I am, reading gibberish from a typewritten ms and constantly popping the mike. As customary at these events in the Necessary Voices series, the hall includes a number of lunatics with questions. A Chinese-Canadian woman, clearly audible but scarcely understandable, takes the floor to tell us that we need to accept Jesus as our Saviour. She can't be stopped from going on in this vein until the mike is passed, forcibly, to a woman demanding to know why Emma Goldman was opposed to abortion (which of course she wasn't). A well-spoken and cheerful middle-class woman at the rear (a teacher, as it happens) tells us that all the members of the Bush cabinet except Rice are members of a hitherto undetected Jewish conspiracy. Undetected but apparently not undocumented, for she presses on me a newspaper article on the subject. It is written in Hungarian, a language I of course do not read – and neither does she. I crumple it and put it in the rubbish, but Zaslove retrieves it. He also tells me that Peter Buitenhuis died a few days ago.[12] There's been no death notice in the *Globe* or the *Vancouver Sun*: his wish evidently. He had cancer for a couple of years and apparently decided against continuing with treatment. Ann was at his side, as were his children, I'm told. I remember how in 1969, long before we ever met, he called me a hippie in the *New York Times Book Review*.

SATURDAY, 25 DECEMBER / TORONTO
I struggle down to Massey College and keeping my parka on manage to do half a day's work at the desk, which looks out on Devonshire Place, facing north, towards the spot where the old Varsity Stadium (where I once talked with John Lennon) stood. Then I finish unpacking, and by tending a large fire manage to chase at least some of the damp out of the

---

11   Warren Tallman (1921–1994), literary theorist and professor; Lionel Kearns (b. 1937), experimental poet, author of *Assaults on the Interface* and other works.
12   Peter Buitenhuis (1925–2004), professor and critic, author of *The Grasping Imagination: The American Writings of Henry James*.

room. I'm hopeful that I'll be able to work here. In the past, I've had to find ways of sending people away in order to get important work done, as when (back in the days when I had at least some money) I despatched J on holidays to Hongkong or her ancestral homeland, the Orkneys. Now (without money) I must contrive to get others to send me away, as with the U of T in this instance.

MONDAY, 27 DECEMBER / TORONTO
A bitterly cold morning again. I have much wood but no kindling, and find none in the woodpile. So I tear off bark where I can, and lug a small bag of the stuff back to my rooms and soon have a fire up and running. Being here when there are no other people around is certainly calming, though some of my neighbours in this part of the college – House II – should be interesting. For example, Bob Rae, the former NDP premier, and Moses Znaimer, the television entrepreneur, both of whom I know very slightly. If only there were heat to accompany the silence.

THURSDAY, 30 DECEMBER / TORONTO
M and I meet up in the afternoon and take in the exhibition of Picasso ceramics being held at the University Art Centre in Sig Samuel owing to the reconstruction under way at the Gardiner. She hasn't seen this stuff before even in reproductions and is taken, as I am, with the fish platters especially, some of the animal jugs, and the ceramic portraits of Françoise and particularly Jacqueline. To me the most revealing gallery is the one illustrating his homage to ancient Hellenic ceramics and other antiquarian sources. The exhibit is also quite enlightening as to process. The whole affair well presented, considering the ad hoc nature of the space.

FRIDAY, 31 DECEMBER / TORONTO
My chest cold is much worse. On what is already a low-oxygen day, and me with an arthritis flare-up to boot, this is problematic. M and I go to the Modigliani show at the AGO. Having read the catalogue, I am well prepared, but am surprised by the low level of specifically Jewish content, as I had been led to expect that showing Modigliani's Judaism was the primary purpose of the Jewish Museum in New York in organising the exhibition. Very crowded.

2005

Jericho proved a minor publishing failure. Finishing the term at Massey College in Toronto, I went back to Vancouver and renewed work on the novel *Walt Whitman's Secret*, which would not be published until 2010.

MONDAY, 3 JANUARY / TORONTO

John Fraser knocks on the door. He has just returned from Africa (Elizabeth is still there), naturally looking heavier and less hirsute than when I saw him last. For some reason, his complexion has turned a light caramel colour (the African sun?). He tells me not to worry about Bob F's silence, for he (Bob) has been having some heart concerns and was in hospital having something implanted ("not a pacemaker"). The news makes me sad. He also tells me that my stay here is secure for an extra two months, paid for by an anonymous donor whom he immediately identifies as Peggy A.

TUESDAY, 4 JANUARY / TORONTO

My first begowned dinner, with Latin prayers at beginning and end. As with most everything else at Massey, the eccentricity is a bit forced. But talking with my table mates I do appreciate their high degree of socialisation and the mark of promise they all wear on their faces.

I've used up the last of the wood. I write until the fire goes out at 10:00 p.m.

FRIDAY, 7 JANUARY / TORONTO

This evening, High Table with all its rigmarole. I sit next to Haroon Siddiqui of the *Star* and PEN and across from Peggy A. Everyone is accomplished, often in odd ways, and everyone is charming, none more so than Fraser, who is quick-witted and gracious for the occasion. When he finishes, he places the text of his prepared remarks by his salad plate. Reading it upside down (a trick of those who grew up with hot metal in the composing room), I notice that the last page has a note, TURN OFF MIKE. This derives, I understand, from a High Table a few years ago at which he forgot to do so and the assembled diners listened in silent glee as he and Peggy gossiped for twenty minutes.

Peggy gives me a kiss when she first arrives in the Common Room. Her hair is fair these days. Later in the evening, when all the High Table denizens are seated in the Upper Library, with the port passed in one direction and the Madeira in the other, we talk easily of politics and writing, and she tells of the patent she's received for a device that allows authors to sign books electronically from anywhere in the world. When the snuff horn is passed, she takes a pinch with the best of them and sniffs away. Later we all return to the Common Room to mingle with the junior fellows. When I finally leave, I catch sight of her being chatty and generous with a small knot of them.

SATURDAY, 8 JANUARY / TORONTO

A cold dark morning, and I am blue and tense, always a poor combination. I do my laundry, then take the streetcar out to Riverdale for a quite excellent massage. Coming down Devonshire, grocery bags in both hands, I see a familiar face but chubbier than I had remembered it from, most recently, Vancouver: Dennis Duffy, whose eyes are still full of bereavement. I ask if he's still intending to teach at the new Sea to Sky University in BC when and if it finally opens. "No, my life is here," he says. "I like being in a place where I can pick up the phone and talk to someone I've known a very long time. I spent forty years of my life here before Mary Anne's death." I remember him very nearly that long ago, teaching at Trinity with the mercurial Dave Godfrey and doing good works.

I'm deeply disappointed at not having written a single word in the *Tales* draft yesterday, owing to High Table. This evening I manage only one partial page in the notebook.

TUESDAY, 11 JANUARY / TORONTO

I'm a trifle late for dinner, because I have been doing a phone interview for the *Calgary Herald*'s freestanding books section. The reporter sounds extremely young and inexperienced. Her questions are of the "What inspired you to write this?" variety. In short, exactly the sort of journalist I was at her age – or what I take to be her age.

WEDNESDAY, 12 JANUARY / TORONTO

I telephone Bob F, as Fraser has suggested, and am relieved to find that all is quite well between us. We lunch next week. Bob tells me of his health scare. In his recounting of it, two of the chambers of his heart lost their syncopation. Ever the jazz enthusiast, Bob calls it a be-bop heart. The irregularity was corrected by electric shock but is likely to recur, in which case a pacemaker is one option. He sounds cheerful but elderly.

I see Rubin (Hurricane) Carter [the famous middleweight boxer of the 1960s] on the subway. What he's doing on the subway I have no idea. At dinner, one student tells another to "stop universalising your axioms."

THURSDAY, 13 JANUARY / TORONTO

At the evening meal, Molly climbs the stone stairs and enters the room like she owns the joint, strolling up and down each aisle sniffing not the food, for she's too close to the ground to get a good whiff, but rather the diners. Everyone is amused. Finally, her mistress Elizabeth appears in the doorway wearing a track suit and says, "Will someone *please* get the damn dog?" Molly is carried from the hall, looking as though she's riding in a sedan chair. I sit next to a former engineering student, soon-to-be-former law student, who is having the première of his one-hundred-and-ten-minute feature film set in sixteenth-century Japan that he has made for $250 (as compared with the $700 he is paying to rent a cinema for the screening). It is his fifth such feature, and seemingly his career has now chosen him. All he needs now is talent.

One of the rooms in the cellar of this place is stuffed with the gifts that Vincent Massey was given by potentates, Native chiefs, diplomats, and so on.[1] One of them is a clay bust of himself with a light bulb inside so that one may illuminate the cranium and bathe in the warm glow.

I enjoy life here despite all the noise of conscious résumé-construction, for there are indeed some remarkable people doing remarkable things.

---

1   Vincent Massey (1887–1967), diplomat and philanthropist; Canada's first native-born governor general, 1952–59.

TUESDAY, 18 JANUARY / TORONTO

I meet Bob F at Mercurio's. He has a plate of sausages, suggesting that he has yet to adopt the healthy-heart diet, though he confesses to doing a half hour on the treadmill each day, exercise, he says, being the only thing that regulates his sleep. "Six and a half hours is a rare good night's sleep for me. Four and a half is more the usual." He looks far older than when we last met, as of course I do to him; he will soon be seventy-three. The tone is both serious and lighthearted. He apologises for being out of touch for a while and for not being able to read the novel – it just didn't hold his interest (my words based on his response). Fair enough. He says selling the house on Lynwood and moving to a condo was trying and taxing and took up months of their lives, though the actual move re-quired only a couple of days. He sold two-thirds of his books, some to Mason and the art books to Asher Joram. He is understandably sad to be shutting down his life in such an orderly fashion but it is typical of him at his best that it should *be* so orderly. He has extended the pride he has long displayed in his family by enjoying the fact that two of his sons-in-law have books coming out soon that already have been sold in other jurisdictions. I then ask him questions relating to the think-tank projects and he speaks for quite a while about what I call the outsourcing of news – does so with great precision, the kind that derives from years of thought never publicly expressed. I've long understood the reason he keeps writ-ing several columns a week is because of momentum and the fear of letting go. Why the *Post*? Because it's a non-union shop that won't limit how much it can use from a freelance contributor. I've known Bob for nearly forty years and he has taught me as much as he has entertained me and helped me, which is a great deal indeed.

WEDNESDAY, 19 JANUARY / TORONTO

Al Moritz arrives for lunch, full of good fellowship and searing intelli-gence as usual. He brilliantly analyses *Singer, An Elegy*, and we have a long talk about the low-level miracle of Whitman. At 2:00 I have to rush off to teach my seminar, and barely get any real work accomplished be-tween the end of that and dinner, where I learn some facts about this particular suite. It is the one always occupied by Pierre Trudeau when he would stay at Massey for weeks at a time after leaving public life. Its most recent occupant, however, was the former mayor of Winnipeg who's now here at the university teaching a seminar on urban blight (or something like that).

Reluctant as I am to avoid not being self-critical enough, I must say I perform quite well indeed at lunch with the English Department chair and Sam Solecki at the Hart House Grill. I speak with maximum fluency and am (I believe) witty and charming. The chair has been in the department thirty-five years and is a Restoration drama specialist educated at the University of Chicago. He looks somewhat like a Daguerreotype image. Sam is Sam, thirty-four years in the job, perhaps a bit – a tiny bit – more polished now than in the '70s when he had a brief tenure as editor of the *Canadian Forum* to which he still refers, though few now remember the *Forum*, which did not survive ownership by Jim Lorimer. Hart House has never been shy about displaying its huge art collection, and in the Grill I am delighted to see a Lemieux, one much more vibrantly coloured, to say the least, than his most typical work. Our table overlooks the Great Hall. I believe my last visit to that room was when I took Allen Ginsberg there in 1968 for a reading so crowded that kids seemed to be hanging from the rafters.

I return to find an email from Susan Walker telling me that Doug Marshall has died from booze at sixty-seven. Indeed drinking always seemed to be his primary occupation in life, with a bit of competent journalism on the side. A difficult and often befuddled person, as I recall, who had the good fortune to be married to Sarah, whose brow I always feared he would lower.

Wake to find the north window is ice-stencilled in what looks like a Star of David pattern. One of the coldest days of the year, warmed only by a long phone talk with Howard Engel, who has made considerable – very considerable – headway recovering from his stroke, as he says he now reads and writes, though more slowly than he once did. Has a new book coming out from Penguin.

Early this morning as I sit in the Common Room reading the *New York Times*, John arrives with Molly in tow and says, "She has two tricks, which is one more than her master, the Master." Whereupon Molly lies down on command, fully stretched out, and remains immobile even after a milk bone is placed near her nose. But then, on hearing the word "Free," she gobbles it up and does a little dog curtsy.

WEDNESDAY, 26 JANUARY / TORONTO
This morning at 10:00 a one-hour chat with Anne about *Jericho*, *Tales*, writing, and publishing in general. She is a bit stiff in her movements, explaining that she has had to shovel snow at the farm. "To drive downtown on a morning like this, I have to get up early to start the tractor." Weariness and also fatigue of the more immediate sort are obvious on her face. These she can't hide. Otherwise, though, she keeps herself under wraps as always, doling out little glimpses of herself as reader, writer, parent and spouse. For no one knows Anne but all wish to. She controls everyone's access to understanding. Fascinating as always. At 11:00 she passes me over to Kendall Anderson so that Kendall and I can go over corrections to the Vintage edition of *The Book of Assassins*. As she leaves me to this task, Anne, I notice, lowers her mask for just a second and I catch a glimpse of her scepticism (about me? – not sure).

FRIDAY, 28 JANUARY / TORONTO
Fraser takes me to lunch in Harbord Street. I volunteer to walk Molly some morning if he can't get away. He picks right up at the offer. "She likes to run round the yard at Trinity," he says. This naturally leads to a discussion of his fellow Anglicans, and he tells me that a highly sociable priest of our acquaintance was discovered by his wife to have been gay all along. (She might have known, John goes on to say, as their two grown sons – one of whom was the beloved of one of the Fraser daughters – were both conceived through artificial insemination. A trusting woman, evidently.) Anyway, no harm seems to have been done to anyone. John of course prides himself on being Toronto's most prolific gossip and never fails to get himself into trouble and likewise always fails to learn his lesson.

SATURDAY, 5 FEBRUARY / TORONTO
At 5:00 a.m. I go to the *Globe* website. The reviews aren't posted, not yet in any event, but I discern that they're using an excerpt of *Jericho* for online purposes, and this gives me hope that they are taking it seriously.

So an hour later when I get the paper I'm gladdened to read a review by Michel Basilières (whose first novel I read with pleasure last year) for he gets it: understands, and explains well, the fact that these characters live through the individual voices with which they speak. Such a review quite changes the whole complexion of the book's reception, for this is after all the *Globe*, the only place that matters in terms of actually making people aware of the book's existence. I am of much better cheer.

MONDAY, 7 FEBRUARY / TORONTO

Coming up St George from the U of T Bookroom I run into Howard Engel again, and we chat on the street corner for quite a while. HarperCollins has him writing a memoir that is to deal mostly with his stroke and recovery. Of course he naturally wishes it to be broader, and is eager to get me to lunch to share memories of Marian. We go into the matter reasonably far for two chaps standing on the pavement, but I agree that a longer conversation is needed.

Then down to Random to tape a radio interview, after which I pop in to see Anne, who's wearing one of Eric's sweaters. She is in good form, though still looking a bit tired. She astonishes me by saying that she felt the overall effect of the *Globe* review was negative, owing to its last sentence, speculating that though the novel may well be praised critically, it will not sell.

Sometimes I leave Anne's office feeling sad and awkward, at other times feeling happy and uplifted. This is one of the former.

Terribly sad news today as well: Anne tells me that Bill Cameron has cancer of the oesophagus, diagnosed last May. How horrible. Such a sweet man.

TUESDAY, 8 FEBRUARY / TORONTO

I have to back out of a dinner with Susan Swan to go to a buffet dinner at the Master's Lodgings for twelve or fourteen people, junior and senior fellows together, smoothly done, practised. I sit on the right of a judge's wife in a pêche-coloured suit who wishes to know about the season's novels and also whether my homosexuality is a burden to me. She's obviously never been rude to anyone in her life and would be horrified to know that she misinterpreted my speech difficulty. So after making mention of a few books I say noncommittally, "On the other matter – well, society continues to evolve but its lash can still sting." She is satisfied and looks at me with sympathy for my plight. Several glum theology students are dining as well. Molly the dog goes back and forth between the tables wearing an expression that seems to say "One does not fetch, does one?"

MONDAY, 14 FEBRUARY / VICTORIA
Awake every hour on the hour all night, evidently concerned about my talk at 7:30 to booksellers at the Victoria Book Fair. But in fact, when the time comes, I am evidently relaxed, polished, and funny, or so I am told not only by the Random rep but by the audience as well. Rebecca from the *Sun* is there, looking smashing and scribbling notes, as is John Burns from the *Straight*. Also Robert Wiersema, the bookseller, who has a first novel coming out next year from Random. He and I go for coffee in Bastion Square. Then, feeling a cold coming on, I decide to take an earlier than planned seaplane back to Vancouver.

MONDAY, 21 FEBRUARY / TORONTO
I have temporarily run out of wine and so at 6:00 p.m. when the bar opens I mosey down to the Common Room only to find it full of be-suited big-money men like Hal Jackman and John Honderich: I have stumbled into the pre-dinner congregation of the Monday Club.[2] The sea parts and I see Roy MacLaren for the first time in a decade at least. He's seventy now and is, I'm sure, a disappointed man (who is not?), for after having three posts in the Trudeau and Turner governments he was, many felt, spurned by Jean C, whom he always had made sport of; shunted off to be High Commissioner in London. We chat amiably, as I remember how I respected his panache when he was in his early forties and inter-ested in publishing. Then he and the others suddenly disappear up the stairs to the private dining room and I am left looking at Jeff the Barman.

WEDNESDAY, 23 FEBRUARY / TORONTO
I meet Al Mortiz for a drink in the Common Room. While he and I are debating Whitman's mental health in the late 1850s, John Fraser wad-dles over, greeting Al as an old acquaintance and asking if we're going to

2   Henry Jackman (b. 1932), financier and philanthropist.

attend a talk by the *New York Times* ombudsman. "No," says Al, "we're just having a drink before going off to an anarchist meeting." John wanders away looking perplexed. Al has a fine mind, quite fully stocked and refreshed, and is certainly the most enviably articulate person of my acquaintance. He takes me down Spadina to a second-storey Vietnamese restaurant below Dundas for a meeting of the discussion group he and I founded in the early '90s. The people sitting at the big round table are all new to me, save for Susan Brown. I feel out of place in other ways as well. The Ring has grown too accepting of state authority, preferring to focus mainly on ecological concerns, etc. This leaves me sad. But a pleasant evening all the same, and Al and I walk home in frostbite conditions, with snow falling on all the illuminated Chinese signs.

MONDAY, 28 FEBRUARY / TORONTO
Have a pleasant phone call with Ken McGoogan, who mentions that he's teaching two writing classes for U of T Continuing Studies, which sounds to me as though his relocating from Calgary has not yet proved financially rewarding. I know, for I've taught those courses myself. Ken is a decent fellow, honest and hardworking, and deserves more successes like his most recent book. No doubt his biography of Lady Franklin will prove quite popular, particularly if he can find some way (others have failed) to make her appear interesting.

WEDNESDAY, 2 MARCH / TORONTO
Dr Morose comes by at 4:30 to lug the heavy boxes of books down to the Common Room for my launch. Anne C turns up shortly thereafter, looking absolutely stunning in a black and white silk dress with a leaf pattern. I never see Anne without realising all over again how much I have wished over the years to know more about her; I rarely part from her without feeling happy simply to have seen her again; in between, I'm always just in awe. She orders bourbon, of all things, to prepare for her little speech to the perhaps fifty people present. She says touchingly how, since I find it so hard to communicate orally, I try harder to communicate by other means and that this novel is one of the wonderful results. Something like that. Very well done. I am gratified at seeing so many people from my past there. I'm also somewhat dizzy from the combination of painkillers for my dental problem and the social exertion of

having to meet everyone's eyes and make pleasant small talk: hard work for someone with my limited gifts. I believe I have sold a thousand dollars worth of books.

THURSDAY, 3 MARCH / TORONTO

Plumbers have the water at Massey shut off between 9:30 and 4:30. So when Esther Vincent arrives from Peterborough at noon (causing Fraser to cock an eyebrow on spotting her bowler and her many piercings) she and I must eat lunch from paper plates using plastic cutlery. Then we come down here to my rooms where she interviews me on tape about the '60s more generally and Toronto's '60s in particular. Her dramatic ideas for [a stage adaptation of] *Travels* are beginning to take form. The action will take place on 31 December 1969 at a New Year's Eve party, or rather in the room containing the bed on which the guests' coats are thrown. Allen Ginsberg and Gwen MacEwen will be major characters, entering and exiting throughout. Working with Esther is delightful, notwithstanding a certain amount of feistiness on her part. I've long sought this kind of cross-disciplinary relationship. When we're speaking of actors and of the Peterborough arts scene, she mentions that she once was photographed nude on horseback, arms spread wide in salute, in the local listings mag.

SUNDAY, 6 MARCH / TORONTO

After the gym, I go to see [Al] Pacino's *Merchant of Venice*, not knowing what to expect except that Shylock will have a New York accent. The film is neither too slick nor too rough, with the individual actors far superior to the direction they receive or the editing. Seeing a play unstaged is always interesting. In this case, the palette is especially pleasing with its rich earth tones; the use of red is kept in check. Of course the play always comes down to the question of whether its depiction of anti-Semitism is itself anti-Semitic. A non-Jew can't enter into the matter with the same intense emotion as a Jew but can only say that Shylock is beautifully full and believable for his understandable reaction to how he and his fellow Jews are treated: surely one of the most memorable characterisations in Western literature, more so even than Lear, I think. Pacino is surprisingly effective in the role, yet, strangely, is less so in a way than Mel Gibson (of all people) was in *Hamlet*. Pacino is only acting whereas Gibson seems to have a genuine little streak of madness from which to draw.

MONDAY, 7 MARCH / TORONTO

The only media for *Jericho* that the Random House publicist has managed to find for me is a live interview today on the York University radio station, all five hundred watts of it. Everything else I've had to arrange myself, often after she has failed: *Books in Canada*, CBC Radio, the *Star*, the *Globe*, the U of T Reading Series. Not that I'm complaining; I'm happy to do the strategic work and let her bill Random (she's a former staff publicist, now freelancing). Still, she thinks that the old student radio dodge will work. This particular interview, about forty minutes, consists of my phoning the student host, who can hear me plainly though I can barely make her out. She keeps cutting me off accidentally, so I must phone back more than once. Other mechanical failures cause her to announce a "musical interlude" now and then, a VERY LOUD African drum solo that each time seems to go on forever. I bear up with my usual good humour.

THURSDAY, 10 MARCH / TORONTO

Not certain how swollen or sore I would be the other day after the dental work, I arranged for one of the students in my seminar at UC to help me do the poetry reading tonight in the Upper Library to satisfy the St George Campus part of my obligation. She is one of George Clarke's students, and what's more – you begin to see my method – is a trained actor with experience at Stratford (though she's only twenty-three). In fact, I feel better than I expected to, and we end up sharing the lecture, alternating poems from the *Selected*. I introduce her well, I believe (after Solecki introduces me rather nastily). The brief English Department reception afterwards is dry, and so I'm not surprised in a way to see Rudy Wiebe there, looking outdoorsy and disciplined; we chat amiably for a while. No books sold at the reading. I ask Fraser whether there can possibly be any sense to the assertion being made loudly in the papers that Ignatieff will be the next leader of the federal Liberals. "If that's true," he sniffs, "then I'll be Finance!"

FRIDAY, 11 MARCH / TORONTO

At the end of the day I go down to the *Globe* (such a frightening newsroom – the ceiling is extra low and the light otherworldly) to meet Val

Ross, who takes me home to the West End to have dinner with her and Morton, who's going to England soon to complete the last requirement of his PhD at Sussex. Hebrew prayer, breaking bread, and so on. A long, talkative, and charming evening.

SATURDAY, 12 MARCH / TORONTO
Howard Engel has won the $20,000 Matt Cohen prize from the Writers' Trust, and I stop round his place in Major Street to congratulate him. He is recovering nicely from his stroke but at seventy-four his short-term memory is failing, and I sense that the money is welcome: the exterior of the house is decaying badly (and the interior shows the absence of the love brought to it by dear departed Janet, whose photo is everywhere).

Howard then tells me tragic news: that Bill Cameron, who I learned only two days ago had entered palliative care, has died. This sets us to having the long conversation about Marian that H has asked me to have with him, to aid his recollection for the memoir that HarperCollins has asked him to write. This is tricky ground, but he implores me to be fully candid and seems to appreciate it when I am – as when, for example, I tell him that so many people presumed, not unreasonably, that she was an individual who, had she grown up in a later time, might have arrived at a different understanding of her sexuality. He nods sadly. Likewise, when we discuss her anti-Semitism.

SUNDAY, 13 MARCH / TORONTO
This morning's obituaries for Bill Cameron are long and sad, and I struggle to write a letter of condolence to Cheryl, while in Devonshire Place, beneath my window, the St Patrick's Day parade marshals itself – fat people dressed in green, struggling under the burden of out-of-tune tubas.

MONDAY, 14 MARCH / TORONTO
Today I go to the Mississauga campus to give a reading for a decent number of students and faculty who buy a decent number of books. The point man is Richard Greene, a friendly fellow who comes from Memorial in Newfoundland. I believe this to be one of my more successful performances. I'm interested to learn that Greene is a friend of Kildare Dobbs, who has an Irish publisher for his memoirs and is shopping the proofs around Toronto. If the book is successful, Kildare is saying, he will do a collection of portraits of Can lit figures.

TUESDAY, 15 MARCH / TORONTO
Setting out this morning, I run into David Silcox, the president of Sotheby's. I haven't seen him in years but have had slight dealings with him in all his previous jobs – Canada Council, Ontario Arts Council, Toronto Arts and Culture, and of course in his role as an author of art books, especially those on Milne and Thomson. Always a hale fellow with a very slight edge of mockery. He tells me the art business is rebounding.

THURSDAY, 17 MARCH / TORONTO
Today a private lunch for Lord Black. There are eleven of us in addition to Fraser. The guest of honour is twenty minutes late. He is looking quite a bit trimmer than when I saw him last and with attractively silver hair (today, with a rather prominent cowlick), but his skin is blotchy in an obviously unhealthy way (stress?). He plays down the pinstripes some-what but wears his Order of Canada pin. He has been quite well briefed – so well as to suggest he's gone to far more trouble than simply getting Fraser to send him a memo. For example, he knows all the vital facts about those he is meeting for the first time, and when I shake his hand he says, "You had your other Christian name when last we met." Even though we have all been introduced and exchanged a few words, Fraser makes everyone round the table introduce himself or herself, which is a trifle ridiculous – as when Bob Fulford, who quit as editor of *Saturday Night* when Black bought it but has since ridden to Black's rescue in print, has to say, "I'm Robert Fulford and ..."

When my turn comes, I say, "I'm George Fetherling, and I was Your Lordship's most inconspicuous servant as literary columnist of the *Vancouver Sun*."

To which he replies, "Oh not *that* inconspicuous!"

So I say, "Well, either the most inconspicuous or not inconspicuous enough."

Sitting round the table are an Economist, a Scientist, and so on: it's like Noah's Ark except that there is only a single specimen of each spe-cies. In order to complete the set, one needs, of course, a Poet.

While discoursing on FDR, Lord Black holds his left hand by the wrist, allowing four fingers to rest lightly on the tablecloth. I take this as a part of his public-speaking style. The discussion inevitably strays into other areas: economics, for example, but other more personal ones as well. He is charming, and he lets drop a small bombshell by reminding everyone of what they don't actually know: that he has first refusal on buying back the *National Post* if the Aspers decide not to keep it going, which he admits is a possibility in the short to medium term. (Of course, to own the paper, he would need to be a Canadian citizen again, though I suppose there are ways of getting round this, by being the controlling but not the majority owner.) When the talk drifts into US foreign policy, he says (graciously, not menacingly), "Now, George, some of these will be hot-button issues for you, but ..."

FRIDAY, 18 MARCH / TORONTO

With minutes to spare I remember that I'm to be at the last High Table of the term, the one at which choirs sing, guards are changed, and endless prizes are given out. The dining hall overflows, and so I am put with ten or so others in the private dining room, with Elizabeth as host. Thus do I see for the second time in as many days John Polanyi's Nobel medal hanging on one wall and a portrait of William Southam on the other. Southam is shown holding a rolled-up copy of his first newspaper, the *Hamilton Spectator*. He in fact might be said to be squeezing the paper, as though to extract every cent.

TUESDAY, 22 MARCH / TORONTO

I wake to find the first true spring day, when, for example, junior fellows are sitting on the benches in the quad. My greatest accomplishment today – other than writing, advising a junior fellow on her career, working at the library, preparing for tomorrow's seminar, going to the U of T Press, and shopping – is happening to be in Bloor-Yonge station to see a busker's dog, a smiling uncombed fellow of uncertain heritage, sitting up in his master's open guitar case, into which the occasional passerby drops a coin or two. My guess is that the presence of the dog doubles the take, at least.

SATURDAY, 26 MARCH / TORONTO

This morning's *Globe* has a devastating review of Subway's kids' book: a real sales-stopper. I regret the economic waste but mostly I feel bad for Jen and M, for this is the first time that either of them has had her name on the cover of a book. M is rushing off to Sechelt later today, and though we exchange email I don't inform her of the review, preferring not to dampen her break. And poor Jen is coping with her newborn; she doesn't need the stress she will get when she sees the paper. All I can do is to send them both a note.

WEDNESDAY, 30 MARCH / TORONTO
I read from *Jericho* at Hart House in the company of Steven Hayward, author of a comedic novel of Jewish life around Christie Pits in the '30s, and Stephen Marche, whose first novel is an urban (and urbane) young cynical romance story. Marche, as it happens, is husband to Sarah Fulford, who's become so gracious. I'm told that I read well. I certainly practised.

FRIDAY, 1 APRIL / TORONTO
A long lunch today at which I renewed my friendship with Ramsay Derry, strained but not severed these past twenty years. He must be sixty-five now, though he seems not to have aged at all. One usually has the opposite perception in the case of a person one has seen so seldom. His gentle fussy humour is unchanged as well. Sitting in the Common Room, he tells me of having been awarded a school prize by Vincent Massey. "He stood there like a wooden Indian and said a few words to each boy, something on the order of 'Good show.'"

Then I spend two hours having coffee on Bloor Street with one of my seminar students. Astonishingly she is only twenty. She's also wonderfully talented, poised, and well-read – and lacking in the boastfulness of other young people who practise the cult of the extraordinary (as so many junior fellows at Massey do, for example). I try to advise her as best I can.

SATURDAY, 2 APRIL / TORONTO
Walking along Bloor, I see Stephen Marche at the entrance to Philosophers' Walk, and we go for a quick coffee. He tells me that he received his doctorate only a few days ago. Of course the market for a Shakespearean scholar is rather limited, and he agonises. He impresses me favourably.

MONDAY, 4 APRIL / TORONTO
Happily the forecast – gossip actually – is completely mistaken. A springlike day: the gods are forgiven.

Lunch with John Macfarlane from *Toronto Life* after he gives me the tour of St Joseph Media, which the proprietors, the rags-to-riches Gagliano family, have actually named after the saint, in gratitude. I have a nicely broiled salmon steak, John has a selection of oysters from various oceans, the owner coming out from the kitchen to give full genealogical and biographical particulars on each one. John walks with a limp now, and the two of us look like a pair of Chelsea pensioners going along Adelaide Street to Yonge after leaving the restaurant. We've known each other, though not well, since I was twenty-one and he twenty-eight.

Later I go up to Random and see Anne, who, unlike me of course, is looking tired. We calculate that *Jericho* needs to sell another five hundred copies to be a successful failure. Then across the corridor to the boardroom, which Knopf has turned into a champagne reception for Ian McEwan.[3] Many familiar faces indeed. As I'm chatting with McEwan, a woman floats over purposefully and begins flirting with him outrageously, holding his forearm as she does so. This being their first meeting, she evidently does not feel it proper to hold his cock, for she is bound by the Old World protocols of decorum and deportment. McEwan bears up patiently as only a poor jetlagged author can do who's touring Canada having promoted America into submission through saturation charm and bonhomie. His smile says, "If I don't get home to London soon I'm going to die in one of these godforsaken places."

TUESDAY, 5 APRIL / TORONTO
As Anne feared and I confirmed, I've had to do all the publicity on *Jericho* myself, as the freelance publicist doesn't even read the *Globe*. Suits me fine.

WEDNESDAY, 6 APRIL / TORONTO
I meet Maggie Helwig, who has come into the poise and sophistication she (like the rest of us of course) lacked in her younger days, such as a decade ago when she worked for Nicky Drumbolis at his bookshop. Of course she's grown as a writer, too, while sticking with peace activities – so admirably.

---

3 Ian McEwan (b. 1948), English novelist and playwright, author of *Amsterdam* and other works.

MONDAY, 11 APRIL / TORONTO

I climb to the Grill Room for lunch with Rosemary Sullivan. She is difficult to dislike, she's so unselfconsciously educated working-class and with a big open heart. Peggy and Graeme are a few tables distant, and they come over to chat on their way out, Peggy wearing a large pea-green summer hat. It's good to see a couple who've been together so happily for so long still able to just take off and have a fancy lunch together on a spring afternoon. Rosemary and I sit beneath that wonderful Lemieux, talking of Banff and of creative writing at the U of T, where it is a new discipline. As I return to Massey, I find the back quad full of student actors, a dozen or more, rehearsing their stage duelling with one another, their swords shining in the sun, contesting the same patch of grass where each morning I see all the neighbourhood dogs having breakfast: a kind of kibbleklatch.

TUESDAY, 12 APRIL / TORONTO

I have been pondering the matter of what I call social muscle. When one is prosperous and confident, and enjoying a period of public activity, one builds up social muscle that can be used to ward off attacks, hurtful remarks, and misunderstandings generally. When one is reclusive for a while, out of the fray, the muscles atrophy, the batteries run down. Journalism always has been the source of whatever social muscle I possess, and also the only reason to require it. With journalism of any type now of less interest to me (and I to it) than at any previous time, I am somewhat vulnerable, except that a) I am under less threat, and b) age has given me more confidence (in place of the energy it has taken away).

WEDNESDAY, 13 APRIL / TORONTO

This morning there are two ducks – a government-issue brown one, and one of these contemporary private-sector ones with a green bill – sitting in the heavily populated fish pond without so much as a by-your-leave. Anyway, they pause for a harmless paddle and then are gone. Migrating northward, I presume.

Today is the final session of the poetry seminar. One student brings me a bottle of wine, then she and three others take me out for a drink at Hart House. The two talented ones promise to stay in touch.

THURSDAY, 14 APRIL / TORONTO

[One of the students] still has many questions about becoming a writer and so we meet for breakfast once again. We talk for a couple of hours, then I walk with her down to the E.J. Pratt Library. Leaving her there, I wander through the rest of Victoria College, the most atmospheric of the U of T colleges, I think. I try to imagine Peggy's time there and how it shaped her. (The imagining is quite easy.) I think even more of Janet Hamilton, taken away by a brain tumour so young; her spirit seems to be all through the place, an impression heightened perhaps by the fact that the corridors and grounds are almost entirely empty, as everyone is studying for exams later this week and all next.

SUNDAY, 17 APRIL / TORONTO

Dinner at the McGoogans' place in the Beach for what turns out to be a most pleasant evening's worth of talk about books, travel, and the like. Ken has managed to land on his feet since the tragic strike at the *Calgary Herald*, where he did a heroic job putting out the book section. His books on Arctic exploration do well and like me he picks up the occasional residency or equivalent. Sheena, who tells me we were introduced once on the street long ago, is a former teacher, now a painter, who wears bangs, making her look somewhat Quakerish in an attractive way. The three of us, not counting Cody, the part-Cocker spaniel, talk for six hours or so in the tiny living-room of their Arts and Crafts house. They would be good people to travel with. I have particular affection for Ken despite his love of Kerouac. He was an intern at the *Star* – his first job out of Ryerson – when I worked there. For me, a very late night indeed.

MONDAY, 18 APRIL / TORONTO

A busy day. I do some research at the Robarts and then meet Martin Levin of the *Globe* for lunch in King Street. Whether for my benefit or not, possibly just out of awkwardness, he makes a big display of being an outsider today. My guess is that he seeks to project outsider solidarity. A rushed but pleasant time, talking about his books section and how it's fared under different bosses. I like him.

Then home to read and rest before walking, slowly, up to Bloor to meet George Clarke at the Intercontinental Hotel, his watering hole evidently. We get to talk candidly for a while before a friend of his, an old mate from Waterloo, now a high school teacher, turns up. I tell him that I'm concerned about him. I tell him he must be prepared psychologically for the inevitable fact that he will not go on indefinitely winning all the awards and being the media darling. That of course a new generation will come along, and he may find himself in a crisis of self-confidence. He thanks me – sincerely, I believe – as though he is already thinking about what isolation might do to him, for he is quite the extrovert: voluble, endearing, articulate (at least during the first two of the three double martinis I'm astonished to watch him consume), a singular talent. I offer to see him home to the Danforth at evening's end, but he insists he can manage. And so I watch him stagger a bit as he enters St George station.

WEDNESDAY, 20 APRIL / TORONTO
Glancing up from the table at Mercurio's where I'm sitting in plain view, I see Howard Engel, the lunch companion I'm waiting for, sitting at the bar, looking bewildered. He wears a green tweed hat and a fisherman's vest not done up, and carries no umbrella though it's pouring out.

The lunch is sad. Howard has been telling me conflicting stories about how much of his ability to read he's recovered since the stroke, but I observe that he cannot read the bill of fare on the chalkboard and must point to various dishes. His memory for common words is poor, so I must negotiate a path between supplying enough of them to enable his conversation to proceed and not supplying so many that he feels uncomfortable. That he's quite deaf now doesn't help (and I've chosen such a noisy restaurant). A frustrating experience in a way, but touching.

"You're the only reason I'm a writer," he says at one point, exaggerating mightily. "I knew people who wrote but never thought I'd be a writer too until you encouraged me." He's so lonely. His son has inherited his late mother's depression, and I can tell that Howard feels terrible that he's not going to be around to see the matter through (though in fact Howard is likely to go on a long time – his father lived into his nineties). I offer to take him to a film on Friday, followed by cheap Indian food on Yonge Street. He doesn't get out of the house much because, as he says, he finds it confusing if everything's not in its usual place – including himself.

FRIDAY [SEEMS LIKE SATURDAY], 22 APRIL / TORONTO
I fall asleep reading Northrop Frye's notebooks, including this passage, which I agree with, recognise, and am somewhat awed by: "One doesn't know anything about an after-life, but one can always invent. We read (experience) a text linearly, forgetting most of it while we read; then we study it as a simultaneous unit. While we live we learn fast but not enough, like a bull in a ring. Meanwhile our dreams store up commentary while we sometimes remember but don't understand. At death we enter into & become the total dream-world we've constructed. We understand it then. The slave, the captive, the exploited, become the compensation worlds of release & freedom they dream of. Others help & teach us to read. Not so much an inner-world as a world of which one is the circumference, seeing it all simultaneously, as we're said to do before death. A world where youth knows and age can."

Howard Engel and I go see a Hollywood thriller about African politics. Unfortunately, some of the plot turns on stuff written in notebooks, which the viewer gets to see. Poor Howard can't make out the words quickly enough. Then as I am walking him home along Bloor we see that UTS on Bloor is being mocked up as a New York high school for a film shoot. "See that?" I say. "They've changed all the street signs. And look at those New York newspaper boxes." But of course they all look the same to him.

Other notes: Howard becomes uncharacteristically sharp-tongued speaking about his Jewish upbringing in St Catharines. He also recalls – mistakenly, I'm pretty sure – that he, I, and others (Jack Jensen, I suspect) ate dinner with Earle Birney in Chinatown hours before his famous crash in the taxi.

Also, I've been thinking of Ken McGoogan's manner of speech – how he speaks loudly and in a declarative way as though wishing to make certain he's understood the information he's about to pass along. Very distinctive and effective.

WEDNESDAY, 27 APRIL / TORONTO
At the reception for Peggy A preceding her Quadrangle Society lecture, I'm sitting with Austin Clarke when Kildare Dobbs, now eighty-two, enters the Common Room wearing a pop art necktie. He says that the memoir he has coming out in Ireland will be published over

here by Dundurn. But aside from imparting this one bit of information, he's decidedly cool to me all evening, even dismissive towards the end. This is in contrast to the last time I saw him, when he was actually rather jolly. Maybe he's not feeling well. The dinner for Peggy is quite well done, the dining hall transformed by candles, tablecloths, the seldom-seen good silver. I sit opposite a very actressy English actress who flirts and tells me of once having performed in Fort McMurray and Prince Rupert. Then we all troop down to the Upper Library for Peggy's talk. Fraser, just off a plane from Europe with moments to spare, makes one of his signature introductions, saying "I've had a long intimate relationship with Ms Atwood." He goes on to explain that she was a counsellor at a rich kids' summer camp attended by both him and Conrad Black. "Conrad brought binoculars and rented them out to the other boys so we could watch the counsellors skinnydipping." Sandra Martin is an even more skilled host. In fact I've been quite impressed with how she has remade herself as the charming diva.

A packed house. Looking around, I see Norman Jewison and other notables.[4] Peggy speaks wittily of "the writing life." She begins with the familiar narrative of her apprenticeship, including the story of how she taught English to engineers in a Nissen hut at UBC. "I had them doing writing exercises based on Kafka's short parables. I thought they would find this useful in their later careers." She then moves on to discuss how she wrote *The Edible Woman*, *Alias Grace*, and *The Handmaid's Tale*. She is a polished lecturer, and of course quick-witted. The lectern is too tall for her and she asks Fraser, "Can you make this go lower?" He replies: "No, but I can make you go higher." She: "Oh, many people have tried that."

TUESDAY, 3 MAY / TORONTO
Stumbling along Bloor Street to breakfast, I see William Thorsell standing on the north side opposite the ROM, whose director he now is. He is viewing with evident pride the hideous crystal tank-trap under construction.

4 Norman Jewison (b. 1926), film director.

SATURDAY, 7 MAY / TORONTO

I'm starting to wind up my affairs here, seeing how much I can pack into my luggage and so on. My main accomplishments have been finishing *Tales* and making twenty grand to carry me a while longer. My attempt to find some assignments has been less successful.

I'm greatly disappointed that *Jericho* has been a publishing failure yet I'm heartened by the reviews both it and *Singer, An Elegy* have received thus far.

SATURDAY, 14 MAY / TORONTO

After getting back from the gym and resting, I walk over to Howland Avenue for Roger Hall's sixtieth birthday celebration. To say that Roger and Sandra now live in splendour is an understatement, a far cry from 1972 when, just back from England, they had a tiny apartment on Lyndhurst after first staying with Rachel and me only a block up from where they are now. Today their lavishly redone place stuffed with expensive art and artefacts is full of people who are materially successful, expensively dressed, and talking incessantly about their real estate acumen.

TUESDAY, 17 MAY / TORONTO

Good communications today from Dean, about how to circulate *Tales* to the prospective publishers; from Esther V, about the very rough plot outlines she's written for *Travels*; and from Anne, about the paperback *Book of Assassins*.

SUNDAY, 22 MAY / TORONTO

I speak to no one all day: what a relief. Instead I go through the file of unpublished poems, revising and rewriting, sometimes even cannibalising for parts. This last procedure sounds ridiculous when described this way, but I usually find myself, as others do, performing it. Why it works for me is that I tend to be consumed for short though intense periods by one or two or three situations, modes, and experiences, as shown by the patterns of key words that came to light during editing. Really I'm writing a single discontinuous poem, or a couple of them, over a certain period, and so I can combine and recombine modules, so to call them, until I am more satisfied with the material. Viewed from the inside, nothing about the habit is terribly strange.

TUESDAY, 24 MAY / TORONTO

At 5:00 I go over to the Fisher [Rare Book Library] for the opening of
an exhibition of Canadian literary manuscripts. How odd to see some of
my own stuff under glass. I'm surprised to see Greg Cook from Saint
John who's here working in the Ernest Buckler papers. He, Leslie, and I
go out for Indian food later and end up talking for four hours. They will
be coming through Vancouver in October en route to Brisbane. Leslie
will be on sabbatical.

FRIDAY, 27 MAY / TORONTO

At 12:30 I meet Dean in the King Eddy bar so that we can confirm plans
for our lunch with Anne C at one o'clock. Anne is wearing peg-legged
jeans, a silk jacket, and a sort of loud floral frockcoat that she picked
up in Portobello Road. I give her a birthday present five days early. We
lunch at some expensive wine bar at the foot of Church Street but she's
careful not to become tipsy. Productive talk about business. Then she
talks about menopause. When Dean points out that he turned fifty last
December thirty-first, she says, as though talking to another woman and
not a gay man, "But you've kept your figure."

MONDAY, 30 MAY / TORONTO

A knock on the door shortly before noon and there's Howard Engel, out
of breath from the climb, as I sometimes myself am. He's lonely and has
come by to take me to lunch at the Faculty Club. A long and enjoyable
chat about former CBC Radio colleagues living and dead. Howard's memory takes odd directions. For example, he orders clam chowder and a roast
beef sandwich. He is finished with soup and is half way through the sandwich when he suddenly puts it down and says, "I can't taste the seafood
in this at all." One of his stories takes a confusing narrative turn when he
keeps saying *hotel* when he means *apartment block*. But he appears to be
happy, indeed serene, for he refuses to become frustrated. He tells me that
he was asked to give a reading in the U of T Bookstore series and brought
along an actor friend to do the actual reading for him. "I could have got
started but every five sentences I would have stopped making sense."

Coming back to Massey, I see Malcolm Lester, who returns the *Tales*
manuscript with his very helpful comments and suggestions about character, plot, and Jewish references.

WEDNESDAY, 8 JUNE / VANCOUVER

No real work accomplished, although I feel I am nearly ready to sit down and attack the *Walt* novel. Civilians, and indeed most writers, don't understand how writing gets written: by getting oneself psyched up and then writing a set number of sentences each day for a long period, working out the thoughts that have come to one during the preceding twenty-four hours: labour from which one is all too easily distracted.

FRIDAY, 10 JUNE / VANCOUVER

Dream situated in "St Clair and Bathurst times three" where I'm looking for a flat that I can make into a safe house.

WEDNESDAY, 15 JUNE / VANCOUVER

I finally settle down to work on the *Walt* book. My intention is to do so each morning, working at the new kitchen table, before moving to the freshly reordered office to write other things and generally carry on.

THURSDAY, 16 JUNE / VANCOUVER

Second morning of work on *Walt*. The problem will be figuring out how to spring the subplot and how to properly distinguish Horace's voice from Walt's. The former's voice is younger, of course, and more earnest, perhaps even a bit prissy. The latter's is marked by opinions about everything and a belief that good old American slang is expressive of his crackpot democracy; though Walt's health is giving out rapidly, his speech is still vigorous – indeed it takes up the slack covered by the body's retreat from usefulness.

FRIDAY, 17 JUNE / VANCOUVER

A dream in which writers, meeting at SFU, are being trained by the RCMP for some type of police work.

SUNDAY, 19 JUNE / VANCOUVER

I get some more work on *Walt* done. I'm now beginning to draft the second chapter, which will be the third in time. I see the core of the Horace/Walt stuff being about 60,000 words. As always, I need to find ways of keeping the story moving. This is difficult when the primary character is confined to his bed and his rocker.

MONDAY, 20 JUNE / VANCOUVER

More *Walt*, but I find concentrating difficult today. I must take to heart the lesson of Massey, which is that I need to say no to petty intrusions and distractions and refuse to be diverted: first things first.

TUESDAY, 21 JUNE / VANCOUVER

Dream in which the actor George Segal, or someone he is portraying, buys a Ford. This is in the 1920s. "I've got the first payment right here. Let's send it with the papers." Dream in which I lend my ID. "The wisdom of the old, let me have it, please." I wake thinking of the effect of the Internet on exiles. Positive, I should think. At least more positive than negative.

WEDNESDAY, 22 JUNE / VANCOUVER

I work a bit on *Walt* in the morning before turning to other tasks. I know I can't get away with writing a whole work in the first person again. So *Walt* will have an authorial narrator in some sections as well. In italics? Possibly but probably not. I must make Booth a little sinister (of course) as well as socially accomplished and vain, while Horace is defeated by his lack of talent but won't admit it; Walt himself must carry the burden of his past. I know, I know, I'm supposed to be at work on the other novel, but I'm going with this roll as long as I can.

THURSDAY, 23 JUNE / VANCOUVER

Dream in which I'm lying prone in tall grass with a group of other trappers, listening. From somewhere comes the sound of CBC Radio. I recognise Anne C's voice.

MONDAY, 27 JUNE / VANCOUVER

Dream in which I am wearing a leather tux and I mistake someone else for me and myself for someone else.

THURSDAY, 30 JUNE / VANCOUVER

Dream in which firefighters are supporting dictators: "The idea is really starting to take off." I lie in bed thinking how various people's reactions to Bishop in *Jericho* have been useful to me in terms of social mapping.

THURSDAY, 14 JULY / VANCOUVER
I'm just about ready to return to *Walt*. I have decided to do without Flora
D as a third narrator, though she will still be present. Instead I'll alternate
between Traubel (quoting a great deal from W) and the unmanned all-
seeing dead person (who pushes the narrative along – indeed is a narrator
in the classic sense rather than in any way the protagonist).

FRIDAY, 15 JULY / VANCOUVER
Dream about moving cartons of correspondence from place to place, all
round the city, trying to stay one move ahead of some unknown adversary.

TUESDAY, 19 JULY / VANCOUVER
Dream in the middle of the night, in which it is 10:30. The numbers eight
and eighteen dominate, though this phrase occurs as well – "ten linear
shrink lives."

THURSDAY, 21 JULY / VANCOUVER
Moderate progress on *Walt*. I suppose I should get comfortable with the
possibility that this manuscript may never be published or at least not in
my lifetime. This doesn't deter me in the slightest.

THURSDAY, 28 JULY / VANCOUVER
Obituaries in the papers for Arthur Crook, the long-serving editor of the
TLS. I met him when he made a triumphal visit to Toronto years ago. He
looked and sounded like the Scotland Yard inspector in any of a hundred
films made in the '30s.

MONDAY, 1 AUGUST / VANCOUVER
I should be able to resume work on *Walt* now, having figured out the
skipped opening chapter as well as the Booth one – figured out in the
sense of having a rough (though pliable) chronology and ideas about
the action, even a few scraps of dialogue.

FRIDAY, 5 AUGUST / VANCOUVER
To Lincoln Clarkes' studio in Strathcona to look at the results of the
photo shoot re: the cover of *Tales*. It's way out East Georgia and full of

his work, of course. Behind it is a barn he owns; in front is the accompanying house and a related structure that evidently began life as a Chinese grocery. He is tall, lean, square-jawed, forty-six, with mischievous eyes and a high thin voice. We choose a photo, one that billboards the book's eroticism without being explicit in any way that would put off readers who are ortho. I am saying to myself that he is a real mensch to give me a photo for only a hundred bucks.

THURSDAY, 1 SEPTEMBER / VANCOUVER
Dream in which I am in desperate need of a strong magnifying glass. Rejecting those available in shops, I decide to buy a powerful stand-mounted one owned by Conrad Black, and discourse on how it will alter my life for the better.

Lunch at Stepho's with Dan Francis, such a genial fellow and such a fluent writer. We talk of his progress on the prostitution book, and then he tells me of his early days selling books at the Fraser Book Barrel on Robson, writing editorials on the *Medicine Hat News*, reporting for the *Ottawa Journal*, and editing *Horizon Canada*, that strange weekly magazine of Canadian history. The last of these, he says, was a patronage scam by the Liberals aimed at repaying a few francophone federalists.

Found in Anne Carson's new book, a collection of experimental mixed-genre essays: "Going to visit my mother is like starting in on a piece by Beckett."

SATURDAY, 3 SEPTEMBER / VANCOUVER
Looking at emails that came in yesterday, I see that those people at the SFU publishing programme, having invited me to be a panellist at next year's symposium on the novel, have now disinvited me.

SATURDAY, 10 SEPTEMBER / VANCOUVER
Dream in which a man is praying to gipsies along Queen East in Toronto and I'm walking with my stick.

FRIDAY, 23 SEPTEMBER / VANCOUVER
Breakfast with Katherine Govier, who's in town to read at the VPL. She is looking about as old as I am. I steer us into serious conversation about

how despite our extreme dissimilarities – the piece of foreign rabble and the native-born Society divorcee – we are as one in establishment's dislike of us. As always she is wise and thoughtful. (When we part, she gives me a hug – a first.)

Then, in the early afternoon, off to a top-floor suite at the Hotel Vancouver to speak with Salman Rushdie about his new novel. The last time we talked was by phone shortly before the events of 11 September 2001. He is the nearly perfect author to interview because he does not appear to repeat himself – no rehearsed talk, no sound bytes – and is so supremely articulate and curious about everything without being artificially up, looking out at the world from beneath his cobra eyes. He is cleanshaven now and even more bald than I am, wears casual clothes badly, and sports an expensive digital watch.

FRIDAY, 30 SEPTEMBER / VANCOUVER
I work until shortly before 4:00 p.m. when I go to the unfortunately renovated bar of the Sylvia to meet with the Joy Kogawa group about trying to save her former home from demolition at the hands of its new owner, a woman in Taiwan who intends to build a monster home on the site. Jim Green is there, smart and easygoing. He's going to face quite a struggle to become mayor in November with Sam Sullivan in the race. Alas. His platform is of course progressive and what's more I'm very attracted to the idea that Vancouver should have a former Vietnam-era deserter as its mayor. Others at the meeting include several members of the younger generation of Chinese-Canadian media and political people who really know how to get things done.

TUESDAY, 11 OCTOBER / VANCOUVER
Today I send bound proofs of *Tales* to John Burns and tomorrow will send same to *Quill & Quire* and the *Globe*. This is the point in my own work when I often waver, the result of all those years, 1968 to 1985, when I was panned and torn up by reviewers almost unanimously. I can recall two occasions when I have precluded books of mine getting any attention at all. I'm at least slightly less insecure these days, and am determined to send out about a hundred review copies with press kits and see what happens.

WEDNESDAY, 12 OCTOBER / VANCOUVER

I'm to meet [a colleague] at 8:30 in the lobby of the Sylvia. She's late of course: a mix-up. I treat her with my special gloves, knowing how difficult and thin of skin she can be, but in fact she seems fine this morning, dressed to the nines in somewhat bohemian fashion and using her official Author voice.

FRIDAY, 14 OCTOBER / VANCOUVER

Greg Cook and Leslie Jeffrey got in late last night and we sat up talking, the four of us, until about 1:00 a.m., when I walked them next door to the Oceanview where I've had to see them put up for a few days because M hasn't found the time to ready her suite for them. Greg looks far younger than his sixty-three years, is planning to spend the half year he and L will be in Brisbane working away on his Ernest Buckler biography.

WEDNESDAY, 26 OCTOBER / TORONTO

Dream about Conrad Black and a stylish young woman whose first name seems to be O'Leary and who wears a business suit and serious shoes and sounds like an academic appearing on television.

FRIDAY, 25 NOVEMBER / VANCOUVER

I get a chance finally to examine in detail the first finished copies of *Tales*, which arrived yesterday: a small batch, well in advance of the bulk shipment. Try as one might, one can never approach the thrill of holding one's first book in one's hands. The publicity campaign for *Tales* is proving very difficult to organise in the string-of-firecrackers way that is the most desirable. Such is always the case, I find. One makes do with a ragged response that will not be so effective. In any case, one never ever knows which book, if any, might attract readers. It's true what people say: that the best publicity is word-of-mouth.

WEDNESDAY, 30 NOVEMBER / VANCOUVER

Another example of how my resolve, like my leg joint, stiffens. All this idealising I once did trying to make friends more interesting than they really are shows I require more honesty in the perceptions I voice. And I need to be far less lazy in my habits. My priorities are health, financial survival, the condo mess, and of course work. I need to re-double my efforts in all of these, and while I do so, to reposition myself vis-à-vis Toronto. It is the city I must monitor more closely from out here. I have always done best observing and analysing from an external position like this. In this way I have kept a lid on the chaos and benefited myself in terms of growth. All this sounds pompous, but I believe I speak the truth as I know it.

SATURDAY, 3 DECEMBER / VANCOUVER

Have been out of town. Returning here, I find I have no food in the fridge and so go to the supermarket where, waiting in the check-out queue, I am forced by boredom to read the gossip tabloids. Thus do I become aware that Paris Hilton has been dissing Britney Spears for not being sufficiently serious in her study of Kabbalah. Not since a fellow inmate stabbed my childhood acquaintance Charles Manson in an argument about God have two such major theologians been at loggerheads this way.

SUNDAY, 4 DECEMBER / VANCOUVER

This is the weekend that visitors to the Denman Mall can confide their wishes to Santa and have their picture taken with him. I spot the obviously gay Santa, his scratchy beard lowered, taking a cigarette break and grabbing the ass of whoever is occupying the reindeer suit. Then I stop for a browse at the remainder bookstore, only to have my knee buckle, sending me crashing into the Health and Spirituality section, the works of Mary Baker Eddy breaking my fall. Coming back down our *soi*, I find a dead rat the size of a lapdog at the end of our walkway.

The dinner party seems a great success. Tim Brook comes, without Fay, alas, as she is in India, and he's very gentle, and learned, and wise in his remarks about China. He leaves me the ms of his new book on the seventeenth-century world for comments. Don Stewart is relaxed and fun, as he usually is away from the pressures of his shop, and Ann is friendly and at ease and appears to strike up a special relationship with M. Also here: Heike from Kate Walker's and her husband Christoph; they're both native speakers of German but he seems rather more so than she does, speaking with a slight formality despite being fully idiomatic. M and I manage to merge our two sets of dinnerware, stemware, etc. to serve seven people, and there is much talk of books and politics, much consumption of absinthe and red wine and Indian food buffet style. A success for certain.

SUNDAY, 11 DECEMBER / VANCOUVER

From Bei Dao: "In the land where the king is dead/the old rifle sprouting branches and buds/has become a cripple's cane." Well, not quite yet unfortunately. I think of the Iraq war whenever I read of literary prizes, and vice versa. Book prizes, the cult of celebrity, ignorance, torture, nuclear blackmail: all part of the same inanity.

MONDAY, 12 DECEMBER / VANCOUVER

This morning when I go to the photocopy shop on Denman to courier an envelope to Jen in Edmonton, I find three city cops there, one with his evidence kit open. A druggie with a knife tried to hold up the tobacconist's next door, and the screams of the ill-tempered proprietress and the sound of inventory falling from shelves alerted Rob and Marian, who held the robber by force until the cops arrived in response to the shop manager's call. Rob was bitten on the hand and now must have a blood test for AIDS, as the druggie would seem to be a needle-user. A small horror to begin a day of wet fog and darkness.

TUESDAY, 13 DECEMBER / VANCOUVER

Miracles! I have returned to *Walt*, however undramatically. The breakthrough is that I find the way to begin, find the framing device needed for the opening chapter, for which I have had only false starts until now.

FRIDAY, 16 DECEMBER / VANCOUVER

I have taken the *Tales* publicity into my own hands and arrange to meet Alexandra Gill from the *Globe* bureau, who is identified as the West Coast arts reporter but in fact is simply a really nasty restaurant reviewer. She suggests a drink at 6:00 p.m. at the Oasis on Davie, cautioning that she will be coming straight from the office. She arrives forty minutes late, whereupon the proprietor kisses her on the lips. She wears a low-cut little black dress. I say: "I presume that either you're not coming straight from the office after all or else that the *Globe* is a far more interesting place to work than I ever imagined." She does what she thinks is a Veronica Lake impression, and flirts throughout the meeting. She will write her usual hatchet piece. I don't care.

The first outside reaction to *Tales* comes this morning in the form of a total but civil rejection of it by Bob F, who says he's simply not the reader for it and it's not the book for him. I respond in jovial fashion, hiding my brief mind-storm (just long enough and sharp enough to remind me of the value of such episodes in quickly dealing with a crisis before it worsens but also the inconveniences of them – how they instantly drain attention and concentration needed elsewhere). Down through the years Bob has never seen any merit whatever in my imaginative work, though he has sometimes praised my cultural journalism; indeed, he commissioned a great deal of it at *Saturday Night*, 1969–88. In fact, he's probably the only important journalist who actually accepted me as a fellow journalist. This is contrast to Neil, who saw that I've been on the journalistic fringes since I was sixteen but am actually a different sort of being entirely and not really a journalist at all – except in the obsolete literal sense of someone who keeps a daily journal.

About the Author

George Fetherling has been a wide-ranging and prolific figure in Canadian literature since the mid-1960s. The Montreal *Gazette* has called him "a mercurial, liberal intelligence ... the kind of which English Canada has too short a supply." *Xtra* described him as "something of a national literary treasure." He is a poet, novelist, and writer of literary travel narratives. He is also a visual artist. Some of his more familiar books are *Travels by Night: A Memoir*, *The Sylvia Hotel Poems*, *The Book of Assassins*, *Three Pagodas Pass*, and the novel *Walt Whitman's Secret*. He commutes seasonally between Toronto and Vancouver.

"One of the benefits of being a Canadian writer," he says, "is that you have periods of being somewhat footloose, as opportunities come up that allow you to connect for a while with many different parts of the country." For example, he has been writer-in-residence at Queen's University, the University of New Brunswick, Berton House in the Yukon, and the University of Toronto. Similarly, he has spent years as the regular books columnist of the leading newspapers in five cities: Toronto, Kingston, Saint John, Ottawa, and Vancouver. But his cultural commentary and criticism range far more broadly than that suggests: he has published numerous books in such areas as Canadian art, film, and social history. He was awarded the Harbourfront Festival Prize for "a substantial contribution to Canadian letters." Later, St Mary's University conferred on him a DLitt *honoris causa* for "his instrumental role in the development" of Canadian writing.

Despite such connections with the established order, Fetherling is considered to be happily independent of the accepted centre in somewhat the same way that "independent scholars" are understood to be apart from the academy without necessarily being at hazard with it. W.H. New makes the point cogently in the *Encyclopedia of Literature in Canada* when he writes: "Fetherling's constant subject is Canada, its history, mores, and culture, and his writings can be read as a dialogue between the personal and the political, as inquiries into the values of Canadian society and the writer's relation with them, and hence into the depths of his personal passion for independence. Almost any one of his books provides an access point to this exchange."

Fetherling, born in 1949, says he was "lucky enough to come of age, chronologically if not otherwise, in time to take a small part in the great explosion of Canadian culture that began around the time of Expo '67 and rattled on noisily for many years afterwards." It is in this period that *The Writing Life*, with all its major and minor personalities – some famous, some obscure, all of them neatly sketched with a few strokes of Fetherling's brush – sets off on its mission to chronicle, reveal, and entertain.

Index